EXPEDITIONARY POLICE ADVISING AND MILITARIZATION: BUILDING SECURITY IN A FRACTURED WORLD

Modern Military History

Series Editors

ALARIC SEARLE, Professor of Modern European History, University of Salford, UK

DONALD STOKER, Professor of Strategy and Policy, US Naval War College, Naval Postgraduate School, Monterey, CA, USA

This series is dedicated to making available, at a reasonable price, quality academic military history, based on innovative and thorough scholarly research. While the main emphasis is on the publication of single-authored monographs, there will be scope for edited collections which focus primarily on new perspectives and evidence, as well as occasional translations of important foreign-language studies. *Modern Military History* will be framed in an 'inclusive' fashion, so that it encompasses armies, navies and air forces. While the traditional core concerns of military history—such as tactics, combat experience, technology, strategy and officer education—remain important fields of consideration, the encouragement of new angles and original approaches, whether methodologically, geographically or thematically, form a significant part of the editors' agenda.

Titles

No 1 *Genesis, Employment, Aftermath: First World War Tanks and the New Warfare, 1900-1945* edited by Alaric Searle (ISBN 978-1-909982-22-2)

No 2 *Naval Advising and Assistance: History, Challenges, and Analysis* edited by Donald Stoker and Michael T. McMaster (ISBN 978-1-911512-82-0)

No 3 *Expeditionary Police Advising and Militarization: Building Security in A Fractured World* edited by Donald Stoker and Edward B. Westermann (ISBN 978-1-911512-86-8)

Expeditionary Police Advising and Militarization

Building Security in a Fractured World

Modern Military History No.3

Edited by
Donald Stoker and Edward B. Westermann

Helion & Company Limited

To Chikara Hashimoto, 1975-2016

Helion & Company Limited
26 Willow Road
Solihull
West Midlands
B91 1UE
England
Tel. 0121 705 3393
Fax 0121 711 4075
Email: info@helion.co.uk
Website: www.helion.co.uk
Twitter: @helionbooks
Visit our blog http://blog.helion.co.uk/

Published by Helion & Company 2018
Designed and typeset by Mary Woolley, Battlefield Design (www.battlefield-design.co.uk)
Cover designed by Paul Hewitt, Battlefield Design (www.battlefield-design.co.uk)
Printed by Lightning Source Ltd, Milton Keynes, Buckinghamshire

ISBN 978-1-911512-86-8

British Library Cataloguing-in-Publication Data.

A catalogue record for this book is available from the British Library.

For details of other military history titles published by Helion & Company Limited contact the above address, or visit our website: http://www.helion.co.uk.

We always welcome receiving book proposals from prospective authors.

Contents

About the Contributors

STEPHEN CONNOR holds a BA from the University of Windsor and MA and PhD from Wilfrid Laurier University. Dr. Connor is a recipient of a Social Sciences and Humanities Research Council Fellowship, the Holocaust Educational Foundation's Christopher Browning Research Fellowship, and the Charles Revson Foundation Research Fellowship at the Center for Advanced Holocaust Studies. He was also the recipient of the Wilfrid Laurier University Teaching Award of Excellence in 2008, and the Nipissing University Chancellor's Award for Excellence in Teaching in 2012. Dr. Connor has presented his research in a variety of forums, including the Laurier Centre for Military Strategic and Disarmament Studies Conference, the Institute on the Holocaust and Jewish Civilization at Northwestern University in Evanston, IL, the United States Holocaust Memorial Museum in Washington, DC, and the Society for Military History Conferences in Washington, DC, and New Orleans, LA Dr Connor's most recent publication entitled *Bringing in the Harvest: The German Civil Administration and Occupation Management in Brest-Litovsk, 1942-1944*, is forthcoming in *Global War Studies*. Dr. Connor is currently an Assistant Professor of History at Nipissing University where he teaches courses focused on military history.

ROBERT N. DILLON is a Colonel in the US Army Military Police Corps and is currently the chief of the Human Dimension Division at the US Army Capabilities Integration Center. Most recently, Colonel Dillon was the Director, National Security Justice Development for US Forces Afghanistan after commanding the 89th Military Police Brigade, and Fort Hood Director of Emergency Services. With over 25 years of US Army service, Colonel Dillon has commanded at every level from platoon to brigade, and on staffs from battalion to Headquarters. He was the Chief of Policy and Plans in the Office of the Provost Marshal General, leading the effort to devise the strategic plan for the US Army Military Police Corps for the next 20 years. Colonel Dillon has a master's degree in Public Administration from the University of Texas and a Master of Strategic Studies from the US Army War College. In addition, he holds a graduate-level certification in Law Enforcement Intelligence Operations from Michigan State University.

Lieutenant-Colonel BRIAN ERICKSON serves with the Royal Canadian Air Force and is currently the J3 Africa/Asia-Pacific at the Canadian Joint Operations Command Headquarters in Ottawa, Ontario, Canada. In 2011-12, he was the Deputy Director-Police Plans at the NATO Training Mission-Afghanistan where he had the opportunity to work with the international efforts to develop, advise, and assist the Afghanistan National Police. He earned a NATO Meritorious Service Medal for work in developing police capacity. He is a 2013 graduate of the United States Air Command and Staff College where he was recognized as the top international officer in his class.

JASON E. FRITZ is a senior consultant at the Noetic Corporation where he leads research on a number of issues related to violent non-state actors, stability operations, and land power capabilities. He is also a doctoral student in the Department of Justice, Law, and Criminology at American University's School of Public of Affairs, where his studies focus on the intersection of political violence and policing in late- and post-conflict states, and on quantitative methods. Previously, Jason worked as a consultant and researcher providing analysis on a wide array of defense and diplomatic issues. Before his research and consulting career, Jason was an armor officer in the US Army, and served multiple tours of duty in Iraq in positions ranging from platoon leader to brigade planner. He is a senior editor at *War on the Rocks*, and is a graduate of the United States Military Academy at West Point with a degree in mathematics.

Prof. Dr. Ir. GEORG E. FRERKS holds a chair in Conflict Prevention and Conflict Management at Utrecht University and a chair in International Security Studies at the Netherlands Defence Academy. He worked nearly 20 years for the Dutch Ministry of Foreign Affairs, both at its headquarters and abroad, serving as an inspector at the Ministry's Policy and Operations Evaluation Department, as well as in other positions. He was also head of the Conflict Research Unit of the Netherlands Institute of International Relations 'Clingendael' from 1997-2004. Frerks has carried out studies on conflict-related subjects for academic and multilateral, governmental, and non-governmental agencies. He has conducted a number of studies on Afghanistan: *Evaluation (Dutch) Peace Fund, Flexibility with Vision* (with Bart Klem) (The Hague: Netherlands Institute of International Relations 'Clingendael', 2003); *Evaluation (Dutch) Stability Fund 2004 and 2005* (with Bart Klem) (Amsterdam: Wageningen University, 2007); *Principles and Pragmatism. Civil-Military Action in Afghanistan and Liberia* (with Bart Klem, Stefan van Laar and Marleen van Klingeren) (Utrecht/Amsterdam: Utrecht University, 2006); and *The Struggle after Combat, the Role of NGOs in DDR Processes: Afghanistan Case Study* (with Geert Gompelman, Stefan van Laar, and Bart Klem) (The Hague: Cordaid, 2008). Together with Dr. Mario Fumerton, professor Frerks also wrote the *Independent Quality Assurance Team's (IQAT) Evaluation Report* of the *Contextual Analysis of Police and Justice System in Kunduz: 2011 Baseline Assessment*, and the *2012 and 2013 Progress Reports on the Dutch Integrated Police Training Mission in Kunduz, Afghanistan.*

BIRTE JULIA GIPPERT is a Teaching Assistant at the War Studies Department of King's College, London. She holds a PhD from the University of Reading. Her work focuses on local legitimacy of international peacebuilding operations, local compliance, resistance, and contested spaces. Birte previously worked as a policy researcher for the Kosovar Stability Initiative, a local think tank in Pristina, Kosovo.

CHIKARA HASHIMOTO (1975-2016) received his PhD in International Politics from Aberystwyth University, in the UK. He was Assistant Professor in International Relations, University of Sharjah, the UAE, and Assistant Editor of *Intelligence and National Security*. His doctoral thesis was awarded the British Society for Middle Eastern Studies (BRISMES) Leigh Douglas Memorial Prize for the best PhD dissertation on a Middle Eastern topic of 2014. His book based on his PhD work, *British Intelligence and Counter-Subversion in the Middle East, 1948-1963*, was published by Edinburgh University Press in 2017.

Major NICHOLAS J. KRAMER is a US Army Foreign Area Officer specializing in the Middle East and North Africa. In 2006, he served as a trainer to an Iraqi Army battalion in central Baghdad, and subsequently as a mechanized infantry company executive officer in western Baghdad partnered with a second Iraqi Army battalion. Between 2010 and 2012, Major Kramer spent 19 months as a Special Forces Detachment Commander in Dand Wa Patan District, Paktia Province, Afghanistan, advising and training Afghan National Army Special Forces and Afghan Local Police. He also worked closely during that time with the Afghan National Police, the Afghan Border Police, and the District Sub-Governor. Major Kramer is currently completing a Master's in Nonproliferation and Terrorism Studies at the Middlebury Institute of International Studies at Monterey in Monterey, California.

DAVID LIVINGSTONE is a PhD candidate at the University of California, San Diego. He is presently writing a dissertation focused on West Germany's federal border police force, the *Bundesgrenzschutz*, and its influence on re-civilizing civilian policing from 1951 to 1978. He is a veteran municipal police officer with the City of Simi Valley, California, where he has served in a variety of positions over the past 27 years. He is currently a Commander assigned to the Detective Unit and also leads the Department's Special Weapons and Tactics Team. He has previously taught Strategy and Policy for the United States Naval War College, College of Distance Learning at Port Hueneme, California, and history in a variety of undergraduate and Community College programs.

Dr. MARK MOYAR has published five books and numerous articles and book chapters. His most recent book is entitled *Aid for Elites: Building Partner Nations and Ending Poverty Through Human Capital* (Cambridge University Press, 2016). His recently completed history of American special operations forces will be published in 2017 by Basic Books. He has served as a professor at the US Marine Corps

University, where he held the Kim T. Adamson Chair of Insurgency and Terrorism, and as a Senior Fellow at the Joint Special Operations University. A frequent visitor to Afghanistan and other foreign conflict zones, he has acted as a consultant to the senior leadership of US Central Command, the International Security Assistance Force in Afghanistan, US Special Operations Command, and the NATO Training Mission-Afghanistan. He holds a BA *summa cum laude* from Harvard University and a PhD from Cambridge University.

NIELS TERPSTRA holds an MA in Conflict Studies and Human Rights (*cum laude*) and is currently a PhD candidate at the Centre for Conflict Studies, Utrecht University, the Netherlands. In this capacity he focuses on issues of human security, state fragility, rebel governance, insurgency and counterinsurgency in Central and South Asia. In 2013 Terpstra carried out fieldwork in Kabul, Kunduz, and Mazar-e-Sharif and wrote a case study on the IPM, focusing on the experiences of Afghan community members with formal and informal justice mechanisms. His study received the J.C. Baak prize of the Royal Holland Society of Sciences and Humanities. Terpstra also provided methodological and theoretical input for the above-mentioned *Independent Quality Assurance Team's (IQAT) Evaluation and Progress Reports.*

DONALD STOKER was Professor of Strategy and Policy for the US Naval War College's Monterey Program at the Naval Postgraduate School in Monterey, California, from 1999-2017. The author or editor of a number of books, his most recent work, *Carl von Clausewitz: His Life and Work* (Oxford University Press, 2014), was recently placed on the British Army professional reading list. His *The Grand Design: Strategy and the US Civil War, 1861-1865* (Oxford University Press, 2010), won the prestigious Fletcher Pratt award for the best non-fiction Civil War book of 2010, was a Main Selection of the History Book Club, and is commonly used as a text in history graduate seminars and strategic studies courses. It is also on the US Army Chief of Staff's reading list. His other works include an edited volume on strategy in the War for American Independence, and works on military advising, conscription, and the arms trade. He has written for numerous magazines such as *MHQ (Military History Quarterly)*, *North & South*, and *Naval History*. In 2016, he was a Fellow of the Changing Character of War Programme at the University of Oxford's Pembroke College. He is writing a book on limited war for Cambridge University Press and co-editing a number of other works. During the 2017-2018 academic year he was Visiting Fellow and Distinguished Diplomatic Academy Fulbright Professor of Political Science at the Diplomatic Academy in Vienna, Austria.

EDWARD B. WESTERMANN is a professor of history at Texas A&M University–San Antonio. He teaches courses on European History, the Holocaust, and War and Society. He has been a Fulbright Fellow, a German Academic Exchange Service Fellow, and a Fellow at the US Holocaust Memorial Museum. He is the author of numerous publications including *Hitler's Police Battalions: Enforcing Racial War in the*

East and *Flak: German Anti-Aircraft Defenses, 1914–1945.* His latest book, *Hitler's Ostkrieg and the Indian Wars: Comparing Conquest and Genocide*, was published in 2016.

CRAIG WHITESIDE is Associate Professor of Theater Security Decision Making for the Naval War College at the Naval Postgraduate School in Monterey, California. Craig came to the War College from Washington State University, where he earned a PhD in Political Science and taught American Government and National Security Affairs. Prior to this, Professor Whiteside was a career infantry officer in the US Army. He is an Iraq War veteran and served with the Geronimos of the 1st Battalion, 501st Parachute Infantry during 2006-7. He finished his military service as the Professor of Military Science at Washington State University. Professor Whiteside's dissertation investigated the political worldview of the Islamic State of Iraq and al Sham (ISIS). He is a graduate of the United States Military Academy and the US Army Command and General Staff College.

ATHOL YATES works at the Institute for International and Civil Security, Khalifa University, which offers a Master's Degree aimed at Emirati security professionals. He teaches civil security, which covers professional security practice, internal security, and disaster management. Prior to joining Khalifa University, Dr. Yates was the Executive Director of the Australian Security Research Centre, a think-tank examining domestic security issues. His current major research is on the contribution that expatriates have made to the security services of the UAE and Trucial States such as the Dubai Police, Abu Dhabi Police, Abu Dhabi Defence Force, Ras al-Khaimah Mobile Force, Dubai Defence Force, Sharjah National Guard, Umm Al Quwain National Guard, Union Defence Force, and the UAE Armed Forces.

Introduction

Edward B. Westermann and Donald Stoker

Since the attacks on 11 September 2001 the US military has been involved in a series of conflicts that paradoxically have highlighted the greatest strengths and the greatest weaknesses of the world's most advanced combat forces. On the one hand, the overwhelming technological advantages enjoyed by US forces in the areas of firepower, communication, logistics, and battlefield surveillance were applied with devastating effect during the initial invasions of both Afghanistan in 2001 and Iraq in 2003. However, the ability to defeat the enemy's fielded forces and to capture Kabul and Baghdad did not result in outright victory as insurgencies developed in both countries that successfully adopted strategies and tactics designed to minimize US and coalition partner advantages in technology and firepower. The wars in Afghanistan and Iraq and the continuing conflicts throughout the Levant and North Africa have evolved into classic insurgency campaigns that offer a number of challenges for conventional military forces.

One of the most critical elements for defeating an insurgency involves the issue of gaining popular support and providing security to the local population. Not surprisingly, these are not distinct and separate issues, but interrelated factors. In his classic work, *Counterinsurgency Warfare: Theory and Practice*, David Galula argued, 'the population's attitude . . . is dictated not so much by the relative popularity and merits of the opponents as by the more primitive concern for safety'. He continued, 'Which side gives the best protection, which one threatens the most, which one is likely to win, these are the criteria governing the population's stand.'[1] If one accepts the premise of the fundamental importance of providing security to the local population then it clearly follows that such protection will be provided by a combination of military forces along with local civil police forces. Indeed at specific times and in specific locations, local police and security forces will be the primary if not sole representatives

1 Galula, David, *Counterinsurgency Warfare: Theory and Practice* (Westport, CT: Praeger Security International, 2006), pp. 8-9.

of the government, and may provide the margin between success and failure in a counterinsurgency (COIN) campaign.

With respect to the importance of police forces in COIN operations C. Christine Fair and Sumit Ganguly asserted, 'the task of restoring public order invariably involves careful and sustained police work. Among a host of other matters, winning the support of an aggrieved or fearful population requires a neutral, competent, and reliable police force'.[2] While undoubtedly true, this assertion begs the question of the methods by which such a 'neutral, competent, and reliable police force' can be trained and organized. Therefore, one of the objectives of this volume is to provide a broad historical and analytical examination of the role of police advisors in training, equipping, and organizing foreign police forces both for standard policing as well as counterinsurgency warfare. This volume provides a brief history of expeditionary police advising and the advantages and disadvantages inherent in its use, the specific model or organizational ideal used in training and creating local police forces, as well as the growing concerns related to the militarization of police forces and the effects of such militarization on the way in which police view their role in society and the methods by which they enforce the rule of law. As in the case of security and popular support, it should be apparent that issues related to the model used for developing police culture, the effects of militarization, and the pros and cons of police advising are applicable to police activities in peacetime environments as well as during times of major public unrest or insurgency.

Police Advising: The Pros and Cons

There are of course many reasons for nations to involve themselves in police advising, as well as solid reasons not to. One of the most obvious advantages is the crafting of effective police forces that might actually provide a solution to a security problem, one that eventually enables the local population to assume responsibility for their own safety. The post-Second World War US efforts to train democratic police forces in Germany, Japan, and Austria worked very well and left these nations with competent, independent, professional policing arms.[3] But one could also consider these best case scenarios for police advising because of their relatively secure post-war situations and the availability of significant resources.

The establishment of an effective police force can also be very useful in the suppression of an insurgency. Police are particularly valuable as sources of intelligence in a counterinsurgency situation because they generally have more intimate contact

2 Fair, C. Christine and Sumit Gangly, 'Introduction: The Police in Counterinsurgency Operations', in Fair, C. Christine and Summit Gangly (eds), *Policing Insurgencies: Cops as Counterinsurgents* (Oxford: Oxford University Press, 2014), p. 1.

3 Phelps, James, 'Lessons in Developing Democratic Police from Post-Second World War Successes', *International Journal of Comparative and Applied Criminal Justice*, 34:1 (Spring 2010), p. 112.

with the people than members of the armed forces.[4] One of the primary roles of the reformed Philippines constabulary in the war against the Hukbalahap (Huk) Rebellion (1946-54) was the collection of intelligence.[5] Not having what the British called a 'Special Branch' arm in the Cyprus police severely injured Britain's ability to counter the insurgency that erupted there in 1956.[6]

But the downsides are more numerous. Arguably, the biggest of these is the possibility of failure, and in police advising the risks of failure are quite high. We have discovered no empirical study that presents the actual rates of success or failure, but the historical record does not bend one toward optimism. Military forces and international organizations doing stability operations are often tasked with building local police forces, but political scientist Lawrence Cline notes that 'Thus far, the record of such local police has been questionable at best'.[7] Historian William Rosenau argues that US police reform abroad has been generally unsuccessful for two reasons. The first is the organizational and bureaucratic difficulty of the US government determining which of its prongs is best for handling such a task. The second is the raw political challenge in the nation in which reform is being attempted. In some parts of the world the police are considered part of the problem, and indeed are.[8] Such issues sometimes escape the notice of reformers.

Another downside of police advising, particularly if the military has been tasked with the creation or redevelopment of the police, can be the creation of paramilitary forces (e.g., militias). This produces follow-on problems, especially the question of the suitability of such forces for police work, and the loss of actual police functions. For example, militia forces generally offer a poor solution to a policing problem. Militia are often badly trained, neither professional police nor soldiers (usually having other jobs), difficult to control (the various Iraqi militias arising since 2003 provide some of the worst examples of this), sometimes become a shadow army that threatens the state, and usually have little knowledge of police work. They can offer useful local, stopgap measures against insurgents, and supplements to the regular army, but to use them for policing missions is often asking for failure.

Other drawbacks of police advising can arise from the advisors themselves. Advisors—even police advisors—sometimes get killed. One of the earliest examples

4 Rosenau, William, *'Low-Cost Trigger-Pullers': The Politics of Policing in the Context of Contemporary "State Building" and Counterinsurgency* (Santa Monica: RAND, Oct. 2008), pp. 4-5.

5 Ladwig, Walter C., III, 'When the Police are the Problem: The Philippine Constabulary and the Hukbalahap Rebellion', in Fair, Christine, and Ganguly, Sumit (eds), *Policing Insurgencies: Cops as Counterinsurgents* (Oxford: Oxford University Press, 2014), p. 30.

6 Corum. James S., *Training Indigenous Forces in Counterinsurgency: A Tale of Two Insurgencies* (US Army War College, Carlisle, PA: Strategic Studies Institute, March 2006), p. 32.

7 Cline, Lawrence E., 'The New Constabularies: Planning US Military Stabilization Missions', *Small War and Insurgencies*, 14:3 (2003), p. 173.

8 Rosenau, *'Low-Cost Trigger-Pullers'*, pp. 15-17.

of this occurred in Albania. In July 1914, Lodewijk Thomson, the commander of the Dutch gendarmerie mission was killed by anti-government forces.[9] Nothing has changed here in the last century: three contractors training police in Jordan were killed by a trainee in 2015.[10] Casualties among police advisors greatly increase when police forces are being stood-up or reformed in an area with an active insurgency. In the face of heavily armed insurgents, police are *not* the answer to the security challenge. That is a job for regular troops.

Charles Gwynn, the author of the classic *Imperial Policing*, points out a challenge faced by military officers doing police duties that also applies to military personnel acting as police advisors, and which can cause problems for the sending nation: the military officers have to identify 'the minimum force they must employ rather than how they can develop the maximum power at their disposal'.[11] The obvious difficulty and complexity in making these decisions under pressure can produce unexpected consequences.

Police advisors, just like military advisors, can also go rogue.[12] When the First World War began in 1914, 20 of the Swedish officers acting as police advisors in Persia remained behind when their mission departed. Some of these Swedes helped the Germans dabble in Persia during the war, and one even convinced his Persian gendarme regiment to join the Germans.[13]

The Militarization of Policing

Closely linked to the disadvantages of expeditionary police advising is the challenge of police militarization. The effects of militarization on police forces has emerged as a growing topic in contemporary US political discourse concerning the role and action of the police. With respect to US police forces, Peter Kraska highlighted the move away from a community policing model and a new trend towards 'certain militarization' as 'reflected by a precipitous rise and the widespread mainstreaming of police paramilitary units (PPUs)' such as SWAT (special weapons and tactics)

9 Goslinga, Gorrit T.A., 'The Dutch in Albania (A History of the First Albanian Gendarmerie Organized and Directed by Dutch Officers, 1913-1914)' [Part 3], *Shêjzat*, 16 (1972), pp. 27-29, 37.

10 Al-Khalidi, Suleiman, 'Jordanian Officer Shoots Dead Two Americans, One South African at Security Training Site', *Reuters* (9 Nov. 2015).

11 Gwynn, Charles, *Imperial Policing* (London: Macmillan, 1939), p. 6

12 For a related article on this see Simons, Anna, 'The Military Advisor as Warrior-King and Other "Going Native" Temptations', in Frese, Pamela R., and Harrell, Margaret C. (eds), *Anthropology and the United States Military: Coming of Age in the Twenty-first Century* (New York: Palgrave MacMillan, 2003), pp. 123-130.

13 Fazlhashemi, Mohammad 'Sweden ii, Swedish Officers in Persia, 1911-1915', *Encyclopedia Iranica*, <http://www.iranicaonline.org/articles/sweden-ii> (15 Aug. 2006).

teams that are specifically modeled along the lines of US special operations units.[14] Kraska's work not only raised the issue of the domestic effects of the militarization of police forces, but also highlighted the increasing trend of using US military forces and assets in law enforcement operations such as the 'war on drugs' or the interdiction of undocumented aliens entering the US across the southern border. In a similar vein, Radley Balko addressed the issues of 'direct militarization' and 'indirect militarization' in *Rise of the Warrior Cop: The Militarization of America's Police Forces* by describing the former as 'the use of the standard military for domestic policing' and the latter as a process that occurs 'when police agencies and police officers take on more and more characteristics of an army'.[15]

The issue of police militarization is not new. Indeed, the diversity of the nature of police tasks, their equipment, and their ethos was reflected in differing European approaches to policing in the nineteenth century. At one extreme, the formation of gendarmerie forces in France and Germany during the nineteenth century composed largely of former military members and armed with swords or sidearms served in many respects as paramilitary forces for enforcing state control in the countryside. In contrast, the unarmed London 'bobby' emerged as a 'new style' police force and 'created a law enforcement standard that would be widely emulated' and that embodied the community policing ideal.[16] Uniformed police forces in the German state of Prussia adopted a more authoritarian approach, especially in the wake of the growth of the working class and Socialist political parties, which 'bred a lively animosity particularly among the poorer classes. . . . the police represent[ed] the imperial government, and thus the domination of the bureaucracy'.[17] The use of rifle butts and fixed bayonets by the Cologne police to disperse a crowd on 1 September 1830 in many respects reflected the general military inclination of nineteenth century police forces within Germany in general, and the practice of hiring former soldiers helped to reinforce the military orientation of German police forces into the twentieth century.[18]

During the Third Reich, the militarization of the uniformed police forces and the creation of a martial identity within the police became a major focus of Nazi police leaders such as Chief of the Order Police (*Ordnungspolizei*) Kurt Daluege who

14 Kraska, Peter, 'The Military-Criminal Justice Blur', in Kraska, Peter (ed.), *Militarizing the American Criminal Justice System: The Changing Roles of the Armed Forces and the Police* (Boston: Northeastern University Press, 2001), pp. 6-7.

15 Balko, Radley, *Rise of the Warrior Cop: The Militarization of America's Police Forces* (New York: Public Affairs, 2013), p. 35

16 Johnson, Herbert A., Nancy Travis Wolfe, and Mark Jones, *History of Criminal Justice*, 4th ed. (Newark, NJ: Matthew Bender and Company, 2008), p. 220.

17 Chapman, Brian, *Police State* (New York: Praeger, 1970), p. 48.

18 Lüdtke, Alf, *Police and State in Prussia, 1815-1850* (New York: Cambridge University Press, 1989), p. 70, and Nipperdey, Thomas, *Deutsche Geschichte, 1866-1918*, Vol. 2, *Machtstaat vor der Demokratie* (Munich: C.H. Beck, 1992), p. 128.

proclaimed, 'To be sure the soldierly thought and feeling within the new police of the National Socialist state can no longer be denied'. He continued, 'Although the member of the German police corps is also a civil servant, so will and must he feel himself to be a soldier; his duty demands this from him'.[19] In this case, the promotion of a military ethic bound to the regime's racial ideology within the police led to the creation of a force that became directly involved in acts of mass atrocity and genocide in the occupied eastern territories during the Second World War.

While the Nazi police apparatus provides perhaps one of the most extreme examples of the risks associated with militarization and politicization of the police, many countries have developed paramilitary police forces intended to either serve as the incubus for future military forces or to conduct specific military related missions within the country or on its borders. In the case of the former, the East German *Volkspolizei* (People's Police) included the creation of paramilitary *Bereitschaften (alarm units)* in 1948 that eventually became the kernel the East German National People's Army (NVA). In the words of Richard Bessel, 'the impetus for the growth and militarisation of the East German police appears to have been not a concern about the security needs of the civilian population but rather a determination to secure political control as the Cold War came to dominate European political life'.[20] In fact, one history described the East German garrisoned police force as a 'camouflaged army'.[21] In the case of paramilitary police forces in domestic operations, the actions of the Philippine Constabulary (PC) during the Hukbalahap Rebellion (1946-54) offer a cautionary tale on the efficacy of such forces for internal security tasks. In this case, historian Walter Ladwig asserted, 'Not only does the experience of the PC highlight the problems that result from the politicization of police forces, it also raises questions about the utility of paramilitary-police style forces in counterinsurgency'.[22] As readers of this volume will see, the questions related to the value and efficacy of paramilitary police forces remain a major concern with respect to contemporary counterinsurgency and can be seen clearly in current debates concerning the role and equipping of the Afghan National Police.

Police in Counterinsurgency Operations

Whether 'militarized' or not, there can be no doubt about the importance of the police to effective counterinsurgency operations, something with a long history. The Mughal rulers of sixteenth and seventeenth century India possessed a police

19 Westermann, Edward, *Hitler's Police Battalions: Enforcing Racial War in the East* (Lawrence: University Press of Kansas, 2005), p. 70.

20 Bessel, Richard, 'Policing in East Germany in the Wake of the Second World War', *Crime, History, and Societies*, 7:2 (2003), p. 9.

21 Diedrich, Torsten and Rüdiger Wenzke, *Die getarnte Armee: Geschichte der Kasernierten Volkspolizei der DDR, 1952-1956* (Berlin: Christoph Links Verlag, 2001).

22 Ladwig, 'When the Police are the Problem', p. 19.

force and established *thanas*—permanent police posts—especially when mounting counterinsurgency operations.[23] Police are generally the first line of defense versus insurgents. They also are often the first target of insurgents as they are visible representatives of state authority and control, as well as sometimes the only source of weapons. French counterinsurgency expert David Galula described the police as 'the eye and arm of the government in all matters pertaining to internal order'. As such he warned, 'they are the first counterinsurgent organization that has to be infiltrated and neutralized [by the insurgents]'.[24] The important role of legitimate and fair police forces in the defeat of an insurgency was recognized by the authors of US Army Field Manual 3-24, *Counterinsurgency* with the contention that 'If the HN [Host Nation] police have a reasonable reputation for competence and impartiality, it is better for them to execute urban raids; the populace is likely to view that application of force as more legitimate. This is true even if the police are not as well armed or as capable as military units. However, local circumstances affect this decision. If the police are seen as part of an ethnic or sectarian group oppressing the general population, their use may be counterproductive. Effective counterinsurgents thus understand the character of the local police and popular perceptions of both police and military units. This understanding helps ensure that the application of force is appropriate and reinforces the rule of law'.[25]

David Kilcullen, one of the preeminent contemporary theorists of insurgency warfare, emphasizes the differences between traditional policing in peacetime and policing in a counterinsurgency environment. Moreover, he identifies the three 'key components' needed to ensure effective counterinsurgency policing as (1) the use of 'community police officers, who act to secure and protect population centers and deliver basic public order and rule of law'; (2) the availability of 'field police (paramilitary organizations sometimes called constabulary or gendarmerie units), who conduct normal police duties but in a higher threat environment and typically are better armed and more mobile than community police'; and (3) the presence of a 'police intelligence or police special operations capability (sometimes called a "special branch") that specifically targets and arrests insurgent underground cells'.[26] Furthermore, Kilcullen recognizes the potential utility of local police auxiliaries charged with basic security functions as an extension of the community police.

Kilcullen's taxonomy of police forces raises several issues for analyzing the use of police forces against an insurgency. First, it is clear that a police force with strong ties to the local population is a critical prerequisite for successful operations. Second, the

23 Black, Jeremy, *Insurgency and Counterinsurgency: A Global History* (London: Bloomsbury, 2016), chapter 3.
24 Galula, *Counterinsurgency Warfare*, p. 20.
25 Headquarters Department of the Army, Field Manual 3-24, *Counterinsurgency* (Washington, DC: Department of the Army, December 2006), p. 1-25.
26 Kilcullen, David, *The Accidental Guerrilla: Fighting Small Wars in the Midst of a Big One* (Oxford: Oxford University Press, 2009), p. 61.

use of paramilitary police forces should not be discarded outright as it appears that these forces have a necessary role under certain conditions, but their utility must be continually evaluated over the course of the campaign. For example, when an acceptable level of security has been achieved in a given area, it may be more prudent and effective to shift security duties to community police forces or to change the organizational model and approach of the existing paramilitary forces by deemphasizing their martial character and use in combat operations in favor of tasks aimed at promoting the public order. Third, the use of police intelligence or police special operations capabilities carries an inherent risk since these types of forces have the potential to operate beyond the boundaries of acceptable police behavior and have the potential to transform into 'death squads' or assume political police functions whose actions ultimately prove counterproductive in winning the hearts and minds of the local populace.[27] One of the clearest illustrations of this danger can be found in the actions of the secret intelligence unit created by the French military officer Paul Aussaresses during the battle of Algiers; a unit that used torture and summary execution on a routine basis between 1955 and 1957.[28] Finally, the employment of local auxiliaries may also prove to be counterproductive if these forces are not sufficiently trained and equipped or if they become the force of choice instead of remaining primarily as adjunct forces as intended. In this case, the South Vietnamese Self-Defense Corps and the Civil Guard offer a cautionary lesson as both 'were poorly trained and equipped, miserably led, and incapable of coping with insurgents . . . [and] they proved to be an asset to the insurgents in two respects: they served as a source of weapons; and their brutality, petty thievery, and disorderliness induced innumerable villagers to join in open revolt against the GVN [Government of Vietnam]'.[29]

The example of policing in South Vietnam (and in Iraq and Afghanistan) in fact offers another important point with respect to the role of the police in counterinsurgency. In many respects, the war against insurgents is primarily a battle of information in which the side with the best intelligence gains a tremendous advantage over their adversary. Because of this it is essential that police develop a cooperative relationship not only with the local population, but with the host nation military force as well. Such a relationship allows for the timely sharing of crucial intelligence, but also allows for the coordination of operations and initiatives. Stuart Herrington, a US Army officer attached to the Phoenix program in a rural district near the Cambodian border in 1971, after studying the security situation in Duc Hue came to the apparently simple realization that the key to success involved getting the South Vietnamese military and the police to work together. Herrington recalled, 'Our mission: to get Mr. Phung of

27 Ibid., p. 62.

28 For a revealing and frank discussion of these activities see Aussaresses, Paul, *The Battle of the Casbah: Terrorism and Counter-Terrorism in Algeria, 1955-1957* (New York: Enigma Books, 2002).

29 Quoted in Nagl, John, *Learning to Eat Soup with a Knife: Counterinsurgency Lessons from Malaya and Vietnam* (Chicago: The University of Chicago Press, 2002), p. 121.

the police and Lieutenant Bong of district intelligence to share their information with one another . . . or at least get them talking to one another about the attack on the Vietcong organization'.[30] To Herrington's chagrin, despite the ostensible agreement of Phung and Bong to his plan, neither had any intention of cooperating and viewed the American advisor as a 'meddler' in their own affairs.[31]

In the case of the war in Algeria, Galula also emphasized the importance of close cooperation between the police and other branches of the government by stating that the efficiency of the police was in large part a function of 'the backing they get from the other branches of the government—particularly the judicial system'.[32] Similarly, US forces learned the same lesson again in Afghanistan and Iraq; a lesson expressed in the doctrinal statement that 'A formal link or liaison channel *must* exist between the HN [Host Nation] police and military forces. This channel for coordination, deconfliction, and information sharing enables successful counterinsurgency operations'.[33] The British counterinsurgency campaign in Malaya between 1952 and 1957 provides a positive example of such cooperation and proved to be a key factor in the ultimate defeat of the communist insurgency in that country. In his analysis of the conflict, John Nagl highlighted the important role of coordinated operations between the army, the police, and civil authorities. One British report noted, 'The secret of the change is not so much the new type of training as the integration of Army and Police together as a single anti-Bandit force and the close association with them of the District Officers and other civil authorities on the ground'.[34]

Some Reflections on Police Advising

In addressing the issue of police advising, this volume in some respects raises more questions than it answers. The historical case studies presented here, as well as the historical overview presented by Donald Stoker, demonstrate that there is no single template for successful advising, especially advising in a counterinsurgency environment. However, the following chapters do highlight several key issues related to police advising, the question of the militarization of police, and the role of the police as counterinsurgents.

1. Police advisors must understand the organizational and cultural terrain within which they operate and adjust their actions and expectations accordingly; in

30 Herrington, Stuart, *Stalking the Vietcong: Inside Operation Phoenix. A Personal Account* (New York: Presidio Press, 1982), p. 19.
31 Ibid., p. 21.
32 Galula, *Counterinsurgency Warfare*, p. 20.
33 FM 3-24, pp. 6-19 (emphasis added).
34 Quoted in Nagl, *Eating Soup with a Knife*, p. 105.

short there is no universal model for effective police advising or for instituting police reform.
2. The training, equipping, and organizing of police forces, especially in an insurgency environment, is not a goal in itself, but must be linked to a broader strategic vision that links the role and mission of the police to other civil and military institutions.
3. Regardless of the nature of the security environment, competent, reliable, and legitimate police forces are a crucial element in ensuring stability and promoting good governance.
4. The militarization of police forces and/or the use of paramilitary style police forces carry a significant level of risk related to the potential for the abuse of such forces within both peacetime and conflict environments.

With respect to the first point, Birte Gippert's analysis of police reform efforts in Kosovo and Bosnia clearly shows that preexisting models of organizational behavior and the processes of decision-making that predated European and US reform efforts needed to be understood and taken into consideration prior to attempts at implementing reforms from the bottom up. As she notes, 'Targeting reforms to the right level of the police means working "with the grain", utilizing the power of the local organization, and ideally winning their legitimacy and respect for showing knowledge and consideration to local organizational practices'. Similarly, Mark Moyar's entry on Village Stability Operations (VSO) and the Afghan Local Police (ALP) highlights the attempts by US special operations forces to create grassroots security and police capability at the village level. He shows, however, the challenges associated with such efforts and notes that ultimately reform from the grassroots required both buy-in and support from higher levels such as provincial and district governors in order to be successful. He concludes, 'One of the most important lessons of VSO and ALP was that permanent village stability required building partner capacity beyond the village level. The Afghan government needed capacity at the district and provincial levels in order to sustain the ALP once the Americans departed, and it needed capacity at the regional and national levels to manage the provinces and direct national programs and resources'. In his chapter, Athol Yates examines the move by the United Arab Emirates to adopt a strategic management model to guide the modernization of the Abu Dhabi Police by hiring foreign police advisors. He contends that the UAE's experience offers a template 'for other developed police services wanting to leap-frog stages of organization evolution'.

Not surprisingly a number of these chapters explore the use of police in counterinsurgency operations and seek to define the appropriate relationship between military forces and civil police forces in establishing domestic security. Brian Erickson looks at the varying approaches to police advising and development in Afghanistan and contrasts the differing imperatives of police and military forces in such environments. Georg Frerks and Niels Terpsta use the Dutch-led Integrated Police Training Mission in Kunduz, Afghanistan, as a case study for evaluating the success of this effort in strengthening the capacity of the Afghan police, enhancing cooperative efforts between the police and the criminal justice system, and improving the awareness, acceptance, and access to this system among the local population. Ultimately, they find that 'the IPM has planted some nice seedlings, but whether these will bud and flower is far beyond its ability to control'. The chapter by Jason Fritz and Robert Dillon in many respects stands this paradigm upon its head by arguing for the greater use of Military Police forces for training their foreign civilian police counterparts in traditional police roles within the framework of Foreign Internal Defense (FID) efforts.

Nicholas Kramer and Craig Whiteside reflect on the reasons behind the failure of the US and its coalition allies to develop credible police forces in Iraq and Afghanistan as part of a fundamental misunderstanding related to the organization, training, and equipping of these forces within a high risk environment. Their chapter addresses the wicked problem related to the benefit of civil police in the maintenance of public order, but the susceptibility to attack of such civil forces in areas of high insurgent activity. In addition to creating a model to analyze these advising missions, they emphasize the important role of foreign advisors in helping to determine the appropriate transition points for civil policing, paramilitary security forces, and military operations. Similarly, Chikara Hashimoto examines British efforts in the wake of decolonization to advise and train Middle Eastern governments. In contrast to expectations, the efforts to strengthen Middle Eastern security services in support of anti-communist efforts and the maintenance of Britain's interests in the region served mainly to prop-up increasingly unpopular authoritarian regimes and resulted in a backlash of anti-British sentiment. Hashimoto asserts that 'certain Middle Eastern governments actually undermined their own security as the repressive nature of their regimes alienated and bred resentment among their own populations. In this regard, Britain's anti-Communist policy in the region was arguably flawed in the first place'.

With respect to issues of militarization of police forces, Edward Westermann discusses the organization and training of auxiliary police forces from the conquered eastern territories in support of Nazi occupation policies and as adjuncts for the conduct of mass murder and atrocity, especially against the region's Jewish population. He demonstrates that the Nazi embrace of the direct approach in its counterinsurgency and the brutal punishment strategy not only failed to pacify these areas, but in fact stands as a definitive argument against its use in such operations. He concludes, 'Despite the overwhelming use of draconian measures against the subject populations in the occupied East, the German reliance on the direct approach failed to achieve its goal of pacifying these territories and transforming them into a "German Garden of Eden", but instead created a literal "dead zone" that ultimately consumed both victims and perpetrators'. In another analysis of the militarization of German security forces, David Livingstone discusses the debate within the Federal Republic of Germany after the Second World War concerning the need for a militarized police adjunct to the existing police forces, an issue of extreme concern to West Germany's European neighbors and the country's own socialist political party. In the end, the government of Konrad Adenauer chose to create a paramilitary *Bundesgrenzschutz* (BGS-German Border Police) as the requirements and arguments for increasing security overruled calls for reform to the traditional model of German policing. He asserts, 'Throughout the 1950s and beyond, the BGS retained its paramilitary character and its personnel were regarded as West Germany's "special police troops". Then in 1968, West German civilian policing finally began to gradually reject militarization following a series of internal reforms prompted by the anti-authoritarian activism of the student movement. These reforms culminated with the National Police Law of 1972, which professionalized the riot police and BGS so their personnel were trained in traditional crime detection and suppression rather than warfighting.' Finally, Stephen Connor's entry considers the role of the US effort in the development, deployment, and operations of the National Police Field Force (NPFF) for the conduct of pacification operations in South Vietnam. Despite their paramilitary capabilities, the NPFF was seen as the only permanent local security forces capable of assuring civil development by their ability not only to patrol the countryside but to extend a viable and credible security presence in rural areas while also improving the government's image. Despite high expectations, Connor provides important insights on the organizational dysfunctionality and the managerial mentality that ultimately contributed to the failure of the NPFF.

In the final analysis, these entries taken as a whole provide a number of insights both historical and contemporary for evaluating the challenges and opportunities associated with the organization, training, and equipping of police forces. It also offers evidence for evaluating the efficacy of such efforts specifically related to police advising in a peacetime environment and the role of police forces in wartime. Considering the contemporary global security environment, these chapters should offer a number of insights for both scholars and practitioners.

1

Expeditionary Police Advising: A Brief History

Donald Stoker

Introduction

Policing expert Otto Marenin observed that 'Police forces are the capstone in the construction of the modern state'.[1] This is a particularly cogent remark with which to begin an examination of the history of police advising, a field possessing no history and one in which historians have shown scant interest. This is despite the fact that since at least the turn of the nineteenth century, numerous nations have expended large amounts of blood and resources raising new police forces or reforming existing ones in other states.[2]

Like every field, writing about police advising presents its own conceptual and definitional problems. What writers mean by 'police' and 'security assistance' is often nebulous. One should also differentiate between police advising and policing; these are not the same thing. The latter is doing the act while the former is the teaching of it. Defining foreign police advising in a manner that does not lead the reader to believe we are discussing the advising of local US police forces is also a necessity. The best term I have heard is one I have blatantly stolen from a colleague who served as a police advisor in Iraq: Expeditionary Police Advising. The name explains itself.

The dispatch of police advising missions has generally been connected to a modernizing impulse, whether from the sending or the receiving state. This has also generally been an optimistic effort, particularly on the part of the sender. They often

1 Marenin, Otwin, 'Police Performance and State Rule: Control and Autonomy in the Exercise of Coercion', *Comparative Politics*, 18:1 (Oct. 1985), p. 102.

2 Giustozzi, Antonio, Artemy Kalinovsky, with Paul Robinson, Bob Spencer, and Alfia Sorokina, *Missionaries of Modernity: Advisory Missions and the Struggle for Hegemony in Afghanistan and Beyond* (London: Hurst, 2016), p. 120.

have been frustrated by the difficulty in efforts to create new organizational models and mindsets within host nation police forces, particularly when building new police forces from the ground up. This should not be surprising. Western states did not begin with professional, modern police forces. These evolved—sometimes over centuries—and after the development of many other building blocks of a functioning civil society that emerged as a reflection of the respect for the individual and their basic rights. But for more than a century these same Western states (and not a few non-Western ones) have been sending teams to less developed nations and expecting them to give birth to models of modern, western, metropolitan police. Military forces and international organizations doing stability operations are generally the ones tasked with building police forces. This is distinct from the colonial policing practiced by the traditional imperialist powers, though this is certainly a similar and related field of study from which much can be learned, and which is touched upon lightly here in relation to using police as a counterinsurgency tool.

Differing views regarding what kind of police should be created are also generally part of the advising equation. The intended role of the force often plays a key part here. Is the force to be responsible for general, local law enforcement tasks and should thus be built along a 'community policing' line? Or will the police be one of the state's security arms and tasked with fighting an insurgency or defending the nation from foreign or internal enemies and thus should have a more militarized structure? For example, the United States does not have a tradition of gendarmerie or constabulary forces, which are usually national and more militarized arms of policing exemplified by France's *Gendarmerie* and Italy's *Carabineri*. But when doing stability operations the US military is often being used in a classical, constabulary-style role—even though its leaders and members have traditionally disliked using this term for peacekeeping-style deployments. In the early twentieth century US forces often did lengthy service of this type in the Philippines, the Caribbean, and Central America, they did similar duty while performing post-World War II occupation roles. The British and French did the same in their respective colonial empires.[3] Additionally, non-Americans sometimes do not know that American policing is extremely fragmented. Most US municipalities have their own police forces, but there are also county and state level forces, as well as national-level agencies such as the Federal Bureau of Investigations (FBI).

Layered on top of this is the issue of the suitability of militia for local security or as police auxiliary forces. Militias are often seen as a solution to provide security against insurgents and terrorists. The US has its own militia tradition dating to the Colonial era. George Washington famously insisted that governors use their militia for local security against the British because he did not want to fritter away his scant regular Continental troops on local defense. Debates over the utility of militias in policing are

3 Cline, Lawrence E., 'The New Constabularies: Planning US Military Stabilization Missions', *Small War and Insurgencies*, 14:3 (2003), p. 159.

often connected to one of the primary roles of police advising: to create police forces that are useful as counterinsurgency tools. Indeed, some of the earliest examples of police advising concern the creation of police for this role.

Police Advising Before the First World War

The earliest European expeditionary police advising effort I have discovered (and it is possibly the first) took place in Southeastern Europe. In January 1897, an insurgency among Crete's Greek population began against the island's Muslim Turkish rulers. The Greek government backed the insurgents and landed on Crete in February 1897. The fallout from this crisis sparked an international effort among the European 'Great Powers' that designated Crete an 'international protectorate'. A 3,000 man multinational peacekeeping force arrived in March. Its Italian members trained a Cretan gendarmerie while the British trained militia forces.[4]

Similar issues led to the dispatch of another multinational European mission. The instability in Turkish-controlled Macedonia resulting from guerrilla and bandit activity, as well as a desire to maintain the regional status quo, led the half-dozen European 'Great Powers' to impose a settlement on the Ottoman Empire. In October 1903, the various parties signed the Mürzsteg Reform Plan. Its provisions included a proposal from France's consul in Salonika for the dispatch of foreign personnel to train and command a Macedonian gendarmerie to help stabilize the area. The blueprint called for 60 officers initially with plans to increase the number to 200. But between 1904 and 1908, only 48 advisors journeyed to Macedonia because of Turkish resistance to the effort. The first six military officers reached Macedonia in 1904 and were from Belgium, Norway, and Sweden. They were given ranks in the Turkish Army one grade above those they had held respectively in their national services.[5] One of the mission's participants was Swedish army officer Lieutenant Wilhelm Unander, whose work from 1903-06 earned international praise.[6] The Muslim population generally resented the foreign advisors as an alien, Christian influence imposed upon them by foreign, Christian powers. Not surprisingly, the Turkish government generally resisted the recommendations of the advisors until 1908.[7]

In 1906, the governor of Brazil's São Paulo province invited a French mission to assist in the modernization of the state's police force, Brazil's decentralized structures allowing for such a move. The French took up the task to curb German influence and

4 Savich, Carl, 'International Intervention in Kosovo and Macedonia, 1902-1908', *Serbiana.com*, <http://www.serbianna.com/columns/savich/092.shtml> (3 Sept. 2007).

5 Ibid.; Akhund, Nadine, 'Stabilizing a Crisis and the Mürzsteg Agreement of 1903: International Efforts to Bring Peace to Macedonia', *Hungarian Historical Review*, 3:3 (2014), pp. 590-591, 595.

6 Fazlhashemi, Mohammad 'Sweden ii, Swedish Officers in Persia, 1911-1915', *Encyclopedia Iranica*, <http://www.iranicaonline.org/articles/sweden-ii> (15 Aug. 2006).

7 Akhund, 'Stabilizing a Crisis and the Mürzsteg Agreement of 1903', p. 597.

gain trade advantages. France also sent police missions to Peru and Uruguay in the early 1900s. The Germans, for their part, sent advisors to work with the police forces of Argentina, Brazil, and Chile before the First World War. France and Germany, like the United States, sought to expand their regional influence through police advising.[8] There are undoubtedly many more example of European police advising missions during this era.

What seems to have been the first US police expeditionary advisory efforts were rooted in the American victory in the Spanish-American War (1898). After taking Cuba from Spain, personnel from the United States Marine Corps setup a constabulary force to police the island. Additionally, Havana's municipal police force was formed under the direction of former New York City police officers.[9] The US also trained Liberia's National Guard in 1912.[10]

The results of this same war also led to perhaps the first US expeditionary effort to create a police force as a counterinsurgency tool. This took place in the Philippines and provides an example of how using a police force to tackle an insurgency—even a paramilitary and thus militarized police force—can lead to disaster. On 18 July 1901, the American Philippine Commission created the Philippine Constabulary as a native 'semi-military police' organization. Its job was to chase bandits and guerrillas, thus removing this task from the purview of US troops. The force was under civilian control and was initially trained at the local level. In the southern areas of the island of Samar, US commanders used these new constabulary forces as the primary counterinsurgency tool. But the constabulary had been slowly and inadequately recruited, and had not been able to build a basis of local support that US planning assumed would act as a force multiplier. It also simply lacked enough men. An insurgency on Samar that had been on the ropes in 1902 was so strong by July 1905 that the US Army had to be called in to address the worsening security environment. The Philippine Constabulary's task on Samar had been made even more difficult by the corruption and incompetence of the local municipal police. The role of the constabulary was focused primarily on policing, but it also took on many civic development projects that siphoned off men and money. It could not simultaneously do development and counterinsurgency, and ultimately failed at both.[11]

8 Huggins, Martha K., *Political Policing: The United States and Latin America* (Durham, NC: Duke University Press, 1998), pp. 34-36.

9 Ibid., p. 26.

10 Kuzmarov, Jeremy, *Modernizing Repression: Police Training and Nation-Building in the American Century* (Amherst, MA: University of Massachusetts Press, 2012), p. 171.

11 Ibid.; Mihara, Robert, 'Employment of the Philippine Constabulary (1901-1917) and Haitian Gendarmerie (1916-1934) in Civic Tasks, Such as Anti-Corruption, Against the Background of Counterinsurgency Campaigns', in Gott, Kendall D. (ed.), *Security Assistance: US and International Historical Perspectives* (Leavenworth, KS: Combat Studies Institute Press, 2006), pp. 393-394, 396-400, 409-410.

One of the earliest efforts at using expeditionary police advising as a tool of modernization occurred in Persia. In 1906, there was a 'Constitutional Revolution' in what is now Iran, the fallout from which wrecked Persia's police and military and led to increasing disorder and banditry along Persian highways. The next year Russian and British competition in the 'Great Game' ended with an Anglo-Russian agreement splitting Persia into spheres of influence. In 1910, after a threat from the British to intervene and solve the problem of unrest in the nation's southern and southwestern areas, the Persian government decided to establish a 'highway gendarmerie' trained by Europeans. The Persian elite also hoped that by having Europeans responsible for reorganization of national administrative bastions they could temper foreign interference as well as modernize their state.[12]

The Persians looked to neutral nations for instructors for its new gendarmerie, first approaching Italy (which declined), and then Sweden, which accepted even though it had no gendarmerie. The Persians viewed the Swedes as competent professionals in such matters, something proven by the above mentioned Wilhelm Unander's work. For its part, the Swedish government believed the mission would open the door to Swedish economic interests in Persia, which happened during the subsequent interwar period. The men who staffed the mission went for a variety of reasons: adventure, the chance of rapid career advancement, higher wages, etc. But one of the dominant drivers was a sense that theirs was a 'civilizing mission', meaning that they could lead Persia into the modern world. General Harald Hjalmarsson led the 38 Swedish military officers and non-commissioned officers who went to Persia. They departed in August 1911 and formed the nucleus of what became a 60 member Swedish colony. The officers, in addition to signing a contract, also swore a loyalty oath to the Shah. The tasks of the new gendarmerie were to police the highways against bandits, making them safe for trade and travel, guarding Tehran's highways, and keeping an eye on potentially rebellious nomads.[13]

Hjalmarsson quickly grasped the reins. He created a Central Bureau of the Gendarmerie and raised seven gendarmerie regiments. He opened a gendarme officer training school in October 1911, a troop training school in February 1912, and a third school that trained both non-commissioned officers and enlisted troops in April 1912. The training, based upon Swedish practice, lasted six months. Six months of highway patrolling followed. The best of these men then went to the NCO course. After another six months the standouts here could attend the one-year officer course. The final step before commissioning was an exam. The Persian gendarmerie numbered 200 officers and 7,000 men by 1914, and the Persian government considered the Swedish mission an unqualified success.[14]

12 Fazlhashemi, 'Sweden ii, Swedish Officers in Persia, 1911-1915'.
13 Ibid.
14 Ibid.

The advisors had no qualms about using force and the gendarmerie came to look very much like the Swedish army. Court-martials and summary executions by firing squad or hanging were seen simply as parts of their civilizing mission and necessary to instill discipline in the Iranian people and insure order and the rule of law. In this respect, their behavior was not unlike other European powers in the developing world at the time.[15]

When the First World War broke-out in 1914, some of the Swedish advisors succumbed to what anthropologist Anna Simons has described as the 'going native danger'. Russian and British fears of pro-German sentiments among the Swedes led to pressure to end the mission, which closed in February 1915. General Hjalmarsson and most of his men left, but 20 remained and under contracts with the German army. The Shah was swayed toward the Germans, and the Swedes who stayed behind helped plot a revolt against the Russian Cossacks who patrolled Persia's northern lands. This was to take place in November 1915, and the intention was to create a situation where the Shah had no choice but to declare war on both Russia and Britain. But the plan leaked and the Russians were prepared beforehand.[16]

The Germans kept trying their hand in Persia and the Swedes helped them. The November 1915 German-Ottoman expedition to Persia included two former Swedish gendarmes. One of these, Gunnar Källström, later succeeded in convincing his gendarme regiment to come over to the German side. April 1916 saw the remaining Persian gendarmerie being renamed *amniya* after a nineteenth century patrolling force. It then went into decline and the British South Persian Rifles absorbed their duties. At least four Swedes died of wounds in Persian service.[17]

Another pre-First World War European effort was launched in Albania. This small state has hosted several police missions in its history and there are a number of works examining them.[18] Independent Albania arose in the wake of the Balkan Wars of 1912-13, a neutral creation of the European 'Great Powers' initially administered by an international control commission. But a significant multinational force had

15 Ibid.

16 Ibid.; Simons, Anna, 'The Military Advisor as Warrior-King and Other "Going Native" Temptations', in Frese, Pamela R., and Margaret C. Harrell (eds), *Anthropology and the United States Military: Coming of Age in the Twenty-first Century* (New York: Palgrave MacMillan, 2003), pp. 123-130.

17 Fazlhashemi, 'Sweden ii, Swedish Officers in Persia, 1911-1915'. The Persian mission has been the subject of extensive study. See especially Fazlhashemi, Mohammad, 'Kolonialt medvetande utan kolonier. Svenska officerare på uppdrag i 1910 talets Persien', in Berg, Magnus, and Veronica Trépagny (eds), *I andra länder: historiska perspektiv på svensk förmedling av det främmande: en antologi* (Lund: Historika Media, 1999), pp. 111-134; Ineichen, Markus, *Die schwedischen Offiziere in Persien (1911-1916),* (Bern: Lang, 2002); Persson, S.A., 'Det svenska gendarmeriet i Persien', in Ådahl, Andreas (ed.), *Iran genom seklerna, en svensk antologi* (Stockholm: Norstedt, 1971).

18 See most recently Ruis, Edwin, *Vechtmissie: Nederlande Militairen in Albanie, 1913-1914* (Uitgever: Just Publishers, 2013).

to be dispatched to prevent Serbia and Montenegro from dismembering their new neighbor. On 4 May 1913 this force of 500 landed in Shkodra, Albania, and assumed control from the departing Montenegrin occupiers. They quickly established a city government and began fighting epidemics of smallpox and typhoid. A British Royal Marine lieutenant set up a small police force of 24, which was soon supplemented by 40 mounted gendarmes. Royal Navy officers organized a court system that included a court of appeals. The most stunning detail is that this took just a few days.[19]

To reorganize a gendarmerie for all of Albania the coalition decided to recruit an advisory team. They approached the Swedes initially, but Stockholm begged-off because of its advising responsibilities in Persia. The coalition then turned to the Dutch, and Holland's eventual gendarmerie mission arose from a 29 July 1913 agreement settling the Second Balkan War.[20] A Dutch Royal Decree of 22 October 1913 approved the dispatch of a study group to Albania to prepare the ground for a gendarmerie mission. The three officers and the two NCOs who toured Albania planned to raise 1,000 men in three weeks, a quarter to be mounted—if the foreign powers of the International Control Commission (ICC) would immediately provide the necessary funding of 150,000 francs. While waiting, they drew-up a plan for a national gendarmerie of 5,000 men at an annual cost of eight million francs. The Dutch advisors decided against creating a separate militia, but did consider conscripting men for the gendarmerie. On 24 December 1913, Holland's Queen Wilhelmina approved the creation of an official gendarme mission and Colonel de Veer assumed command of the Albanian gendarmerie.[21]

One thing critically important to understand is why the members of the small Dutch team agreed to serve in such a mission. The officers saw two benefits from the work: honor and prestige. They believed it brought great humanitarian benefit to a people in need of foreign help, but also saw it as a means—if done well, and if it helped Albania's Muslims—of increasing Dutch prestige among the Muslims in Holland's overseas colonies. Dutch Foreign Minister Jonkheer J. Loudon expressed similar reasons, though he emphasized the honor that Holland would accrue from its effort.[22] Agreement on the part of Holland's government was also partially driven by prestige, though on an international scale as the mission was seen as a means of showing the flag.[23]

19 Schmidl, Erwin, 'The International Operation in Albania, 1913-14', *International Security*, 6:3 (Autumn 1999), pp. 1, 5-6.
20 Ibid., p. 7; Goslinga, Gorrit T.A., 'The Dutch in Albania (A History of the First Albanian Gendarmerie Organized and Directed by Dutch Officers, 1913-1914)' [Part 1], *Shêjzat*, 15 (1971), pp. 120, 122.
21 Goslinga, 'The Dutch in Albania' [Part I], pp. 125-128, 130.
22 Schmidl, 'The International Operation in Albania, 1913-14', p. 7.
23 Goslinga, Gorrit T.A., 'The Dutch in Albania (A History of the First Albanian Gendarmerie Organized and Directed by Dutch Officers, 1913-1914)' [Part 3], *Shêjzat*, 16 (1972), p. 37.

The mission's members quickly found themselves immersed in Albania's political maelstrom. In 1914, the gendarmerie they raised helped foil a Turkish-backed plot to seize Albania. The International Control Commission declared martial law and brought the local police under control of the gendarmerie, which among other things arrested and disarmed the plotters and quickly quashed the revolt. The gendarmerie also helped fight a war against Greek-backed rebel forces in Albania in the months before the outbreak of the First World War.[24] The gendarmerie proved an inadequate tool for dealing with Greek insurgents in southern Albania, as well as sundry local groups unwilling to recognize the leadership of the newly named king, Prince William of Wied.[25]

The Dutch advised gendarmerie soon began to function essentially as a militia (an early example of police militarization) during what became an Albanian civil war, one in which the Dutch advisors fought and their leader, Lodewijk Thomson, was killed. In July 1914, the Dutch advisors were ordered to resign by their government when Austrian and Italian advisors entered the country to begin training a militia. The resignations were completed by 27 July 1914. The looming war also contributed to the Dutch desire to end the mission.[26]

Influence and Modernization: Police Advising Between the World Wars

This was an era when foreign advising in general emerged as a growth industry. The Soviet Union entered the advising realm with its mission in Mongolia.[27] The victors of the First World War found fertile advising ground in the newly independent states of Eastern Europe, while also continuing to work in Latin America and Asia. Eastern Europe also became an arena for police advising, though little research seems to have been done in this realm.

In 1919, Italian *Carabineri* and French *Gendarmerie* collaborated in the creation of a post-Ottoman Turkish police force. Their solution to preventing local prefects from using the police as tools for their own ends was the institution of strict military discipline (sometimes elements of the militarization of police become part of the solution). The Turkish government hesitated to take the actions recommended by occupation forces, but the government of Mustafa Kemal Atatürk later implemented some of the mission's advice.[28] Italians began training Ecuador's police in 1927, advised Bolivia's constabulary from 1936, and also served as instructors to the police

24 Goslinga, Gorrit T.A., 'The Dutch in Albania (A History of the First Albanian Gendarmerie Organized and Directed by Dutch Officers, 1913-1914)' [Part 2], *Shêjzat*, 15:7-9 (1971) pp. 225-228, 230-234.

25 Schmidl, 'The International Operation in Albania, 1913-14', p. 7.

26 Goslinga, 'The Dutch in Albania' [Part 3], pp. 27-29, 37.

27 Kuznetsov, Ilya I., 'The Soviet Military Advisors in Mongolia, 1921-39', *The Journal of Slavic Military Studies*, 12:4 (Dec. 1990), pp. 118-137.

28 Giustozzi, et al., *Missionaries of Modernity*, pp. 12-13.

in Peru and Venezuela.[29] These efforts under Italy's fascist regime offer another area needing additional study.

The British, like the other European powers, were involved in expeditionary police advising in the aftermath of the First World War, which is yet another area open for further research. There was a short-lived British police mission to newly reborn Poland after the First World War, and an an officer of the British police in Darjeeling, India, went to Lhasa in 1920 to help retrain the Tibetan police force.[30] More famously—and controversially—the British created two militarized police groups largely recruited from former soldiers to fight the insurgency in Ireland, the Royal Irish Constabulary (RIC) (known as the 'Black and Tans' because they initially wore British army khaki and police dark green), and the Auxiliary Division of the Royal Irish Constabulary (ADRIC).[31]

A British police advisory mission during this era that has been examined is the British gendarmerie mission to Albania from 1925-38. It was not an 'official' British mission and London's reluctance to become officially involved always remained, but the British government took unofficial interest because it wanted professional trainers assigned to the advising roles. London's interest in Albania had political and economic foundations. The British desired to create stability in Albania and Yugoslavia, and thus throughout the volatile Balkans, as well as block Italian penetration while possibly securing newly discovered Albanian oil reserves and opening the country to British economic interests.[32] Albania's President Ahmet Zogu (later King Zog) wanted the mission because he felt the country's first need was internal security. This was the only thing that could make it peaceful and allow development. He believed he couldn't have the Italians train the gendarmerie because it would put him too much in Benito Mussolini's thrall. He also believed British trainers would be more effective and more likely to act in Albania's interests. Zog personally recruited Colonel F.W. Stirling, who had been advising the Albanians on administration since 1925, to lead the mission.[33]

29 Huggins, *Political Policing*, pp. 34, 55.

30 Stoker, Jr., Donald J., 'Undermining the *Cordon* Sanitaire: Naval Arms Sales, Naval Building, and Anglo-French Competition in the Baltic, 1918-1940—Poland—Finland—The Baltic States' (PhD dissertation, Florida State University, 1997), p. 87 fn. 114; Marshall, Julie G., *Britain and Tibet, 1765-1847: A Select Annotated Bibliography of British Relations with Tibet and the Himalayan States, Including Nepal, Sikkim, and Bhutan* (London: Routledge, 2005) pp. 348, 478.

31 There is much literature on this. See for example Leeson, D.M., *The Black and Tans: British Police and Auxiliaries in the Irish War of Independence, 1920-1921* (Oxford: Oxford University Press, 2011).

32 Martin, Simon, 'The Gendarme Mission in Albania, 1925-38: A Move on the English Chess Board?', *Contemporary European History*, 7:2 (July 1998), pp. 145, 150-151, 157-158.

33 Oakley-Hill, D.R., 'The Albanian Gendarmerie, 1925-1938, and its British Organizers', in *Albania* (Roma: Comité National-Démocratic 'Albanie Libre', 1962), p. 403.

The mission certainly seems to have been needed. The Albanian gendarmerie had done a poor job of providing public security and reportedly had interfered in the recent elections. In addition to Stirling, nine more British officers were retained to help mold a new force. They were contracted to the Albanian government and not actually in British pay.[34] Stirling was replaced by Major-General Sir Jocelyn Percy in 1926, and Percy led two major reorganizations of the gendarmerie, the first not succeeding as well as he had hoped, and established training schools to instill professionalism and loyalty.[35]

The British government lost interest when Italian penetration became inevitable (largely because the Italians were training and advising the Albanian Army), the oil reserves proved poor and thus unprofitable, and Albanian corruption and oppressive taxation killed any chance of British business prospering along this piece of the Adriatic coastline.[36] Nevertheless, the mission remained in place until the Italian invasion of 7 April 1938. Overall, it is considered successful because it greatly increased the efficiency of the Albanian gendarmerie and helped maintain peace in the Balkans.[37]

The US became even more heavily involved in expeditionary police advising after the First World War. Instead of American-style police forces, US administrations generally insisted upon the creation of constabulary or gendarmerie-type units, which are essentially quasi-military or paramilitary police forces. These constabularies were intended for both internal law enforcement as well as defense against foreign powers.[38] These paramilitary forces were also to serve as apolitical agents of security while reducing corruption and providing stability so that the US would not again need to intervene.[39] US police advising focused generally upon the Western Hemisphere and US Army and Marine Corps members either continued or embarked upon new missions to train police and army forces in Panama, Nicaragua, Haiti, Cuba, Puerto Rico, the Dominican Republic, and the Philippines. There were also American naval and military missions to Brazil, Guatemala, and Peru. For the US, the primary purpose of these missions was furthering political stability in a region considered strategically and economically important.[40]

34 Simon, 'The Gendarme Mission in Albania, 1925-38', pp. 145, 148-151.
35 Oakley-Hill, 'The Albanian Gendarmerie, 1925-1938', pp. 404-405.
36 Simon, 'The Gendarme Mission in Albania, 1925-38', p. 153.
37 Ibid., pp. 156, 158.
38 Rosenau, William, Melissa McAdam, Megan Katt, Gary Lee, Jerry Meyerle, Jonathan Schroden, Annemarie Randazzo-Matsell, with Cathy Hiatt, and Margoux Hoar, *United States Marine Corps Advisors: Past, Present, and Future* (Washington, DC: CNA, 2013), p. 11.
39 Millett, Richard L., 'Limits of Influence: Creating Security Forces in Latin America', *Joint Forces Quarterly*, 42:3 (2006), p. 14.
40 Pach, Chester J., *Arming the Free World: The Origins of the United States Military Assistance Program, 1945-1950* (Chapel Hill, NC: The University of North Carolina Press, 1991), p. 8; Huggins, *Political Policing*, pp. 27, 30-31.

A well-studied example of a US police advising mission of this era was that to Haiti, which has been the recipient of several police advisory efforts over the last century. US Marines landed in Haiti on 28 July 1915 in the wake of the 1914 revolution and the subsequent collapse of order. The US Marine Corps received instructions to organize a new gendarmerie under the terms of a protocol of a treaty signed between US and Haitian representatives. The US swept away the thoroughly corrupt existing army and five police forces and designed and built a new force to replace them: the *Gendarmerie d'Haiti*, which was officially created on 16 September 1915.[41]

USMC Major Smedley Butler assumed command of the new gendarmerie on 3 December 1915. He and the other Marines faced a number of obstacles. Haitian officials, for example, resisted the change because of efforts to reduce corruption. The gendarmerie's members also generally suffered from poor health, which increased the difficulty of creating and maintaining an effective force. In 1916, 95 percent of its 1,200 members had syphilis infections as well as many other problems such as hookworm. Also, until 1921 the police suffered constant attacks from guerrillas and bandits. But the Marines succeeded in laying a firm foundation and wisely brought the prison system under the control of the gendarmerie, which ensured it was professionally run. Additionally, after one earlier failed attempt at moving Haitians into leadership positions, the Marines made an intense effort to do this from 1926-29, partly by establishing a military school to train gendarmerie officers.[42]

The US also intervened in Nicaragua from 1923-27. The US police advising effort here was done via the State Department, which arranged contracts between the Nicaraguan government and American policing experts. This was perhaps the first time the US government actively used private contractors for police training. Part of the reasoning for arranging the Nicaraguan effort in this manner was that US law forbade the military from training foreign police or military forces if the US had not actually occupied the country, a restriction removed by Congress in 1926. The initial US effort in Nicaragua became a victim of the nation's unstable politics. In 1927, US Marines disbanded the existing constabulary and established a new one for which they provided the officers. The Marines left in 1933.[43] The US Marine Corps was so frequently involved in the construction of constabulary forces that instructions on their creation were included in the 1940 USMC *Small Wars Manual*.[44]

The 1930s saw the first expeditionary advising effort of the US Federal Bureau of Investigation (FBI) when it dispatched a mission to Chiang Kai-Shek's Chinese

41 McCrocklin, James H., *Garde d'Haiti: Twenty Years of Organization and Training by the United States Marine Corps, 1915-1934* (Annapolis, MD: Naval Institute Press, 1956), pp. v, 21-22, 55-59; Mihara, 'Employment of the Philippine Constabulary (1901-1917) and Haitian Gendarmerie (1916-1934)', pp. 404-405.

42 McCrocklin, *Garde d'Haiti*, pp. 65-66, 69-70, 86, 90-92, 186-187.

43 Huggins, *Political Policing*, pp. 30-31, 33-34, 41.

44 US Marine Corps, *Small Wars Manual* (Washington, DC: USGPO, 1940, Reprint, 1987), chapter 12, pp. 1-25.

Kuomintang government.[45] In 1939, the FBI sent an agent to Brazil and Colombia to help their respective police establish secret services, but little came of these efforts. Beginning in 1943, the FBI helped Brazil form a national police force that mirrored the functions of the FBI.[46]

In the long term, none of the many US police advisory efforts in Latin America and the Caribbean succeeded as planned, and the created forces sometimes instead became instruments of anti-democratic repression. Later, the US found itself intervening again in some of these same lands.[47]

An Arm of Ideological Struggle: Expeditionary Police Advising and the Cold War

The British and Americans were the dominant Western forces doing foreign advising during the Cold War (including police advising), and were generally driven by Cold War security concerns and fears related to the spread of communism. The Soviet Union was hardly less active in the advising realm and had advisors working in nearly 50 different nations in the Cold War era. Unfortunately, Soviet advising in general has been little studied. Another factor driving the post-Second World War dispatch of police advising missions was decolonization. This necessitated the creation of new police forces, or the retraining of former colonial personnel.[48]

Many US postwar police advising efforts were rooted in the course of the Second World War or arose from its aftermath. For example, the US sent a mission to Iran during the war to train Iranian gendarmerie and counter pro-Axis sentiment there while laying the groundwork for the future US-Iranian relationship.[49] After the war, the mission to advise the police became part of the struggle against Soviet and Communist expansion. It, along with an army advising mission, remained after the war and in 1950 US President Harry S. Truman partially credited Iran's survival in the face of Soviet pressure to this support. The gendarme mission was commanded by an experienced army officer and former policeman, Norman Schwarzkopf, Sr., the father of the future US commander in the 1990-91 Persian Gulf War.[50]

The post-war occupation and reconstruction of Germany, Italy, and Japan meant further US involvement in police advising. We also see in post-war Germany, Japan, and Austria successful US involvement in the construction of democratic police

45 Kuzmarov, *Modernizing Repression*, p. 7.
46 Huggins, *Political Policing*, pp. 53-56, 62.
47 Millett, 'Limits of Influence: Creating Security Forces in Latin America', p. 14.
48 Giustozzi, et al, *Missionaries of Modernity*, pp. 31, 119.
49 Pach, *Arming the Free World*, p. 97
50 Motter, T. H. Vail, *United States Army in World War II, The Middle East Theater, The Persian Corridor and Aid to Russia* (Washington, DC: Center of Military History, 1952; Reprint 2000), pp. 462-465, 475-477. See also Ricks, Thomas M., 'US Military Missions to Iran, 1943-1978: The Political Economy of Military Assistance', *Iranian Studies*, 12:3/4 (Summer—Autumn, 1979), pp. 163-193.

forces in the decade after the end of the war.[51] The Allies had made some advanced preparations for rebuilding a German police force and established schools to aid in its creation. But the new police were unarmed and thus vulnerable to criminals who were not. The Allies also had destroyed existing stocks of captured weapons, which made it more difficult to equip what became the West German police when it was decided to arm it.[52] In occupied Italy the US assisted in the construction of a new paramilitary *Carabineri*, a role of which was to help counter Communist subversion.[53]

No wartime plan existed for creating a new Japanese police. The 1947 Police Law created decentralized training programs that produced uneven results, though a subsequent 1954 statute birthed standardized recruiting, training, and instruction. The US was enforcing the demilitarization of Japan, but Communist Chinese success in China and North Korea forced a rethinking of this approach and led to the creation of a militarized Japanese police force equipped with US weapons and clothed in American uniforms. Something considered critical to Allied success in both Japan and Germany was the de-politicization of the police by removing from their purview everything not related to dealing with crime and general policing functions.[54]

US forces also occupied what became known as South Korea at the end of World War II. One of the earliest US actions was the reconstitution of a Korean police force to maintain internal order and relieve US troops of these duties. But as rapid US demobilization saw US troop numbers drop, American leaders realized Korea needed its own defense organization, as well as a police reserve. In December 1945, the US launched Plan Bamboo to build a South Korean Constabulary force of 25,000 to serve as a police reserve. This was intended as the nucleus of the South Korean army, and became just that. Recruiting began in January 1946.[55] The Korean National Police saw the growing Constabulary as a threat to their business interests and extortion rackets. Police harassment of constabulary members was met by a June 1947 shootout between Constabulary and police forces when Constabulary troops attacked a police station to free a comrade. The attack left three men dead. Simultaneously, the Soviets constructed four police forces in North Korea: the Railway Constabulary, the Coast Guard, the National Police, and a militarized Border Guard that numbered 40,000 by the end of 1948.[56]

51 Phelps, James, 'Lessons in Developing Democratic Police from Post-Second World War Successes', *International Journal of Comparative and Applied Criminal Justice*, 34:1 (Spring 2010), p. 112.

52 Ibid., pp. 129-130.

53 Kuzmarov, *Modernizing Repression*, pp. 168, 189.

54 Phelps, 'Lessons in Developing Democratic Police from Post-Second World War Success', pp. 127-129; Huggins, *Political Policing*, pp. 72-73.

55 Clemens, Peter, 'Captain James Hausman, US Military Advisor to Korea, 1946-48: The Intelligent Man on the Spot', *The Journal of Strategic Studies*, 25:1 (Mar. 2002), pp. 165-167.

56 Millett, Alan R., *The War for Korea, 1945-1950: A House Burning* (Lawrence, KS: University Press of Kansas, 2005), p. 104, 107-108.

The Hukbalahap (Huk) Rebellion (1946-54) in the Philippines, a US possession until 1946, became not only an arena for the US to do police advising as part of the Cold War's global ideological struggle, but also marks an example of one of the other primary roles for police in the Cold War: as tools of counterinsurgency. The Huks emerged as the Philippines' most effective resistance group in the wake of the 1941 Japanese invasion. Drawn largely from Luzon's farmers and Communist Party labor unionists, its wartime strength peaked at 15,000 full-time and 30-50,000 part-time fighters, and 100,000 people in secret political organs, all supported by as many as two million other sympathizers. The post-war Manila government refused official recognition of their wartime status, which meant they received no compensation from the US like other resistance fighters. Manila also replaced local Huk political leaders and kept Huk politicians from taking the six seats in the Congress that they won in the 1946 elections. The large landowners began taking back holdings the Huks had distributed to peasants during the war, sometimes using private militias known as 'civil guards' to do so. The Huks responded by returning to their guerrilla ways. They enjoyed abundant public sympathy and their military prowess, combined with the tendency of the government constabulary and 'civil guards' to abuse the people, soon saw their numbers match those of government forces while enormous tracts of rural Luzon fell under their control.[57]

Initially, the Filipino security forces consisted of the 24,000 men of the paramilitary national police force, the Philippine Constabulary. The Constabulary's structure and composition aligned more with that of a national, European-style gendarmerie as it was more heavily armed and more militarized than a US-style police force. Its armament included tanks and artillery and it looked more like light infantry than police. It focused upon defending the state rather than the population, and the fact that its head was a presidential appointee made the Philippine Constabulary a political tool often used by the Liberal Party to insure that its candidates won elections. Organizationally, the Philippine Constabulary answered to the Minister of the Interior, who generally worked for the interests of the large landowners. This politicization contributed to corruption and crony-style leadership.[58]

Philippine president Manuel Roxas declared the Huks an illegal group and in 1948 had the Philippine Constabulary try to suppress them by force in a generally unsuccessful offensive. This lack of success injured the Constabulary's morale, which when combined with the government's lack of interest in the struggle and its failure to provide proper material support worsened the problems. The Constabulary generally performed poorly against the Huks as its members had no real command and control

57 Ladwig, Walter C., III, 'When the Police are the Problem: The Philippine Constabulary and the Hukbalahap Rebellion', in Fair, Christine and Sumit Ganguly (eds), *Policing Insurgencies: Cops as Counterinsurgents* (Oxford: Oxford University Press, 2014), pp. 20-22.

58 Ibid., pp. 24-26, 36-37.

system or strategic direction. Meanwhile, their abuses of the population fed the insurgency.[59]

The Filipino government appealed to the US for emergency military aid in 1949. The US was certainly willing, but attached a stipulation. US officials understood the problems caused by the Constabulary's abuses and the head of the Joint US Military Assistance Group (JUSMAG) insisted in mid-1950 upon shifting COIN operations to the army. The Constabulary would also be placed under the Ministry of Defense, which then meant the US military could use military assistance funds for training. The government of President Elpidio Rivera Quirino resisted the reforms, but a mid-1950 Huk offensive saw him bend to the US demand. A new 7,000-man Constabulary and a separate 17,000-man army emerged, alongside an air force and navy.[60]

When the post of Secretary of National Defense came open shortly after the reorganization, the US pushed for the appointment of the former Second World War guerrilla resistance leader and Liberal Party Congressman Ramon Magsaysay. His leadership proved transformational. Magsaysay made the police force a police force and the army an army. He depoliticized the military and reduced corruption. He attacked army abuses that fed the insurgency by curbing their actions against civilians and paying and feeding the soldiers better so they didn't loot the civilians (junior enlisted personnel had been so poorly paid that their wages would not even cover the cost of their meals). The police became a tool for law and order—not counterinsurgency—which became the army's job. Magsaysay shrank the size of police companies by one-third, increased training (limited funding slowed this), tossed out corrupt, incompetent, and politically controlled members, and replaced their heavy weapons with batons. The police did have some functions in the war against the Huks: intelligence collection, maintenance of local law and order, and, if the Huks attacked a town or city, the police were to fight the insurgents until the army arrived. Unfortunately for the police though, promising officers were too often poached by the army.[61]

Magsaysay's reforms and his elimination of abuse by the 'civil guards' won much support for the government while causing many defections among the Huks. By 1951 the Filipino forces were killing 40-50 Huks weekly. The insurgency's numbers shrunk to about 8,000 active guerrillas in early 1952, and it was reduced to a nuisance by the following year. Historian Walter Ladwig wisely notes, 'Although subordinating the police to the army when conducting COIN operations is contrary to the advice of most theorists, the Huk Rebellion illustrates that there are no cookie-cutter solutions to insurgency'.[62]

Just as with the Americans, one of Britain's tools in the ideological struggle was police advising. The British had a police mission in Greece after the Second World

59 Ibid., pp. 24-25, 31-32.
60 Ibid., pp. 27-28.
61 Ibid., pp. 28-30, 37.
62 Ibid., pp. 23, 35-36, 40.

War run by Sir Charles Wickham, who had established the Royal Ulster Constabulary. This gendarmerie was further expanded by the US State Department. The US also modernized the police forces in Greek cities. All were expected to act aggressively against Greece's Communist insurgency.[63] Similarly, one of Great Britain's methods of stopping the spread of communism in the Middle East was the introduction of police or security advisors in Lebanon, Iraq, and Jordan.[64]

The British were also heavily involved in conducting counterinsurgency operations as part of the Cold War anti-Communist struggle. One of the best known examples is found in the Malayan Emergency (1948-60). The British—based on their extensive colonial experience—viewed handling insurgencies as largely a police task to be supported by the military. In June 1948, when Britain declared the Malayan Emergency, it embarked upon a crash increase of the police. By 1951 the 20,000 regulars were supplemented by 30,000 special constables who made up a weakly trained paramilitary force designed to fight the insurgents.[65]

One can certainly hold up the British approach of relying on the police to fight insurgents as an ideal, but this is not always the best option, and sometimes counting on the police to carry the counterinsurgency weight is simply mad. The Malayan insurgency was very small in numbers, which meant it could be addressed with different means than a massive insurgency such as the one launched by the North Vietnamese against South Vietnam. The bigger the insurgent force, the less likely police, militia, and home guard units can deal with it without army support. If the insurgents are supported by regular troops, or guerrilla forces that have essentially become light infantry such as Main Force Viet Cong units, opposing them with regular military forces is the primary rational counter. If one does otherwise, the police will simply be killed by the insurgents, a fate often also suffered by militia used in a policing role in a counterinsurgency environment.

The British threw a large number of men at their Malayan problem, which is exactly what counterinsurgency guru John McCuen later advised in *The Art of Counter-Revolutionary Warfare*. By 1950 there were enormous numbers of auxiliary police and home guards. This stabilized the situation, but the insurgency was still growing and in 1951 reached its peak strength of 8,000, the Emergency's most violent year. This was also the year the problems with the Malayan police became horribly clear. The new police were poorly trained, poorly led, too often corrupt, and often extremely abusive of the population, particularly the ethnic Chinese, all of whom were often treated as insurgents simply because they were Chinese. Some of the heavy-handedness was a result of the employment of veterans of Britain's defunct Palestine Police, who

63 Kuzmarov, *Modernizing Repression*, pp. 190-192.
64 Hashimoto, Chikara, 'British Security Liaison in the Middle East: The Introduction of Police/Security Advisers and the Lebanon-Iraq-Jordan "Anti-Communist Triangle" From 1949-1958', *Intelligence and National Security*, 27:6 (2012), p. 848.
65 Corum, James S., *Training Indigenous Forces in Counterinsurgency: A Tale of Two Insurgencies* (US Army War College, Carlisle, PA: Strategic Studies Institute, March 2006), p. 5.

could be exceptionally brutal. A 1950 Police Commission report revealed extensive corruption throughout the Malayan government, but found it particularly endemic in the lower ranks of the police. They were identified as 'a major source of the people's dissatisfaction with the government'. Corruption was particularly bad among the rural police. They were too often prone to bribe taking, often reluctant to act against the guerrillas, and even turned over their weapons to them. This was supposed to be the first line of defense against the insurgents.[66]

Beginning in April 1950, Lieutenant General Harold Briggs led the British military effort in Malaya and helped develop the counterinsurgency strategy that eventually broke the Communist guerrillas. His reforms included better military and police cooperation, particularly in regard to collecting intelligence. Moreover, the primary instructors at the new police schools were policemen, not soldiers. This was done to give the police their own identity and to lessen what was already seen as a tendency toward militarization.[67]

An early plank of the Malayan government's counterinsurgency effort was a stopgap measure: the establishment of village home guards. A home guard unit would have 60-100 men to stand watch in guard towers or at the village gates. They would only have about a dozen weapons between them and these would be given to the men standing watch. About 100,000 men had been organized in this manner by 1951. They had no uniforms, were not paid, and were used only for their appointed security task. The British eventually had 200,000 men in local defense units and the effort was generally judged a success. One reason for this is that the British didn't ask much from them, which was wise because they provided very little training. They never asked the home guard to take the lead in active operations, but made successful use of the natural tendency of locals to want to organize for their own defense and security. On the formation and use of such militia-style organs, 'controlling and managing the process' is the big problem.[68]

This is relevant because the Malayan home guards were in many respects militia, but lacked the military power, organization, and capabilities of most militia. This meant that they were easier to control, easy to disband when no longer needed, and possessed less ability to coerce and abuse the civilian population, especially since they *were* a part of the civilian population. Their limited military capacity meant that military and police commanders were not tempted to move them somewhere else and use them the way US commanders employed Civilian Irregular Defense Group (CIDG) units in Vietnam in the early 1960s. Their disadvantage was this same lack of military capability that made them a useful alternative to militia. Against any type of concerted insurgent attack they were little more than a tripwire. But in Malaya, where

66 Ibid., pp. 7, 13-14.
67 Ibid., pp. 14-15, 40.
68 Ibid., pp. 13, 47-48.

guerrilla bands tended to be small, if they were properly supported by police or army forces, a tripwire was all that was needed.

In Cyprus, the British faced another insurgency in which police advising played a role. The insurgency against British rule in Cyprus began on 1 April 1955. The Greek insurgents, EOKA, never had more than 200-300 fighters among their ranks and generally waged their war through bombings and small attacks, but they benefited from broad popular support. The Cyprus police were poorly paid, led, trained, and equipped, few in number, notoriously corrupt, and suffered from infiltration by insurgent sympathizers. Guerrilla attacks on the police incapacitated the force further and the British relied heavily upon Turkish Cypriots recruited to fill the forces' ranks and expand them. The British also raised an Auxiliary Police force from this community, which performed local guard and security duties. In this regard, growing the police freed up troops for active operations against the insurgents. The British also drastically increased their troop numbers and by early 1956 had in Cyprus 20,000 British soldiers and 20,000 other military and police personnel to deal with about 200 insurgents.[69]

But the British lacked an intelligence gathering capability in Cyprus as they had no local 'Special Branch', a critical fixture of such British operations. They also had a largely Turkish police force to use against a Greek population that in turn provided them with almost no intelligence. The ethnically Turkish police were badly selected, were known to loot Greek homes, and sometimes had criminal pasts. The British neglected the necessary reform and training of the police in Cyprus, believing this could wait until after the insurgency was quashed. This resulted in a badly trained police force whose members often abused detainees (allegations of torture were made). This quickly lost Britain the strategic public information war abroad. In contrast, the insurgents made very effective use of the Greek media against the British. The shifting of world opinion against London was a key factor influencing Britain's move to grant Cyprus independence in 1959.[70]

The Cyprus case—like many of the examples of Cold War police advising (especially those involving counterinsurgency)—raises the question of whether one should initiate police reform while fighting. The scale and intensity of the insurgency is certainly one of the key factors to consider when making this decision: the larger the insurgency, the more difficult this will be because of the challenges being faced. But often the police and police ineffectiveness are causes of the insurgency, or at least feeding it. If the police aren't sufficiently professionalized and reformed, executing an effective counterinsurgency strategy might not be possible.

Meanwhile, the US was also deepening its involvement in the Cold War struggle and one of the planks of US grand strategy became police advising and assistance. By the end of the administration of US President Dwight Eisenhower, the Central Intelligence Agency (CIA), the Department of Defense (DOD), and the Agency

69 Ibid., pp. 25-32.
70 Ibid., pp. 31-33.

for International Development (AID) did almost all US overseas foreign internal security assistance, with the CIA taking the lead in training foreign police as well as paramilitary organizations. The Eisenhower administration dispatched police missions to nations as varied as Brazil, Indonesia, and South Vietnam. In all of these countries the US government attempted to export the US policing model, but did not achieve the results hoped for.[71]

One of the key institutional instruments of US police advising was what came to be called the 1290-d program launched by Eisenhower's State Department. In 1955, National Security Council Action Memorandum 1290, sub-clause 'd', became the legal and administrative foundation for expeditionary police advising efforts. The many subsequent 1290-d police advising efforts were seen as a tool in the Cold War against Communist subversion, and police forces of all kinds were seen as the first line of defense in the global struggle against communism. The catalyst for this measure was the 1954 French defeat at Den Bien Phu. Later, this effort became known as the Overseas Internal Security Program (OISP).[72] The US was soon also providing police assistance to Cambodia, Indonesia, Afghanistan, Pakistan, Saudi Arabia, and Jordan.[73]

The Eisenhower administration also established the Office of Public Safety (OPS) to train foreign police officers. The US personnel came from the CIA, the FBI, and the Special Forces. In addition to being a tool of modernization, one of the most important roles of an OPS trainer was the establishment of intelligence wings within police forces. The primary purpose of this was to identify and suppress leftist (i.e., Communist) anti-government elements. A downside of these efforts was that some client states used these assets for repression.[74]

OPS training also often went hand in hand with the militarization of police forces. In the 1950s the CIA built a paramilitary police for Thailand to use against Communist insurgents. But the US advisors did not understand that a strengthened Thai police was viewed by the army as a threat to its position in the nation. When the Thai army seized power in 1957, it immediately stripped the police of its paramilitary functions, responsibilities, and equipment. The US returned in 1964 to train the police. The force was rapidly expanded as a counterinsurgency instrument and deployed to the countryside, but its corruption and atrocious behavior handed the insurgents a propaganda weapon. The Thai army also did what it could to ensure the effort failed. US advisors began training the Laotian police in 1955 and used the Thai police as a model on the mistaken assumption of cultural similarity between the two nations.[75]

71 Rosenau, William, 'The Kennedy Administration, US Foreign Internal Security Assistance and the Challenge of "Subterranean War", 1961-63', *Small Wars and Insurgencies*, 14:3 (2003), pp. 82, 90. See also Rosenau, William, *US Internal Security Assistance to South Vietnam: Insurgency, Subversion, and Public Order* (London: Routledge, 2005).

72 Kuzmarov, *Modernizing Repression*, p. 9; Huggins, *Political Policing*, pp. 79-80.

73 Giustozzi, et al, *Missionaries of Modernity*, pp. 102-103, 138, 202-206.

74 Ibid., p. 120.

75 Ibid., pp. 120-122.

One of the most unique police advising programs was that run by Michigan State University (MSU) in South Vietnam beginning in 1955. It advised on a variety of governmental functions including policing. The program was plagued by a general ignorance among its advisors of Vietnam and the country's specific conditions. South Vietnamese president Ngo Dinh Diem also disagreed with the MSU advisors regarding the type of police force suitable for South Vietnam. Diem (as did his US military advisors) wanted a more militarized police to counter the North Vietnamese insurgency. The MSU advisors wanted a US-style, lightly armed police.[76]

US expeditionary police advising efforts intensified under the administration of President John F. Kennedy. His administration's officials saw police and paramilitary advising and assistance as the first line of defense against communism in the Third World. They also believed the Eisenhower administration had not done enough here. To review police and paramilitary training responsibilities and assistance the Kennedy administration established the Interagency Committee on Police Assistance Programs in Newly Emerging Countries. It became known as the Johnson Commission after its director, U. Alexis Johnson.[77]

The Johnson Commission report concluded that the most critical function of such assistance was countering Communist subversion. The Commission believed police assistance programs should have three objectives: improving the ability of civilian police and other government security forces 'to maintain public order with a minimum of violence', thus making these forces better able to counter subversion; and 'developing humane policing methods and upgrading the image and character of internal security forces'. It also urged pressuring US allies, such as France and Great Britain, to increase their efforts along these lines as police and internal security advising had become yet another realm of Cold War competition. If the West provided such help—went the reasoning—emerging nations would be less likely to seek Chinese or Soviet assistance.[78]

A question that one must ask is whether or not the Johnson Commission's approach should be the purposes of expeditionary police advising. If the emphasis is placed upon building police forces designed to counter specific ideological threats, it could be difficult to create a police force that fulfills the basic law and order functions communities expect from a professional force. It also raises the question of whether or not the intense focus on anti-subversion work means the police will be properly trained and supported to perform core law and order enforcement in a manner where everyone is treated equally. Fair, effective, and impartial conduct on the part of the police is part of what builds the credibility of the state in the eyes of the people and thus makes them not as susceptible to subversion, threats, and propaganda.

76 Ibid., pp. 123-125.
77 Rosenau, 'The Kennedy Administration', pp. 83, 90-91.
78 Ibid., p. 84.

On 1 November 1962, the Kennedy administration made the Office of Public Safety (OPS) a sub-branch of the United States Agency for International Development (USAID) to give an organizational home to police advising and assistance and act as the central office for police missions and assistance run by the USAID and the State Department.[79] Over the next 12 years, the Office of Public Safety advised police in 52 different nations, while 5,000 police personnel from 77 nations completed the full International Police Academy curriculum. This effort was further supported in 1963 by the opening of the International Police Academy in Washington, DC.[80] The Kennedy administration also spent heavily on police advising all over the world. Together, in the 1962 fiscal year Costa Rica, Iran, Nicaragua, Panama, the Philippines, and South Vietnam, received $17.8 million in Department of Defense funding; $12 million of this went to South Vietnam. USAID doubled its fiscal year police assistance budget in 1963 to $33,744,000. The same year the US had 171 people in police advising roles in 30 nations, especially in Thailand, Indonesia, and South Vietnam. More than one million foreign personnel were in AID policing programs in August 1963.[81]

Much of this interest in police advising was rooted in the ideas of a key member of the Kennedy (and later Lyndon Johnson) administration, Walt Rostow. He brought with him what became known as 'Modernization Theory'. Many in this era thought social science was the key to winning the Cold War, and while at MIT Rostow had argued that modernization could counter the spread of communism in the developing world. To Rostow, modernization theory also explained the problems of the developing world, and gave the foundations for a course of action. In modernization theory, the US stood at the developmental pinnacle. Its institutions provided the models for what the developing world needed to address its problems and shortcomings. Strengthening state institutions was key; police forces were one of these. Moreover, foreign aid would help these less-developed nations grow and leap into the modern world. Rostow assumed development was always in a straight line—always upward. To make this work one had to increase the power and efficiency of state institutions. They also firmly believed the US government could replicate these measures abroad. While the theory lacked an empirical grounding and a basis in historical reality, the administration also assumed universal application. Rostow and others even frowned upon being given information that was specific to a certain nation, such as South Vietnam.[82]

Early US counterinsurgency doctrine in Vietnam argued for police, military, and civil action against the insurgents at the same time, but the growing US presence

79 Ibid., pp. 84-85.

80 Ladwig, Walter C., 'Training Foreign Police: A Missing Aspect of US Security Assistance to Counterinsurgency', *Comparative Strategy*, 26:4 (October 2007), pp. 288-289.

81 Rosenau, 'The Kennedy Administration', pp. 82, 85.

82 Ibid., pp. 66, 73-74.

made it unclear who ran the myriad programs.[83] US leaders also wanted US-style law enforcement, but without US-style fragmentation, believing that centralization better utilized scant resources while also achieving the important goal of strengthening the authority of the state. The US does not have a national gendarmerie or constabulary, but has state-level National Guard forces under the general control of the governor (unless the president federalizes them). The National Guard—it was believed—resembled a paramilitary force closely enough for it to be used as a model for the Third World.[84] Unfortunately, too often the result was that American 'progressive' statism created the foundation for totalitarian governments. This and other forms of militarization of police forces emerged as a frequent issue during the Cold War.

Other areas of the globe also saw intense US Cold War efforts to advise and assist police and gendarmerie forces. The US involvement in the Caribbean and Latin America intensified. The Marines returned to Haiti from 1959-1963 to build another gendarmerie. In addition to protecting US interests and furthering stability, the mission was also seen as a bulwark against Communist subversion. Unfortunately, upon its departure the mission had little to show for its hard work.[85] The US had a police advisor in Bolivia in 1955, and after the Cuban Revolution in 1959 police training programs became an important US tool of the Cold War struggle in Latin America. Soon, the US was providing police advisors and aid to Venezuela, the Dominican Republic, Guatemala, El Salvador, Costa Rica, Peru, Bolivia, Uruguay, Chile, Argentina, Brazil, and Paraguay.[86]

African nations also received much American police assistance. The US State Department supported Liberia from 1955 to 1971 with over $3.4 million in police aid and training to modernize its force. The US spent heavily to build a militarized police force in the Congo after 1963, provided aid and support to Chad in the mid-1960s, and aided the Ivory Coast in the late 1960s with the support of French advisors. The 1960s also saw the US provide police advising or assistance to Ghana, Dahomey (Benin), Niger, the Central African Republic, Rwanda, Burundi (with Belgian help), Kenya, Tanzania (alongside British advisors), and Uganda (with British and Israeli assistance). The US also worked with Nigeria from 1970-1972.[87]

The US police advisors were active in the Middle East and its bordering areas, particularly in the early decades of the Cold War. In post-Second World War Iraq, the US trained Iraqi police until Nuri al-Said's government was overthrown in 1958. US aid money helped build Baghdad's central jail, Abu Ghraib. In the 1950s

83 Daddis, Gregory A., 'CORDS in Charge: Organizing for Pacification Support in the Vietnam War', in Seidule, Ty, and Jacqueline Whitt (eds), *Stand Up and Fight! The Creation of US Security Organizations, 1942-2005*, (Carlisle, PA: Strategic Studies Institute, US Army War College Press, 2015), p. 142.

84 Rosenau, 'The Kennedy Administration', p. 81.

85 Rosenau, *United States Marine Corps Advisors*, pp. 18-19, 22-23.

86 Kuzmarov, *Modernizing Repression*, pp. 208-230.

87 Ibid., pp. 170-173, 177-178, 181-186.

Turkey received a US mission led by a veteran of the Detroit police force, Charlie O'Brien, who was later killed in Vietnam. Working in conjunction, the US and Italy advised Somalia's police in the 1950s in an effort to thwart the rise of leaders with Soviet sympathies. The Departments of Defense and State supplied more than $4.5 million in OPS aid and worked in Somalia until it aligned with the Soviet Union in 1972. The US also provided training to the police of Libya's King Idris before he was overthrown by Muammar Gaddafi in 1969.[88] Ethiopia approached the US about police assistance in 1961. Under the OPS program, the US provided advisors and more than $2 million in material support before the OPS program ended in 1973. US efforts were supplemented by West German and Israeli advisors. Beginning in 1965, West Germany reportedly supplied around $8 million in equipment over the next three years. Israeli trainers largely provided instruction at the Abab Dina Police College and criminal and paramilitary training.[89]

Partially as a reaction to the US experience in Vietnam, and partially due to unclear US policy, Congress killed the Office of Public Safety in 1974 via the Foreign Assistance Act, which also imposed tight limits on how US agencies could use funds to train foreign police. This left the US without an institutional framework for doing police advising as no US government agency had responsibility for such tasks. Congress sometimes subsequently granted exemptions, but this often resulted in confusion, program and effort duplication, and inappropriate training.[90]

Expeditionary Police Advising in the Post-Cold War World

The decades since the end of the Cold War have been by far the most active for police advising and police training activities. The US and Great Britain again have been among the most active nations here, but other European states have helped carry the burden, often under the auspices of NATO, the United Nations, or the European Union. Multinational efforts at police advising became increasingly common in the late twentieth and early twenty-first centuries. There were efforts to establish democratic police forces in many places: Afghanistan, Bosnia, Cambodia, El Salvador, Guatemala, Haiti, Iraq, Kosovo, Mozambique, Namibia, Nicaragua, Somalia, South Africa, Timor-Leste (East Timor), and others.[91] Moreover, not a few nations traditionally classified as 'developing' took up expeditionary police advising.

88 Ibid., pp. 168-169, 200-201; Agyeman-Duah, Baffour, *The United States and Ethiopia: Military Assistance and the Quest for Security, 1953-1993* (Lanham, MD: University Press of America, 1994), pp. 88-89.
89 Agyeman-Duah, *The United States and Ethiopia*, pp. 85-88.
90 Ladwig, 'Training Foreign Police', p. 289.
91 Phelps, 'Lessons in Developing Democratic Police from Post-Second World War Successes', pp. 119, 122.

The United Nations dramatically increased its role in police advising in the post-Cold War era, particularly in post-conflict environments.[92] For example, a 10 June 1999 agreement led to the establishment of the United Nations Mission in Kosovo (UNMIK) to train police. The US-led multinational force of 7,000 included 800 US personnel. Working under the authority of Security Council Resolution 1244, this was the first UN 'armed executive police mission in a region where there was no host government'. The mission was to restore order and perform general policing functions while it trained the new, multiethnic Kosovo Police Service (KPS). The Organization for Security and Cooperation in Europe ran the training, which eventually included instructors from 20 nations. But the first units deployed only in April 2000. This slow implementation left the population unprotected from the worst possible depredations. US troops began taking up the slack and doing police tasks, something that did not make their commanders happy.[93] The great lesson of the mission is that such forces need to arrive with the ability to establish not just police, but a law enforcement system that included courts and prisons. If this is not done it feeds disorder and lawlessness.[94] By April 2015, a decade-long police United Nations Police (UNPOL) mission to Liberia had put 4,904 police officers in the field.[95]

Arms of the European Union have also become increasingly involved in police advising, very often under UN auspices. In Mostar, Bosnia Hercegovina, from 1994-96, the Western European Union (WEU) built the Unified Police Force. There was a European Union Police (EUPOL) mission in Macedonia from 15 December 2003. Macedonia was one of the most important routes for trafficking drugs, as well as women forced into the sex trade. The WEU also set up the Multinational Advisory Police Element in spring 1997 to help build Albania's police force. The EU assumed control of this in June 2001.[96]

The December 1995 Dayton Accords that ended the war in Bosnia established the Federation of Bosnia and Hercegovina (dominated by Bosnians and Croats) and the Serbian controlled Republic of Srpsa. At the time, there were three ethnic police forces. Under a slow and difficult process, reformed, ethnically integrated police and security forces were created in each state, all under the guidance of a UN International Police Task Force (IPTF), which took over at the end of 1996.[97] The International Criminal Investigation, Training, and Assistance Program (ICITAP) funded and

92 Giustozzi, et al., *Missionaries of Modernity*, p. 1.

93 Bayley, David H. and Robert M. Perito, *The Police in War: Fighting Insurgency, Terrorism, and Violent Crime* (Boulder, CO: Lynne Riener Publishers, 2010), pp. 44-45; Perito, *US Police in Peace and Stability Operations*, pp. 8-9.

94 Bayley and Perito, *The Police in War*, pp. 47-48.

95 Zanker, Franzisca, 'A Decade of Police Reform in Liberia: Perceptions, Challenges, and Ways Ahead', *Centre for Security Governance SSR 2.0 Brief*, 4 (Sept. 2015), pp. 1-12.

96 Ibid., pp. 544-545, 550.

97 Osland, Kari M., 'The EU Police Mission in Bosnia and Herzegovina' *International Peacekeeping*, 11:3 (Autumn 2004) pp. 548, 550.

supplied the training done by the IPTF. The US conducted the subsequent police training mission in Bosnia under the ICITAP umbrella and its efforts helped get control of street crime, but this wasn't backed by the creation of judicial and prison systems. This prevented the police from effectively addressing organized crime, 'which turned Bosnia into a criminalized state over time'.[98] On 1 January 2003 the EU took over the UN effort. The European Union Police Mission (EUPM) in Bosnia and Hercegovina became the European Union's first mission under the aegis of its European Security and Defence Policy (ESDP). The EU saw the mission as a means of addressing two concerns: organized crime and possible state failure.[99]

A non-UN mission not backed by the US or an EU member state was the Regional Assistance Mission to the Solomon Islands. Beginning in July 2003, it was composed of Australian and New Zealand troops and civilian personnel and began as an effort to stabilize a failing state. It included police reform and advising elements and had devolved by mid-2013 into a police assistance program.[100]

Since the mid-1990s Britain's Ministry of Defence Police (MDP) has done much in the international police assistance realm. On occasion it supplied about half of the UK police serving overseas and since 2007 its personnel have worked in Afghanistan in Helmand province and in Kabul.[101] In 2000, after intervening to support a threatened UN mission in Sierra Leone, the British established the International Military Advisory and Training Team to prepare Sierra Leone's police and army.[102]

In 2009, the British established an International Policing Assistance Board (IPAB) to coordinate and improve British police assistance overseas. This was replaced in June 2010 by the Association of Chief Police Officers International because IPAB lacked the authority to deal with counterterrorism or international policing. The new organization became the clearinghouse for Britain's growing international policing efforts, the personnel for which are drawn broadly from UK constabularies and the Ministry of Defence Police. Supporting this since 2004 has been an interdepartmental

98 Perito, Robert M., *US Police in Peace and Stability Operations* (Washington, DC: United States Institute of Peace, 2007), pp. 6-8.

99 Osland, Kari M., 'The EU Police Mission in Bosnia and Herzegovina', pp. 544-545.

100 Bergin, Anthony, and Karl Claxton, 'Shock Without Awe: Military Lessons of the Regional Assistance Mission to the Solomon Islands', *PRISM*, 5:3 (2014), pp. 161-173; McLeod, Abby and Sinclair Dinnen, 'Police Building in the Southwest Pacific—New Directions in Australian Regional Policing', in Goldsmith, Andrew and James Sheptycki (eds), *Crafting Transnational Policing: Police Capacity-Building and Global Policing Reform* (Oxford: Hart Publishing, 2007), pp. 295-328.

101 Sinclair, Georgina, '"Insider"/"Outsider" Policing: Observations on the Role of UK Police (MDP) in Afghanistan and the Application of "Lessons Lernt"', in Johnson, Robert, and Timothy Clack (eds), *At the End of Military Intervention: Historical, Theoretical, and Applied Approaches to Transition, Handover, and Withdrawal* (Oxford: Oxford University Press, 2015), p. 415.

102 Miller, Paul D., *Armed State Building: Confronting State Failure, 1898-2012* (Ithaca, NY: Cornell University Press, 2013), pp. 139-140.

Stabilization Unit, and later the Stabilization Unit Policing Team stood-up in April 2011. As of 2015, the British government had police officers seconded to the European Union Police Mission in Afghanistan (EUPOL), and similar EU missions in Georgia, Iraq, and Kosovo, and the NATO Training Mission in Afghanistan.[103]

US police assistance to developing nations jumped after the end of the Cold War.[104] The US was conducting 125 overseas programs assisting police in the early 1990s. Much of this work was being done by the Defense Department's Program to Assist National Police Forces and its clients included Bolivia, Colombia, Ecuador, Mexico, Panama, and Peru. The State Department had police advisors in Bosnia, while the US military was helping create police forces in Haiti and Somalia.[105] Between 2000 and 2015, the US dispatched more than 5,000 police personnel on UN missions and spent nearly $1 billion via the Global Peace Operations Initiative to equip and train other states to do peacekeeping. Police advising remained an element of US foreign policy during the administration of President Barack Obama.[106]

The earliest US post-Cold War police advisory effort occurred in Panama. After the US overthrew Panama's dictator in 1989, the US military could not train a replacement police force because it was illegal for US military forces to do this in peacetime. The Justice Department was given the task and over the next two years opened a police academy and built a new Panamanian police. The US military patrolled with the new force, but this was done as a 'liaison and operational activity', not as training.[107]

The 1992 UN-sponsored, US-led Operation Restore Hope in Somalia did not have a police component. The Somali National Police Force had been destroyed by the civil war, but when the intervention occurred members of the force began reappearing and helping the intervening units by taking up their former policing functions. The US military soon began helping establish an Auxiliary Security Service around former Somali police officers but did not provide training as that was prohibited by US law. This force disappeared when the UN forces departed. The US did try and build a Somali police force under UN auspices beginning in March 1994 and even received a Congressional waiver allowing the military to be involved. But by this time US troops were leaving and the police mission was withdrawn in June 1994 as Somali descended

103 Sinclair, '"Insider"/"Outsider" Policing', p. 417.

104 Pino, Nathan and Michael D. Wiatrowski, 'Implementing Democratic Policing and Related Initiatives', in Pino, Nathan, and Michael D. Wiatrowski (eds), *Democratic Policing in Transitional and Developing Countries* (Aldershot, UK: Ashgate, 2006), p. 112.

105 Huggins, *Political Policing*, p. 1.

106 US Government, White House, 'Fact Sheet: US Support to Peace Operations 2015 Leaders' Summit on UN Peacekeeping', <https://www.whitehouse.gov/the-press-office/2015/09/28/fact-sheet-us-support-peace-operations-2015-leaders-summit-un> (28 Sept. 2015).

107 Perito, *US Police in Peace and Stability Operations*, p. 4.

into civil war.[108] Similarly, a local police force was established in Timor-Leste (or East Timor) in 2002.[109]

The post-Cold War era saw Haiti once again as the recipient of a police advising mission. On 28 April 1995, Haitian President Bertrand Aristide dissolved the army, which was officially disbanded by an act of parliament on 6 February 1996. Half of the 7,000 former soldiers joined the newly created interim police force, which proved a disaster. Since its leaders and members came from the former army—an institution popularly viewed as corrupt and oppressive—the people of Haiti saw the new police in the same light. The International Criminal Investigation, Training, and Assistance Program (ICITAP) provided six days of training, but this was too scant to correct old ways. US leaders had insisted upon using the former soldiers in the police force because this was seen as a way of preventing the US from having to take on policing duties, something seen as 'mission creep'. The force lacked the physical means and necessary trust of the population to be successful and proved a contributor to lawlessness. It was dissolved on 6 December 1995.[110]

The new permanent police that followed was intended to be a civilian force that many hoped would rely on community policing practices. But the people with weapons and security training—and thus best qualified to join the new police force—were former members of the hated army, and 1,500 of these joined the new police. Initially the population trusted the force, but this changed quickly with poor police behavior that produced thuggery, crime, and constant scandals. The trust level deteriorated more quickly in urban areas because rural areas did not hear as much about urban police corruption.[111]

Why was this force so bad? It was very young and inexperienced, and its terrible human rights practices led people to believe it would become just as repressive and brutal as the army. The people were inclined to distrust security forces because of the history of brutality of such forces against the Haitian people. But the core problem was poor training. The police received four months training, but half of the courses were taught by foreigners who had to instruct via an interpreter. One year of training was considered proper. Another problem was that half the training took place at US Army bases because of the lack of Haitian facilities. This robbed the new force of credibility because the US had trained the old, hated army. Haitians wanted a civilian police force, yet its training was in the US military's hands. At least one Canadian instructor working alongside the Americans felt this approach created a 'might makes right force'. Meanwhile, the Canadians wanted to build a force based around the community policing model. Other issues included minimal human rights training,

108 Ibid., pp. 4-5.
109 Cline, Lawrence E., 'The New Constabularies: Planning US Military Stabilization Missions', *Small War and Insurgencies*, 14:3 (2003), p. 173.
110 Mobekk, Eirin, 'International Involvement in Restructuring and Creating Security Forces: The Case of Haiti', *Small Wars and Insurgencies*, 12:3 (Autumn 2001), pp. 102-103.
111 Ibid., pp. 103-104.

insufficient training in the use of weapons, police procedure, and crowd control. There were also frequent human rights violations, especially by special police units. Overall, Haitian leaders 'refused to create an efficient control system for the force'.[112]

US police advisors in Kazakhstan used a 'train the trainer' model to develop a post-Communist police force. US trainers initially did most things, and then gradually transitioned responsibilities to local trainers. From 2001-2003 the trainers held eight, three-day sessions attended by 20 Kazakhstani police officers.[113]

In November 2005, as a result of the wars in Iraq and Afghanistan the US Department of Defense officially recognized the importance of postwar stability operations to securing the peace after a war. Part of this recognition included direction to the US military that building police, correctional, and judicial systems after the end of a war was part of its responsibility. This was supplemented by President George Bush's 7 December 2005 order placing coordination of the various related Federal civilian efforts in the hands of the State Department. Its Office of the Coordinator for Reconstruction created a reserve corps of civilian experts that included police and constabulary officers to assist the military.[114]

One of the longest-lived and diverse expeditionary police advisory efforts has been that launched in Afghanistan after the 2001 US invasion that toppled Kabul's Taliban government. Police advising has been consistently part of the intensive foreign development efforts here. For example, at its peak in 2009, the International Security Assistance Force (ISAF) in Afghanistan included military personnel from 51 nations.[115] Since 2001, Afghanistan has probably received more advisory assistance on policing—from more nations—than any country before. The American efforts are well known and have been widely studied, but gendarmerie-type units from the Netherlands, Italy, Turkey, France, and Romania have also served in Afghanistan.[116]

112 Ibid., pp. 104-107.

113 Snajdr, Edward, 'Creating Police Partnerships with Civil Society in Kazakhstan Through US-Funded Domestic Violence Training: A Step Toward Democratic Policing', in Pino, Nathan and Wiatrowski, Michael D. (eds), *Democratic Policing in Transitional and Developing Countries* (Ashgate: Aldershot, Hampshire, 2006), pp. 179, 186-187.

114 Perito, Robert M., *US Police in Peace and Stability Operations* (Washington, DC: United States Institute of Peace, 2007), pp. 2-3.

115 See Brian Erickson's contribution to this volume.

116 Clutterbuck, Lindsay, 'The Other Side of COIN: New Challenges for British Police and Military in the Twenty-First Century', in Johnson, Robert, and Timothy Clack (eds), *At the End of Military Intervention: Historical, Theoretical, and Applied Approaches to Transition, Handover, and Withdrawal* (Oxford: Oxford University Press, 2015), p. 454.

There is extensive literature on this.[117] In February 2013, the Afghan National Police was receiving assistance from 32 different nations.[118]

Like Albania and Haiti, Afghanistan has been a frequent recipient of police advisory assistance. The US sent a police advisor and aid in the late 1950s. In the 1960s and 1970s both the East German and West German governments provided Afghanistan with police advisory assistance. During the Soviet occupation, the Soviets built a police force along the Soviet two-track model of using both conscript and professional police personnel, which resulted in the militarization of the force. There was essentially no real police force in Afghanistan during the civil war between the various warlords and the Taliban, though in 2002 there were some 50,000 men who nominally served as police for the local warlords or military commanders.[119]

After the American intervention, Afghanistan became an inadvertent laboratory for every possible type and vision of policing, particularly in a violent environment. The combination of an unstable security situation, Afghanistan's particular cultural conditions, and so many hands sharing the work resulted in an explosion of police forces. Depending upon how one counts them, since 2001 Afghanistan has seen the creation of at least 13 different policing arms. One must ask the following of this: Does a country with a population of 30 million need so many different police forces?

The Germans developed the initial program to build a modern Afghan police staffed by professionally trained personnel. The 2001 Bonn Agreement produced a two-stage plan for constructing Afghanistan's new security sector. First, in order to build legitimacy for the central government, it was necessary to establish or reestablish the rule of law. Second, the local police would be enabled to take over from the military forces. Germany donated money and vehicles, and dispatched a team of police advisors that reached Kabul on 16 March 2002. They had the police academy reopened by 22 August. The five-year program planned for 1,500 officer cadets and established a three-month training course for police non-commissioned officers. They planned a force of 70,000, but the model chosen by the Germans would have taken decades to produce this.[120]

The US responded in 2003 by establishing a parallel program to retrain personnel in existing police forces run by the State Department, which subcontracted many functions to DynCorp International (something similar had been done it the Balkans). The main center was in Kabul, but seven regional training centers quickly followed. Basing the instruction on a curriculum used to train police in Kosovo,

117 The most comprehensive study to date is Giustozzi, Antonio, and Isaqzadeh, Mohammad, *Policing Afghanistan: The Politics of the Lame Leviathan* (New York: Columbia University Press, 2012). See also the bibliography at the end of this volume.

118 Planty, Donald J., and Robert M. Perito, *Police Transition in Afghanistan* (Washington, DC: United States Institute of Peace, 2013), pp. 3-4.

119 Perito, Robert, *Afghanistan's Police: The Weak Link in Security Sector Reform* (Washington, DC: United States Institute of Peace, 2009), p. 3.

120 Perito, *Afghanistan's Police*, pp. 3-4; Sinclair, '"Insider"/"Outsider" Policing', pp. 420-421.

they offered three short courses lasting from 15 days to eight weeks. By July 2007, 71,147 personnel had completed at least one of the courses. The quality of much of the instruction was weak, particularly because as many as 70 percent of the attendees were illiterate. Unfortunately, the American 'training program also failed to provide the type of follow-on field training that had been a constant feature of similar programs in Panama, Haiti, and the Balkans'.[121]

In 2005, the US military took over the police training program from the State Department. It now fell under the Combined Security Transition Command-Afghanistan (CSTC-A), which also trained the Afghan National Army. Things did not improve and a December 2006 State and Defense Department joint report concluded that after spending $1.1 billion, the Afghan police were ineffective.[122]

Early 2006 saw the signing of the Afghanistan Compact as an effort to further cooperation between the Afghan government and donor nations, while at the same time giving the Afghans the lead in their fight. This included efforts at police reform and planned for a combined strength of 62,000 in the Afghan Border Police and Afghan National Police by 2010. Two subsequent Afghan National Police Strategies were developed in 2009 and 2011, respectively.[123]

In 2007, the US created the Afghan Civil Order Police (ANCOP) as an 'elite gendarmerie' to help maintain public order after the May 2006 Kabul riots. They were subsequently assigned to temporarily replace Afghan Uniformed Police (AUP) undergoing training. In this role ANCOP units suffered 75-80 percent attrition. In 2010 ANCOP units, because they possessed heavier firepower, were essentially used as troops in a counterinsurgency role as part of the US 'surge' in Afghanistan. When they were used in the 'hold' phase of the Marjah offensive they suffered horribly—as police usually do in such an environment—as they were committed to areas that had not been first cleared of enemy forces. They later received better training and by 2011 had become 'an elite rapid reaction force and counterinsurgency force' held in generally good regard by both Afghans and coalition forces.[124]

The Afghan National Police Auxiliary (ANPA) was launched in late 2006. This allowed district governors in particularly dangerous areas to recruit a militia to support the ANP. This force recruited locals and operated (badly) from July 2007 until its disbandment in May 2008.[125]

The British began conducting counterinsurgency operations in Helmand province, Afghanistan, in April 2006, but it probably took until 2010 for them to recognize how important policing was to conducting a successful counterinsurgency campaign as well as performing general policing duties. But both the British and the Americans

121 Perito, *Afghanistan's Police*, p. 4.
122 Ibid., p. 5.
123 Sinclair, '"Insider"/"Outsider" Policing', pp. 420-421.
124 Perito, Robert, *Afghanistan's Civil Order Police: Victim of Its Own Success* (Washington, DC: United States Institute of Peace, 2012), pp. 1, 7.
125 Perito, *Afghanistan's Police*, p. 9.

were more interested in building counterinsurgency capacity in the Afghan National Police (ANP). Eventually, a British Stability Unit staffed by UK police officers and British troops began delivering police training to the ANP.[126]

British police began serving in Helmand in 2008. Beginning in 2011 they served with the UK Stability Unit and thus worked independently of the British military, though they relied upon the military for transport and their security. Moreover, since military needs generally take precedence, civilian police advising is sometimes simply fitted in when it can be. This is unfortunate because when properly trained, local police are particularly valuable in gathering intelligence. They know the strangers in their areas, increasing the chances that insurgents can be picked out by local police. But neither the British military nor police in Helmand trained the police in intelligence gathering procedures. In 2010, the US Marines launched in Helmand a duplicate of a successful intelligence training program they had instituted in Iraq. It was quickly picked up by ISAF and expanded into Kandahar, other provinces in Eastern Afghanistan, and Kabul. The US military controlled the program, but former UK police officers (many of whom had served in Kosovo, Northern Ireland, or Iraq) did the actual training. It provided regular intelligence on the insurgency while also laying the foundation for future Afghan work along this line after the NATO withdrawal. Having both US and British advisors working in the same area sometimes caused competition between the advisors for 'facetime' with the senior Afghan National Police officers who were being advised. Seconded British police officers also needed time with them.[127]

One of the problems here was that the British and US military advisors doing the training rarely had police experience. This applied even to the members of a Police Mentoring and Advisory Group (PMAG) appointed to advise senior Afghan police officers. Sometimes the Afghan police superior they were supposed to mentor had immense experience and superior rank. At other times the Afghan official had no police experience or training. Sometimes US military reservists serving in Afghanistan provided actual police experience. The US also utilized police officers working in Helmand as part of the Law Enforcement Professional Program (LEPP) who were attached to a US Army Security Forces Advise and Assist Team (SFAAT) or US Marine Corps Province Police Advisory Team (PPAT).[128]

In 2007, the European Union Police (EUPOL) mission in Afghanistan replaced Germany as the primary police training partner.[129] The European Union authorized the dispatch of 400 police advisors as members of the European Union Police mission. EUPOL emphasized democratic policing and saw the police 'as the key instrument

126 Clutterbuck, 'The Other Side of COIN', p. 449.
127 Ibid., pp. 450-452.
128 Ibid., pp. 449-450.
129 Perito, *Afghanistan's Police*, p. 1.

of securing and protecting the population'.[130] EUPOL also wanted to introduce community-style policing, but the problem is doing this with an active insurgency.[131]

The initial EUPOL mandate ran from 31 May 2007 to 31 May 2013. EUPOL then tried to unite the non-US programs. But this resulted in an overly complex bureaucratic monster that was taken over by the Combined Security Transition Command-Afghanistan (CSTC-A). The EUPOL mission was supposed to build a functioning Afghan police force to hand off to Afghan control. Twenty-two EU members, plus Canada, Croatia, and New Zealand contributed personnel. What followed were contradictory policies because as one observer commented, 'there is no "Europe" in Afghanistan'. The larger emphasis, though, was on community policing. EUPOL, the UK, and Germany favored community policing. France and Italy favored a gendarmerie approach. Another layer of complexity followed from the US paramilitary and counterinsurgency approaches.[132]

Another program was launched in November 2007. Focused District Development (FDD) aimed to train all the members of the Afghan National Police in a particular district at the same time. Afghan National Civil Order Police (ANCOP) were to temporarily replace them during their training cycle. Seven weeks of training, vetting, and reequipping followed. The training cycle was supposed to take nine months, but all required longer than this, and the program was supposed to complete the retraining by December 2010. Afghanistan had 365 police districts and by January 2009, 52 of these districts had police that were being retrained. January 2009 saw the birth of the Afghanistan Public Protection Force Program (APPFP). This force recruited local villagers to defend themselves against the Taliban.[133]

On 16 November 2009 France sent *Gendarmerie* trainers to Afghanistan as part of a Police Operational Mentoring Liaison Team (POMLT) under NATO command. They sent 100 personnel to teach ethical and professional practices. *Gendarmerie* official General Guy Cachet believed it was important for the local police to learn to be in contact with the population and to build trusting relationships. Another 50 personnel went to train the Afghan National Civil Order Police (ANCOP).[134]

Other nations did the same, and often in an uncoordinated manner. Italy first sent *Carabineri* to Afghanistan to train Afghan police in 2002. Italy, Britain, and Canada conducted their own police advising missions in Afghanistan—unconnected to the EUPOL effort. Canadian police advisors worked in Kandahar as part of a Police Operational Mentor Liaison Team (POMLT), as well as through their Provincial Reconstruction Team (PRT). The large number of missions generated confusion in the

130 See Brian Erickson's contribution to this volume.
131 Sinclair, '"Insider"/"Outsider" Policing', p. 420.
132 Ibid., pp. 422-423.
133 Perito, *Afghanistan's Police*, pp. 5-6, 9-10.
134 'Cent Cinquante Gendarmes Française en Mission en Afghanistan', *Le Monde*, 16 Nov. 2009.

Afghan National Police.[135] Directly resulting from this has been a long-running debate among the various international partners about what kind of police force Afghanistan should have. The US Army pushed for a more militarized police, while the Germans and other Europeans wanted a more civilian-style police system. The paramilitary version was eventually judged the most realistic.[136] The largest police training partner was the US military, which resulted in the Afghan National Police being militarized and its members being used as 'little soldiers' in the counterinsurgency struggle. They were not suited for this role and as a result suffered three times the casualties as their Afghan army counterparts. Distributed in small packets without proper support, the Afghan National Police units became easy targets for insurgents.[137]

None of this produced the results any of Afghanistan's partner nations hoped for. In 2009 the Afghan National Police was 'riddled with corruption and generally unable to protect Afghan citizens, control crime, or deal with the growing insurgency'. An extensive drug trade fed the corruption. This was despite the fact that from 2002-9, the international community spent $10 billion building police in Afghanistan. By 2009, the force's numbers had reached 68,000, and in 2009 the eventual target end strength for Afghan police forces was set at 86,000.[138]

When US President Barack Obama escalated the US war in Afghanistan the administration also changed its police advising effort and set new targets for its end strength. This was increased in October 2010 to 109,000, and to 134,000 in October 2011.[139] A 2011 report insisted it would take five or ten more years to construct a successful police force in Afghanistan.[140]

In February 2013 Afghanistan had four police forces and two auxiliary police forces, all under the direction of the Ministry of the Interior. The ANP had four branches: The Afghan Uniformed Police (AUP), the Afghan Border Police (ABP), the Afghan National Civil Order Police (ANCOP), and the Afghan Anti-Crime Police (AACP). The auxiliary forces include the Afghan Local Police (ALP) and the Afghan Public Protection Force (APPF). The ALP was raised for local defense and had around 19,000 members in February 2013. The APPF was launched under the initiative of President Hamid Karzai in 2011 to replace the private security contractors in Afghanistan after he essentially outlawed them.[141]

135 Perito, *Afghanistan's Police*, pp. 1, 11.
136 Giustozzi, Antonio and Mohammad Isaqzadeh, 'Afghanistan's Paramilitary Policing in Context: The Risks of Expediency', *Afghan Analysts Network Thematic Report*, 7 (November 2011), p. 2.
137 Perito, *Afghanistan's Police*, p. 1.
138 Ibid., pp. 1-2.
139 Planty, Donald J., and Robert M. Perito, *Police Transition in Afghanistan* (Washington, DC: United States Institute of Peace, 2013), p. 3.
140 Sinclair, '"Insider"/"Outsider" Policing', p. 423.
141 Planty and Perito, *Police Transition in Afghanistan*, pp. 3-5.

The aforementioned Afghan Local Police (AFP) have been one of the many controversial elements of police advising in Afghanistan. The idea for the Afghan Local Police came from the Sons of Iraq program, though it did not show the same dramatic success. The ALP is inextricably linked to the US Village Stability Operations (VSO) counterinsurgency effort. It is also an example of militarization. How successful this program has been is a point of debate.[142]

Tied to the development of the ALP is what is sometimes termed 'the militia problem'. As we've seen, militia organizations, especially ones used for policing, can sometimes cause as many problems as they address. Brookings' scholar Vanda Felbab-Brown correctly observes that in Afghanistan 'the embrace of militias and other irregular proxies had been a key feature of the war since 2001'. After a short-lived effort in the beginning of the war to demobilize the militias, the US turned to creating them as another tool in the war against the Taliban, with their primary task being to weaken the enemy's grip while increasing security, particularly in areas where the Afghan National Army (ANA), Afghan National Police (ANP), and NATO forces were thin on the ground. Early attempts at this included the Afghan National Auxiliary Police (ANUP), the Afghan Public Protection Program (APPP), as well as the Local Defense Initiative (LDI), or Community Defense Initiative (CDI), and the CIA trained Counterterrorism Pursuit Teams, which earned a reputation for abusing civilians. The Soviets built militias in Afghanistan the 1980s as part of their strategy for getting out of the country.[143]

The Afghans also created their own militias outside of American command. Kabul's intelligence agency, the National Directorate of Security (NDS), and others, encouraged Tajik units as a counterweight to Pashtun forces. Tajiks ran the NDS, which was at one time under the control of Bismullah Khan Mohammadi, who was branded 'notoriously corrupt' and ran the 'ethnically factionalized Ministry of Interior (MoI)'.[144]

The biggest and most well-known of these 'militia' efforts is the aforementioned Afghan Local Police, though ISAF and the US refused to call them militia and argued that the program was rooted in traditional Afghan defense organizations such as the *arbakai*, which were essentially tribal militia. In September 2014, there were 30,000 ALP. They served in 99 sites at a cost of $120 million annually. Militiamen cost one-quarter that of an ANP member, a bill paid by the US. The program was

142 For some example see Strandquist, Jon, 'Local Defence Forces and Counterinsurgency in Afghanistan: Learning from the CIA's Village Defense Program in South Vietnam', *Small Wars and Insurgencies*, 26:1 (2015), pp. 90, 105-106; Felbab-Brown, Vanda, 'The Dubious Joys of Standing Up Militias and Building Partner Capacity: Lessons from Afghanistan and Mexico for Prosecuting Security Policy Through Proxies', *Brookings* (21 July 2015), pp. 8-9; and Mark Moyar's contribution to this volume.

143 Felbab-Brown, 'The Dubious Joys of Standing Up Militias and Building Partner Capacity', pp. 3-4.

144 Ibid., pp. 4-5.

supposed to end in 2018, but Kabul wanted the ANP to grow to 45,000 and to extend it—at the minimum—to 2024.[145]

Overall, since 9/11 there have been three main waves of police reform in Afghanistan: 2003-5, in 2006, and 2008-10. Each occurred under a different Afghan Minister of the Interior, and each produced very limited results. These failures eventually led to making the police a paramilitary force, one that largely arose as a means of addressing Afghanistan's dismal security situation.[146]

The US-led police advisory effort in Iraq required even heavier lifting than the long effort in Afghanistan. When the US invaded Iraq, its leaders assumed that they could simply remove the upper tiers of leaders and keep the structures and personnel underneath. The assumption was that the regime's existing police and military forces would remain intact and enforce order. This, of course, proved utterly incorrect. When US forces captured Baghdad on 9 April 2003, Iraqi army and police personnel simply took their weapons and went home. The complete collapse of public order followed, the hallmark being extensive looting. But this proved only the initial problem and what followed was a wave of criminality mixed with murderous political and personal retribution.[147]

Initially, the US had no plan for rebuilding the Iraqi police, and no intention to do so. Before the invasion, retired Lieutenant General Jay Garner, the head of the short-lived Office of Reconstruction and Humanitarian Affairs (ORHA), asked for a Kosovo-style constabulary and police force to maintain order. This was refused as the administration believed the assurances of Iraqi exiles that the Coalition forces would be welcomed by the Iraqis. The only Saddam-era security force to remain intact was its lowest tier organization, the Iraqi National Police (INP), which dealt with petty crime and traffic. It had a reputation for corruption and incompetence and had grown accustomed to doing very little because it could rely on the work of the many other Iraqi security arms.[148]

The US soon launched an assessment of the problem and the Department of Justice's International Criminal Investigative Training Assistance Program (ICITAP) police assessment team issued its report in May 2003. It recommended deploying 6,600 police advisors to train Iraqis in policing and border control duties. It also urged the dispatch of 2,500 police constabularies to help the military restore order and train Iraqis to do the job. Coalition Provisional Authority (CPA) head Paul Bremer approved this in June 2003, but couldn't fund it. It was also discussed at June 2003 White House meetings, but seen as too big and rejected. US Central Command chief

145 Ibid., pp. 4-5.
146 Giustozzi and Isaqzadeh, 'Afghanistan's Paramilitary Policing in Context', p. 2.
147 Bayley and Perito, *The Police in War*, pp. 6-7.
148 Ibid., pp. 8-9.

General John Abizaid asked for responsibility for police training in September 2003, but Bremer kept police training under the Coalition Provisional Authority.[149]

The Iraqi National Police became the Iraqi Police Service (IPS), and by the summer of 2003, US Lieutenant General Ricardo Sanchez, the commander of the coalition ground forces in Iraq, was running a program that provided police recruits with three weeks of training and then put them on the street. Soon, 40,000 Iraqi police had received this training, which was conducted by US military police under the guidance of the Department of Justice's Transition and Integration Program (TIP).[150] Bremer ordered this shuttered, partially because of the weakness of its recruits, though the Coalition Provisional Authority had no replacement program.[151]

The CPA had its first 24 police trainers on the ground in December 2003.[152] The initial Department of State effort to recruit 1,000 police advisors died from lack of funding, but was revived in fall 2003 when the State Department contracted with DynCorp to provide police advising. It was spring 2004 before these advisors reached Iraq in significant numbers. Their number had also been cut to 500 due to funding shortfalls. There were only 283 of them in Iraq in June 2004.[153]

After the 2003 invasion of Iraq, the British had in their area of operations no police force. The British attempt to create police in Basra drew upon local militia for much of the personnel, creating a force loyal only to their respective leaders and that grew hostile toward the British. The Serious Crimes Unit of the Basra police came to function as a death squad that used police equipment and uniforms to commit crimes and murder political opponents.[154]

December 2003 saw the opening of a State and Justice Department program in Amman at the Jordan International Police Training Center. Thirty-thousand police received eight weeks of training here over the next year. The curriculum was one that had been used to train police for Kosovo and included three months of follow-on instruction in the field after completing the initial course. The Coalition Provisional Authority proved unable to manage the influx of such a large number of police so quickly, and failed to properly and efficiently equip them or to provide them with proper facilities, many of which had been destroyed in the looting that followed the US capture of Baghdad.[155]

Unfortunately, much of the initial US police training effort in Iraq repeated some of the mistakes the British made in Cyprus in the 1950s. It built upon the existing abusive and corrupt force and failed to provide adequate preparation. During the Malayan

149 Ibid., pp. 10-11; Hammes, T.X., 'Raising and Mentoring Security Forces in Afghanistan and Iraq', *Orbis*, 60:1 (Winter 2016), p. 312.
150 Bayley and Perito, *The Police in War*, pp. 11-12.
151 Hammes, 'Raising and Mentoring Security Forces in Afghanistan and Iraq', pp. 312-313.
152 Ibid., p. 313.
153 Bayley and Perito, *The Police in War*, p. 11.
154 Clutterbuck, 'The Other Side of COIN', pp. 445-446.
155 Bayley and Perito, *The Police in War*, p. 13.

Emergency, for example, new recruits had received six months training. Thorough training (or retraining) is one of the keys to building an effective police force.[156]

Bush administration officials concluded that the Department of Defense (DOD) was the only organization with the resources to handle the police training mission and in May 2004 was given the task. A Civilian Police Advisory Training Team (CPATT) was established under the command of what soon became known as Multi-National Security Transition Command-Iraq (MNST-I).[157] The Civilian Police Advisory Team (CPATT) initially ran the police advising and training effort. Commanded by a British Brigadier, it had a civilian US State Department deputy and a mixture of military and civilian personnel. It was supported by the US Army's 89th Military Police Brigade.[158]

What followed was a fight over what kind of police Iraq should have, one that produced terrible results. The CPA (and the State and Justice Departments) wanted a community police force, while the Department of Defense wanted a more militarized organization to address the growing violence and help fight the insurgency. This drove the DOD effort to raise 54,000 police, which, they argued, could be converted into a community policing force later.[159] The Department of Defense cut the Kosovo-based training curriculum from the original five months of classroom and field work, to 10 weeks overall, and then used the community policing force in a counterinsurgency role for which they were not trained or equipped.[160]

The results were disastrous. Policing expert Robert Perito correctly notes that in Iraq the 'Use of the police in combat operations pitted poorly led and inappropriately trained and equipped patrolmen against heavily armed former military personnel, veteran security operatives, and foreign terrorists'. From 2004-6, the Iraqi police suffered 12,000 casualties, including 4,000 killed. In April 2004, Iraqi police units in Fallujah, Karbala, Najaf, and Kut came apart under insurgent attacks.[161]

There were less than 100 civilians training police in Iraq in June 2004 at the time of the transition to Iraqi control. When the CPA departed, the Iraqi Ministry of the Interior became responsible for the police, but the US still carried the water. By late 2004, in an effort to stem the growing violence and protect the Iraqi government from militias and insurgents, MNSTC-1 commander Lieutenant General David Petraeus allowed the creation of police battalions of 750 men. They were raised almost entirely from Sunni former special operations soldiers and immediately went into action

156 Corum, *Training Indigenous Forces in Counterinsurgency*, p. 38.
157 Bayley and Perito, *The Police in War*, p. 13.
158 Perito, Robert, *The Iraq Federal Police: US Police Building under Fire* (Washington, DC: United States Institute of Peace Press, 2011), pp. 2-3.
159 Hammes, 'Raising and Mentoring Security Forces in Afghanistan and Iraq', pp. 313-314.
160 Bayley and Perito, *The Police in War*, pp. 14-15.
161 Perito, *The Iraq Federal Police*, pp. 3-4.

alongside coalition forces. Meanwhile, Iraqi Interior Minister Falah Hassan al-Naqib independently raised police commando units from the same source.[162]

On 3 May 2005 the Iraqi transitional government came to power. The new Shiite interior minister, Bayan Jabar Solagh (or Baqir Jabr al-Zubeidi), reorganized and consolidated the various police forces into the 8th Police Mechanized Brigade, the Public Order Division, the Special Police Commando Division, and the Emergency Response Unit. Jabr, who was a member of the Shiite Supreme Council of the Islamic Revolution of Iraq (SCIRI), also appointed members of his organization's armed wing—the Badr Brigade—to prominent police positions. The purge of Sunnis and the recruitment of Shia turned the police into a Shia tool for murder and ethnic cleansing.[163]

The US responded in 2006 with a focus on developing the Iraqi police that consolidated the police commando battalions raised by the US with the similar units raised by the Iraqi government into the Iraqi National Police. This supported the regular street force, the Iraqi Public Service police. The US also began cracking down on police abuses by taking units off duty and arresting leaders, something that continued into 2007.[164]

Simultaneously, Italian *Carabineri* arrived to retrain national police units.[165] The Italian *Carabineri* trainers in Iraq had worked under NATO command in Kosovo and Bosnia to train police forces there. In the opinion of policing scholar Robert Perito writing in 2011, they proved effective instructors and 'the key to transforming the INP from a rogue force into a competent constabulary. Without the involvement of professional European *gendarmes*, US military and contract police personnel would not have had the technical skills or the corporate culture required to transform the INP'.[166]

The US also established advising and training teams for the Iraqi police and had deployed 117 of them to the Iraqi Police Service by November 2006. The various training efforts included Police Transition Teams (PTTs), Border Transition Teams, National Police Transition Teams, and Customs and Border Support Teams. Their personnel included civilian police trainer contractors hired by the State Department and US military members.[167] By December 2006, MNST-I had trained 135,000 Iraqi Police Service personnel, 28,400 Border Police, and 24,400 Iraqi National Police. Another 100 personnel advised the Iraqi Ministry of the Interior, which oversaw the police.[168]

162 Hammes, 'Raising and Mentoring Security Forces in Afghanistan and Iraq', p. 314; Perito, *The Iraq Federal Police*, p. 4.
163 Hammes, 'Raising and Mentoring Security Forces in Afghanistan and Iraq', pp. 314-315.
164 Ibid., pp. 315-316.
165 Ibid.
166 Perito, *The Iraq Federal Police,* pp. 9-10.
167 Hammes, 'Raising and Mentoring Security Forces in Afghanistan and Iraq', p. 316.
168 Bayley and Perito, *The Police in War*, pp. 15-16.

Despite this massive effort, by July 2007 the various police branches had become little fiefdoms for their respective heads whose members settled disputes by killing one another. The Iraqi Ministry of the Interior became a corrupt, violently sectarian entity riven by political infighting. Violence was tamped down by December 2007, and some progress was made with the police. Its total strength grew to over 370,000 and the US had at one point 247 PTTs working in Iraq. But the police remained corrupt, inefficient, and unable to manage their own logistics.[169]

In Iraq in 2008, under the auspices of Multi National Force West (MNF-W) in Anbar province, the USMC launched an experimental project called the Legacy Program to teach local police to build human intelligence gathering (HUMINT) capacity. The successful program was later expanded to four other provinces and then duplicated in Afghanistan beginning in 2010.[170]

In 2010, after his party's victory in the elections, Iraqi Prime Minister Nouri al-Maliki took on the portfolios of the Interior, Defense, and National Security Ministries. Shia sectarianism now reigned supreme.[171] On 1 October 2011, the US State Department again took over responsibility for training Iraqi police forces.[172] The total number of Iraqi police had reached 650,000.[173] Much of this force collapsed in the face of the Islamic State offensive in 2014.

A final element that remains a part of expeditionary police advising (one used in Iraq as well as many other places) is the hiring of independent contractors who work directly with the foreign government desiring their services, or are dispatched under the auspices of a sending government. For example, in 2015 the US was using contractors in Jordan to train members of the Palestinian police forces. Unfortunately, this is also an example of an area where the US suffered 'green on blue' deaths (meaning trainees killing instructors) as it too often has in Afghanistan.[174]

Conclusion

This brief survey barely touches the historical scope of expeditionary police advising. Today, numerous nations conduct police advising, and not just the traditional Western powers. Police advising and assistance is something far from being merely the purview of European nations and the United States. For example, Brazil helped establish

169 Hammes, 'Raising and Mentoring Security Forces in Afghanistan and Iraq', pp. 316-317.
170 Clutterbuck, 'The Other Side of COIN', p. 452.
171 Hammes, 'Raising and Mentoring Security Forces in Afghanistan and Iraq', pp. 317-318.
172 Perito, *The Iraq Federal Police*, p. 13.
173 Hammes, 'Raising and Mentoring Security Forces in Afghanistan and Iraq', p. 318.
174 Al-Khalidi, Suleiman, 'Jordanian Officer Shoots Dead Two Americans, One South African at Security Training Site', *Reuters*, 9 Nov. 2015.

Guinea-Bissau's police academy and train this African nation's police.[175] Expeditionary police advising will likely remain a growth industry, partly because policymakers see it as a low cost option requiring minimum commitment. But as we look back over the history of police advising, the difficulty of the task becomes even more apparent. Hopefully, this volume will contribute to increasing our understanding of the many problems of police advising.

175 Aguilar, Sérgio Luiz Cruz, 'South Atlantic: Brazil-Africa Relations in the Field of Security and Defense', *Austral: Brazilian Journal of Strategy and International Relations*, 2:4 (July/Dec. 2013), p. 60.

2

Paramilitary Police Auxiliaries and Counterinsurgency Warfare: The Failure of the Direct Approach in the Nazi East, 1941-1944

Edward B. Westermann

Introduction

The wars in Afghanistan and Iraq reintroduced the U.S. military to the challenges of fighting and winning a counterinsurgency war. From a historical perspective, the difficulties in combating insurgents were nothing new for the U.S. military as the experience in Southeast Asia between 1963 and 1972 fully revealed the problems associated with this form of warfare. In his theory on guerrilla warfare, Mao Tse-Tung used the analogy of a fish swimming in the water in describing the relationship of the insurgent to the population.[1] In general, counterinsurgents have chosen one of two strategies for defeating insurgent forces, the direct or the indirect approach.[2] The direct approach has been most often associated with a strategy aimed at the complete destruction of insurgent forces as well as their means of support, while the indirect approach seeks to separate the insurgent from his sources of support especially among the population. In its most extreme form, the direct approach 'pollutes' the water accepting the destruction of both the insurgent and the population, while the indirect approach attempts to separate the insurgent fish from his protective habitat and to preserve the local population.

The direct and indirect approaches are not mutually exclusive, but the employment of the former clearly influences the success of the latter in the counterinsurgency environment. Regardless of the approach taken, however, the value of professional,

1 Tse-Tung, Mao, *On Guerrilla Warfare* (Norwalk, CT: Easton Press, 1996), p. 113.
2 Galula, David, *Counterinsurgency Warfare: Theory and Practice* (Westport, CT: Praeger Security International, 2006), pp. 44-45.

well-equipped, and legitimate police forces has been emphasized in theory and can be clearly seen in practice in numerous historical cases.[3] In his classic work on counterinsurgency, David Galula remarked on the role of the police by noting, 'Their efficiency depends on their numerical strength, the competency of their members, their loyalty toward the government, and, last but not least, on the backing they get from other branches of the government'.[4] The importance of capable and reliable police forces is even more vital when the insurgency itself is directed against a foreign military force attempting to occupy and pacify subject populations. In this case, the recruitment, training, and employment of indigenous police forces may provide a critical adjunct to support the efforts of the occupation power in administering and pacifying the conquered area. The specific composition, capabilities, and activities of these indigenous police forces are key aspects related to their employment. Indeed, such police forces are merely one of many potential tools to be considered within the overarching counterinsurgency strategy of the direct or indirect approach.

The German use of indigenous police forces during the National Socialist occupation of Eastern Europe between 1939 and 1945 provides insights into the rationale, methods, and effectiveness of German occupation policies during World War II. In fact, Nazi policies for the subjugation and exploitation of these territories offers one of the most vivid examples of the direct approach in counterinsurgency operations and also exposes the methods by which indigenous police forces were transformed into militarized adjuncts for SS and police forces and became key instruments in a racial war of annihilation.

Dreams of a German Garden of Eden

In the case of Nazi Germany, Hitler preached a gospel of 'national salvation' that depended on 'the "removal" of the Jews and the acquisition of *Lebensraum* or "living space" in the east'.[5] In fact, this idea of a racialized living space in the East became the one of the fundamental pillars of Hitler's worldview and an essential planning factor in his war against Poland in 1939 and the subsequent invasion of the Soviet Union in 1941.[6] This concept involved a plan of military conquest by an army of Nazi Party bureaucrats with visions of establishing a Nazi agrarian colony where the indigenous peoples either would be reduced to the status of slaves or eliminated.

As a foreign policy goal, hegemony could only be accomplished through war and conquest. In *Mein Kampf*, Hitler claimed that 'State frontiers are man-made and can

3 Fair, C. Christine and Sumit Ganguly, 'Introduction', in Fair, C. Christine and Sumit Ganguly (eds), *Policing Insurgencies: Cops as Counterinsurgents* (Oxford: Oxford University Press, 2014), pp. 1-16.

4 Galula, *Counterinsurgency Warfare*, p. 20.

5 Kershaw, Ian, *Hitler: 1889-1936. Hubris* (New York: W.W. Norton, 1998), p. 252.

6 Weinberg, Gerhard, *A World at Arms: A Global History of World War II* (New York: Cambridge University Press, 1994), p. 44.

be altered'. He then underlined the necessity for war and conquest by recognizing that 'only the might of a triumphant sword will in the future assign us territory, and with it life for our nation'.[7] The purpose of *Lebensraum* focused not only on the material and geographical dispossession of the Slavic population, but also included the planned racial restructuring of the East through a process of large-scale physical extermination. According to Nazi ideology, the East would be 'cleansed' of millions of its inferior peoples and replaced by a new race of Aryan soldier-farmers.

In the case of Hitler's war against the Soviet Union, racial considerations provided the primary justification for launching a war of extermination and enslavement against the native populations of Eastern Europe. In fact, Hitler lectured German military leaders on 30 March 1941 about just such a war of extermination and the 'massive demographic revolution' that it entailed.[8] The captured lands in the East were designed to serve as the agricultural heartland of the Third Reich; an area that would be dominated by martial agricultural settlements in which German farmers ruled the land with the rifle and the plow. Above all, racial beliefs and Nazi ideology formed the bedrock upon which National Socialist policy in the East was based.

The invasion of the Soviet Union on 22 June 1941 unleashed a lethal maelstrom upon the Red Army and the Soviet people. During the attack and over the course of the German occupation, violence, atrocity, and mass murder as well as a colossal program of economic exploitation emerged as the defining characteristics of German rule. Literally on the eve of the German invasion, Reich Leader of the SS Heinrich Himmler, in his role as Reich Commissioner for the Strengthening of German Nationality, reviewed plans for a vast demographic restructuring of the occupied and incorporated territories. The initial drafts of the General Plan East (*Generalplan Ost*) were completed in the summer of 1941 and envisioned a program of Germanization that included the transfer of millions of German agrarian settlers into the East and the expulsion or elimination of tens of millions of the indigenous inhabitants.[9] One historian described the plan as nothing less than 'a timetable for the extinction of the entire population of Eastern Europe'.[10]

Operation Barbarossa

The planning for the invasion of the Soviet Union far exceeded in scale and resources earlier Wehrmacht campaigns of conquest. Despite the vast size of the Soviet military, Hitler firmly believed that the Russian colossus had 'feet of clay' and would crumble quickly in the face of the German onslaught. Indeed, the German invasion force of

7 Hitler, Adolf, *Mein Kampf* (New York: Reynal and Hitchcock, 1939), p. 949.
8 Weinberg, *World at Arms*, p. 190.
9 Rutherford, Phillip, *Prelude to the Final Solution: The Nazi Program for Deporting Ethnic Poles, 1939-1941* (Lawrence: University Press of Kansas, 2007), p. 218.
10 Tooze, Adam, *The Wages of Destruction: The Making and Breaking of the Nazi Economy* (New York: Viking, 2006), p. 468.

3,600 tanks, 2,500 aircraft, 600,000 motorized vehicles, and three million men was the largest military assembly fielded for a single operation in the history of warfare.[11] Divided into three army groups, Army Group Center constituted the main thrust of the invasion with the objective of moving across central Russia towards Moscow. Army Group South pushed into Ukraine in order to capture the 'breadbasket' of the Soviet Union and secure the coveted 'black earth' country of Nazi colonial fantasy. Finally, Army Group North was to strike through the Baltic States with the aim of capturing the strategic and symbolic city of Leningrad. In addition to these military forces, Hitler personally ordered the employment of 23 police battalions, consisting of 400 police officers and 11,640 policemen, to accompany the Wehrmacht into Russa with orders to 'cleanse' the area of security threats and for the 'combat of criminal elements, above all political elements'.[12] A Higher SS and Police Leader (HSSPF) was assigned to each of the Army Groups with command of all SS and police forces in his area and made responsible for security behind the lines of the advancing Wehrmacht forces. The inclusion of HSSPFs into the Wehrmacht's organizational structure prior to the invasion was critical as the HSSPFs emerged as the 'central coordinators of mass murder' in the Soviet Union.[13]

Prior to the invasion, Hitler repeatedly stated to Wehrmacht leaders that this was to be a 'war of annihilation' and the army leadership had planned accordingly. The army's planning directive described the operational strategy: 'During the initial phase the bulk of the Russian Army stationed in western Russia is to be destroyed in a series of daring operations spearheaded by armored thrusts'.[14] In short, the armored forces would serve as iron wedges to rapidly penetrate Soviet forward defenses and thrust deep into their rear in order to cut off, encircle, and then destroy the Russian armies.[15] Army planners envisioned a campaign that incorporated the speed and mobility embodied in Blitzkrieg combined with the maneuver and firepower of *Kesselschlacht* (cauldron battle) to overwhelm Russian forces.

The success of the initial operations by all three army groups appeared to vindicate Hitler's prediction of a rapid campaign and to justify the army's plan of attack. On 3 July. General Franz Halder, the chief of staff of the German Army, gloated, 'It is thus probably no overstatement to say that the Russian campaign has been won in the space of two weeks'.[16] Halder's celebration may have been premature, but it was not

11 Kershaw, Ian, *Hitler: 1936-1945 Nemesis* (New York: W.W. Norton, 2000), p. 395.
12 Westermann, Edward, *Hitler's Police Battalions: Enforcing Racial Policy in the East* (Lawrence: University Press of Kansas, 2005), pp. 163-165.
13 Pohl, Dieter, *Die Herrschaft der Wehrmacht: Deutsche Militärbesatzung und einheimische Bevölkerung in der Sowjetunion 1941-1944* (Munich: Oldenbourg, 2008), p. 73.
14 Citino, Robert, *The German Way of War: From the Thirty Years' War to the Third Reich* (Lawrence: University Press of Kansas, 2005), p. 292.
15 Megargee, Geoffrey, *War of Annihilation: Combat and Genocide on the Eastern Front, 1941* (Lanham, MD: Rowman and Littlefield, 2006), p. 25.
16 Kershaw, *Nemesis*, p. 391.

based on wishful thinking. All along the thousand mile front, German armored forces advanced at an astounding pace, the tanks in Army Group Center advanced 270 miles towards Moscow in the first week of the invasion and the German army successfully completed a series of large-scale encirclements that had inflicted 'appalling' losses on Soviet forces and netted almost a two million prisoners by the end of August.[17]

Organizing the Police Auxiliaries

In a meeting at his field headquarters on 16 July 1941, Hitler discussed the initial success of the campaign and his determination to take 'all of the necessary measures' including mass shootings and mass deportations to ensure that the area was brought under German control. Furthermore, he emphasized that no 'foreign' military forces would be allowed west of the Urals and declared his 'iron principle' that 'Never would it be permitted that anyone but a German can bear arms [in this region]'.[18] Despite Hitler's reluctance to arm non-Germans, events on the ground in the opening weeks of the campaign created a fait accompli as auxiliary units composed of indigenous Estonians, Latvians, and Lithuanians became involved in mass murder. The commanders of the *Einsatzgruppen* (Special Mission Units) received orders early in the campaign to encourage 'self-cleansing measures by anticommunist and anti-Jewish circles', a charge accepted by auxiliaries in the first days of the German occupation.[19] In the case of the *Einsatzgruppen*, these units were created prior to the invasion and specifically tasked with the mass murder of the putative racial and political enemies of the Third Reich including Communist functionaries and Jews.[20]

One example involving the employment of indigenous auxiliary police in support of the *Einsatzgruppen* included the actions of Latvian auxiliaries under the command of Victor Arājs, a Latvian nationalist. In early July, a detachment of auxiliaries herded a group of Jews into a city synagogue and burned them alive. Some two weeks later, Arājs and his men under the command of *Einsatzgruppe A* escorted a group of Jews into Bikernieki Forest and executed them at the site.[21] In total, the auxiliaries under Arājs murdered an estimated 26,000 civilians and facilitated the killing of another 60,000 men, women, and children.[22] Such actions were not limited to Latvia alone.

17 Citino, *German Way of War*, pp. 293-294.

18 Meyer, Gert (ed.), *Wehrmachtsverbrechen: Dokumente aus sowjetischen Archiven* (Cologne: PapyRossa Verlag, 1997), pp. 51-52.

19 Matthäus, Jürgen and Frank Bajohr (eds), *The Political Diary of Alfred Rosenberg and the Onset of the Holocaust* (Lanham, MD: Rowman and Littlefield, 2015), p. 431.

20 Golczewski, Frank, 'Die Kollaboration in der Ukraine', in Dieckman, Christoph, Babette Quinkert, and Tatjana Tönsmeyer (ed.), *Kooperation und Verbrechen: Formen der "Kollaboration" im östlichen Europa, 1939-1945* (Göttingen: Wallstein Verlag, 2003), p. 171.

21 Snyder, Timothy, *Bloodlands: Europe Between Hitler and Stalin* (New York: Basic Books, 2010), p. 193.

22 Stranga, Aivars, 'The Holocaust in Occupied Latvia, 1941-1945', in Nollendorfs, Valters and Oberländer, Erwin (eds), *The Hidden and Forbidden History of Latvia under Soviet and*

In a diary entry of 11 July 1941, Otto Bräutigam, a senior Nazi bureaucrat who had traveled to Kovno remarked on 'numerous Jewish pogroms conducted by the Lithuanian auxiliary police', pogroms being conducted with German approval.[23]

On 17 July, Hitler transferred authority for the security of the newly occupied eastern territories to Heinrich Himmler in his role as Reich Leader of the SS and the Chief of the German Police. Hitler ordered Himmler to work with local Nazi Party leaders in the East to establish a police structure designed for the expropriation of these conquered areas and their subsequent Germanization.[24] For his part, Himmler quickly realized that the vast conquered territories could not be secured with the SS and police forces available for duty in the East and he subsequently notified the Higher SS and Police Leaders that the planned 'tasks' associated with the occupation of these areas required support from within the indigenous populations. In a letter of 25 July, he stated his intention to create auxiliary formations (*Schutzformationen*) from 'suitable' ethnic groups from the Ukraine, the Baltic States, and Belorussia to provide support to German uniformed and security police forces. Himmler noted that further details concerning equipment, uniforms, supply, and the specific duties of these units would be provided later. He also explicitly referred to the prior use of such auxiliaries by the *Einsatzgruppen*.[25]

The fact that Himmler, in the conception and creation of auxiliary police formations, referenced the role of these forces in the mass murder of the Jews cannot be overemphasized. Indeed, the conceptualization of these forces as adjuncts to Nazi plans for the exploitation and mass murder of indigenous populations from the first weeks of German occupation clearly demonstrates the method by which the radical demographic restructuring of these lands was to take place and set the precedent for the use of auxiliary police forces as a key instrument in support of draconian German occupation policies.[26]

Less than a week after his initial order authorizing the formation of police auxiliaries, Himmler's office provided additional guidelines concerning the formation of *Schutzmannschaften* (Police Auxiliaries). The first step in the process required that all applicants be vetted by the local German security police for political reliability and general fitness. Not surprisingly, the majority of applicants were volunteers from the local police and from the ranks of former Soviet soldiers, in many cases released

Nazi Occupations, 1940–1991 (Riga: Institute of the History of Latvia, 2005), p. 167.

23 Matthäus, and Bajohr (eds), *Diary of Alfred Rosenberg*, p. 435.

24 Meyer, *Wehrmachtsverbrechen*, p. 59.

25 US Holocaust Memorial Museum Archive (USHMMA), RG11.001M.15: Der Reichsführer SS und Chef der Deutschen Polizei im Reichsministerium des Innern, O-Kd, Nr. 24/41 (g.), [25 July 1941].

26 Breitman, Richard, 'Himmler's Police Auxiliaries in the Occupied Soviet Territories', *Simon Wiesenthal Center Multimedia Learning Center*, 7:2, <http://motlc.wiesenthal.com/site/pp.asp?c=gvKVLcMVIuG&b=395183> (accessed 9 June 2016).

prisoners of war.[27] The fact that former soldiers were favored for these positions was apparent in the remark that applicants would be able to wear their former Russian uniforms, but with all former insignia removed and the inclusion of an armband with the word *Schutzmann*, an identifying number, and the place of origin (e.g., *Schutzmann* 304 Riga). The auxiliaries were initially to be provided with a wooden or rubber baton with provisions for the issuing of rifles and pistols if necessary. Of crucial significance was the fact that these units were to be commanded by Germans, specifically by SS and police officers or experienced senior enlisted personnel from the uniformed police.[28] In fact, German control of the auxiliaries was a paramount consideration with the lowest ranking German policemen exercising authority over the most senior non-German auxiliary.[29] In other words, they were not being trained to act independently, but under the supervision of SS and police personnel and in support of German occupation policies.

One attempt to ensure the allegiance of these auxiliaries involved the requirement for these men to take the following oath after completing four weeks of duty, 'As a member of the auxiliaries, I swear to be loyal, brave, and obedient and to consciously fulfill my duties, especially in the battle against genocidal Bolshevism. I am prepared to give my life for this oath, so help me God'.[30] The taking of the oath certainly did not guarantee the allegiance of every auxiliary, but it does emphasize the importance of ritual and ceremony within the police, even with regard to the employment of foreign nationals. In truth, the problem of auxiliaries deserting their posts for the partisans, especially after the German defeat at Stalingrad in February 1943, became a growing issue and led to orders that such persons were to be shot on the spot.

The issue of command authority was emphasized repeatedly as the auxiliary units, whether organized into small posts or precincts or in larger company and battalion sized formations, were seen as adjuncts to existing German security and uniformed police forces under direct German control. In an order on 6 November 1941, Himmler stressed that auxiliary forces only would be allowed to operate under German command. Further, he noted that individual and small groups of auxiliary policemen within cities, towns, and throughout the countryside were primarily tasked with general police duties and intended to mirror the existing German police organization in these areas. In addition, he ordered the establishment of police auxiliary battalions and companies with these units being subordinated to the HSSPF in the army rear

27 National Archives and Records Administration (NARA) T 580, reel 96: Vortrag über den Kräfte- und Kriegseinsatz der Ordnungspolizei im Jahre 1941, [February 1942].

28 USHMMA: RG11.001M.15: Der Reichsführer SS und Chef der Deutschen Polizei im Reichsministerium des Innern, O-Kdo. I. g. Nr. II/41 (g.), [31 July 1941].

29 Tessin, Georg, 'Die Stäbe und Truppeneinheiten der Ordnungspolizei' in Neufeldt, Hans-Joachim, Jürgen Huck, and Georg Tessin (eds), *Zur Geschichte der Ordnungspolizei* (Koblenz: Schriften des Bundesarchivs, 1957), p. 56, and Tec, Nechama, *In the Lion's Den: The Life of Oswald Rufeisen* (Oxford: Oxford University Press, 1990), p. 85.

30 BAB: R 19, folder 304, page 222: Vereidigung der Schutzmannschaft [31 August 1942].

areas.[31] These battalions, consisting of three companies of approximately 140 men each, were to be led by German police officers and senior enlisted personnel.[32] These auxiliary battalions, like the German uniformed police battalions and the *Einsatzgruppen*, emerged as paramilitarized, purpose built instruments for imposing Nazi control over the occupied territories and critical adjuncts for the prosecution of racial policy and mass murder.

Militarizing the Police

By December 1941, the failure of German forces to seize Moscow and end the campaign in the East, combined with a Soviet counteroffensive, revealed the strategic illusion that had blinded German generals during the initial advance into Russia. Likewise, the severe losses faced by the *Ostheer* (Eastern Army) by the end of 1941 threatened the German offensive with collapse.[33] In fact, the situation was so desperate that the German High Command citing 'urgent' military necessity reached agreement with Himmler allowing for the deployment of all available German police forces stationed in the East, including in Poland, on the frontlines.[34] Forced into the battlefront with insufficient winter clothing and handicapped by a lack of heavy weapons, the police battalions 'demonstrated their military abilities' but suffered significant casualties from combat and frostbite.[35] Not coincidentally, it was at this very time that the senior police leaders in the East called for the 'accelerated' formation of auxiliary police battalions for the conduct of combat operations alongside Wehrmacht forces.[36] In fact, Hitler approved the formation of auxiliary police battalions at the end of January 1942 and SS and police leaders launched a major recruitment campaign the following month.[37]

31 Bundesarchiv-Berlin (BAB) R 19, Band 281: Der Reichsführer SS und Chef der Deutschen Polizei im Reichsministerium des Innern, O.Kdo. I O (1) Sch. Nr. 1/41, [6 November 1941].

32 BAB: R 19, Band 281: Der Befehlshaber der Ordnungspolizei für das Ostland, o. Abt I, [4 December 1941].

33 Stahel, David, *Operation Typhoon: Hitler's March on Moscow, October 1941* (Cambridge: Cambridge University Press, 2013), pp. 262-266.

34 Westermann, *Hitler's Police Battalions*, p.186 and Witte, Peter, Michael Wildt, Martina Voigt, Dieter Pohl, Peter Klein, Christian Gerlach, Christoph Dieckmann, and Andrej Angrick, *Der Dienstkalender Heinrich Himmlers 1941/42* (Hamburg: Christians, 1999), p. 294.

35 NARA: T 580, reel 96: Vortrag über den Kräfte- und Kriegseinsatz der Ordnungspolizei im Jahre 1941, [February1942].

36 BAB: R 19, Band 281: Der Befehlshaber der Ordnungspolizei für das Ostland, o. Abt I, [4 December 1941].

37 Kangeris, Kārlis, '"Closed" Units of Latvian Police—*Lettische Schutzmannschafts-Bataillone*: Research Issues and Pre-History', in Nollendorfs, Valters and Erwin Oberländer (eds), *The Hidden and Forbidden History of Latvia under Soviet and Nazi Occupations, 1940-1991* (Riga: Institute of the History of Latvia, 2005), pp. 120-121. Hitler's authorization for

In a speech to senior police leaders in February 1942, Chief of the German Order Police Kurt Daluege remarked that manpower shortages within the police by the end of 1941 required the creation of 'auxiliary forces from the occupied territories . . . organized, trained, and equipped for the fulfillment of police tasks'. In the Reich Commissariat Ostland, auxiliary police forces drawn from ethnic Latvians, Lithuanians, Estonians, and Belarussians numbered 31,652 men, almost 10 times the size of German police forces in the commissariat. Similarly, the Reich Commissariat Ukraine mobilized 14,452 police auxiliaries from ethnic Germans and Ukrainians in support of the commissariat's 3,880 German uniformed policemen. Daluege praised the auxiliaries assigned to these companies and battalions for their efforts in the economic exploitation of the conquered territories and especially their performance in the 'never-ending battle against partisans, [Soviet] paratroopers, and communist criminals'.[38]

Daluege's comments offer a number of insights into the role and importance of the auxiliaries in the eastern campaign. First, German control over the occupied territories could hardly have been possible without the assistance of these forces. Indeed, auxiliaries formed the vast preponderance of total police forces in these areas. Second, Daluege's emphasis on the military organization of these forces, and, especially their employment in anti-partisan operations is a critical point. Already at the end of September 1941, a three-day conference on anti-partisan warfare including representatives from the Wehrmacht, the SS, and the police had been held at Mogilev in Belorussia. Guidelines prepared as part of the conference dictated that 'the enemy must be completely annihilated' and further argued, 'The constant decision between life and death for partisans and suspicious persons is difficult even for the hardest soldier. . . He acts correctly who fights ruthlessly and mercilessly with complete disregard for any personal surge of emotion'.[39] Not only did this conference establish annihilation as the standard for combating partisans, but it also introduced the equivalency of partisans with Bolsheviks and with Jews. Indeed, the equation of Jews with partisans was made by Hitler in a meeting with Himmler on 18 December 1941 and resulted in the latter's telegraphic remark 'Jewish question. [To be] exterminated as partisans'.[40] In other words, as Daluege delivered his speech in February 1942,

the formation of these battalions on 25 January 1942 coincided closely with the Wannsee Conference and offers further evidence of the ways in which Hitler and Himmler sought to seek the implementation of the "Final Solution' by using auxiliary police formations as a key instrument in the process of mass murder.

38 NARA: T 580, reel 96: Der Chef der Ordnungspolizei, Vortrag über den Kräfte- und Kriegseinsatz der Ordnungspolizei im Jahre 1941.

39 Beorn, Waitman W., 'A Calculus of Complicity: The Wehrmacht, the Anti-Partisan War, and the Final Solution in White Russia, 1941-1942', *Central European History*, 44 (2011), pp. 316-317, 324.

40 Witte, et al., *Dienstkalender Heinrich Himmlers*, p. 294.

the terms 'partisans' and 'communist criminals' had been already linked and tied the mission of the police formations to the annihilation of the Jews.

Like their uniformed police counterparts, German Security Police units faced their own manning crisis by early 1942 as they prosecuted their own campaign of racial cleansing. As a result the Reich Security Main Office issued orders on 19 January, 1942 calling for the creation of auxiliary police battalions of the Security Police based on the existing model of the auxiliary police battalions of the Order Police. These Security Police auxiliaries like their uniformed counterparts were tasked primarily with 'anti-partisan combat' and 'security duties' and most tellingly were assigned for duties with each of the four *Einsatzgruppen*. In fact, each *Einsatzgruppe* received authorization to establish 10 battalions of auxiliary security policemen.[41] The timing of the augmentation of the *Einsatzgruppen* with these auxiliaries once again offers a critical clue related to their mission. At a meeting devoted to the implementation of the 'Final Solution to the Jewish Question' on 20 January 1942, Chief of the Security Police Reinhard Heydrich openly discussed the plans for the mass murder of all European Jews under German control.[42] In this endeavor, the newly organized auxiliary police formations would provide critical assistance in the conduct of mass murder.[43]

Instruments for Mass Murder

By the fall of 1941, the use of auxiliary police formations for the mass murder of Jews was a common practice in the occupied territories. For example, a company of Lithuanian auxiliaries under German command, after torturing many of the victims, executed 864 Jewish men, 2,019 Jewish women, and 817 Jewish children in the Ponary Forest on 2 September 1941 as part of an operation aimed at clearing the Wilno Ghetto.[44] Likewise, a Lithuanian auxiliary battalion conducted 'the first act of mass murder of Reich Jews' near Kaunas at the end of November 1941 by murdering 4,934 Jews deported from Germany.[45] The auxiliary formations were not limited to the Baltic nationalities as Ukrainians and even Crimean Tatars were recruited to serve under German police command.[46] In the case of the former, Ukrainian

41 Birn, Ruth Bettina, *Die Sicherheitspolizei in Estland, 1941-1944: Eine Studie zur Kollaboration im Osten* (Paderborn: Ferdinand Schöningh, 2006), pp. 28-31.
42 Burleigh, Michael, *The Third Reich: A New History* (New York: Hill and Wang, 2000), pp. 646-650.
43 Golczewski, 'Kollaboration in der Ukraine', p. 173.
44 Sakowicz, Kazimierz, *Ponary Diary, 1941-1943: A Bystander's Account of Mass Murder* (New Haven, CT: Yale University Press, 2005), pp. 24-28.
45 Arad, Yitzhak, *The Holocaust in the Soviet Union* (Lincoln: University of Nebraska Press, 2009), p. 389.
46 Angrick, Andrej, 'Die Einsatzgruppe D und die Kollaboration', in Kaiser, Wolf (ed.), *Täter im Vernichtungskrieg: Der Überfall auf die Sowjetunion und der Völkermord an den Juden* (Berlin: Propyläen Verlag, 2002), pp. 71-84.

auxiliaries assisted *Einsatzkommando 4a* in the murder of Jewish men in the town of Sokal in the first week of the invasion. By the fall of 1941, Ukrainian auxiliaries emerged as an important adjunct assisting both the *Einsatzgruppen* and Order Police battalions in mass executions at numerous killing sites including Kamenez-Podolsk, Dnepropetrovsk, and Babi Yar near Kiev; killing actions that claimed the lives of 23,600, 34,000, and 11,000 Jewish victims, respectively.[47]

Continuing the practice established at the start of the invasion, pogroms aimed at the Jews in the East often were perpetrated by auxiliaries but instigated by German Security Police forces. The Germans then sought to place the blame for these 'spontaneous' actions at the feet of the local populace.[48] Not all these men were necessarily anti-Semites, but many of them came from a social background in which anti-Semitism was not an uncommon trait and their training did include political education involving virulently anti-Semitic material.[49] This social background combined with German ideological education proved a two-edged sword as some German officials worried about maintaining discipline in the ranks of men who 'had lost all moral restraints' during their participation in the 'liquidation of the Jewish population'.[50] In addition to ideological affinity, 'material expectations provided from early on a major incentive for locals to join the ranks of auxiliary police units'.[51] For example, the promise of plunder gained from the murdered Jews or the chance to receive additional food rations or alcohol provided practical incentives for the participation of some auxiliaries in genocide.[52]

The importance of Ukrainian auxiliaries in the annihilation of Jews in the East increased with the clearing of the Jewish ghettos in 1942, the 'killing year' of the Holocaust during which some three million Jews perished, as these forces assisted Order and Security Police units in a murderous campaign stretching from Poland into Russia.[53] In the case of the auxiliary police battalions, these men were used in a variety

47 Pohl, Dieter, 'Ukrainische Hilfskräfte beim Mord an den Juden', in Paul, Gerhard (ed.), *Die Täter der Shoah: Fanatische Nationalsozialisten oder ganz normale Deutsche?* (Göttingen: Wallstein Verlag, 2002), pp. 212-213.

48 Ibid., p. 212.

49 Dean, Martin, 'The German Gendarmerie, the Ukrainian *Schutzmannschaft*, and the "Second Wave" of Jewish Killings in the Occupied Ukraine', *German History*, 14 (1996), p. 179.

50 Browning, Christopher with Jürgen Matthäus, *The Origins of the Final Solution: The Evolution of Nazi Jewish Policy, September 1939–March 1942* (Lincoln: University of Nebraska Press, 2004), p. 274.

51 Ibid., p. 274.

52 Westermann, Edward, 'Stone Cold Killers or Drunk with Murder?: Alcohol and Atrocity in the Holocaust', *Holocaust and Genocide Studies,* 30 (Spring 2016), pp. 1-19.

53 Browning, Christopher, *Ordinary Men: Reserve Police Battalion 101 and the Final Solution in Poland* (New York: Harper Collins, 1992), pp. 78-113, and Pohl, 'Ukrainische Hilfskräfte', pp. 214-217. For a discussion on Ukrainian accomplices and their motivations see Radchenko, Yuri, 'Accomplices to Extermination: Municipal Government and the

of roles, including the surrounding of ghettos and killing sites to prevent escapes and as execution squads for mass shootings.[54] In the case of Jewish survivors in Ukraine, one historian notes that 'there is barely a story from a survivor that does not reference how Ukrainian auxiliary policemen herded Jews together, shot the old and the sick on the spot or beat them to death, and then delivered the remaining [Jews] to German authorities for execution'.[55]

Stalin's Partisans

As the German police accelerated their conduct of genocide in a 'second wave' of mass killing, these SS and police forces were now facing an increasingly well organized and equipped partisan threat organized by the Soviet Army General Staff (Stavka). In fact, Soviet partisan forces numbered about 72,000 by the spring of 1942. In order to further strengthen these forces, Soviet commandos parachuted into German occupied territories to organize partisan groups and the Soviet Air Force delivered supplies and munitions. By the summer of 1942, the Soviet partisan force was 'solidly established' and numbered 125,000 women and men. Operating primarily in small groups, the partisans concentrated on actions aimed at interdicting German supply lines or attacks on isolated garrisons or facilities.[56] German forces met the growing partisan activity by instituting increasingly draconian measures, including the use of reprisal killings and scorched earth attacks aimed at the local inhabitants as the partisan war became a contest in which quarter was neither asked for nor given.[57] This hard line tact was further reinforced by Hitler's appointment of Himmler to head the anti-partisan effort in the summer of 1942, along with the *Führer's* demand for the 'elimination' of the partisan threat. Himmler's chief of staff, Gottlob Berger, captured the guiding principle for this effort with his advocacy of a policy of 'better to shoot one Pole too many than one Pole too few'.[58] The translation of this theory into practice can be seen in police operations in the vicinity of Chotimsk in the summer of 1942 against suspected partisans during which a former police platoon leader remarked that he could not remember a single instance in which prisoners were

Holocaust in Kharkiv, 1941-1942', *Holocaust and Genocide Studies,* 27 (Winter 2013), pp. 443-463.

54 Matthäus, Jürgen, 'What about the 'Ordinary Men'?: The German Order Police and the Holocaust in the Occupied Soviet Union', *Holocaust and Genocide Studies,* 10 (Fall 1996), p. 139.

55 Golczewski, 'Kollaboration in der Ukraine', p. 173.

56 Grenkevich, Leonid, *The Soviet Partisan Movement, 1941-1944* (London: Frank Cass, 1999), pp. 205, 207-208.

57 Steinhoff, Johannes, Peter Pechel, and Dennis Showalter (ed.), *Voices from the Third Reich: An Oral History* (Washington, DC: Regnery Gateway, 1989), pp. 269-270.

58 Westermann, Edward, 'Partners in Genocide: The German Police and the Wehrmacht in the Soviet Union', *The Journal of Strategic Studies* 31 (October 2008), pp. 791-792.

taken.[59] With Himmler and his SS and police forces at the helm, murder and atrocity emerged as institutional standards. The historian Kenneth Slepyan aptly described the German use of the direct approach: 'German counterinsurgency tactics, which emphasized brute force over winning the hearts and minds, increased the alienation of the occupied population. . . .The more vicious German reprisal became, the more the peasantry turned to the partisans as their only viable alternative'.[60]

Police Auxiliaries and the Anti-Partisan War

In the face of the growing partisan threat, German police forces and auxiliary police formations focused their efforts on the 'pacification' of the countryside and the economic exploitation of industrial and agricultural resources in the occupied territories.[61] In an order of 18 August 1942, Hitler referred to the 'serious danger' posed by partisan attacks to the supply of the troops at the front and called for the 'extermination' of these groups by the use of 'active combat' and the 'hardest measures' aimed at both the partisans and their supporters before the start of the winter. He also emphasized that the SS and police formations had primary responsibility for such actions.[62] Interestingly, it was at this time that Hitler not only agreed to the employment of more SS and police units in the partisan campaign, but he also changed his views on the arming of auxiliaries and gave his belated support to the formation of auxiliary police units; a clear signal on the increasing importance of these forces as in both the anti-partisan role and as instruments of mass murder.[63]

With Hitler's approval the number of foreign police auxiliaries under German command exploded by the end of 1942. In September, there were 1,000 German uniformed policemen in Latvia compared to 18,000 foreign police auxiliaries, a number that included 19 auxiliary police battalions with an average of 400 auxiliaries per battalion. In Lithuania the number of German uniformed police was a mere 450 men compared to 16,600 foreign auxiliaries, including 20 auxiliary police battalions.[64] For the entire Reich Commissariat Ostland, an area of almost 200,000 square miles

59 Zentrale Stelle der Landesjustizverwaltungen (ZStl) 208 AR-Z 30/62, folder 1, page 108: Testimony of Erwin L.

60 Slepyan, Kenneth, *Stalin's Guerrillas: Soviet Partisans in World War II* (Lawrence: University Press of Kansas, 2006), p. 39.

61 NARA: T 580, reel 3: Dientsbesprechung der Befehlshaber und Inspekteure der Ordnungspolizei im Januar 1943 in Berlin, [1 February 1943].

62 Bundesarchiv-Militärarchiv (BAM) RW 4: Weisung Nr. 46 Richtlinien für die verstärkte Bekämpfung des Bandenunwesens im Osten [18 August 1942] and Witte, et al., *Dienstkalender Heinrich Himmlers*, p. 501.

63 BAB: NS 19, reel 1671, frame 11: Der Reichminister für den besetzten Ostgebiete, II 1 d 963/42 GRs, Betr.: Verstärkte Bekämpfung des Bandenunwesens in den besetzten Ostgebieten [25 August 1942].

64 BAB: R 19, Band 119: Niederschrift über die Besichtigung der Verwaltungsdienstellen des Kommandeurs der Ordnungspolizei in Riga [30 September 1942] and Niederschrift

and over 19 million inhabitants, there were only 4,428 German police personnel compared to 55,797 auxiliary policemen including 23,758 auxiliaries serving in some 60 auxiliary police battalions.[65] By the end of the year, the total number of uniformed police auxiliaries stood at 300,000 men, including 100,000 Ukrainian auxiliaries alone, an increase that coincided with a massive wave of killing aimed at the Jews and the growing partisan movement.

In his annual address to police leaders in Berlin at the start of 1943, Daluege not only praised the performance of the auxiliaries. He also admitted that the increasing demands placed on the police in the occupied territories could only be accomplished with the assistance of the auxiliary police and he underscored the growing importance of these forces for 'security duties principally anti-partisan operations (*Bandenbekämpfung*)'.[66]

Accomplices and Perpetrators in the Countryside

In a speech celebrating the tenth anniversary of the Nazi seizure of power on 30 January 1943, Daluege was even more explicit concerning the role of SS and police forces in the East. He declareded, 'This corps of the SS and the police represents Adolf Hitler and his struggle for a Greater Germany, for Europe, and for the world. Their task is the annihilation of the eternal enemies of all *völkisch* and racially conscious nations'.[67] If the goal for SS and police forces was annihilation, then the massive expansion of auxiliary police formations in the occupied East throughout 1942 created a ready-made force for the murder of East European Jews, operations against partisan forces, and even combat at the front. In the case of the first two missions, auxiliary policemen in precincts and in posts joined their counterparts in the auxiliary police battalions for these actions. In fact, it was the auxiliaries stationed at small rural posts under the supervision of German gendarmes who played a significant, if sometimes overlooked, role in the destruction of the remnants of Jewish communities throughout the East.

Despite their small size and relative isolation, gendarmerie forces, including auxiliary police forces, became 'an agency of prime importance for the successful implementation of the "final solution"' in the occupied East.[68] While the operations of the police battalions were notable by the scope and scale of killing these forces

über die Besichtigung der Verwaltungsdienstellen des Kommandeurs der Ordnungspolizei in Kauen [21-22 September 1942].

65 BAB: R19, Band, 119: Der Reichsführer SS usw. O-VuR. Pers. 45 Nr. 1/42, [29 October 1942]. Interestingly the report noted that 10 of the auxiliary battalions were involved in operations outside of the Reich Commissariat *Ostland* at the time.

66 NARA: T 175, reel 3, frames 2503392-93: Dienstbesprechung der Befehlshaber und Inspekteure der Ordnungspolizei im Januar 1943 in Berlin [1 February 1943].

67 NARA: T 580, reel 216: SS und Polizei im großdeutschen Freiheitskampfe [30 January 1943].

68 Matthäus, 'Ordinary Men', p. 136.

participated in, the actions of the policemen stationed at small posts in the countryside were distinguished by the independence of these units and the cumulative effects they achieved over time. In fact, the relative physical isolation of these posts did not prevent many of these men from becoming active and willing participants in the mass murder of the Jews as well as anti-partisan operations.

The German gendarmerie post Choiniki near Zhitomir, Ukraine, offers one clear example of the importance of the auxiliaries. The post consisted of only five German gendarmes, an ethnic German translator, and 100 Ukrainian police auxiliaries, and was the only German outpost within 60 miles along a main road.[69] In fact, this lopsided distribution of German gendarmes to auxiliary policemen proved the rule and not the exception. For example, the cases of the gendarmerie posts at Kulikowka with six German gendarmes and 99 auxiliaries, at Gorodnja with 10 German gendarmes and 136 auxiliaries, and at Ostor with only three German gendarmes and 227 auxiliaries were not atypical and highlight the disproportionate importance of auxiliaries for operations in these areas.[70] While the German gendarmes exercised complete authority over the assigned auxiliaries, it is clear that they could not have conducted their duties, including anti-partisan operations and the mass murder of Jews, without the auxiliary forces under their command.[71] Likewise, the leaders of such posts had great personal authority and exercised significant freedom of action on a daily basis, and many demonstrated initiative in their daily duties. Indeed, by March 1942 in Ukraine, the gendarmes had received authorization to murder Jews on their own authority without prior approval of the SD (Security Service) and 'began routinely to shoot smaller groups of remaining Jews, such as Jewish families hiding in the forests'.[72]

In one example, the leader of a gendarmerie post at Stoplce in the General Commissariat of White Russia (Belorussia) reported that he and his men had 'liquidated' 293 Jews on 31 January 1943 after escape attempts from the town's ghetto.[73] In another example, auxiliary policemen from a regional police station in Belorussia routinely cooperated with German policemen in the murder of the region's remaining Jews, a population mostly scattered throughout the countryside in small towns and villages. According to one account, 'Belorussian policemen and German gendarmes used to come to a village or small town, collect all the Jewish inhabitants, and then murder them. Each killing operation resulted in 10 to 40 victims, depending

69 Ibid., p. 138.

70 ZStl: II 204 AR-Z 278/67: Stärkenachweisung zur Gliederung des SS und Pol. Führers Tschernigow [24 November 1942].

71 BAB: R 19, folder 464: Vorläufige Richtlinien für den Einsatz der Gendarmerie in den besetzten Ostgebieten [8 January 1942].

72 Lower, Wendy, "Anticipatory Obedience'and the Nazi Implementation of the Holocaust in the Ukraine: A Case Study of Central and Peripheral Forces in the Generalbezirk Zhytomyr, 1941-1944', *Holocaust and Genocide Studies,* 16 (Spring 2002), p. 8.

73 Matthäus, 'Ordinary Men', p. 138.

on how many Jews resided in a specific place'.[74] Oswald Rufeisen, a translator with the police, witnessed one such combined action in the town of Kryniczno under the command of a German gendarme, Karl Schultz, a man he described as being of 'low intelligence, a pathological murderer and a sadist'. Schultz, a baker before the war, kept a personal log of the names of his victims, except for those under the age of 16 who he simply noted as 'pieces' (*Stücke*). Rufeisen recalled the killings, especially the actions of one Belorussian policeman who had taken particular interest in two beautiful Jewish girls: 'To my horror I saw him bend down. Next I realized that he was busy taking off the dead girl's handmade sweater. . . . The others too continued to examine the rest of the bodies impassively, methodically. When they discovered any signs of life they shot again'.[75]

The actions of the auxiliaries illustrate not only the willing participation of some segments of the indigenous populations in the murder of the Jews and the execution of their own countrymen, but more importantly these actions once again demonstrate the key role played by German police forces in organizing and commanding these operations. German authorities proved adept at taking advantage of the auxiliaries' knowledge of the local terrain, customs, and languages as well as any existing anti-Semitic or anti-Communist prejudices to facilitate the conduct of genocide. In this respect, one point is clear, without German guidance and encouragement, these auxiliaries might have conducted atrocity on their own, but certainly not on the scale that they eventually did.

The Auxiliary Police Battalions

While the auxiliary policemen at small precincts and posts generally killed their victims in small groups, the auxiliary police battalions were critical adjuncts for mass murder reaching into the thousands and tens of thousands as in the case of the Ukrainian and Russian auxiliary formations praised by the commander of *Einsatzgruppe B* in a situation report on 15 September 1942.[76] In fact, Himmler recognized the increasing importance of the auxiliary police battalions with an order creating the position of the 'Commander of the Auxiliary Police' (*Kommandeur der Schutzmannschaft*) subordinated to each of the HSSPFs in the Reich Commissariat Ostland and Reich Commissariat Ukraine. These positions were staffed by German policemen with the rank of Lieutenant Colonel and were ordered to focus their efforts 'above all on the weapons training and employment duties of the closed formations [auxiliary police battalions] of the *Schutzmannschaft*'.[77]

74 Tec, *Lion's Den*, p. 89.
75 Ibid., pp. 94-95.
76 USHMMA: RG 53.002M, fond 658, reel 5, folder 1, Polizeilicher Lagebericht für die Zeit vom 1. bis 15.9.1942 [September 1942].
77 USHMMA: RG 11.001M.15, reel 80, folder 51: Der Reichsführer SS und Chef der Deutschen Polizei im Reichsministerium des Innern, O.Kdo. I O (1) Nr. 405/42,

The increased focus on the weapons training and tactical employment of the auxiliary police battalions signaled a shift in focus for their employment. The case of Auxiliary Police Battalion 282 (APB 282), composed of Latvian auxiliaries under German command, highlights the increased focus on combat operations. The order authorizing the formation of the battalion on 5 March 1942 noted that 'the training of the men is to be conducted intensively and placed exclusively on anti-partisan operations'.[78] By the end of 1942, however, units that had been closely involved with mass murder and the Final Solution were being sent into combat at the front and in anti-partisan operations.[79] The nature of the anti-partisan operations can be seen in guidelines issued to German forces in the East on 16 December. The guidelines directly addressed 'the battle against the partisans' by arguing for the 'utmost brutality ... to master this pestilence ... without any restraint, also against women and children, as long as it leads to success'.[80] In one respect, such guidelines were a natural extension of the existing practices pursued by SS and police forces in dealing with Third Reich's putative racial enemies; practices that were now extended to those suspected of active or passive opposition to the German occupation.

Operation Winter Magic, a planned six week long operation starting in February 1943, highlights the key role of the auxiliary battalions in large-scale anti-partisan operations during this period. The operation included German Order and Security Police forces, Luftwaffe aircraft, and a Wehrmacht anti-aircraft section; however, one Ukrainian and seven Latvian auxiliary police battalions comprised the majority of the forces.[81] The objective of the operation involved creating a 'dead zone' (*tote Zone*) using a 'hammer and anvil' maneuver to sweep through the Latvian countryside. In addition to sweeping the area for 'bandits' [i.e., partisans], the German and auxiliary police forces were ordered to confiscate all available agricultural products, including livestock, grains, and feed.[82]

One clear indication of the military emphasis of the operation among the auxiliary police battalions involved their equipping with heavy and light machine guns as well

[9 September 1942]. In addition to the Reich Commissariats, Himmler assigned a Commander of the Auxiliary Police to the HSSPF Central Russia (*HSSPF Russland Mitte*)

78 USHMMA: RG 18.002M, reel 8, folder 7: Aufstellung des Schutzm.-Batl.282 [6 February 1943].

79 NARA: T 175, reel 3, frames 2503393: Dienstbesprechung der Befehlshaber und Inspekteure der Ordnungspolizei im Januar 1943 in Berlin [1 February 1943].

80 Hébert, Valerie, *Hitler's Generals on Trial: The Last War Crimes Tribunal at Nuremberg* (Lawrence: University Press of Kansas, 2010), p. 89

81 USHMMA: RG 18.002M, reel 8: Einsatzbefehl Nr. 2 für das Unternehmen Winterzauber [6 February 1943].

82 USHMMA: RG 18.002M, reel 8: Einsatz Sicherheitspolizei und SD. im Rahmen des Unternehmen Winterzaubers [15 February 1943].

as mortars for the operation.[83] Police Colonel Max Knecht, the commander of the Order Police (KdO) in Latvia, referenced the brutal measures to be used by reminding his subordinates that 'necessary executions' were to be the primary responsibility of the Security Police forces and not the auxiliary police forces. The rationale for this order, however, was not due to a perception of unreliability among the auxiliaries or to protect the auxiliaries from the psychological effects of mass murder, but rather it related to the attempt to have the SD first interrogate those captured. It also reflected Himmler's efforts to ensure that the bodies of the victims needed to be completely destroyed to obliterate the evidence of Nazi crimes in the East. In 1942, Himmler even created a special unit *Sonderkommando 1005* that traveled throughout the East to previous mass killing sites, disinterring and burning the remains of the victims and even employing enormous 'bone crushing machines' to grind the victims remains into dust.[84]

In the case of Operation Winter Magic, Knecht's order did note, 'In the event that executions [are] necessary by the [auxiliary] troops, because the SD is not in the vicinity, executions are to take place in houses. The bodies are to be covered with hay and straw and the houses set on fire'.[85] In any event, the order did not prevent the auxiliaries from executing suspected partisans as Auxiliary Police Battalion 278 shot 10 'bandits' and 10 'suspected bandits' during a patrol sweep on 14 February.[86] Likewise, Auxiliary Police Battalion 279 reported the execution of 30 persons alongside of a road on 21 February. Importantly, the unit's report did not mention the capture of any weapons or resistance from those killed, but did note that there was no possibility of burning the bodies as ordered.[87] A week later, destruction by fire was not an issue as the battalion requested and received permission to raze the village of Zerkowno after a firefight with partisans.[88] Upon the completion of Winter Magic, a summary report concerning the actions of the Order Police and the Latvian police auxiliaries detailed the killing of 77 'bandits' in combat, the capture of nine others, the 'special handling' [i.e., execution] of 875 bandits and bandit helpers, and the turnover of an additional 1,389 persons to the SD in the period between 16

83 USHMMA: RG 18.002M, reel 8, folder 6: Zusammenstellung über den Munitionsbestand der Batln. 276, 277, 278, u. 279 [14 February 1943].
84 Spector, Shmuel, 'Aktion 1005-Effacing the Murder of Millions', *Holocaust and Genocide Studies*, 5 (August 1990), pp. 157-173, and Arad, *Holocaust in the Soviet Union*, pp. 348-352.
85 USHMMA: RG 18.002M, reel 8, folder 7: Message traffic for Auxiliary Police Battalion 276, 277, 278, and 279 [18 February 1943].
86 USHMMA: RG 18.002M, reel 8, folder 4: War Diary entry [February 1943].
87 USHMMA: RG 18.002M, reel 8, folder 7: Radio message from Auxiliary Police Battalion 279 [20 February 1943].
88 USHMMA: RG 18.002M, reel 8, folder 7: Message traffic from Gruppe Berta [27 February 1943].

February and 31 March 1943.[89] A separate report compiled by the Security Police, noted 132 enemy casualties, 2,588 executed 'bandit helpers', 22 arrests, and the forced deportation of almost 4,000 persons. In addition to those executed as either 'bandits' or 'bandit helpers', the operation also involved the destruction of numerous villages and farmsteads that were razed to the ground. While acknowledging the importance of German police leadership in the conduct of Winter Magic, one historian analyzed the operation and emphasized the key role played by the auxiliary police units.[90]

The discussion of the victims in the police reports raises a key point when looking at the German approach to counterinsurgency in the East. The justification for the execution of men, women, and children was given as 'bandits' and 'bandit helpers', two terms that proved extremely elastic in application by the police formations throughout the period of the German occupation. In fact, the 'linguistic criminalization' of any acts of resistance became a standard practice in police reports that served to vindicate mass atrocity; words such as 'bandit helper', 'asocial', 'mentally ill', or 'vagrant' in addition to categories such as bandits, Jews, and 'gypsies' emerged as ready-made justifications for murder that could be applied essentially at the whim of individual police officials.[91] The use of euphemism to validate murder becomes even more apparent when one considers that during the six week operation, German and auxiliary police losses totaled 22 killed-in-action (KIA) and 77 wounded-in-action (WIA).[92] In other words, police losses totaled *less than one percent* of the losses experienced by the partisans and their alleged helpers. This fact perhaps more than any other highlights the brutality associated with the Nazi policy of the direct approach in the partisan war in the East.

The Police Rifle Regiments

The formation of Police Rifle Regiments (*Polizei-Schützen-Regimenter*) in April and May 1943 created a new model for integrating German and auxiliary police forces into larger combat formations, especially for the conduct of anti-partisan operations. These regiments consisted of three battalions; the first battalion was composed solely of German uniformed policemen while the second and third battalions were comprised of auxiliary policemen under German command. The major difference between the German police battalion and the auxiliary police battalions was that the

89 ZStl: UdSSR folder 245 Af, pp. 161-164, 191: Befehl über Abschluß des Unternehmens 'Winterzauber' [30 March 1943]. The high number of transferred persons is a direct reflection of the initial orders given to the policemen prior at the start of the operation.

90 Birn, Ruth Bettina, "'Zaunkönig" an "Uhrmacher", Partisanenaktionen 1942/43 am Beispiel des 'Unternehmens Winterzauber', *Militärgeschichtliche Zeitschrift*, 60 (2001), p. 115. Birn lists another report showing 137 enemy combatant deaths, 51 arrests, and the execution of 1,807 "suspects."

91 Westermann, *Hitler's Police Battalions*, pp. 127, 221-223.

92 USHMMA: RG 18.002M, reel 8, folder 4: Report on losses [31 March 1943?].

former included a heavy weapons company.[93] As implied by their designations, these regiments were classified as light infantry forces. The addition of the heavy weapons company was needed based on the rapidly growing partisan network throughout the occupied East, a situation that resulted in the German decision also to train the auxiliaries in the use of heavy weapons, including heavy machine guns, anti-tank weapons, and mortars.[94]

The need for larger formations of German and auxiliary policemen and greater firepower was reflected in part by the increasing number of Soviet partisans. In January 1943, there were 102,562 partisans (both male and female); a number that almost doubled to 181,392 by January 1944. In some areas the growth of partisan forces was no less than explosive, as in the case of Belorussia, which saw Soviet partisans increase from 68,498 in April 1943 to 121,903 by January 1944.[95] Paradoxically, part of this growth came at the expense of German auxiliary police forces as increasing numbers of auxiliaries began defecting throughout 1943 to the partisans, taking with them their weapons and their knowledge of German tactics and troop dispositions. In one example, Ukrainian police auxiliaries conspired with local partisans to turnover their entire unit in April 1943. In a nighttime raid with the assistance of the Ukrainian police auxiliaries working on the inside, Soviet partisans killed 12 German policemen and wounded five others, while 180 of the Ukrainian auxiliaries defected to the partisans. In an after action analysis, the Germans explained the event as a result of the weakening situation along the front and the increasing use of propaganda by the Soviet government urging the auxiliaries to defect.[96] In fact, from 1942 onwards, the Soviet government conducted a concentrated propaganda campaign calling on auxiliaries serving with the German occupiers to defect and 'to atone for their guilt'. In the case of Belorussia alone, more than 6,500 auxiliaries had defected to the partisans by January 1944.[97] In one case, rumors of an impending defection in September 1943 by a group of Russian police auxiliaries led a German police battalion to place all the auxiliaries under 'house arrest' for eight weeks before deporting them to Germany and refilling their ranks with newly recruited auxiliaries.[98] In another example, an

93 BAB: R 19, folder 330: Aufstellung von Pol.-Schützen-Regimentern [25 May 1943]. A total of eight Police Rifle Regiments were formed during the war. See Tessin, Georg and Norbert Kannapin, *Waffen-SS und Ordnungspolizei im Kriegseinsatz, 1939-1945* (Osnabrück: Biblio Verlag, 2000), p. 557.
94 ZStl: V 205 AR-Nr. 2684/1965, Band I: Testimony of Johann B. [18 January 1968].
95 Slepyan, *Stalin's Guerrillas*, p. 188.
96 BAM: RW 4, folder 309a: Bandentätigkeit im Bereich Einsatzgruppe B [4 April 1943].
97 Slepyan, *Stalin's Guerrillas*, pp. 221-223.
98 ZStl: V 205 AR-Nr. 2684/1965, Band I: Testimony of Alfred G. [18 January 1968]. It is unclear if these men were deported to a concentration camp or sent to forced labor duties within Germany.

'unreliable' Ukrainian auxiliary policeman was handed over to Special Detachment 10 of *Einsatzgruppe D* for execution.[99]

Despite growing concerns of their reliability, the auxiliary police battalions continued to play a key role in enforcing German occupation policies throughout 1943. The use of these forces in the conduct of mass reprisals against villages and communities highlighted the continued German use of the direct approach and a reliance on terror to maintain their rule. For example, Police Rifle Regiment 34, a unit consisting of Germans and Ukrainian auxiliary policemen, received orders on 2 May, to conduct a reprisal against the village of Laski in response to increased partisan activity in the district of Bialystok, Poland. The unit was ordered to surround the village, a community of approximately 40 farmhouses and 220 inhabitants, and to execute 'the entire population' and to raze the village to ground.[100] Later that summer, the same regiment participated in the liquidation of the Bialystok ghetto, an operation that resulted in the murder of approximately 2,000 Jews and the deportation of an additional 15,000 Jews to the death camps in Poland. The 'liquidations' of the remaining Jewish ghettos in occupied Poland during the summer of 1943 was partly in response to the Warsaw Ghetto uprising in April of that year and reflected the Nazi administration's intent to murder the remaining Jews in these areas; a process in which Ukrainian and other auxiliary policemen played a major role.[101]

A former German policeman recalled two anti-partisan operations involving Auxiliary Police Battalion 57. In the first operation the battalion entered a small village, after which the German police officer in charge of the battalion determined that the entire population of some 20 men, women, and children belonged to the partisans. At the police commander's order, the battalion executed all the men, women, and children and burned down the village's houses and barns. During a subsequent action, another village experienced the same fate as the battalion murdered the entire population and burnt their homes to the ground.[102] When questioned after the war, a German policeman from the battalion mentioned that the unit followed the motto 'Whoever was regarded as a Jew or suspected partisan was bumped off'.[103] In the fight against the partisans and the extermination of the Jews, the auxiliary police battalions, like their German police counterparts, proved to be an effective and deadly instrument for prosecuting racial policy.

99 ZStl: Verschiedenes 301 Cd Bd 163: Lagebericht für die Zeit vom 16. Juni bis 15. Juli 1942 [19 July 1942].

100 ZStl: Verschiedenes 301 AAe, Band 131: Vergeltungsmassnahmen [May 2, 1943].

101 Geldmacher, Thomas, *'Wir als Wiener waren ja bei der Bevölkerung beliebt': Österreichische Schutzpolizisten und die Judenvernichtung in Ostgalizien, 1941-1944* (Vienna: Mandelbaum Verlag, 2002), pp. 122-124.

102 ZStl: 202 AR 165/61, folder 1, pages 62-63: Testimony of Erwin Z.

103 ZStl: 202 AR 165/61, folder 1, page 80: Testimony of Johann H.

The Collapse of the Eastern Front and the End of the Auxiliaries

The Soviet winter offensive from December 1943 into May 1944 essentially broke the back of the German army on the Eastern Front as Soviet forces pushed the *Wehrmacht* back by as much as six hundred miles, leaving 'the physical and material strength of the troops exhausted'.[104] In addition to the catastrophic losses suffered by the *Wehrmacht* during the Soviet attacks, numerous German police forces and their auxiliaries were literally 'wiped out' in early 1944 as they were thrown into the frontlines in a desperate effort to halt the Soviet advance. As a result of catastrophic combat losses, Police Rifle Regiments 33, 35, and 37 as well as the SS Police Mounted Detachments I and II were deactivated in March 1943 and their remaining forces parceled out to supplement other depleted police regiments.[105] The spiraling losses of German police and auxiliary policemen extended to all branches of the police, including among the rural gendarmerie, and was apparent in the lengthening lists of death notices compiled by administrators in the occupied territories. For example, the commander of gendarmerie forces in Zhitomir listed 21 gendarmes KIA while conducting anti-partisan operations between 21 March and 7 May 1943, while the commander of the Order Police in Belorussia listed 38 policemen, including 14 auxiliaries, who fell in the 'battle against Bolshevism' between 2 May and 27 May 1943.[106] In truth, senior police leaders, like Daluege, who praised the auxiliary units for conducting their duties in a 'courageous' and 'determined' manner, always had based this evaluation on the willingness of these men to sacrifice their lives in support of the German occupation.[107]

Conclusion

In a 1944 speech to SS and police leaders, Himmler exclaimed, 'We have only one duty, to stand firm and to conduct this racial war (*Rassenkampf*) without mercy'.[108] If war without mercy was the charter, then Himmler's SS and police forces had more than fulfilled their mandate in the East. In Belorussia alone, Soviet sources estimated that German anti-partisan operations claimed more than two million victims from 200 cities and 9,200 villages.[109] In the end, foreign auxiliaries whether serving in

104 Fritz, Stephen, *Ostkrieg: Hitler's War of Extermination in the East* (Lexington: University Press of Kentucky, 2011), p. 398.
105 BAB: R 19, folder 330: Message concerning police losses [28 March 1944].
106 USHMMA: RG 53.002M, reel 5, folder 3 and reel 3, folder 1: Daily Orders listing casualties [12 May, 31 May, and 15 June 1943].
107 NARA: T 580, reel 3: Dientsbesprechung der Befehlshaber und Inspekteure der Ordnungspolizei im Januar 1943 in Berlin, [1 February 1943].
108 Smith, Bradley and Agnes Peterson (eds), *Heinrich Himmler Geheimreden 1933 bis 1945* (Frakfurt/Main: Propyläen, 1974), p. 189.
109 Matthäus, 'Ordinary Men', p. 143.

German Security or Order Police units, in the labor and death camps in Poland, or with armed formations of the *Waffen-SS* and the *Wehrmacht*, proved a key adjunct to overstretched German forces and critical instruments for mass murder in the East. As Peter Black correctly asserted, 'The Nazis could not have implemented their "Final Solution of the Jewish Question" without assistance from ethnic German and non-German auxiliaries'.[110]

In discussing counterinsurgency warfare, David Kilcullen argues that there are three necessary components for 'effective police work' in this environment:

1. Community police officers, who act to secure and protect population centers and deliver basic public order and rule of law;
2. Field police (paramilitary organizations sometimes called constabulary or gendarmerie units), who conduct normal police duties but in a higher threat environment and typically are better armed and more mobile than community police;
3. Police intelligence or police special operations capability (sometimes call a 'special branch') that specifically targets and arrests insurgent underground cells.[111]

With respect to the last, Kilcullen warns that the lack of a special operations capability is 'not necessarily a bad thing' as the formation of such units 'can result in "death squads" or "secret police" activity, which (besides being morally repugnant) is fundamentally counterproductive in this environment'.[112] The case of the German use of auxiliary policemen in general, and the formation and employment of the auxiliary police battalions in particular, not only provides a historical case study supporting Kilcullen's assertion, but the employment of the police auxiliaries also points to a more important fact of counterinsurgency. Despite the overwhelming use of draconian measures against the subject populations in the occupied East, the German reliance on the direct approach failed to achieve its goal of pacifying these territories and transforming them into a 'German Garden of Eden', but instead created a literal 'dead zone' that ultimately consumed both victims and perpetrators.

110 Black, Peter, 'Foot Soldiers of the Final Solution: The Trawniki Training Camp and Operation Reinhard', *Holocaust and Genocide Studies,* 25 (Spring 2011), p. 1.
111 Kilcullen, David, *The Accidental Guerrilla: Fighting Small Wars in the Midst of a Big One* (Oxford: Oxford University Press, 2009), p. 61.
112 Ibid., p. 62.

3

A Hidden Dimension of Britain's 'Informal Empire': British Police and Security Advisors and Anti-Communist Measures in the Middle East, 1949-1958

Chikara Hashimoto

Introduction

In recent years, the 'War on Terror' has raised the public profile of British intelligence liaison with foreign governments, and documentary evidence of such dealings has also been found in Tripoli as a result of the recent turmoil in Libya.[1] This is not a new phenomenon, however. Sir Stephen Lander, former Director-General of the Security Service (MI5), reminds us that the British Intelligence Services had maintained a relationship with their Middle Eastern counterparts long before the 'War on Terror'.[2] A former Israeli intelligence officer also testified over three decades ago that the British Intelligence Services had been instrumental in developing the Arab security services.[3] The British preoccupation with keeping the Middle East under British influence in the early Cold War has long been well known—the culmination of which can be seen in the Suez debacle of 1956.[4] The British presence and effort to maintain its own influence in the Middle East has often been portrayed as part of Britain's

1 Cobain, Ian, et al., 'How MI6 Deal Sent Family to Gaddafi's Jail', *The Guardian,* 9 Sept. 2011; Hopkins, Nick, 'The Libya Papers: A Glimpse into the World of 21st-Century Espionage', *The Guardian*, 9 Sept. 2011.

2 Lander, Stephen, 'International Intelligence Cooperation: An Inside Perspective', *Cambridge Review of International Affairs,* 17:3 (2004), pp. 483-484, 489.

3 Caroz, Yaacov, *The Arab Secret Services* (London: Corgi, 1978), p.13.

4 On the Suez Crisis, c.f. Kyle, Keith, *Suez* (London: St. Martin's Press, 1991); Lucas, Scott, *Divided We Stand* (London: Hodder & Stoughton, 1991).

'informal' empire.[5] It has also been demonstrated that, as Communist Parties were largely prohibited in the Middle East, the communist movement and influence in the region was less prominent throughout the Cold War.[6] This was perhaps helped by the undemocratic characteristics of most Middle Eastern regimes, chiefly supported by strong domestic security forces which were central to the existence of these regimes.[7] Nevertheless, there is a 'missing dimension' in the literature, which is the lack of discussion about the existence of an intimate British-Arab intelligence relationship in fighting against Communist Parties in the region during the period.

Using newly released and previously unexploited records, this chapter will prove the existence of a British-Arab (Lebanon, Iraq and Jordan) security liaison from 1949 to 1958. It will show that Britain was instrumental in developing the Lebanese, Iraqi and Jordanian security services as an anti-communist measure, and how the need to counter communist subversion in the possible event of war against the Soviet Union was shaped by competition with France and the United States. By looking at the 'missing dimension', it will argue that these measures were not, however, just in the British interest, but actually also based on similar requests from Middle Eastern governments. Thus, the continuation of Britain's 'informal empire' was also influenced by invitation of Middle Eastern governments secretly seeking British assistance to fight against communist activities in their countries.

The Official Committee on Communism and Anti-Communist Measures in the Middle East

A distinctive characteristic of the communist movement in the Middle East was that by the late 1940s communism was illegal in most Middle Eastern countries.[8] Communist Parties had not then gained popular support in the region. However, the communist movement was by no means non-existent: as their activities were prohibited, the members of the Communist Parties, and their sympathisers, went underground. According to the first post-war comprehensive survey conducted by the Joint Intelligence Committee (JIC), these underground communist movements sought to exploit nationalist elements for 'opposition to the interests of "Anglo-American

5 A reference to the 'informal' empire: c.f. Balfour-Paul, Glen, 'Britain's Informal Empire in the Middle East', in Brown, Judith M. and Roger Louis (eds), *The Oxford History of the British Empire*, Vol. IV (Oxford: OUP, 1999), pp. 490-514; Sluglett, Peter, 'Formal and Informal Empire in the Middle East', in Winks, Robin W. (ed.), *The Oxford History of the British Empire*, Vol. V (Oxford: OUP, 1999), pp. 416-436.

6 C.f. Laqueur, Walter, *Communism and Nationalism in the Middle East* (London: Routledge and Kegan Paul, 1956); Ismael, Tareq, *The Communist Movement in the Arab World* (London: Routledge, 2005).

7 C.f. Caroz, *op. cit.*, ch.1; Batatu, Hanna, *The Old Social Classes and the Revolutionary Movements of Iraq* (New Jersey: Princeton University Press, 1978).

8 The exception was Israel.

Imperialism"'.[9] By the late 1940s, the post-war strategic planners, the British Chiefs of Staff, were beginning to envisage a potential war against the Soviet Union, and these local communist parties and their sympathisers were inevitably regarded as 'potential fifth columnists', whose activities might threaten an allied war effort in the event of war against the Soviet Union.[10] The defence of the Middle East was in fact regarded as one of the foundations of post-war British strategy, owing to its geostrategic location for communicating with the Commonwealth and colonial countries, as well as its natural resources for fighting wars.[11] The problem with the communist movements in the region, from the British point of view, was that, because they operated underground, it was difficult to obtain a clear picture of the extent of the communist influence. More importantly, the local security services were considered ill-prepared for war, especially, in terms of their anti-communist security measures.

Records declassified since 2010 reveal that a highly secret cabinet committee, the Official Committee on Communism (Overseas), alias the AC (O), was the engine for facilitating security liaison with Middle Eastern countries. This hitherto unexplored committee deserves a brief note. The AC (O) was established in December 1949 at the suggestion of the Foreign Secretary, Ernest Bevin, in response to pressure from the Chiefs of Staff for the co-ordination and initiation of 'any measures' which 'appeared desirable in the conduct of the Cold War'.[12] 'Any measures' included propaganda by the Information Research Department (IRD) and clandestine paramilitary operations by Secret Intelligence Service (MI6).[13] The committee was chaired by a senior official from the Permanent Under-Secretary's Department of the Foreign Office, and the permanent members included Chairman of the JIC, the Chief of MI6, and the representatives of the Ministry of Defence and of the Chiefs of Staff.[14] The existence

9 The National Archives (TNA), London: Public Record Office (PRO) [thereafter TNA: PRO] CAB158/9: JIC (50)20: memorandum, 'Communist Influence in the Middle East', 21 Apr 1950.

10 TNA: PRO CAB81/133: JIC (46)70(0)(FINAL), 'The spread of Communism throughout the world and the extent of its direction from Moscow', 23 Sept. 1946; PRO CAB159/5: JIC (49) 28th meeting, 'Scale and Nature of Attack on the Colonies', 16 Mar. 1949; also Annex to JIC (48) 128 (Final) Revise, 'Fifth Column Activities', 11 Jan. 1949.

11 TNA: PRO CAB79/46: COS (46) 51st meeting, 'strategic position of the British commonwealth', 29 Mar. 1946. Also c.f. Bullock, Alan, *Ernest Bevin* (London: W.W. Norton, 1983), p. 215; Ovendale, Richie, 'William Strang and the Permanent Under-Secretary's Committee', in Zametica, John (ed.), *British Officials and British Foreign Policy 1945-50* (Leicester: Leicester University Press, 1990), p. 217.

12 On the AC (O), see also Cormac, Rory, 'The Pinprick Approach: Whitehall's Top-Secret Anti-Communist Committee and the Evolution of British Covert Action Strategy', *Journal of Cold War Studies*, 16:3 (2014), pp. 5-28.

13 TNA: PRO PREM8/1365: minute by Ernest Bevin to Clement Attlee, 19 Apr. 1949; CAB134/4: AC (O) (50) 1st meeting: minute, 'terms of reference and procedure of the committee', 25 Jan. 1950.

14 C.f. TNA: PRO PREM8/1365: note by Sir Norman Brook to Mr. Helsby, 13 Feb. 1950; PRO CAB134/3: AC (O) (49) 1: note by the Secretary of the Cabinet, 'composition and

of the committee was kept secret, and knowledge of its activities was confined to British officials on a *need to know* basis. Sir Ivone Kirkpatrick, the Permanent Under-Secretary of the Foreign Office, later warned all his departments as to the secrecy of the committee, so much as that even the name of the committee 'should never be mentioned to posts abroad, and quotations from its minutes or papers should only be made after consultation with the OPS [Overseas Planning Section, sub-committee of the AC (O)]' and that it should be referred to as the 'ACO' Committee.[15] The activities of the committee were supervised by the Ministerial Committee on Communism, alias AC (M).[16]

The AC (O) attached special importance to the Middle East as a pillar of the British post-war strategy. Michael Wright, Assistant Under-Secretary of the Foreign Office, the chief expert on Middle Eastern affairs, was invited to the committee meeting to express his opinion and pronounced that the danger of the spread of communist influence in the Middle East was 'very real'.[17] More importantly, the AC (O) considered the training of foreign police officers an essential element of anti-communist measures throughout the world. The motivation behind offering foreign police training in anti-communist measures stemmed not only from British experience in the colonial territories such as the Malayan Emergency, but also from concerns about the communist seizure of Eastern Europe following the war. Sir Gladwyn Jebb of the Foreign Office, the chairman of the AC (O), commented that:

> in countries which have been communized since the war the role of the police force has invariably been decisive, and it has been represented that it would help to prevent Communist infiltration of police forces in countries outside the Orbit if it were possible to offer increased facilities for the training of foreign policemen in this country.[18]

The minutes of the meeting on 19 May 1950 distinguish between two branches of foreign police training: training in ordinary police methods to create 'good will' for Britain on the one hand, and in anti-communist 'police' work on the other.[19] The AC (O) tasked the representatives of MI6, as well as the Foreign Office, to 'stimulate

terms of reference', 31 Dec. 1949.

15 TNA: PRO CAB21/2992: memorandum by I. Kirkpatrick, 23 Feb. 1955.

16 C.f. TNA: PRO CAB134/2: AC (M) (49) 1: note by the Secretary of the Cabinet, 31 Dec. 1949.

17 TNA: PRO CAB134/4: AC (O) (50) 18th meeting of the AC (O): minute, 'Communist Influence in the Middle East', 2 June 1950.

18 TNA: PRO FO371/80199: J1641/1G: minute by Gladwyn Jebb, 24 Feb. 1950.

19 TNA: PRO CAB134/4: AC (O) (50) 16th meeting: minute, 'Training of Foreign Police Officers', 19 May 1950.

foreign governments' to ask Britain for 'assistance in training their police in anti-Communist measures'.[20]

During the Second World War, Britain had assumed control of wartime security measures in most Middle Eastern countries, including censorship, port and travel control, and the internment of any suspects; during this time, local security forces acted as though they were a part of the British security services and remained loyal to Britain.[21] The problem in the post-war period was that the organisation of these security measures fell into the hands of the Middle Eastern governments. In addition, from the British point of view, these governments were not aware of the 'insidious nature of methods used by Communists' outside the region.[22] The administrative measures taken to check the spread of communist infiltration even by the most diligent security forces in the region, such as those of the Egyptians and Iraqis, were also considered 'not particularly well-conceived or effective' as they tended to 'make arrests too soon, thus losing valuable intelligence'.[23] The AC (O) felt that providing British advice on a number of the administrative and legislative anti-communist measures to Middle Eastern governments would be desirable to check the spread of communism in these countries.[24] In addition, the encouragement of regional security liaison between Middle Eastern governments, excluding Israel, to exchange information on the communist menace was considered essential to block the infiltration of Soviet influence in the region, especially after 1948. It was also managed and implemented through the regional headquarters of MI5, namely Security Intelligence Middle East (SIME), which was considered the security authority in the region.[25]

In addition to encouraging Middle Eastern governments to adopt administrative and legislative measures, Britain pursued a policy of introducing British police advisors to these governments. This had two objectives. The first objective was to try to control

20 Ibid.

21 C.f. Hinsley, F.H. & Simkins, C.A.G., *British Intelligence in the Second World War*, Vol. 4 (London: Her Majesty's Stationary Office, 1990); Howard, Michael, *British Intelligence in the Second World War*, Vol. 5 (London: Her Majesty's Stationary Office, 1990); Dovey, H.O., 'Operation Condor', *Intelligence and National Security*, 4:2 (1989), pp. 357-373.

22 TNA: PRO CAB134/3: AC (O) (50)28: draft memorandum by the Joint Secretaries, 'Constitutional and Administrative Measures to Combat Communism, particularly in the Middle East', 15 July 1950.

23 TNA: PRO FO371/91177: E1017/2G: letter by Sir Ralph Stevenson to Patrick Reilly, 28 Feb. 1951; E1017/3G: memorandum by H.A. Dudgeon, 'Anti-communist measures in Middle Eastern countries', 1 Mar. 1951.

24 TNA: PRO CAB132/2: AC (M) (51) 4: memorandum by Chairman of the Official Committee, 'the work of the official committee on communism (overseas)': 'activities in the Middle East', 23 June 1951.

25 On the SIME Hashimoto, Chikara, 'Fighting the Cold War or Post-Colonialism?: Britain in the Middle East from 1945 to 1958: Looking through the Records of the British Security Service', *The International History Review*, 36:1 (2014), pp. 19-44.

the spread of communism. The second was to obtain information on communist movements in the region. Chairman of the JIC, Sir Patrick Reilly, recorded:

> Apart from the obvious value of this to our general anti-communist effort, any such strengthening of links with foreign police authorities can be of great advantage both to [MI6] and the Security Service, by paving the way to the exchange of information and operational liaison.[26]

By 1951, the posting of security advisors to local governments had become the preferred method for both advising local authorities on more effective administrative and legislative measures against the communist problem in these countries. It also functioned for checking the spread of communism in the region through liaison with the local police of 'strategically important countries'.[27]

The Lebanese Sûreté Générale and Ousting French Influence

Lebanon is normally regarded in the sphere of French influence owing to its colonial legacy, but was in fact one of the 'strategically important countries' for Britain. In post-war Lebanon the maintenance of internal security was inherited from the French Mandate, in which the *Sûreté Générale*, the Lebanese Security Service, was responsible for internal security, including counter-espionage and counter-subversion.[28]Although the *Sûreté Générale* had already been dealing with communism in the country, it was still insufficient in British eyes due to the complexity of the Lebanese security apparatus, which hampered effective security work. One such 'petty annoyance' which Emir Farid Chehab, the *Chef de Sûreté* [Head of the *Sûreté Générale*] (1948-1958), complained about to Major David Beaumont-Nesbitt, Assistant Military Attaché at the British Embassy in Beirut, was that his official telephone line in the *Sûreté* was 'tapped by agents of the President's brother'.[29] Major Beaumont-Nesbitt was in fact serving as the representative of MI5 in Lebanon and Syria, seconded from the Army on a temporary basis. He reported to MI5 headquarters on the status of the Lebanese security apparatus that 'the mechanics of this preposterous operation, if true, are, as one may imagine, highly complex and there are the usual wheels within wheels, the agents concerned being simultaneously employed by various organisations'.[30]

There were compelling reasons for the need for anti-communist measures in Lebanon from the British point of view. It was recognised that Lebanon housed the

26 TNA: PRO FO371/80199: J1641/1G: minute by Patrick Reilly, 26 Apr. 1950.
27 TNA: PRO FO371/91178: E1018/1G: memorandum by C.E. King, 7 May 1951.
28 C.f. Longrigg, Stephen, *Syria and Lebanon under French Mandate* (Oxford: OUP, 1958), p. 138.
29 TNA: PRO FO371/75319: E8783/G: report by D. Beaumont-Nesbitt to Head Office [MI5] (B1) and SIME (B), 27 June 1949 [thereafter Beaumont-Nesbitt Report].
30 Ibid.

highest number of communist party members (12,000) and sympathisers (50,000) in the Middle East.[31] The Lebanese Communist Party (LCP) was also believed to have been cooperating very closely with the Syrian Communist Party (SCP) under a Joint Higher Committee. The strength of the SCP was estimated at around 2,000 to 2,500 members.[32] A JIC report stated that the LCP also 'kept in close touch with the Soviet Legation', through which it was believed that the Soviets maintained close ties with regional communist parties.[33] When Michael Wright of the Foreign Office was invited to a meeting of the AC (O) to express his opinion on communist influence in the Middle East, he insisted on the need to 'stimulate' the Lebanese government to take necessary action as they were showing 'very little vigour in tackling this problem'.[34]

It is noteworthy that, by the time the anti-communist measures in Lebanon were discussed at the AC (O) in London, there had been a move by the Lebanese concerning the communist influence in the country. The Lebanese Minister of Foreign Affairs, Hamid Franjieh, had already approached Sir William Houstoun-Boswall, the British Minister in Beirut, to ask for a British expert on anti-communist measures. Houstoun-Boswall then reported the Lebanese request to London with great secrecy as 'nobody including the chief of secret police knows anything of this move which it is desired to keep secret and quite unofficial'.[35] The reason for the secrecy was not only due to the sensitivity of the subject, but also to the presence of a French security advisor to the Lebanese government in Beirut. As shown in a recent study on the British-French rivalry in Lebanon, countering French influence in post-war Lebanon had already been a concern of the British before the end of the war.[36] The Lebanese approach thus presented the British with a unique opportunity to establish influence in the French sphere by placing a British senior police officer in the heart of the Lebanese government. It would allow the British officer access to the Lebanese Prime Minister and give personal advice on anti-communist measures. L.G. Thirkell, a senior official of the Eastern Department of the Foreign Office, in charge of Syrian and Lebanese affairs, noted that appointing such an expert without informing the French 'would arouse the worst suspicions', but it was decided not to tell them as notification would 'invite serious criticism and such an appointment would presumably have to be kept secret or have some form of cover'.[37]

31 TNA: PRO CAB134/3: AC (O) (50) 18: report (annex) by JIC, 'Communist Influence in the Middle East', 21 Apr. 1950.
32 Ibid.
33 Ibid.
34 TNA: PRO CAB134/4: AC (O) (50) 18th meeting: minute, 'Communist Influence in the Middle East', 2 June 1950.
35 TNA: PRO FO371/75319: E3456/G: telegram by Houstoun-Boswall to FO, No. 142 of 15 Mar. 1949.
36 C.f.: Zamir, Meir, 'The 'Missing Dimension': Britain's Secret War against France in Syria and Lebanon, 1942-45–Part II', *Middle Eastern Studies*, 46:6 (2010), pp. 791-899.
37 TNA: PRO FO371/75319: E3456/G: minute by L. Thirkell, 17 Mar. 1949.

A meeting was soon held in the Foreign Office, and it was decided that 'the best man' for the assignment, Graham Mitchell of MI5, was to be sent to keep the Lebanese government on track. This recommendation was most likely made by Sir Dick White, then Director of B Division (counter-espionage) of MI5, later Director-General of MI5 and Chief of MI6.[38] Mitchell's mission was to secure a position in Lebanon, which was deemed strategically important to long-term British interests—his failure to do so might cause the Lebanese government 'to approach another Power instead, such as the Americans or even the French'.[39] Mitchell's visit in May 1949 was an appreciable success. During the visit, he convinced the Lebanese Prime Minister, Riad el-Solh, that the Communist movement was a 'formidable enemy', able to act as 'a fifth column in the event of war with Russia', and managed to obtain an oral promise to appoint a British advisor to the Head of the *Sûreté Générale*, Emir Farid Chehab. This appointment was in fact an objective of his visit to boost intelligence collection on the communist movement in the region. Mitchell wrote in his report that:

> [r]epeated reports from various sources have emphasised that from the Russian Legation in Beirut there springs a multitude of espionage and other subversive activities...British control, direct or indirect, of a local Security Service [*Sûreté Générale*] working on efficient lines would therefore hold out a promise of producing material of considerable intelligence value.[40]

Mitchell noted later in his report that it was essential to meet with Emir Chehab, with the permission of Riad el-Solh, to discuss the subject as Emir Chehab was 'thoroughly friendly to British interests and ready to co-operate'. Emir Chehab was above all 'a close contact of our [MI5] representative in Beirut'.[41]

Emir Farid Chehab, still remembered as 'Bay al Amn al Aam [Father of the *Sûreté Générale*]' in Lebanon, retained the post of *Chef de Sûreté* until September 1958.[42] He served his country diligently, but also shared the British vision of what his country needed to do against communist influence. Most of all, Emir Chehab was an anti-communist, believing that communism was a real threat which was detrimental to the values and traditions of the Middle East. He once noted to a Middle East correspondent of *Time*, Keith Wheelock, in 1954 that:

> If it comes to war, the Middle East will fall to the Communists inevitably. Just as inevitably you'll have to take it back. The West could not abide Russia controlling

38 Ibid., 23 Apr. 1949.
39 Ibid., E7476/G: report (Flag C) by Mitchell, 'Lebanon: Defence Against Communism', 17 June 1949 [thereafter Mitchell Report], p. 1.
40 Ibid.
41 Ibid.
42 Quoted in Asseily, Youmna, and Ahmad Asfahani (eds), *A Face in the Crowd* (London: Stacey International, 2007), p. xi.

> the Middle East. It'll be a lot easier to take it back if the people are on your side. If they're not on your side it will be almost impossible to take it back.[43]

Moreover, as Mitchell rightly noted earlier, Emir Chehab was clearly pro-British, as opposed to being pro-American—he regarded the Americans as being 'temperamentally incapable of understanding the complexities of the Levant'.[44] Emir Chehab had an intimate relationship with the British: after his imprisonment by the Vichy French, he had, though indirectly, cooperated with Sir Colonel Patrick Coghill, the head of the British Security Mission in Lebanon in the post-war independence from the French rule; in August 1947, he attended a three-month training course, including counter-espionage, at Scotland Yard's Superior Police Training College. Once he was back from Britain, he was appointed Head of the *Sûreté Générale*.[45]

Written recommendations were left by Mitchell with Riad el-Solh for combating communism suggesting that Emir Chehab be given a 'free hand' for internal security, allowing him to have a technical liaison with the Minister of Posts and Telegram with the 'object of putting at the disposal of the *Sûreté* means for the interception of communications of suspects'. It also stated to set up effective control of frontiers and of 'Russian and satellite aliens' by ensuring that 'no alien enters or resides in the Lebanon' without the knowledge of the government. These were deliberately written in French to conceal 'its face evidence of British origin'.[46] In his report Mitchell recommended that the Foreign Office respond quickly should the Lebanese formally request an advisor, and to make the necessary appointment while 'the iron is hot'. If not, Mitchell wrote that an alternative possibility was to insert a 'technical officer at a lower level' into the *Sûreté* to 'be elevated gradually by Farid [Chehab] as opportunity offers'.[47] Soon after Mitchell's visit, administrative developments indeed emerged: Emir Chehab acquired a new building for the *Sûreté Générale* and strictly compartmentalised sections were established for organisational efficacy.[48] In addition, on 2 September 1950, Riad el-Solh issued a new secret decree for the formation of a special Anti-Communist Bureau, to be also headed by Emir Chehab as the *Chef de*

43 Private Papers of Emir Farid Chehab in possession of the family of Emir Farid Chehab [thereafter Chehab Papers 'F']: report by Keith Wheeler [sic], Middle East correspondence of TIME, 'Subject Communism in the Middle East', 13 Nov. 1954, designated '4Q', p. 14.
44 Asseily et al., *A Face in the Crowd*, p. 191.
45 Ibid., pp. 9, 193-194, 202.
46 TNA: PRO FO371/75319: E7476/G: report (Flag D) by Mitchell, 'Suggested recommendation to be tendered to Prime Minister at second interview', 17 June 1949.
47 Mitchell Report, p. 3.
48 Beaumont-Nesbitt Report.

Sûreté.[49] Shortly after its establishment, Emir Chehab was once again in Britain, but this time was particularly for training in anti-communist measures.[50]

After initial hesitation by the Lebanese President, Bechara El Khoury, who had favoured a French connection, a formal request for an advisor from the Lebanese government eventually reached the Foreign Office via the British Embassy in Beirut.[51] Security Advisor, J.M. Kyles, the former Commissioner of Police in Sudan, with some twenty-years experience in Palestine, was appointed Security Advisor in May 1950.[52] A letter sent by George Clutton, Head of the African Department of the Foreign Office, to Khartoum in September 1949, while finding a suitable candidate for the post, reiterates the advantage of placing a British security advisor in Beirut:

> Lebanon is, as you probably know, the chief centre of communism in the Middle East; and such an appointment would have the double advantage of putting the Lebanese security services into some sort of shape to deal with the local Communist menace and of providing us with first-hand information about communist activities in the Middle East straight from source.[53]

J.M. Kyles was also tasked by the AC (O) to 'stimulate' the Lebanese government 'to repress' the communist menace.[54] About four months after the appointment of Kyles, the special Anti-Communist Bureau was secretly established by Riad el-Solh. Following its formation, Sir William Houstoun-Boswall, the British Minister in Beirut, despatched a letter to Ernest Bevin:

> Mr Kyles, the Police Advisor whose task, as you can well imagine, is not an easy one here, has been trying to influence the authorities to work along more systematic lines. The trouble is, as you will not be surprised to hear, that Mr Kyles' advice is very rarely sought and when given is not acted upon...But now they have at least begun—if only dimly—to appreciate the very real danger presented by Communism. And I do not propose to allow them again to relapse into their pipe dream that Communism must be dead just because it is outlawed.[55]

49 Asseily et al., *A Face in the Crowd*, p. 10.
50 TNA: PRO FO371/91177: E1017/6G: letter by Ronald W. Bailey to Herbert Morrison, 1 June 1951.
51 TNA: PRO FO371/75319: telegram from Beirut to FO, 18 July 1949.
52 TNA: PRO FO371/75319: E10297/G: letter by R.C. Mayall, Sudan Gov. Agency, to Thirkell, 23 Aug. 1949; PRO FO371/82267: EL1015/13G: letter by Ronald Beiley to G.W. Furlonge, 14 Mar. 1950.
53 TNA: PRO FO371/75319: E10297: letter by George.L. Clutton to E.W. Thomas, 8 Sept. 1949.
54 TNA: PRO CAB134/4: AC (O) (50) 18th meeting: minute, 'Communist Influence in the Middle East', 2 June 1950.
55 TNA: PRO FO371/82267: EL1015/16G: Letter by Houstoun-Boswell to Bevin, 28 Nov. 1950.

Thus the Security Advisor was limited in the implementation of legislative measures as the final decision was always in the hands of the Lebanese government. In addition, the assassination of Riad el-Solh in July 1951 caused the implementation of these anti-communist measures to become more strained. It also caused the termination of Kyles' advisory post.[56] As it will be shown later, however, the closer connection made through the appointment of the Security Advisor to Emir Chehab was important in supporting British anti-communist measures in the region.

The Iraqi Connection and Concerns About American Influence

In Lebanon, Britain ousted French influence by planting a security liaison officer in Beirut. In Iraq, their aim was to prevent the growth of American influence, whose participation in strengthening the Iraqi Police in anti-communist measures troubled Whitehall. The CIA-MI6 joint operation in support of the Iranian Coup of August 1953 has been an example of the US-UK special intelligence relationship in the region at the time.[57] However, Britain was less receptive, at least in early October 1953, to the idea of cooperation in the field of security building in Iraq, which was essentially regarded as British province. This was mainly due to the existence of an intimate British-Iraqi cooperation on security matters. The foundation of this was the close connection between MI5 and its Iraqi counterpart, the Criminal Investigation Department (CID) of the Iraqi Police. The Iraqi CID, with more executive power than its British counterpart, had been established in 1947 by the British security delegation in Iraq, headed by J.F. Wilkins, who had been in Baghdad for more than twenty years.[58] This connection was strongly backed by the regional foreign and defence policies of the early 1950s, when the focus of British strategy shifted from Egypt to Iraq.[59]

Given the intimate British-Iraqi security connection, it is no surprise that Iraq was not on the AC (O)'s priority list of countries in need of anti-communist measures in the early 1950s. By then, the Iraqi government had managed to suppress the Iraqi Communist Party (ICP), and according to JIC estimates, there were approximately 2,000 active ICP members in 1950.[60] Since the outlawing of the ICP in January 1947,

56 TNA: PRO FO371/91178: E1018/1G: minute by H.A. Dudgeon, 18 May 1951.

57 To name some important memoirs: Woodhouse, C.M., *Something Ventured* (London: Granada, 1982), chs. 8-9; Roosevelt, Kermit, *Countercoup* (New York: McGraw-Hill, 1979); Wilber, Donald, 'Clandestine Service History: Overthrow of Premier Mossadeq of Iran, November 1952-August 1953', *Foreign Policy Bulletin*, 11:3 (2000), pp. 90-104.

58 C.f. Batatu, *op. cit.*, p. 1157. Also TNA: PRO KV4/384: report, 'report of visit by Mr. A.J. Kellar to the Middle East', p.14, July 1946.

59 On shifting of British strategy from Egypt to Iraq, c.f. Lucas, Scott, 'The Path to Suez: Britain and the Struggle for the Middle East, 1953-56', in Dighton, Anne (ed.), *Britain and the First Cold War* (London: Macmillan, 1990).

60 TNA: PRO CAB134/3: AC (O) (50) 18, JIC report (annex), 'Communist Influence in the Middle East', annex, 21 Apr. 1950.

for instance, the ICP had been severely suppressed, and its most influential leaders had all been imprisoned or executed. In September 1949, the head of the sixth Central Committee of the ICP was also arrested together with some 100 other suspects.[61] As a result, the Foreign Office believed the anti-communist measures in Iraq were to be satisfactory and the Iraqi CID was regarded as the 'most efficient' anti-communist force in the region. Moreover, relations between the Iraqi CID and the representative of MI5 were noted to be 'probably closer than anywhere else in the Middle East'.[62] Sir Henry Mack, the British Ambassador in Baghdad, content with the measures adopted by the Iraqi authority against the communist menace, once wrote to Ernest Bevin that:

> In my opinion these laws and administrative measures have proved an effective check on communist activity and influence in Iraq…The Iraqi Criminal Investigation Department, which owes much to the tradition established by British officers who served in it up till 1947, is by Middle Eastern standards a fairly efficient organization. Doubtless it could be improved if British officers were reintroduced, but the political difficulties in the way of this are very great, and moreover to find a suitable man would not be easy. Even if these difficulties were overcome there would be a risk of prejudicing the present close relation between the Criminal Investigation Department and the representative of the [Security Service].[63]

This situation and British attitude to the co-operative Iraqi CID, would, nevertheless, change in 1953, with the growing communist influence and, more importantly, American interest in Iraqi affairs.

Despite the ICP's low membership, underground communist activities persisted in Iraq, and in October 1953 the British Embassy in Baghdad was approached by the Iraqi Minister of the Interior, Said Qazzaz, who asked for experts to reorganise the Iraqi police and CID. Whitehall was alarmed to learn that Said Qazzaz was also prepared to engage the Americans, who were able to provide support free of charge through the Truman administration's Point Four Program, providing financial aid for development.[64] Sir John Troutbeck, British Ambassador in Baghdad, warned the Foreign Office that this was not only 'the thin edge of the wedge of American penetration in what has been

61 Ibid. Detailed reports on the raid by the Iraqi CID on the ICP in 1949: c.f. PRO FO371/75130; 75131.

62 TNA: PRO FO371/91177: E1017/9G: letter by Sir John Troutbeck to Herbert Morrison, 27 June 1951.

63 TNA: PRO FO371/82410: EQ1019/1G: letter by Sir Henry Mack to Ernest Bevin, 7 Nov. 1950.

64 On the Point Four Program: the National Archives and Records Administration, United States (NARA): RG59: 511.80/4/1653, Clark to Sanger, 16 Apr. 1953, enclosing 'Information Policy for the Point IV Program', 3 Mar. 1953.

our province', but would also lead to the dislocation of the Iraqi CID and police, with 'results potentially disastrous to the security of the whole country'.[65] The Iraqi move was also flagged by Roger Lees, MI5's representative in Baghdad, serving in the guise of the Assistant Air Attaché to the British Embassy in Baghdad,[66] who commented that it would be 'a great pity if the reorganisation of the Iraqi police were to fall into the hands of the Americans'.[67] Indeed, the intimate relationship between the representative of MI5 and the Iraqi CID provided an important first-hand source on communist underground activities in Iraq, as confirmed by Sir Hugh Stephenson, Chairman of the Joint Intelligence Committee in Middle East (JIC/ME), who stated that 'from an intelligence point of view and in our concern with Communism, we are largely dependent in Iraq on our CID liaison'.[68]

The British not only had to provide the advisors free of charge if they were to compete with the Americans, but they also had to avoid financial and political complications in the Iraqi Parliament. Anti-British sentiment in Iraqi politics added to a growing concern that the Iraqis were leaning towards the Americans. While waiting for a formal request from the Iraqi government backed by the Iraqi Cabinet, there was a clear increase in British concern over American influence in Iraq. In his telegram, Sir John Troutbeck commented from Baghdad that:

> An American might well come as a temporary visitor...under the cover of 'Security Advisor to the American Embassy' or something similar rather than as an employee of the Iraq Government...The most effective way therefore of preventing the appointment of an American is for us to evince a more active desire to help the Iraqi Minister of the Interior on the issue...Otherwise, an American advisor—or at least a temporary advisor—may be here before we know it. There are various signs that the Americans are prepared to move rapidly to redeem their diminished prestige here at our expense.[69]

As Iraq was regarded as being under the sphere of British influence, the Foreign Office decided without hesitation to forestall American influence and requested funds

65 TNA: PRO FO371/104719: EQ1641/9G: letter by Troutbeck to Falla, 13 Oct 1953.
66 MI5 also had Norman Himsworth in the guise of the Security Liaison Officer in Baghdad under 'our diplomatic mission' as a part of the SIME network. See Magan, William, *Middle Eastern Approaches* (Michael Russell: Norwich, 2001), p. 150.
67 TNA: PRO FO371/104719: EQ1641/9G: minute by Patricia M. Hutchinson, 19 Oct. 1953.
68 TNA: PRO FO371/111043: VQ1641/5: letter by H.S. Stephenson to R. Allen, 24 Jan. 1954.
69 TNA: PRO FO371/104719: EQ1641/13G: letter by Troutbeck to Falla, 24 Nov. 1953.

from the Treasury for a security advisor. Thus, a British advisor was sent to Iraq free of charge.[70]

The necessity of the intimate collaboration between the representative of MI5, also known as the Defence Security Officer (DSO), in Baghdad and the Iraqi CID can be seen in the requirement for 'war planning', which originated in late 1950.[71] British air bases in Iraq were the keystone of British defence policy, from which the Chiefs of Staff envisaged that they could launch an air assault on the heart of the Soviet Union. Therefore, the maintenance of these bases was regarded as vital for fighting the Cold War. Under instruction by the British Defence Co-ordination Committee in the Middle East (BDCC/ME), via the Air Officer Commanding Iraq Command, the DSO Baghdad shared all necessary intelligence with the Iraqi CID for 'the preparation of lists of security suspects to be arrested on the outbreak of war'.[72] The DSO Baghdad supplied the Iraqi CID with an arrest list which included all known members of the ICP; other known Communists in Iraq; contacts of the Russian Legation, Baghdad; enemy and satellites nationals; and nationalists, leftists, religious leaders, and others likely to engage in subversive activities.[73]

The security measures in place in the event of war in Iraq extended beyond mere intelligence liaison. As these security measures required Iraqi cooperation, in March 1952 Sir John Troutbeck approached the Iraqi Prime Minister, Nuri al-Said, regarding the security plans for war. Agreeing to the suggestion in principle, Nuri al-Said preferred using the police as opposed to the armed forces to 'concoct the planning on the Iraqi side', mainly due to volatile Iraqi sentiments towards the West, particularly Britain. Nuri al-Said worried that the disclosure of war planning would cause 'a serious political storm' in which his government would be accused of 'dragging the country into war on the side of the Western Powers'.[74] He decided to delegate the task to Alwan Hussain, known as Alwan Pasha, Director-General of Police, who would later hand the task over to Bahjat Beg Attiyah, the Director of the CID. On the British side, Sir John Troutbeck nominated Roger Lees of MI5, DSO Baghdad (1951-53), to be the British counterpart for security planning in the event of war in Iraq.[75]

The security planning between the DSO Baghdad and the Iraqi CID was carried out in 'great secrecy', continuing even after the resignation of Nuri al-Said in July

70 TNA: PRO FO371/104719: EQ1641/16G: memorandum by P.S. Falla, 'Police Expert for Iraq', 23 Dec. 1953.

71 For detailed discussions about the war planning and the connections between MI5 and the Iraqi CID, see Hashimoto 'Fighting the Cold War or Post-Colonialism?', pp. 31-33.

72 TNA: PRO AIR23/8605: Joint Standing Instruction No.3: Security Directive, 24 Nov 1950.

73 TNA: PRO AIR23/8605: appendix 'C' to the Air Headquarters Iraq Security Plan, 'Security Measures in Iraq', 30 March 1951.

74 TNA: PRO AIR23/8605: report on 'security planning', by RER Lees, 10 Jun 1953 [thereafter 'British-Iraqi Security Planning Report'], p.2.

75 TNA: PRO AIR23/8605: letter by RER Lees to P.S. Davies, 'Security Measures in Iraq in the Event of War', 19 May 1952.

1952 without the knowledge of subsequent Iraqi Prime Ministers, Ministers of the Interior or Ministers of Defence. As part of these security measures for the event of war, Bahjat Beg Attiyah was trained by MI5 in 'protective security matters' during a visit to London in June 1952.[76] Moreover, in the event of war, the Iraqis agreed to allow a small group of British interrogators to operate at the detention camp where all the suspects on the combined arrest lists would be detained, and, more importantly, they agreed to the provision of British representatives to the central censorship headquarters, controlling postal and telecommunication censorship throughout Iraq.[77] When the report reached Sir Hugh Stephenson, Chairman of JIC/ME, he was 'extremely gratified' to learn of such substantial progress despite the 'difficulties inherent in the unstable political state in the country'.[78] It was in this context that Britain was reluctant to allow the Americans to appoint their own security advisors to the Iraqi Police and CID.

After a series of interviews with candidates for the post of Police and Security Advisor, conducted by the Foreign Office, the post was filled by Duncan MacIntosh, the retiring Commissioner of Police in Hong-Kong (1946-1952). The Colonial Office recommended him to the Foreign Office as a 'first-class all-rounder', who could thus manage the reorganisation of not only the Iraqi Police but also the CID.[79] Although his appointment was delayed due to the dissolution of the Iraqi Parliament and general elections in Iraq, MacIntosh finally arrived as Security and Police Advisor in Baghdad in October 1954 after the thirteenth government was formed under the premiership of Nuri el-Said. Said Qazzaz remained as the Minister of the Interior and was still 'eager for MacIntosh's cooperation in his campaign against the Communists'.[80] Sir Robin Hooper, Counsellor of the British Embassy in Baghdad, observed two months after his appointment that MacIntosh was liked by the Iraqis and was making progress in the Iraqi police and the CID:

> his advice is being sought and readily taken. He has made far-reaching recommendations for the re-organisation of the CID. and the uniformed branches of the Police Force, including...the creation of a Special Branch and integrated reporting of political and subversive activities between the various districts...[and] there is a marked desire among junior officers of the Police Force to better themselves now that they see that the Government is taking steps to

76 British-Iraqi Security Planning Report, pp. 2-3.
77 Ibid., p. 5.
78 TNA: PRO AIR23/8605: letter by Group Captain H.M. White to Air Vice-Marshal J.G. Hawtrey, 'Security Planning in Iraq', 23 July 1953.
79 TNA: PRO FO371/111043: VQ1641/14G: telegram by FO to Baghdad, 31 Mar. 1954.
80 TNA: PRO FO371/111043: VQ1641/27: telegram by Sir J. Troutbeck to FO, 23 Sept. 1954. On the formation of the new government, see: Birdwood, Lord, *Nuri As-Said* (London: Cassell, 1959), p. 227.

reform and improve the Police Force, which has for so many years remained virtually stagnant.[81]

The British-Iraqi security cooperation was closely maintained, and MacIntosh retained his post for about three years. They lasted until the Iraqi revolution in July 1958.

The Arab Legion and the Anti-Communist Triangle

The Jordanian case was unique in the region as the Arab Legion, the chief external and internal security force of the country, was commanded by a British officer, Sir John Bagot Glubb, until March 1956. British personnel were involved in training the Arab Legion, and the development of Jordanian military intelligence has been studied elsewhere.[82] A less well known fact is, however, the British involvement in developing Jordanian civilian political intelligence, especially anti-communist and counter-subversion measures. There was in fact the far from negligible regional security contribution made by Colonel Sir Patrick Coghill, the Director-General of Intelligence of the Arab Legion, who was responsible for internal security in Jordan and foreign liaison.

As in most other Middle Eastern countries, the Communist Party was prohibited in Jordan. Communist activities were almost non-existent in comparison to Lebanon or Iraq: according to a JIC estimate in 1950, members of the Communist Party in Jordan numbered less than fifty.[83] While the AC (O) rightly considered the communist problem in Jordan far less significant than elsewhere, this assessment differed from the perception of the Jordanian government, which since late 1950 had constantly requested the 'special training' of Jordanian police officers in anti-communist measures in Britain, and any information on communist activities known to Britain.[84] These requests were mainly due to the Jordanian government's lack of experience and knowledge of communism, and the assumption that subversive activities against the Hashimite dynasty of King Hussein of Jordan would be associated with communist activities. Additionally, the Jordanian government persistently requested a British advisor in anti-communist measures and help with the reorganisation of the Criminal Investigation Department of the Arab Legion.[85]

81 TNA: PRO FO371/115796: VQ1643/3: letter by R.W.J. Hooper, Bagdad, to R.M. Hadow, of FO, 2 Dec. 1955.
82 Yitzhak, Ronen, 'The Beginnings of Transjordanian Military Intelligence: A Neglected Aspect of the 1948 War', *Middle East Journal*, 57:3 (2003), pp. 449-468.
83 TNA: PRO CAB134/3: AC (O) (50) 18: JIC report (annex), 'Communist Influence in the Middle East', 21 Apr 1950.
84 TNA: PRO FO371/91790: ET1016/4G: minute by J.M. Hunter of FO, 28 Sept. 1951.
85 TNA: PRO FO371/91790: ET1016/4G: letter by Furlonge of FO to Amri Abdul Majid Haidar, 29 Oct. 1951.

At Jordan's request, the aforementioned Colonel Sir Patrick Coghill, the wartime head of the British Security Mission in Lebanon (1941-45), was appointed as security and police advisor to Jordan in April 1952, with the formal title of Director-General of Intelligence of the Arab Legion (1952-56).[86] Owing to the nature of his work, perhaps, he has received inadequate attention from historians, but his role as the Director-General of Intelligence was far from negligible. Jordan had no diplomatic relations with the Soviet Union or other Eastern bloc countries, and technically these nationals were not allowed to enter the country. Colonel Coghill was then responsible for internal security against subversive activities in the country. Despite communist activities being nearly non-existent in Jordan, subversive activities included not only those associated with communists, but also those by the Egyptians and Saudis, who were seen by Colonel Coghill as 'the worst' subversive activity in the country.[87] In addition, Major-General James Lunt, the Second-in-Command of the Arab Legion, recalled that the Free Officers Movement within the Arab Legion was kept under 'a close watch' by Colonel Coghill.[88] These activities, perceived as subversive, were indeed in part instigated by Soviet and Egyptian propaganda, particularly its call to arms against 'imperial powers', and they presented a potential danger to be exploited by local communists. During Coghill's tenure, the Jordanian Police was reorganised and a selected number of Jordanian police officers were sent to Britain for training in anti-communist and anti-subversive measures.[89]

More importantly, Colonel Coghill's work with his Arab counterparts was one of most important factors in developing a regional security liaison for Britain. His private papers testify that Colonel Coghill collaborated closely with Emir Chehab, Head of the Sûreté Générale, and Bahjat Beg Attiyah, the Director of the Iraqi CID, by exchanging information on anti-communist and anti-subversive matters in the region. Based on their personal relationship, the security liaison between Lebanon, Iraq and Jordan became gradually institutionalised and became known in Coghill's own words as the 'Anti-Communist Triangle'.[90] This security liaison also involved intelligence sharing on other subversive activities, most of which were instigated by Egypt and Syria.[91] It included a 'specially strict' surveillance request on the leading figure of anti-British activities in the region, Haji Amin al-Husseini, the ex-Grand

86 A former commander of the Arab Legion, Peter Young, noted Colonel Coghill's title as the 'director of CID [Criminal Investigation Department]'. Quoted in Young, Peter, *Bedouin Command with the Arab Legion, 1953-1956* (London: William Kimber, 1956), p. 174.

87 C.f. TNA: PRO WO216/890: letter by Colonel Sir Patrick Coghill to Major General W.P. Oliver of WO, 27 Nov. 1955.

88 Lunt, James, *The Arab Legion, 1923-1957* (London: Constable, 1999), pp. 140-141.

89 The Documents and Sound Section of the Imperial War Museum [IWM], London: Private Papers of Lieutenant-Colonel Sir Patrick Coghill: memoir/diary, entitled 'Before I Forget…', Vol. 2, pp.108-109.

90 Ibid., p.118.

91 Ibid.

Mufti of Jerusalem, whom Colonel Coghill called 'the most evil power in Palestine Arab Nationalism'.[92] As the Director-General of Intelligence of the Arab Legion, Coghill's role in anti-communist work was appreciated not only by the Jordanians but also the Iraqis too. Before Duncan MacIntosh took up the post of Security and Police Advisor in Baghdad, Said Qazzaz, the Iraqi Minister for Interior, insisted that MacIntosh 'should break his outward journey at Amman to discuss his work with Coghill'.[93] It was no exaggeration when Colonel Coghill described the presence of the Arab Legion in his report to the War Office as 'one of the principal key-stones' in providing stability to Middle Eastern security as a whole.[94]

One of the most important contributions by the Jordan-Lebanon-Iraq anti-communist triangle was perhaps their stimulation of the coordination of anti-communist measures with neighbouring Arab states by establishing closer liaison between the Arab security services. One aspect of this regional initiative came to the fore in 1954 as the foundation for a covert cooperation effort in 'the fight against Communism and Zionism' under the Arab League, with participants from Egypt, Lebanon, Jordan, Iraq, Turkey and other countries.[95] Behind this regional collaboration, the AC (O) acted as a facilitator and their purpose was indeed to enhance the anti-communist measures of Middle Eastern governments by 'means of improving liaison and the exchange of information' between the relevant governments.[96] Britain's most reliable allies, the Lebanese *Sûreté Générale* and the Iraqi CID, were chosen to take the initiative.[97] A senior official at the Foreign Office noted that Emir Chehab appreciated 'the need for and the value of liaison between themselves and their counterparts in other Arab States' and that the Lebanese initiative 'would be less likely to arouse suspicion' than if it came from any other Arab state.[98] This regional collaboration under the Arab League was particularly efficient in combatting communist, and also 'anarchist', activities inside their territories. The united anti-communist campaign led to the discovery of several underground communist cells in the region.[99]

The culmination of the Jordan-Lebanon-Iraq 'anti-communist triangle' activity was a multilateral discussion held in Baghdad in January 1956, when Colonel Coghill, Emir Chehab and Bahjat Attiyah met with Heads of the Turkish and Iranian Security

92 IWM: Private Papers of Patrick Coghill, 'Before I Forget…', Vol. 1, p. 44.
93 TNA: PRO FO371/111043: VQ1641/27: telegram by Sir J. Troutbeck to FO, 18 Sept. 1954.
94 TNA: PRO WO216/890: letter by Colonel Sir Patrick Coghill to Major General W.P. Oliver of WO, 27 Nov. 1955.
95 Asseily, et al., *op. cit.*, p. 68.
96 Quoted from TNA: PRO FO371/91177: E1017/3G: letter by Furlonge of FO, 4 May 1951.
97 TNA: PRO FO371/91177: E1017/10G: letter of FO to Sir John Troutbeck, Baghdad, 4 Oct. 1951.
98 TNA: PRO FO371/91177: E1017/10G: minute by H.A. Dudgeon, 5 Sept. 1951.
99 TNA: PRO FO371/115467: V1016/4: letter from Information Division, Beirut, IRD of FO, 15 June 1955.

Services, and discussed and exchanged intelligence on subversive activities in the region.[100] Before this highly secretive meeting, a preliminary conference outlining their sensitive discussion had been carefully conducted by Colonel Coghill, Emir Chehab and Bahjat Attiyah. In his diary, Colonel Coghill noted that the reason for this carefully-planned arrangement was in order to gain 'mutual confidence in one's opposite number' by showing a united front against subversive activities in the region, which was 'the only way of making this sort of liaison work'.[101] The week-long discussion seems to have been successful.[102] Despite the fact that Lebanon and Jordan did not join the Baghdad Pact, the outcome of this high powered discussion was the foundation of secret anti-communist cooperation under the Baghdad Pact. Under the Baghdad Pact, a Liaison Committee was formed as a committee of the security services of the signed countries, including the United States as an 'observer'.[103] At the first meeting of the Liaison Committee in April 1956, a copy of 'the convention', outlining the cooperation in anti-communist measures, signed by the members (the Jordanian, Lebanese, Iraqi, Iranian and Turkish security services) of the so-called 'Club' at their meeting on 14th January 1956 was submitted by the Turkish delegate. It was later, nevertheless, withdrawn in favour of one submitted by the British government.[104]

Colonel Coghill stepped down as the Director-General of Intelligence of the Arab Legion following the dismissal of Sir John Bagot Glubb in 1956. This appears to have set back the security liaison relationship. Nevertheless, his personal and confidential connection with Emir Chehab continued even after his return to Britain. A personal letter from Emir Chehab to him, for instance, containing detailed information on the internal situation in Lebanon as well as the regional situation during the Lebanon crisis in 1958, was passed onto the Foreign Office. It was treated as 'very top secret', noting that if this was known to the Lebanese, 'he [Emir Chehab] would probably be killed'.[105] In addition, evidence of the strong connection of both Emir Chehab and of Bahjat Attiyah with either MI5 or MI6 is very clear. A biography of Sir Dick White attests that 'the local security service' in Beirut was an 'essential ally' for MI6.[106] Sir

100 C.f. TNA: PRO WO216/890: report by Colonel Sir Patrick Coghill, 'Jordan and the Baghdad Pact', 26 Nov. 1955; PRO FO371/121423: V1691/1: letter from Ankara to E.M. Rose of FO, 9 Jan. 1956.

101 IWM: Private Papers of Sir Colonel Patrick Coghill: Vol. 2, p. 119.

102 The fact of this highly secret meeting is also confirmed by a record of the Turkish counterpart. C.f. Başbakanlık Devlet Arşivleri Genel Müdürlüğü [The State Archives in Ankara]: 30/0/18/12: 141/133/20, 9 Jan. 1956.

103 C.f. documents cited by Aldrich, Richard (ed.), *Espionage, Security and Intelligence in Britain, 1945-1970* (Manchester: Manchester University Press, 1998), pp. 223-225.

104 TNA: PRO FO371/121283: V10710/11: telegram by Shattock, POMEF, to FO, 7 Apr. 1956.

105 TNA: PRO FO371/134116:VL1015/10/G: letter by Sir John Glubb to Rose of FO, 24 Mar. 1958, including 'extracts from a letter dated 26/2/58 from Emir Farid Shehab [Chehab]'.

106 Bower, Tom, *The Perfect English Spy* (London: Heinemann, 1995), pp. 232-234.

Maurice Oldfield, future 'C', also maintained a close friendship with Emir Chehab.[107] Beirut, in neutral Lebanon, even hosted the regional centre of MI6.[108] Brigadier William Magan, Head of SIME (1947-51) and later Director of MI5, stated in his autobiography that Bahjat Attiyah had remained his 'close friend', and even Attiyah visited Magan's house in Britain several times before the events of 1958, when the Nuri el-Said government was overthrown by the 'Free Officers' coup, led by General Abd al-Karim Qasim.[109]

1958: The End of British Security Liaison?

The year of 1958 has been the subject of scholarly attention as the year in which a series of crises in the Middle East formed the turning point for British Middle Eastern policy.[110] It was also certainly a setback for British security liaison in the region. As a result of the Iraqi revolution, the prominent pro-British figures at the centre of the security liaison, such as Bahjat Beg Attiyah, then Director-General of Security,[111] and Said Qazzaz, the Minister of the Interior, were the first civilians to be executed under the new Iraqi regime.[112] Duncan MacIntosh's career as Security and Police Advisor in Baghdad also came to an abrupt end in July 1958. In addition, the Lebanese Crisis in the same year led to the resignation of Emir Chehab from his post as Head of the *Sûreté Générale*. After 1958, when General Fouad Chehab, a former Commander of the Army, became the Lebanese President, the Army, instead of the *Sûreté Générale*, assumed the main responsibility for internal security in Lebanon.[113]

Despite a change in the form of security liaison, however, a certain continuity remained in the British security liaison with the Middle East. Following the foundation laid by the Jordan-Lebanon-Iraq 'anti-communist triangle', the multilateral security liaison remained as the Liaison Committee of the Baghdad Pact, later renamed the Central Treaty Organisation (CENTO). The British delegation was led by MI5, and their regular biannual meetings for the exchange of information on communist activities with their American, Turkish, Pakistani, and Iranian counterparts continued until the dissolution of CENTO in 1979.[114] One of the examples for this cooperation is that, as a part of the security arrangement of the Pact, the Iranian

107 Deacon, Richard, *'C'* (London: Futura, 1984), p. 52; Chehab Papers 'F': letter, designated '17N', from Oldfield was written to Farid on 17 Jul 1975. It was his tenure of 'C'.
108 C.f. Bower, *op. cit.*, p. 232.
109 Magan, *op. cit.*, pp. 146-147.
110 C.f. Louis, Wm. Roger, and Roger Owen (eds), *A Revolutionary Year: the Middle East in 1958* (New York: I.B. Tauris, 2002).
111 The post was created out of the old Special Branch of the CID, presumably a result of MacIntosh's advice.
112 C.f. AP, Beirut, *The Tuscaloosa News*, 21 Sept. 1959.
113 Asseily, et al., *op. cit.*, p. 147.
114 C.f. TNA: PRO FO371/175633: EB1692/1G: a report 'UK submission to CENTO Liaison Committee: assessment of the threat of communist subversion in the CENTO

National Intelligence and Security Service (SAVAK), was established in October 1956,[115] on the joint advice of the British intelligence services, the CIA, and the Israeli intelligence service, MOSSAD, to enhance the internal security of Iran.[116] MI5 was clearly instrumental in establishing and maintaining SAVAK. The aforementioned Roger Lees of MI5, formally DSO in Baghdad, was despatched from London to 'advise' the Head of SAVAK on security matters and also to 'train' Iranian security officers in Tehran. In addition, Iranian female staff working at the Registry of SAVAK were trained in London in protective security.[117]

Moreover, although Colonel Coghill was dismissed in 1956 by King Hussein due to regional and domestic pressures,[118] the Jordanian government still wanted a British security and police advisor. Duncan MacIntosh, the former Security and Police Advisor in Baghdad, soon returned to the Middle East after his escape from the Iraqi coup of July 1958, and was appointed as Police Advisor (1958-62) in Jordan in October 1958. During his four-year tenure in Amman, MacIntosh managed to reorganise the Jordanian Police and laid the foundations for the Jordanian Police and the Security Service, including sections dealing with communists and liaising with foreign services.[119] The latter was later named 'the General Intelligence Department [Dairat al-Mukhabarat al-Ammah]' in accordance with the Act 24 of 1964, which still remains today.[120]

Conclusion

The Middle East was a region where Britain retained a 'predominant' influence over the Arab world and was seen as 'the lion'.[121] As Sir Alan Munro, a former British diplomat, later admitted, his dealings with the Middle Eastern and African affairs were based on 'the legacies of imperial history'.[122] Looking at the British-Arab secret liaison

area', 1 Jan 1964; FO371/180719: EB1692/2: report '13th Session of CENTO liaison Committee', undated.

115 The Iranian cabinet approved a decree to establish SAVAK on 3 Oct 1956, and became effective in 1957. C.f. Ladjevardi, Habib (ed.), *Memoirs of Fatemeh Pakravan* (Cambridge, MA: Center for Middle Eastern Studies of Harvard University, 1998), p. 20 n. 15.

116 Rafizadeh, Mansur, *Witness* (New York: William Morrow, 1987), p. 393 n. 4.

117 C.f. TNA: PRO CAB176/60: JIC/528/57: annex B, 'state of security in Baghdad Pact organisation', by R.S. Crawford, Baghdad, to A.C.I. Samuel of FO, 12 Feb. 1957.

118 C.f. Dann, Uriel, *King Hussein and the Challenge of Arab Radicalism* (Oxford: OUP, 1989), p. 35; Ashton, Nigel, *King Hussein of Jordan* (London: Yale University Press, 2008), ch. 2.

119 TNA: PRO FO371/170335: EJ1641/2: letter by Sir Roderick Parkes, Ambassador to Jordan, to L.C.W. Figg of Eastern Department, 28 Dec. 1962.

120 The information is derived from the official website of the General Intelligence Department, of Jordan: accessible at <http://www.gid.gov.jo/en/home.html> (accessed on 9 Nov 2015).

121 Parsons, Anthony, *They Say The Lion* (London: Jonathan Cape, 1986), p. xiv.

122 Munro, Alan, *Keep The Flag Flying* (London: Gilgamesh, 2012), p. 10.

as a historical enquiry provides us with an insight into the regional dimension of Cold War dynamics, and of interaction between Western powers and local governments. The incentive for British security liaison with their Middle Eastern counterparts originated from British concern with the possibility of war against the Soviet Union. The prevalent feeling about the early Cold War amongst British policymakers and officials was that most Middle Eastern countries lacked the experience required to deal with significant issues, such as fighting international communism. As well as being in the British interest, this policy also dovetailed neatly with the demands of Middle Eastern governments. In the post-war period, Britain was seen as the most reliable and experienced ally by several Middle Eastern authorities, including even Lebanon, where British officials were very much in demand for their advice on anti-communist measures. Britain's 'informal empire' was thus created partly by the invitation of Middle Eastern governments who secretly sought British assistance to fight against communist activities in their countries.

Placing security and police officers in the heart of Middle Eastern governments was indeed advantageous for Britain: the local security services, including police forces, were unique local assets for intelligence and security purposes, and security liaison with them would have been invaluable in at least two ways. Firstly, as communist movements in the region were illegal in these countries, security liaison with regional police meant that Britain was able to access intelligence on communist activities in the region, including police records, which would otherwise be inaccessible. Secondly, a strong security service was regarded as essential to forestall communist subversion. Thus, the training of the security services was seen as the best way of containing the spread of Communism in the region. While it is difficult to isolate the effects of this secret liaison on British anti-communist policies from the many other factors involved, it is at least clear that the anti-communist measures conducted by Middle Eastern countries through their security services were directly or indirectly influenced by the British security and police liaison, directed by British foreign policy objectives. This hidden dimension of the secret liaison at least shows us not only the importance of the role of such specific liaisons, but also the nature of clandestine diplomacy in the broader sense of historical enquiries.

Acknowledgement

This chapter originally appeared in *Intelligence and National Security*, 27:6 (2012), pp.848-874. It has been reproduced as a new version. The original article is accessible at <http://www.tandfonline.com>.

4

'A Theoretical Middle Course:' The Militarization of Civilian Policing in 1950s West Germany

David M. Livingstone

Introduction

On 1 April 1948, tensions erupted between the postwar occupation authorities in the divided city of Berlin. Soviet officials, threatened by the recent introduction of currency reform in the western occupation zones, deployed military and police units to blockade all traffic in and out of West Berlin. The Western Allies responded with a massive airlift that supplied critical resources to the beleaguered residents of the city who were otherwise cut-off from the outside world. At the height of the Berlin crisis, CBS News Correspondent Larry LeSueur asked General Lucius Clay, the Military Governor of the US zone, whether it was time to consider arming German police officers against the threat of communist attacks from the Soviet zone. Clay told LeSueur: 'We are opposed to the creation of a police force which could become a military training school'.[1] General Clay's response reflected the strict postwar Allied policies aimed at demilitarizing all of Germany's indigenous police forces. The American *Handbook for Military Government of Germany* explicitly warned US personnel that, 'The vital role which police forces have played in the execution of the plans of the Nazi leaders and the extent of penetration of the regular German police by the Nazi Party, necessitates that special measures be taken'.[2] The Allies intended

1 Smith, Jean Edward (ed.), *The Papers of Lucius G. Clay, Germany, 1945-1949*, Vol. II (Bloomington: Indiana University Press, 1974), p. 965.

2 Dwight D. Eisenhower Presidential Library (EPL), Walter Bedell Smith Collection of World War Two Documents 1941-1945, Box 35, Handbook for Military Government of Germany.

to completely dismantle Germany's centralized police system and break its traditional ties with the military.

The establishment of separate East and West German nation states in 1949 further polarized Allied-Soviet relations. The communist East Germans had already militarized their civilian police forces during the early period of Soviet occupation. Their paramilitary *Volkspolizei*, or People's Police, was armed with infantry weapons and stationed in barracks along the Inter-German border. For the Allies, remilitarizing West Germany's police was out of the question. The legacies of Germany's Nazi past still shaped the cautious approach of Allied planners involved in its democratic reconstruction. Yet the Allies and West Germany's new civilian government were sufficiently alarmed by the militarized police forces in Eastern Germany to the extent that fears of communist aggression gradually began to outweigh their concerns about the Nazi past. The need for stronger security in West Germany, by now a critical Cold War front, significantly increased in 1950 after the Korean War broke out. West Germany's first Chancellor, Konrad Adenauer, worried that the postwar reduction of Allied military forces in his new nation left it vulnerable to an attack from the east. He believed the communist forces in Korea had demonstrated what might happen in divided Germany.

This chapter focuses on how the Cold War influenced the Allied approach to civilian policing in 1950s West Germany. While they were determined to reform the police to support the accomplishment of their objective of democratizing the Federal Republic, remilitarizing civilian policing was advocated by some authorities as an interim solution to full-scale rearmament. But this approach was not acceptable to all parties with a stake in the reconstruction of postwar West Germany. The French and West Germany's socialist politicians in particular opposed any plans to remilitarize the police, which they believed would increase the power of the federal executive and might be used to abuse its authority or undermine Germany's long term democratization. Adenauer and his conservative government relentlessly pressured the Allies for more autonomy in national security matters. His repeated demands for federal police forces eventually convinced the British and Americans that reinforcing civilian police power was a politically safer alternative than creating a new national army.

The chapter begins with a brief overview of pre-1950s German policing. Allied demilitarization policies were shaped by Nazi Germany's abuse of its police power, but the strong traditional connection between the police and the armed forces, which they were so determined to eliminate, predated the rise of National Socialism. Demilitarization was thus much more problematic and challenging for Allied reformers because militarism was already deeply rooted in German policing. Moreover, there were many police veterans in 1950s West Germany who had served the Nazi regime and took part in war crimes for which they were never held accountable. According to political scientist David Bayley, because post-dictatorial police reform involves working with existing officials, 'The security capacity developed through foreign assistance may be put to repressive uses by whatever regime is in power, even one with aspirations to democracy' such as West Germany.[3] The chapter then investigates the role of policing in the debates over West German rearmament, which has been largely ignored or underemphasized by historians. The onset of the Cold War undermined reforms aimed at demilitarization and led to the emergence of paramilitary civilian police forces such as the *Bereitschaftspolizei* (Riot or Alert Police) and the *Bundesgrenzschutz* (Federal Border Guard). The chapter concludes by examining effects from the global terrorism crisis on police militarization and what lessons contemporary police advising missions can take away from this case study of 1950s West Germany.

Civilian Policing in Germany: A Brief Overview

To fully understand why postwar Allied reformers faced such difficulties demilitarizing the West German police it is first necessary to look back at police development in Germany before the Cold War era. The German police have always had strong ties with the armed forces and were already militarized to a certain extent even before the Nazi seizure of power in 1933. During both the *Kaiserreich* (Monarchy) and Weimar eras, police officers were heavily recruited from the ranks of veteran soldiers.[4] These men made easy transitions into civilian police careers because they shared similar features of the discipline, structure, and *esprit des corps* they were accustomed to in the armed forces. Policing also provided the close-knit masculine camaraderie of the military and space for those with similar political ideologies.[5] Many policemen were sympathetic to conservative political causes while marking groups on the left, especially the communists, as enemies of the state.[6] These widespread conservative, anti-liberal attitudes within Germany's police forces underscored one of the innumerable reasons why National Socialism was so easily accepted by many policemen. During the *Kaiserreich*, policemen resisted internal demilitarization efforts and police reformers were largely unsuccessful because the greater demands for security were more immediate than the larger objectives of professionalization. Chief among these demands was maintaining order and the prestige of the monarchy in the face of increasing activism from trade unions and social democrats.[7] During the Weimar

3 Bayley, David H., *The Changing of the Guard: Developing Democratic Police Abroad* (New York: Oxford University Press, 2006), p. 12.
4 Spencer, Elaine Glovka, 'Police-Military Relations in Prussia, 1848-1914', *Journal of Social History*, 19:2 (Winter 1985), pp. 305-317.
5 For a good discussion of the political polarities between the military and civilian spheres see, Frevert, Ute, *A Nation in Barracks: Modern Germany, Military Conscription, and Civil Society* (New York: Berg, 2004), pp. 201-205.
6 Clark, Christopher, *Iron Kingdom: The Rise and Downfall of Prussia, 1600–1947* (Cambridge, Mass: Harvard University Press, 2006), p. 633.
7 Reinke, Herbert, 'Armed as if for War: The State, the Military and the Professionalization of the Prussian Police in Imperial Germany', in Emsley, Clive and Barbara Weinberger (eds), *Policing Western Europe: Politics, Professionalization, and Public Order, 1850–1940*

era, democratic German police reformers like Interior Minister Carl Severing faced similar challenges. The need for security often outweighed reform efforts. During the 1920s, former soldiers again sought policing careers, especially after the Versailles Treaty limited the size of the national army (*Reichswehr*) to 100,000 men. Despite Severing's efforts, police forces in Germany's first democracy still provided a refuge for veteran soldiers.[8]

The Weimar Republic's *Sicherheitspolizei* (security police—SiPo), with its heavily armed ranks of veteran soldiers and *Freikorps* (Free Corps—paramilitaries) members, reflected the difficult challenges facing police reformers. While Carl Severing tried to modernize the civilian police, he still needed to protect the state and its people from increasing levels of political violence. The SiPo provided the Weimar Republic with a powerful instrument of coercive force against communist strikers and some of its personnel participated in the political murders of Rosa Luxembourg, Karl Liebknecht, and others considered to be enemies of the state.[9] Even though the Allies eventually banned the SiPo as a clandestine army in violation of the Versailles Treaty, its members were quickly absorbed into the regular civilian police forces (the *Schutzmannschaft*).[10] Their influence was especially prominent in police training programs, which featured drill and close quarter combat maneuvers.[11] Thereafter, Weimar policemen began their careers in the riot brigades (*Bereitschaften*) where they remained for up to six years living in barracks before reporting to a precinct for regular patrol duty. This militarized approach to training manifested itself in the tactics and operations employed by the police during strikes and demonstrations where they responded to urban unrest with the force and efficiency of small infantry units.[12] Heavy-handed police responses to these public disturbances could thus be traced back to the militarization trend that began during the *Kaiserreich*.[13]

This trend continued and expanded during the Third Reich. Nazi police officers perpetrated or were complicit in the criminal acts that supported the terroristic

(Westport: Greenwood Press, 1991), pp. 55-73; Lüdtke, Alf, *Police and State in Prussia, 1815-1850* (New York: Cambridge University Press, 1989), pp. 140-145.

8 Bessel, Richard, 'Policing, Professionalization, and Politics in Weimar Germany', in Emsley, Clive (ed.), *Policing Western Europe*, pp. 187-218.

9 Schumann, Dirk, *Political Violence in the Weimar Republic, 1918-1933* (New York: Berghahn Books, 2009), pp. 3-4; Liang, Hsi-Huey, *The Berlin Police Force in the Weimar Republic* (Berkeley: University of California Press, 1970), pp. 43-50. Captain Waldemar Pabst of the Garde-Kavallerie-Schützen-Division, the nucleus of the SiPo, ordered the murders, see Frölich, Paul, *Rosa Luxemburg: Ideas in Action* (Chicago: Haymarket Books, 2010), p. 299.

10 Bessel, Richard, 'Policing, Professionalization and Politics', p. 191.

11 Ibid., p. 199.

12 Ibid., p. 201; Liang, *The Berlin Police Force*, p. 53.

13 Lüdtke, *Police and State in Prussia*, pp. 183-189; Funk, Albrecht, *Polizei und Rechtsstaat: Die Entwicklung des staatlichen Gewaltmonopolis in Preussen, 1848–1914* (Frankfurt Main: Campus Verlag, 1986), pp. 288-289.

policies of their government. Policemen were instrumental, indeed vital, to the National Socialist seizure of power and enforcement of its dictatorship both at home and abroad in conquered territories.[14] Alongside members of Germany's *Wehrmacht* and *Waffen SS*, they arrested and murdered hundreds of thousands of Jews, killed innocent civilians in anti-partisan reprisals, and served as guards in the death camps. Because police officers were so essential for the execution of the regime's criminal policies, the Allies returned authority over civilian policing to the decentralized jurisdiction of Germany's *Länder* (federal states), its traditional base before the Nazis centralized it when they seized power. Although the legacy of German policing was grounded in the armed forces, the shadow of the Nazi past was more influential in shaping the Allied approach to postwar police reform.

West German Policing Before the Korean War

General Lucius Clay reported that there were 22,000 civilian policemen on duty in the American Occupation Zone between July and October 1945. By 1947, the total number of policemen under combined Allied supervision reached approximately 85,000.[15] In the aftermath of the war, West German policemen were busy dealing with minor youth crimes and widespread black marketeering perpetrated by the large masses of displaced persons. According to Clay, all policemen with Nazi records had been purged from the U.S sector of Berlin.[16] The British and French took a more pragmatic approach in their zones by dismissing some former Nazi police officers while keeping those they considered important for maintaining law and order. Thus, there was no new beginning or complete overhaul of German police forces in the western occupation zones before 1949 when the East and West German nation states were established.[17] Nevertheless, under Allied supervision, West German police

14 Browning, Christopher, *Ordinary Men: Reserve Police Battalion 101 and the Final Solution in Poland* (New York: Harper Perennial, 1998); Wilhelm, Friedrich, *Die Polizei im NS-Staat: Die Geschichte ihrer Organisation im Überblick* (Paderborn: Ferdinand Schöningh, 1997); Westermann, Edward, *Hitler's Police Battalions: Enforcing Racial War in the East* (Lawrence: University Press of Kansas, 2005); Schröder, Joachim, *Die Münchner Polizei und der Nationalsozialismus* (Essen: Klartext Verlag, 2013); Schulte, Wolfgang (ed.), *Die Polizei im NS-Staat: Beiträge eines internationalen Symposimus an der Deutschen Hochschule der Polizei in Münster* (Frankfurt: Verlag für Polizeiwissenschaft, 2009).

15 EPL, Walter Bedell Smith Collection of World War Two Documents, 1941-1945, Box 44, Monthly Report of the Military Governor, US Zone (3); European Command, Office of the Chief Historian, *Occupation Forces in Europe Series, 1945-1952* (Frankfurt am Main: Historical Division, US Army Europe, 1947), p. 124.

16 Ibid.

17 Reinke, Herbert, 'The Reconstruction of the Police in Post 1945 Germany', in Fijnaut, Cyrille (ed.), *The Impact of World War II on Policing in North-West Europe* (Leuven Belgium: Leuven University Press, 2004), p. 137. See also Noethen, Stefan, *Alte Kameraden und neue Kollegen: Polizei in Nordrhein-Westfalen, 1945-1953* (Essen: Klartext, 2003), pp. 495-497.

officers had begun taking over responsibility for internal security while upholding the new democratic rule of law.

Policing in the Soviet Occupation Zone developed much differently. In 1946, for example, Soviet authorities unilaterally established paramilitary *Bereitschaftspolizei* (alert/riot police) units. These units were armed with infantry weapons and quartered in barracks like their Weimar era predecessors. The personnel in these units formed the nucleus for East Germany's *Volkspolizei* and eventually the *National Volksarmee* (NVA).[18] Certainly, the militarization of police forces in the east coupled with events such as the Berlin Blockade concerned West Germany's new government. The rapid postwar reduction of British and American combat units added to these insecurities and provided the Soviets with a distinct advantage in conventional fighting power.[19] West German officials estimated the *Volkspolizei* had reached a numerical strength of 70,000 men by 1950.[20]

Against this backdrop, plans for a paramilitary federal police force or gendarmerie as a first step towards rearmament was an approach advocated by certain members of the civil-military establishment developing in West Germany, Britain, and the United States. A year before the Korean War, Lieutenant Colonel Edwards, a member of Allied High Commissioner for Germany (HICOG) John J. McCloy's staff, wrote a top secret analysis advocating the German police system as a 'theoretical middle course' to rearmament that 'might be justified on the grounds that such a course would be necessary to maintain the stability of any government organized under the Bonn Constitution'.[21] This approach was supported by members of the US Joint Chiefs of Staff and unofficially by McCloy despite his public statements to the contrary.[22] In late

18 Lindenberger, Thomas, *Volkspolizei: Herrschaftspraxis und öffentliche Ordnung im SED-Staat, 1952-1968* (Köln: Böhlau Verlag, 2003), pp. 27-28; Diedrich, Torsten and Rüdiger Wenzke, *Die getarnte Armee: Geschichte der Kasernierten Volkspolizei der DDR, 1952-1956* (Berlin: Christoph Links Verlag, 2001), pp. 18-22.

19 US forces were reduced from over three million personnel on 8 May 1945 to 135,000 by 1947. British and French combat troops were similarly reduced. See Swearingen, Bryan T., 'US Force Structure and Basing in Germany, 1945-1990', in Junker, Detlef, Philip Gassert, Wilfried Mausbach, and David Morris (eds), *The United States and Germany in the Era of the Cold War, 1945-1990: A Handbook*, Vol. 1 (New York: Cambridge University Press, 2004), pp. 217-218; Bessel, Richard, *Germany 1945: From War to Peace* (New York: Harper Perennial, 2010), p. 219.

20 Diedrich and Wenzke (eds), *Die Getarnte Armee*, pp. 50-54.

21 National Archives and Records Administration (NARA) RG 466, Records of the Office of the High Commissioner for Germany, Office of the Executive Director, Misc. Files Maintained by Colonel H.A. Gerhardt, Box 2, Top Secret Position Paper, Lieutenant Colonel Edwards to Colonel H.A. Gerhardt, 'Basic Considerations with Regards to Germany', 13 June 1949, p. 2.

22 'Allies Object to Statements on German Rearmament', Associated Press article, *St. Petersburg Times*, 8 Dec. 1949; NARA RG 218, Records of the US Joint Chiefs of Staff: Geographic File 1948-1950, Box 25, Folder 92: US Policy Towards Germany, Memorandum from US Joint Chiefs of Staff to Secretary of Defense, 30 April 1950, p.

1949, the British unilaterally proposed their own police or gendarmerie rearmament option. British High Commissioner Brian Robertson secretly discussed these ideas with former *Wehrmacht* General Gerhard Graf von Schwerin, an early West German advocate of militarizing police forces as an alternative rearmament method.[23] Robertson was open to this approach in part because of his frustration with recent failures by the German police to protect the offices of the British Dismantling Service in Salzgitter against rioters.[24] The British respected Schwerin because of his prewar diplomatic service in London and his reputation for resisting Nazi 'scorched earth' policies while fighting Allied forces in 1944-45. It was Robertson and his assistant, Sir Christopher Steele, among others, who eventually recommended Schwerin as a defense advisor to Adenauer.[25]

In February 1950, a large demonstration involving angry commercial truck drivers upset over increasing gasoline prices forced the adjournment of a plenary session in the *Bundestag* (Parliament). Adenauer used this incident to emphasize the weakness of his government and its lack of sufficient police power. Two days later, while speaking at a press conference in Bochum, he declared, 'The Federal Government has no means of exerting power and no law enforcement agency. What the motorists can do today could be done tomorrow by the unemployed, the expellees, the communists, and finally by strikers…the Federal Republic and, with it, Western Europe would go down'. He used this incident to justify his request for a heavily armed federal police force during his regular meeting with HICOG on 16 February.[26]

2; Amherst College Special Collections, John J. McCloy Papers, Box SP 1, Folder 30, 'Reviving Germany: An Interview with John J. McCloy, US High Commissioner for Germany', *US News and World Report*, 4 Nov. 1949, pp. 26-30.

23 Mawby, Spencer, *Containing Germany: Britain and the Arming of the Federal Republic*, (London: Macmillan Press, 1999), pp. 27-32; Searle, Alaric, *Wehrmacht Generals, West German Society, and the Debate on Rearmament, 1949-1959* (Westport: Praeger, 2003), p. 52.

24 The British Dismantling Commission was responsible for demolishing Germany's industrial warfare capability and often met with resistance from factory workers. See 'Germans Battle Dismantling Squad, Wreck Offices of Commission', *New York Times*, 7 Mar. 1950.

25 Bundesarchiv-Militärarchiv, Freiburg i.Br. (BA-MA), BW/3105: Personal Memorandum, 25 May 1950. Schwerin recalled this recommendation himself in this personal memorandum and claimed he was given the job after a one-hour interview with Adenauer. The British remembered he ignored Hitler's order to destroy the city of Aachen during the war. According to David Clay Large, it was the publisher of *Die Zeit*, Countess Marion Dönhoff, who originally suggested Schwerin to Robertson, see Large, David Clay, *Germans to the Front* (Chapel Hill: University of North Carolina Press, 1996), p. 57.

26 NARA RG 466, Records of the US High Commission for Germany, John J. McCloy, General Classified Records, 1949-1952, 1950 Nos. 410—604, Box 9, Folder: Feb. 50 D (50) 410 to D (50) 455, Minutes of the HICOG Twelfth Meeting with the Federal Chancellor, 16 Feb. 1950; Adenauer's speech at Bochum is recorded in the minutes of the HICOG meeting.

Adenauer outlined and expanded upon these demands in a lengthy letter he wrote to HICOG in April 1950 requesting a 25,000-man federal police force to reinforce internal security. The letter complained that West Germany 'Was unable to take any executive police measures on its own authority'.[27] He claimed he had no need for an army because the Allies already provided for external security. He compared West Germany with Weimar Germany whose 'Police were suddenly faced by well-organized and armed insurgents. Although the police were...better equipped with arms than is the case today, they were not successful in their struggle against an even better equipped opponent and they could not re-establish public order; this was only possible with the support of the *Reichswehr*'.[28] The letter was the first of many examples where Adenauer justified a federal police force by invoking the political violence of Weimar Germany. He was attempting to alarm HICOG by implying West Germany might succumb to a communist insurgency.[29] His use of these memories, however, competed with West Germany's Social Democratic Party (SPD) whose own experiences of Weimar era violence and the heavy-handed police responses against it were reasons to oppose his plans for a federal police force at all costs.[30]

HICOG officials seriously considered Chancellor Adenauer's proposal, especially because it emphasized domestic or internal security rather than national defense. They were concerned over recent intelligence that members of the communist Free German Youth movement (*Freie Deutsche Jugend*—FDJ) were planning large May Day and Whitsuntide (Pentecost) marches from East into West Berlin. Allied and West German officials believed these demonstrations might include up to 3,000-armed members of East Germany's *Volkspolizei*, which amplified the urgency of Adenauer's security demands.[31] Yet the Allies also suspected he might be using these events to justify increasing the symbolic power of his federal government against the influential postwar position which the Allies had given to the federal states (*Länder*). On 12

27 The National Archives of the UK (TNA), Foreign Office Files, FO 371/85324, Letter from Chancellor Adenauer to General Sir Brian Robertson, Chairman of the Council of the Allied High Command, 28 April 1950. He was referring here to the Bonn demonstration and also recent activities by the Free German Youth (FDJ) movement.

28 Ibid.

29 Adenauer regularly emphasized the '*Ohne Mich*' (without me—count me out) peace movement to the Allies and exploited their fear of a rapprochement with the east, see Major, Patrick, *The Death of the KPD: Communism and Anti-Communism in West Germany*, 1945-1956 (Oxford: Clarendon Press, 1997), p. 143.

30 Browder, George, *Foundations of the Nazi Police State: The Formation of Sipo and SD* (Lexington: University of Kentucky Press, 2004), pp. 48-49.

31 NARA RG 466, Records for the US High Commissioner for Germany, John J. McCloy, Classified General Records, 1949-1950, Box 12, Folder: Apr. 50 D (50) 1168 to D (50) 1225, Telegram from HICOG Director of Intelligence B.R. Schute to United States Command, Berlin, 18 April 1950, 'Berlin Situation No. 14'; See also EPL, White House Office, National Security Council Staff: Papers, 1948-61, Disaster File, Box 48, Folder: Germany (4), Frank Pace Jr., Secretary of the Army, 'Top Secret Report to the National Security Council: May Day and Whitsuntide Youth Rallies in Berlin', 28 April 1950.

May 1950, joint Allied discussions in preparation for the London Foreign Ministers Conference proved they were ready to consider his demands. The Allied representatives believed a small national police force would provide him with the ability to 'protect the Federal Government, uphold its prestige, and maintain order in the event of any serious trouble'.[32] Besides HICOG policy, the biggest legal obstacle standing in the way of Adenauer's plans was West Germany's Basic Law (*Grundgesetz*). After the war, civilian policing was returned to the jurisdiction of the *Länder* and Article 91 of the Basic Law strictly limited federal control of police forces to only those emergencies constituting an, 'imminent danger to the existence or free democratic basic order of the Federation or of a *Land*'. Thus, a standing federal police force was explicitly forbidden. And even had such an emergency as defined by Article 91 occurred, it required federal use of *Länder* police officers.[33]

Yet at McCloy's insistence, HICOG secretly recommended that the Foreign Ministers approve Adenauer's request, but limited to 5,000 men instead of the 25,000 he had originally asked for. Realizing the potential for political fallout from this decision, McCloy directed that the unit be designated a 'Republican Guard' rather than a police force.[34] Moreover, it was to have no powers of arrest or conflicting duties with the *Länder* police. McCloy warned his colleagues the decision should not be announced in connection with the conference and was to be presented as an 'allied decision' not a 'concession' to Adenauer.[35] In fact, the official minutes of the London Conference stated: 'With regard to the request for permission to establish a federal gendarmerie, the ministers discussed the recommendations of the High Commissioner, but since neither the French nor the United States had considered the questions, the ministers agreed to postpone action'.[36] McCloy knew militarizing the police was problematic because of the Nazi past and wanted to prevent a public relations blunder by appearing conciliatory towards the Germans. But he also worried about the security threat from the Soviets and hoped to align the Federal Republic

32 TNA FO 371/85324, Memorandum from C.A.E. Shuckburgh, 11 May 1950: 'Ministerial Talks United States/United Kingdom/France, Item No. 3: Germany', p. 1.

33 *Grundgesetz für die Bundesrepublik Deutschland* (Berlin: Bundeszentrale für politische Bildung, 2006), p. 55.

34 EPL, White House Office, National Security Council Staff: Papers, 1948-1961, Disaster File, Box 48, Folder A: Germany, 'NSC 71, A Report to the National Security Council by the Secretary of Defense on United States Policy Towards Germany, June 8, 1950.'

35 The John J. McCloy Papers, Amherst College, Box +HC5, Folder 79: HICOG Correspondence, Top Secret memorandum written on behalf of McCloy by his Assistant, Col. H.A. Gerhardt to the British and French Foreign Ministers, 12 May 1950.

36 United States Department of State, *Foreign Relations of the United States* (hereafter *FRUS*), *1950, Western Europe*, Vol. III, Gleason, Everett, Frederick Aandahl (eds), (US Government Printing Office: 1950), <http://digital.ibrary.wisc.edu/1711.dl/FRUS.FRUS1950vo3> (accessed 4 Aug. 2015), p. 1051

with the West to the extent that he was willing to secretly cooperate with Adenauer to gain his loyalty.[37]

The Korean War and its Influence on Civilian Policing

The attack by communist North Korean forces against the democratic Republic of Korea on June 28, 1950, was a turning point for civilian policing in West Germany. The war generated a significant amount of public anxiety that Soviet and East German forces might try something similar along the Inter-German border. It also convinced HICOG and especially the US State Department that a new approach to European defense was necessary. But while Adenauer was quick to draw parallels between divided Germany and Korea, HICOG still opposed full-scale rearmament.[38] But now, there was much more political support to remilitarize civilian police forces. The decision at the London Foreign Minister's Conference to give West Germany a 5,000-man 'Republican Guard' was postponed indefinitely after the outbreak of the war.[39] Adenauer was frustrated, but was determined to have his police force nonetheless. He cleverly shifted his justifications from internal to external security threats. Communism had replaced Nazism as the new global totalitarian security threat and the Korean War erupted just as the 'red scares' associated with McCarthyism began in the United States.[40] The rise of western anti-communism and its effect on the Allied decision to rearm West Germany, provided Adenauer with new hope that he could pressure HICOG into acting on his plans.

His writings and public statements regularly compared the pre-war strategic situation on the divided Korean peninsula to that of divided Germany. He wanted the Allies and West Germans to believe the Inter-German border was their own 38th Parallel. His renewed requests for heavily armed federal police, which had previously

37 Adenauer specifically told UK High Commissioner Ivone Kirkpatrick that the West Germans would be open to a settlement with Russia because they lacked the ability to defend themselves and had no faith in the west. See United States Department of State, *Foreign Relations of the United States (FRUS), 1950, Central and Eastern Europe, the Soviet Union*, Vol. IV, p. 696, telegram from John J. McCloy to US Secretary of State Acheson, 14 July 1950.

38 The US Joint Chiefs of Staff and particularly General Omar Bradley felt the Korean War was enough to reverse the opposition to rearmament, but President Truman and State Department officials disagreed, See Schwartz, Thomas Alan, 'From Occupation to Alliance: John J. McCloy and the Allied High Commission in the Federal Republic of Germany, 1949-1952' (PhD dissertation, Harvard University, 1985), pp. 295-296.

39 *FRUS, 1950*, Vol. IV, Telegram from US Ambassador Lewis Douglas to Secretary of State Dean Acheson, 6 July 1950, p. 695. The plans were disrupted when US State Department Officials learned that UK Commissioner Brian Robertson had begun unilateral top-secret rearmament discussions with Adenauer.

40 Bragg, Christine, *Vietnam, Korea, and US Foreign Policy, 1945-1975* (Oxford: Heinemann, 2005), pp. 50-51.

omitted references to external security, now emphasized the value of militarized police for western defense. He wanted his own paramilitary police force to counter the East German *Volkspolizei*. From his perspective, the postwar US reduction of combat forces in West Germany mirrored the 1948 withdrawal from South Korea, which he argued, had left the peninsula completely defenseless.[41] He also pointed to the North Korean use of communist 'gangs' or insurgents who paved the way for the inevitable invasion.[42] While these comparisons drove media interest and heightened anxiety amongst the West German population, they were largely unsupported by the facts.[43]

Of course, the US had significantly reduced its postwar combat forces, but unlike its withdrawal from South Korea, it still occupied West Germany in sufficient strength to discourage Soviet or East German aggression. Adenauer's claims omitted nuanced details about the strategic situation in Korea, which differed from divided Germany. In particular, he neglected to mention the Soviets had also withdrawn their forces from North Korea prior to the invasion. The Korean War was a proxy war whereas a similar strike by communist forces against West Germany had greater potential for direct conflict between the two nuclear-armed superpowers—both of which still maintained combat forces in their respective zones. Moreover, pre-war activities by communist supported insurgents in South Korea had caused violent fighting and thousands of deaths. And while there were communist movements in West Germany, their activities never rose to the level of violence experienced with similar groups in prewar South Korea.[44] Finally, the Berlin Airlift demonstrated Western resolve against Soviet intentions in the Federal Republic. According to Petra Goedde, the airlift 'transformed America's role from conqueror to protector' and fostered a postwar consensus that 'deflected German and American attention away from Germany's Nazi past towards an anti-communist future'.[45]

Adenauer was personally frustrated that neither HICOG nor the West German population was initially willing to support his proposal for paramilitary federal

41 Swearingen, 'US Force Structure and Basing in Germany', pp. 217-218. The US still had over 100,000 troops in West Germany as opposed to none in South Korea.

42 Adenauer, Konrad, *Memoirs, 1945-1953*, Vol. 1 (Chicago: Regnery, 1966), p. 271.

43 David Clay Large cites several German newspapers that document increased public fear, see *Germans to the Front*, p. 66. New York Times reporter Jack Raymond claimed the West German public followed developments in Korea so closely that maps of the peninsula were posted throughout its cities so that citizens could chart the war's progress. See Raymond, Jack, 'Germany Views the Border', *New York Times*, 30 July 1950, p. E5.

44 For a good description of the pre-war troubles in Korea, including the Cheju Rebellion that resulted in thousands of deaths, see Cummings, Bruce, *The Korean War: A History* (New York: Random House, 2011), pp. 127-135. Members of the (FDJ) Free German Youth often staged rallies and frequently clashed with state police officers; Adenauer complained to the HICOG the police were too weak even to take streamers and signs away from FDJ demonstrators; Adenauer, *Memoirs*, p. 274.

45 Goedde, Petra, *GI's and Germans: Culture, Gender, and Foreign Relations, 1945-1949* (New Haven: Yale University Press, 2003), p. 170.

police, even though many expressed anxiety over the Korean War.[46] Besides, the Allies already guaranteed him they would defend West Germany against foreign attacks.[47] But this meant very little to Adenauer because, as he later claimed, it was his belief that 'The forces of the Western Allies in Germany were not strong enough'.[48] Adenauer met with HICOG on August 16, 1950, and reiterated his security requests. He told the commissioners that neither the German people nor the decentralized *Länder* police demonstrated a willingness to resist foreign attacks.[49] McCloy wrote to Secretary of State Dean Acheson that in his opinion, Adenauer was 'only seeking means to strengthen his government by the creation of a federal police force and using the Korean incident as a gambit for this purpose'.[50] But Adenauer refused to give up and instead submitted an embellished threat analysis of West Germany's security to McCloy. Adenauer argued that a heavily armed federal police force was the only solution to rapidly improve his substandard national security.[51] McCloy's aide, Samuel Reber, reported that Adenauer's analysis was correct regarding the 'East-West balance...but was written and slanted to stress the alarming nature of the current military situation'.[52]

The State Department's heavily annotated version of Adenauer's letter points out key areas of his analysis they believed was inaccurate and/or exaggerated. For example, he claimed the Soviets would have more than 5,000 fighter jets in their occupation zone by the end of September. The actual number according to US intelligence experts was 400.[53] He also claimed the Soviets built airfields for a strategic air force in their zone, which he considered 'a further clear sign of offensive intentions'. The State Department found this claim to be false. Adenauer alleged, '70,000 men were transferred out of the regular police of the Eastern Zone, organized into paramilitary units and given military training'.[54] US officials called this statement 'misleading' and argued the *Volkspolizei* had only increased to 51,000 men, most of whom came from the general population rather than regular police units. US intelligence sources reported morale in *Volkspolizei* units was generally very low with high desertion rates

46 Geyer, Michael, 'Cold War Angst: The Case of West German Opposition to Rearmament and Nuclear Weapons', in Schissler, Hanna (ed.), *The Miracle Years: A Cultural History of West Germany, 1949-1968* (Princeton: Princeton University Press, 2001), p. 379.
47 *FRUS, Western Europe, 1950*, Vol. III, Communiqué Agreed Upon by the Foreign Ministers, pp. 1106-1107.
48 Adenauer, *Memoirs*, pp. 274-275.
49 Ibid.
50 *FRUS, 1950*, Vol. IV, Telegram from McCloy to Acheson, 14 July 1950, pp. 696-97.
51 NARA RG 466, Records of the Office of the High Commissioner for Germany, Office of the Executive Director, General Hay's Executive Files 1949—1951, Boxes 15-16, Box 2, folder: 'Federal Chancellor Adenauer's Intelligence Estimate, 1950'.
52 Ibid., Reber to McCloy, 31 Aug. 1950.
53 Ibid., p. 1.
54 Ibid., p. 3.

among incoming classes of new recruits.[55] Adenauer concluded his analysis by insisting '[German] police forces are completely inadequate for a commitment against an organized internal enemy, and even less against an intervention by the *Volkspolizei*'.[56] His ambiguous mixing of external with internal security justifications shows how he matched his needs to what he believed might find political favor with the Allies. He clearly gambled all of his hopes for a federal police force on an Allied ruling rather than face political struggles in his own *Bundestag*.

McCloy received this letter just as he was leaving Frankfurt to brief the Foreign Ministers of Britain, France, and the United States in preparation for the upcoming Tripartite Conference in New York City. He already knew Adenauer's position from their meeting on August 17, and had cabled Brigadier General Henry Byroade at the State Department alleging the Chancellor was 'obviously suffering from real anxiety, but was also engaging in his usual pressure tactics'. McCloy also explained his own 'offhand estimate of Adenauer's appraisal of *Volkspolizei* strength and capacity is that he is rather building up their potentials, both as to objectives and timing'.[57] Coincidentally, however, McCloy's official HICOG assessment on security in Berlin was submitted to the National Security Council (NSC) on the same day he received Adenauer's letter. The paper, jointly authored with Generals Thomas Handy and Maxwell Taylor, was entitled: 'A Review of the Berlin Situation'.[58] Surprisingly, in spite of McCloy's comments to Byroade and others, his analysis supported many of Adenauer's embellished claims, especially in regard to the *Volkspolizei* and its potential to attack the West.[59]

McCloy's contradictory statements show his approach to West German policing was driven by competing political concerns. On the one hand, he publicly and privately condemned Adenauer's views for the benefit of those in the State Department and especially his French colleagues who opposed militarized policing. On the other hand, his dealings with Adenauer's supporters, such as British officials and members of the US Joint Chiefs of Staff, reflected his desire to remilitarize the civilian police in West Germany both as a counter to the *Volkspolizei* and as a gesture to secure Adenauer's loyalty. Moreover, policies carried out under the authority of his office in response to the Korean War reflected how McCloy quietly paved the way for Adenauer's

55 NARA RG 466, Records of US High Commissioner John J. McCloy, Classified General Records, 1950-1952, Box 9, Folder: Feb. 1950 D (50) 479 to D (50) 523, 'Self Evaluation of Soviet Zone Alert Police', HICOG Office of Intelligence, Special Intelligence Report No. 1, 25 Feb. 1950, Tab A, 1-3.

56 Ibid., p. 5.

57 NARA RG 466, US High Commissioner for Germany, Officer of Executive Director, Misc. Files Maintained by Colonel H.A. Gerhardt, Boxes 11-12, Box No. 2, Telegram, 'McCloy to Byroade', 18 Aug. 1950, p. 6.

58 EPL, White House Office, National Security Council Staff, Papers: 1948-1961, Disaster File, Box 48, Folder: Germany (5); 'A Review of the Berlin Situation', Joint HICOG, EUCOM, UCSOB Paper, 29 Aug. 1950.

59 Ibid., p. 4.

plans despite what he said in public. For example, on June 27, 1950, McCloy's Public Security Subcommittee struck down the occupation law banning members of Nazi Germany's *Wehrmacht* and paramilitary forces from service in the civilian police.[60]

The Remilitarization of West Germany's Civilian Police

Despite McCloy's unofficial support, the Foreign Ministers rejected Adenauer's federal police proposal during their tripartite meetings in New York City on 19 September 1950. Instead, they authorized the reinforcement of West Germany's *Länder*-based police forces by 30,000 men - a quarter of which (10,000) might be placed under federal jurisdiction whenever an emergency occurred that threatened the free democratic order of the state as defined under Article 91 of the Basic Law. According to the New York Tripartite Agreement, these federally controlled officers, 'would have no normal powers of arrest, and would not perform routine police duties, but would be trained and used solely for the preservation of public order'.[61] This decision paved the way for West Germany's federal states to reestablish the paramilitary Weimar era riot brigades (*Bereitschaftspolizei—BePo*).[62] The New York agreements also permitted the United States to equip and train a special 3,000-man paramilitary police unit in Berlin. Known as 'Force B', its officers lived in barracks and were equipped with mortars, armored cars, and bazookas.[63] While the foreign ministers had agreed to rearm West Germany under supranational control, a national police force was still off limits.

For Adenauer, however, these measures failed to go far enough, especially since his government was still without the means to enforce its authority. Thus, he immediately

60 NARA RG 466 Records of the High Commissioner for Germany, Military Security Board: Military Division, Secret General Records, 1949-55, F-P, Box 2, Folder: German Police, Miscellaneous, Allied High Commission Public Safety Subcommittee Confidential Memorandum: 'Employment in the German Police and Fire Services of Members of the German Armed Forces and Paramilitary Organizations', 27 June 1950.

61 NARA RG 466, General Hays Executive Files 1949-1951, Boxes 15-16, Box 2—Tripartite Meeting, Transcript of New York Foreign Ministers Meeting, 19 Sept. 1950, 'German Mobile Police Forces', pp. 1-2.

62 The BePo was a Weimar Era police force banned under the terms of the Potsdam and Yalta demilitarization guidelines. All *Länder* police officers began their service in the BEPO where they received military training. See Fairchild, Erika, *The German Police: Ideals and Reality in the Postwar Years* (Springfield, Ill: Charles C. Thomas, 1988), pp. 24-25; Raible, Eugen, *Geschichte der Polizei ihre Entwicklung in den alten Ländern Baden und Württemberg und in dem neuen Bundesland Baden-Württemberg, unter besonderer Berücksichtigung der kasernierten Polizei* (Stuttgart: R. Boorberg, 1963) p. 125; Heinrich, Heiner, *Vom Schutzmann zum Bullen: Die Geschichte eines Polizeibeamten in Hamburg* (Nordstedt: Books on Demand, 2009), pp. 28-29.

63 EPL, White House Office, National Security Council Staff: Papers, 1948-61, Box 48, Folder: Germany (7), United States Policy and Course of Action to Counter Possible Soviet or Satellite Action Against Berlin (NSC 132/1), 10 Sept. 1953.

began seeking opportunities to exploit the Allied Tripartite decision to justify the creation of an entirely new paramilitary federal police force. In the years leading up to the New York meetings, his legal advisers had already been striving at his direction to find constitutional exceptions that might justify the lawful establishment of this force. As early as November 1949, Adenauer's Chief of Staff, Hans Globke, instructed Federal Justice Minister Thomas Dehler to research the Basic Law for provisions covering police powers. But Dehler concluded Allied policies prohibited national policing without amending the Basic Law.[64] This helps to explain why Adenauer desperately tried convincing the Allies to grant his security requests. Dehler, however, recommended that Adenauer might be able to achieve his goals under Article 73, Paragraph 10 of the Basic Law, which gave 'exclusive rights for Constitutional protection' to the federal government. But he also cautioned that implementing these rights depended upon the severity and size of the threat to the Basic Law. Moreover, a clause in Article 73 prohibited the federal government from intervening with or exerting direct control over *Länder* police forces.[65]

On the surface, it appeared that Adenauer had exhausted all of his legal means until his administrative law expert Dr. Arnold Köttgen suggested the creation of a new federal border police. Köttgen personified the authoritarian, illiberal continuities still prevalent in postwar West German politics. He had been an ideologically committed member of the Nazi Party and was openly critical of liberal democracy. During the war, he served as the general police councilor at Auschwitz and in the Polish City of Katowice.[66] Köttgen advised Adenauer to create his police force under Article 87 of the Basic Law, which gave the federal government regulatory control over customs and border management. The main problem with this approach, however, was that the Federal Ministry of Finance had jurisdiction over West Germany's borders, which were already policed by its Federal Customs Police (*Zollgrenzschutz*). Moreover, Allied military police and state border guard units such as the Bavarian Border Police also provided law enforcement services at West Germany's frontiers. Nevertheless, Adenauer used Article 87 to introduce a law for the creation of a paramilitary border police force exclusively under the authority of his administration. By proceeding in this manner, the government could establish its own police force with a simple majority vote in the *Bundestag* without enduring the lengthy process of amending the Basic Law.

The move by Adenauer's government to create a paramilitary border police force in this manner drew heavy criticism from West Germany's socialist politicians who accused him of circumventing the rule of law. Walter Menzel (SPD), one of

64 Bundesarchiv Koblenz (BAK) B 144/229, Aufstellung einer Bundesbereitschaftspolizei-Verwaltungsabkommen mit den Ländern, Thomas Dehler to Hans Globke, 'Rechtsgutachten über Möglichkeit, eine Bundespolizei aufzustellen'.

65 Ibid.

66 Dietze, Carola, *Nachgeholtes Leben: Helmuth Plessner 1892–1985* (Göttingen: Wallstein Verlag, 2013), p. 427.

the influential framers of the Basic Law, was determined to expose what he believed was Adenauer's secret attempt to rearm West Germany by militarizing its civilian police. During heated *Bundestag* debates over the new law, Menzel warned his fellow lawmakers that:

> Given the many problems associated with these questions, you will understand that we have made the request to appoint a special Parliamentary Advisory Council for all police matters. We have also requested this from a political-psychological perspective. We want to show those in the outside world, but also those here in Germany, that we do not intend to allow a remilitarization of the police. I want to stress that all of us—not go back in the direction we had gone after 1918.[67]

In spite of the SPD's opposition, Adenauer's bill had the simple majority needed to pass. On February 15, 1951, the *Bundestag* authorized the government to establish the *Bundesgrenzschutz* (Federal Border Police or BGS). The SPD, however, did succeed in attaching measures to the new law limiting the size of the force to 10,000 men and restricting it to a jurisdiction no greater than 30 kilometers from West Germany's borders. Even though the creation of a standing paramilitary police force technically violated the letter and spirit of the New York tripartite agreements, HICOG officials decided against intervening in order to avoid embarrassing Adenauer's government, especially since it was created through a legal and democratic parliamentary process.[68]

Recruitment for the BGS began in earnest and it was an enticing career opportunity for thousands of West Germany's unemployed veteran soldiers who were still trying to deal with the effects of defeat, humiliation, and imprisonment. More than 65,000 men applied to join the new police force.[69] Those selected to fill its 10,000 vacant positions were all veteran soldiers some of which had civilian law enforcement backgrounds. The government deliberately sought soldiers for the BGS because they already had experience handling weapons and were familiar with the discipline of paramilitary and military organizations. Moreover, many of these men were ideologically committed to anti-communism and had experience fighting Soviet troops during the war, especially those selected for leadership positions. In many ways, the BGS replicated the *esprit de corps*, traditions, uniforms, and styles of Nazi Germany's *Wehrmacht*. Its ethos was definitely militaristic and completely antithetical to the democratic policing models the Allies attempted to export to postwar Germany. It was comparable to the French

67 Deutsche Bundestag 97th Session transcript, p. 3543, <http://www.bundestag.de/> (accesed 25 Aug. 2015).

68 BAK B 136/1927, top secret memorandum from Robert Lehr to HICOG, 15 Feb. 1951; *FRUS, 1950*, Vol. IV, telegram from General Hays to Secretary Acheson, 19 Dec. 1950, p. 735.

69 Werkentin, Falco, *Die Restauration der deutschen Polizei: Innere Rüstung von 1945 bis zur Notstandsgesetzgebung* (Frankfurt: Campus Verlag, 1984), p. 92.

Gendarmerie in terms of continental European policing styles even though France had no influence in its creation.[70]

While they were classified as civilian police forces, the BGS and state alert police units (*Bereitschaftspolizei—BePo*) were organized into infantry companies (*Hundertschaften*). They often trained together in exercises that were designed to emphasize their military capabilities. Most of their mock maneuvers, for example, resembled war games with personnel practicing amphibious river assaults, night marches, and anti-tank tactics. Both forces were equipped with light armored vehicles, machineguns, grenades, and mortars, equipment that was generally never issued to American or British police forces. The BePo primarily responded to internal security disturbances such as riots or demonstrations, but BGS units were mainly used to reinforce external security. In 1953, the BGS was expanded to 20,000 men following the violent uprisings against East Berlin's communist government. In fact, it was used as a cadre to build a new national army, the *Bundeswehr*, beginning in 1954-55 when the Allies authorized the West Germans to establish armed forces under NATO. Over 9,000 of its men chose to join the *Bundeswehr*, but this was far short of the government's expectations, which had originally planned on a number closer to 20,000. With nearly half of its personnel choosing army service, the BGS struggled to rebuild and many socialist lawmakers called for its dissolution or incorporation into West Germany's new army.[71]

Nevertheless, Adenauer's government was in favor of retaining the BGS even though it shared parallel external security functions with the *Bundeswehr*. The Federal Interior Minister, Gerhard Schröder, argued his policemen could prevent border incidents from escalating into wider military conflicts. Adenauer was also reluctant to disband his federal police since it was the only armed force at his disposal to enforce the will of his government. Otherwise, he would have had no choice but to rely on the states for police power because his new army was unable to operate outside the supranational authority of NATO.[72] Throughout the 1950s and beyond, the BGS retained its paramilitary character and its personnel were regarded as West Germany's 'special police troops'. Then in 1968, West German civilian policing finally began to gradually reject militarization following a series of internal reforms prompted by the anti-authoritarian activism of the student movement. These reforms culminated with the National Police Law of 1972, which professionalized the riot police and BGS so

70 The personnel lists of the first leaders and NCOs of the BGS show that these positions all went to Wehrmacht veterans. See BA-MA, BW 1/5484-5483, Bundesministerium der Verteidigung–Leitung, Zentrale Stäbe und Zivile Abteilungen, Liste F und G, Hauptman, Majore, und Obersteutnante im BGS.

71 BA-MA, BW 1/5484, Bundesministerium der Verteidigung—Leitung, Zentrale Stäbe und Zivile Abteilungen, Aktennotiz für Abteilungs Leiter III, 20 Jan. 1956, refers to the expectation that more than 18,000 members of the BGS will join the new army.

72 BAK, B 136/1929, Bericht des Bundesministers des Innern über Fragen des Bundesgrenzschutzes, letter from Gerhard Schröder to Chancellor Adenauer, 23 Jan. 1956.

their personnel were trained in traditional crime detection and suppression rather than warfighting. The changes modernized the BGS and state riot police to the extent that both forces evolved from their beginnings as paramilitary forces of *Wehrmacht* veterans into reunified Germany's modern national police forces.[73]

Conclusion: Police Advising and the Global War on Terror

What does the development of postwar West German policing tell us about contemporary police advising missions in the post 9/11 era? This is a particularly relevant question now that the United States and its allies have gone to great lengths in establishing or restoring civilian policing in places like Iraq and Afghanistan. Scholars have argued that there was a lack of planning for this vitally important facet of a functioning government – namely, constructing stable institutions with the legitimate monopolization of coercive force to maintain order and security without undermining the civil liberties of law abiding citizens. The sheer size of and instability in Iraq and Afghanistan, coupled with the widespread postwar violence and chaos, presented challenges for police advisors that greatly exceeded those facing Allied reformers in postwar Germany. Thus, Iraqi and Afghan police were built as paramilitary forces aimed more towards conducting counterinsurgency operations than regular civilian policing duties.[74] Yet why was police militarization a consequence of both postwar efforts even though circumstances in 1950s West Germany were drastically different?

First, in both cases, Allied planners underestimated the long-term development of indigenous policing and the strengths of pre-existing cultures and trends. Their efforts were often fragmented because each entity with a stake in the matter had competing visions of how to reestablish civilian policing. This was especially true in postwar West Germany as each Allied nation had its own law enforcement models they were attempting to export. Moreover, in Germany the strong relations between policing and the army dated back to at least the early nineteenth century. Breaking these bonds and reforming its police ultimately failed because the emergence of the Cold War changed the Allied focus from the Nazi past to the present concern over security. Thus, dealing with the immediate threat of Soviet Communism shifted their focus from demilitarizing to remilitarizing the police.

In Iraq and Afghanistan, police advising missions also attempted to export Western-style democratic policing. But like postwar Germany, prewar indigenous

73 BAK, B 106/83884, Weiterentwicklung von Organisation und Ausstattung des BGS als Folge des neuen Bundesgrenzschutz-Gesetzes, 'Blicktpunkt Bundespolizei 73—Initiativprogramm des Bundesgrenzschutz-Verbands', outlines the plans to modernize the BGS into a national police force.

74 Ladwig, Walter C., 'The Forgotten Force: Police—Building in Iraq and Afghanistan', *World Politics Review* (28 May 2013), <http://www.worldpoliticsreview.com/articles/12976/the-forgotten-force-police-building-in-iraq-and-afghanistan> (accessed 28 August 2015).

policing shared nothing in common with these Western models. And, as the security contingencies of the Cold War encouraged police militarization in 1950s West Germany, so did those associated with terrorism in Afghanistan and Iraq. Thus, the democratization of post-dictatorial policing is often a contested and protracted process, in which there are no guarantees or easy solutions. For as David Bayley has aptly suggested, 'The requirements of security trump aspirations to reform, a pattern to be found in stable as well as struggling democracies'.[75]

75 Bayley, *Changing of the Guard*, p. 69.

5

The Public Safety Division and the National Police Field Force in Vietnam, 1964-1971

Stephen Connor

Introduction

With the end of France's imperial adventure in Indochina and the temporary division of Vietnam into two states, the United States increasingly provided support to the southern regime.[1] Whatever the 1954 Geneva Accords may have allowed, the US proved staunchly unwilling to risk losing all of Indochina to communism. While such support would largely be military aid, US government assistance flowed to a myriad of programs and initiatives aimed at creating a stable, viable state below the 17th parallel.[2] Beginning in 1955, American agencies actively aided the Government of Vietnam (GVN) in building and maintaining a civil police force, something seen as a central element in the creation of a functioning civil society.[3] The result was the

1 An excellent discussion of the origins of US intervention in Vietnam is found Lawrence, Mark, *Assuming the Burden: Europe and the American Commitment to War in Vietnam* (Berkeley, CA: University of California Press, 2007). For the immediate context of the 1965 escalation see Berman, Larry, *Planning a Tragedy: The Americanization of the War in Vietnam* (New York: W.W. Norton, 1982).

2 Office of Public Safety, AID, Department of State (OPS), 'Assistance to Civil Security Forces, Republic of Vietnam', Washington, DC, September 1971, p. 1.

3 National Archives at College Park (NARA), College Park, MD, RG 286 A1 E32 Records of the AID: Office of Public Safety, Operations Division, East Asia Branch, Vietnam, (hereafter RG 286 A1 E 32), Box 53, IPS 3, Organization and Conferences 1966 through 1972, IPS 3 Organization/Administration/Assessment 1968: William Grieves, 'DGNP Organization and Administration Assessment', 6 September 1968. See also Office of Public Safety, AID, Department of State, 'CORDS Public Safety Program Information Handbook', Washington, DC, July 1972, pp. 1-3.

National Police Command (NPC). To provide support and advice, the US Agency for International Development (USAID) established the Public Safety Program through the Public Safety Division (PSD).

Policing Vietnam

By 1960, the challenges of establishing a functioning civil police apparatus were increasingly compounded by the active North Vietnamese controlled National Liberation Front (NLF) insurgency. Faced with this growing threat and the necessity of countering it, the conventional role of policing—maintaining law and order—was profoundly difficult. In this context, the National Police (NP), charged with civil law enforcement was now required to develop a paramilitary capability to help defeat the NLF.[4] To that end, in early 1965 the GVN created the National Police Field Force (NPFF) within the NPC. The PSD played a central role in the program's development, and the NPFF's eventual deployment and operations, and until the end of American intervention in Vietnam, they adopted a decidedly 'hands-on' approach.

In the broadest of terms, pacification was the principal objective of both the NPFF and their US advisors.[5] The question remains: what exactly did this mean for PSD and for the Vietnamese police expected to carry it out? The purpose of this chapter is to consider the relationship between the PSD and the NPC by focusing on the development, deployment, and operations of the NPFF. To highlight significant features of this relationship, central consideration is given to the ways in which PSD and the NP confronted the on-going challenges of establishing standard procedures and conducting missions between 1965 and 1971.

For PSD, the NPFF's primary problem area was not related to its role, organization, or administration, but rather to its ability to execute its mission.[6] Indeed, not only did PSD believe that both advising and operational procedures were sound but, as we shall see, responsibility for key failures lay with other agencies entirely. The NPFF itself then was not the problem, but the failure of other organizations to carry out their duties hindered police operations. Specifically, culpability lay with those most directly connected to NPFF operations: province and district chiefs and the Police Special Branch. The real problems were either misuse (in the case of the former), or the latter's failure to effectively partner with them at all.

Throughout PSD's engagement in Vietnam, the National Police Support Program continuously evolved, ever refining the scope of advisory, material and managerial

4 OPS, 'The Role of Public Safety in Support of the National Police of Vietnam', Washington, DC, April 1969, p. 1.

5 The most complete study of US pacification efforts is found in Hunt, Richard, *Pacification: The American Struggle for Vietnam's Hearts and Minds* (Boulder: Westview Press, 1995). See also Fisher, Christopher, 'The Illusion of Progress', *Pacific Historical Review*, 75:1 (2007), pp. 25-51.

6 NARA: 'DGNP Organization and Administration Assessment 6 September 1968'.

support for the NP. In effect, PSD understood its roles as managers and consultants.[7] As we shall see, their expectation to 'keep in the background', 'prime the pump' and develop their Vietnamese counterparts' ability to eventually 'shoulder the burden' of policing proved impossible.[8]

Building a National Police

With the signing of the 1954 Geneva Accords and subsequent French evacuation, the State of Vietnam's security apparatus comprised a collection of separate agencies that included the *Sûreté*, Gendarmerie, and the Saigon Municipal Police (SMP). At the provincial level, locally raised autonomous militias supplemented these national forces.[9] Predictably, civil policing proved as ineffective as it was chaotic and *ad hoc*.[10]

By the end of 1954, President Ngo Dihn Diem centralized and amalgamated provincial militias, reforming them into a new police agency, the Civil Guard.[11] This new organization, charged with rural policing rural, quickly grew by 1960 to 54,000,

7 OPS, 'The Role', p. 7.

8 Ibid., p. 7.

9 Ibid., p. 5 and OPS, 'Assistance to Civil Security Forces', pp. 1-2.

10 For an early US view of public safety in Vietnam see *US Army Area Handbook for Vietnam*, Washington, DC, September 1962, pp. 265-272 and Nighswonger, William, *Rural Pacification in Viet Nam, 1962-1965* (Washington, DC: American University, 1966). The challenges of establishing security under a "chronically weak GVN administration" is well reflected in Komer, Robert, 'Was There Another Way?' in Thompson, W.S. (ed.), *The Lessons of Vietnam* (New York: Crane, Russak & Company, 1977), pp. 211-230. For a recent insightful examination of factors influencing nation-building and the Diem regime see Chapman, Jessica M., *Cauldron of Resistance: Ngo Dinh Diem, the United States, and 1950s Southern Vietnam* (Ithaca: Cornell University Press, 2013) and Miller, Edward, *Misalliance: Ngo Dinh Diem, the United States, and the Fate of South Vietnam* (Cambridge: Harvard University Press, 2013). The rich historical debate regarding the Diem years is well represented in Moyar, Mark, *Triumph Forsaken: The Vietnam War, 1954-1965* (Cambridge: Cambridge University Press, 2007) *and* Wiest, Andrew and Michael Doidge (eds), *Triumph Revisited: Historians Battle for the Vietnam War* (New York: Routledge, 2010). For the initial development and challenges facing police forces see Rosenau, William, *US Internal Security Assistance to South Vietnam: Insurgency, Subversion and Public Order* (New York: Routledge, 2005), pp. 2-3, 47-76. See also Kuzmarov, Jeremy, *Modernizing Repression: Police Training and Nation Building in the American Century* (Amherst: University of Massachusetts Press, 2012), pp. 17-36, 141-162.

11 National Archives at College Park (NARA), College Park, MD, RG 286 A1 E31 Records of the AID: Office of Public Safety, Operations Division, East Asia Branch, Vietnam, (hereafter RG 286 A1 E31), Box 221, IPS 1, General Policy Guidelines and Background, 1965-1968: 'Some Historical Facts Bearing on the Current Public Safety Program in Vietnam', p. 2. In 1959, MSUG recommended that the Public Safety Division be created within USAID to provide continued assistance to the Civil Guard. NARA: RG 286 A1 E32, Box 24, IPS 2-1 Staff Reports, 1966-1968, IPS 2-1, Action Programs, 1967-1968, MACCORDS-PS Briefing: 'Briefing on GVN National Police and Public Safety Division', 29 June 1967, p. 1.

the single largest component of an internal security apparatus that numbered 70,000. Yet despite organizational changes, police agencies continued to lack adequate central command and coordination, as well as sufficient training and equipment. Consequently President Diem turned to the United States for assistance. Following an assessment by 'US technicians', American support for Vietnam's internal security initiatives came principally through the Michigan State University Group (MSUG) contracted by the International Cooperation Agency and under the 'in-country' authority of United States Operations Mission (USOM).[12] MSUG's major involvement occurred between 1955 and 1959 and encompassed advising, training, and providing aid until the formation of the USOM police office.[13]

In 1961, USAID established the Office of Public Safety (OPS) to oversee paramilitary and police advisory programs first developed in response to President Harry S. Truman's 1949 inaugural speech promising 'technical knowledge' to nations requesting support. In Vietnam, as MSUG's role drew to a close, police advising passed to OPS and its Public Safety Division. In turn, PSD established the Public Safety Program within the broader US Mission to act as the primary American police support agency.[14] While PSD's internal administration and activities remained relatively constant after 1961, on 9 May 1967, the Directorate shifted organizationally to Ambassador Robert Komer's Civil Operations and Revolutionary Development Support (CORDS) under MACV. As the only USAID division to operate fully under CORDS, the effect of the transfer on PSD and the NP would prove significant.[15]

On 27 June 1962, President Diem's decree merged the *Sûreté*, elements of the Gendarmerie, SMP, newly formed Combat Police, and remaining provincial units to

12 Ernst, John, *Forging a Fateful Alliance: Michigan State University and the Vietnam War* (Lansing: Michigan State University Press, 1998), p. 50. For the most complete study of this period see Rosenau, *US Internal Security Assistance*.

13 Agency for International Development, Department of State: *Final Report Covering Activities of the Michigan State University Vietnam Advisory Group for the Period May 20, 1955-June 30*, 1962, Saigon: Vietnam, p. 48. See also Scigliano, Robert and Guy H. Fox, *Technical Assistance in Vietnam: The Michigan State University Experience* (New York, Washington, London: Frederick A. Praeger Publishers, 1965), pp. 14-15, and Alster, Jake, 'Spartans in Vietnam: Michigan State University's Experience in South Vietnam', *Grand Valley Journal of History*, 3:1 (2014), pp. 1-18. Michigan State University continued to provide advisory support to the *Sûreté* until 20 June 1961. NARA: 'Briefing on GVN National Police and Public Safety Division', p. 1.

14 With the establishment of OPS in 1961, police advisory programs in Vietnam were centralized and administered from Saigon until funding ceased in 1973. PSD's priority objective was to assist in building, professionalizing and improving the Vietnamese government's law enforcement capabilities by providing technical and advisory support to the Directorate of Police, Rehabilitation, and Telecommunication under the Ministry of Interior (MOI). OPS, 'The Role', p. 4. See also Attewell, Wesley, 'Ghosts in the Delta: USAID and the Historical Geographies of the Vietnam's "Other War"', *Environment and Planning A*, 47:11 (2015), pp. 2257-2275.

15 OPS, 'The Role', p. 6.

form the National Police (NP), which boasted a strength of about 17,000.[16] However, further significant reforms were undercut by nearly constant military, political, and civil unrest. In early 1964, in the wake of the *coup d'état* against and murder of President Diem, PSD proposed a National Police Plan. The program called for the creation of a truly national, standardized police apparatus to provide law enforcement services that would include an 'extensive police and paramilitary counterinsurgency capability'.[17] To put the plan into action, PSD began expanding its mission and recruiting advisors from a variety of police agencies in the United States.[18] These US advisors were charged with assisting the NP in establishing new law enforcement capabilities that ranged from the creation of the National Police Command (NPC) to the Combined Telecommunications Directorate and reorganized Directorate of Corrections.[19] The focus of the program was managerial and centered on providing police agencies three key elements: advisory personnel, commodities, and training programs.[20]

The post-Diem restructuring of the NPC created four distinct branches: Uniformed Police, Police Special Branch, Marine Police, and the paramilitary National Police

16 Office of Public Safety, AID, Department of State, 'The Public Safety Program Vietnam', Saigon, Vietnam, April 1966, p. 7. *Military Review* lists the 1962 strength at 16,000. See Colonel David Shepherd, 'The Republic of Vietnam's National Police', *Military Review*, June 1971, pp. 69-74.

17 OPS, 'The Role', p. 5. PSD proposed that the NP number 86,000 by the end of 1969. See also OPS, 'Public Safety Program', p. 15.

18 Advisory Personnel would include both US civilians and third-country national employees. OPS, 'The Role', pp. 6-7 and NARA: RG 286 A1 E31, Box 230, IPS 1-1: Briefing Materials, 1971-1972, IPS 1-1 Historical References Miscellaneous Folder I, 1970-1971, 'Public Safety Program Vietnam', 8 January 1970, p. 1, and OPS, 'Assistance to Civil Security Forces', p. 3.

19 For a complete description of specific program-wide objectives and support see OPS, 'Public Safety Program', pp. 15-78.

20 OPS, 'Assistance to Civil Security Forces', p. 3. PSD's commitment to the NPC grew steadily. By the end of FY 1968 total dollar support reached $95.4M and $130.1M in 1969. See NARA: RG 286 A1 E31, Box 230, IPS 1-1: Briefing Materials, 1971-1972, IPS 1-1 Historical References Miscellaneous Folder I, 1970-1971, 'Public Safety Vietnam', p. 1-2. This included $18.5M in DOD funding since 1967 for the NPFF and Telecommunications. In regards to police advisors, numbers rose from six in 1959 to 47 in 1963, and 204 (of 225 positions open) by 1968, significantly more than the 90 in Latin America and 27 in Africa. Further, just a month prior to the signing of the Geneva Agreement in 1973, 154 advisors were 'in country'. See Klare, M.T., *War Without End: American Planning for the Next Vietnams* (New York: Vintage Books, 1972), pp. 382-383. Also NARA: 'Public Safety Vietnam', p. 2. PSD also employed a number of 'Third-Country Nationals', primarily British and Australian. OPS, 'The Role', p. 7 and OPS, 'Public Safety Program', p. 10. For the British Public Safety contributions Beckett, Ian, 'Robert Thompson and the British Advisory Mission to South Vietnam, 1961–1965', *Small Wars & Insurgencies*, 8:3 (1997), pp. 41-63. By 1970 a total of 134 Third Country Nationals were authorized in addition to 41 contract personnel. See NARA: RG 286 A1 E31, Box 230, IPS 1-1: Briefing Materials, 1971-1972, IPS 1-1 Historical References Miscellaneous Folder I, 1970-1971, 'Public Safety Program Vietnam', 8 January 1970.

Field Force (NPFF) based around the former Combat Police.[21] Charged with the 'constitutional processes of law enforcement', a cornerstone of local civil administration, the primary roles of the NP were fourfold: normal police functions, maintenance of law and order, security control, and counterinsurgency activities.[22] These tasks, perceived as central to nation building, would assist the GVN in extending control, influence and services nationwide. However, achieving such goals required policing at the village and hamlet level. Yet not until 1969 were police services effectively extended beyond densely populated, relatively secure provincial and district cities and towns to rural areas.[23] It was into this space that both the GVN and PSD looked to project a civil paramilitary presence..

Throughout the 1950s, MSUG's advisory focus remained primarily centered on Diem's *Sûreté*. Indeed, only in 1959, under the USOM police office did significant work commence on paramilitary security, beginning with the Civil Guard. However, very quickly, and in line with the broader militarization of GVN agencies, efforts to build Vietnam's civil policing capabilities were severely undercut.[24] In December 1960, following the urging of US Military Assistance and Advisory Group (MAAG), control of the Civil Guard passed from the Ministry of the Interior (MOI) to the Ministry of Defense (MOD) and became the foundation for the Regional Forces (RF) and Popular Forces (PF).[25] Given their subsequent 'military orientation and

21 In Vietnamese, the NPFF were designated *Cảnh Sát Dã Chiến* (CSDC). Expansion of the NPC progressed rapidly jumping from 19,000 (1963) to 52,000 (1965) to 90,000 (1971). In 1966, the NP grew to 60,000 and in 1967 reached 70,000. OPS, 'The Role', p. 5. For a brief examination of expansion and militarization of the police (including the NPFF's precursor Combat Police) see Rosenau, *US Internal Security Assistance*, pp. 123-130.

22 Shepherd, 'National Police', pp. 69-70. In 1966, the NP grew to 60,000, in 1967 70,000, and 80,000 in 1968. OPS, 'The Role', pp. 5-9, 11-13. See also OPS, 'Public Safety Program', p. 15 and NARA: 'Public Safety Vietnam', p. 1.

23 Shepherd, 'National Police', p. 70. See also Hunt, *Pacification*, pp. 39, 69.

24 OPS, 'The Role', p. 5.

25 NARA: 'Briefing on GVN National Police and Public Safety Division', p. 1. The move was part of what PSD described, and consistently bemoaned, as the broader 'militarization' of the GVN's security and Public Safety agencies. In early 1969, the Secretary of Defense sent a memorandum to the President briefing him on the NP. SECDEF's view on militarization bears quoting: 'A major characteristic of the NP in general has been its great dependence on the GVN military to provide officers to fill its command slots. All Director Generals of the NP have been Vietnamese Army (ARVN) officers; as of June 1968, 142 ARVN officers occupied the majority of the command positions in the NP.' Records of the Virtual Vietnam Center Archive, Texas Tech University (TTVN), Douglas Pike Collection: Unit 06, Democratic Republic of Vietnam, 'Secretary of Defense Memorandum to the President: National Police in South Vietnam, 1969', <http://www.virtualarchive.vietnam.ttu.edu/>, Item 2321601008. For views on the issue from Chief J.P. Manopoli see NARA: RG 286 A1 E32, Box 24, IPS 2-1 Staff Reports, 1966-1968, IPS 2-1, Action Programs, 1967-1968, 'Memorandum from John Manopoli to Robert Komer, Major Police Problems', 5 July 1967 and, NARA: RG 286 A1 E32, Box 24, IPS 2-1 Staff Reports, 1966-1968, IPS 2-1, Action Programs, 1967-1968, 'Memorandum from L.

training under military auspices', the transfer also ended PSD advice and support.[26] Most importantly, the transition removed the NP's paramilitary arm, ensuring the absence of any police agency in rural Vietnam at the precise time when the NLF insurgency was increasingly active.

In early 1962, Diem's GVN launched the Strategic Hamlet program, an effort to establish and maintain secure bonds between the rural population and the central government. In terms of policing and security, the program quickly exposed the impact of the absence of any civil, paramilitary organization, as the government could not project a police presence beyond urban areas to counter NLF subversion and terrorism in the countryside. Indeed, no central structure existed to coordinate civil police efforts against the NLF at all.[27] To address the problem the GVN established the Combat Police in 1962. While limited in size, the new force did provide the MOI with an armed and mobile paramilitary arm. Yet even with its formation, responsibility for rural security rested with a mixture of civil and military assets, encompassing the Combat Police, Vietnamese Army (ARVN), and Regional/Popular Forces.[28]

1964: Priming the Pump

PSD advocated the civil police as 'the government's first line of defense against subversive insurgency'.[29] To that end, in November 1964 PSD recommended to the DGNP that the Combat Police be reorganized as a paramilitary Police Field Force.[30] Based on their proposal, and concurrent with the wider restructuring of the NP, a presidential decree created the National Police Field Force as a paramilitary, organic branch of the Republic of Vietnam's National Police.[31] From its inception, PSD assumed the principal lead in advising, supporting, and developing the NPFF as part of its broader program of assisting the NPC.[32] The newly formed NPFF was intended to address consistent inadequacies in police efforts to achieve pacification.

Wade Lathram to William Colby, GVN Militarization of National Police Command', 6 September 1967.

26 OPS, 'The Role', p. 5.

27 Ibid., pp. 5, 9.

28 NARA: RG 286 A1 E31, Box 230, IPS 1-1: Briefing Materials, 1971-1972, IPS 1-1: 'Republic of South Vietnam National Police Field Force 1971', p. 1.

29 OPS, 'Public Safety Program', p. 16 and OPS, 'The Role', p. 5. The endgame for PSD would be a 'modern apolitical and professional career service orientated to contribute to the development of a successful representative government'.

30 NARA: RG 286 A1 E31, Box 230, IPS 1-1: Briefing Materials, 1971-1972, IPS 1-1 Historical References Miscellaneous Folder I, 1970-1971, 'Vietnam National Police Field Force: History, Role and Mission'.

31 NARA: 'Briefing on GVN National Police and Public Safety Division'. The NPFF was formed 21 June 1965 following a January 1965 decree ordering its creation. OPS, 'The Role', p. 9 and OPS, 'Public Safety Program', p. 29.

32 NARA: 'Briefing on GVN National Police and Public Safety Division', p. 6.

Based on the counterinsurgency doctrine of clear, hold, and build, planners asserted that only permanent local security forces would allow for sustained civil development with paramilitary policing providing a seemingly viable means to ensure it.[33]

Resisting GVN advances into the countryside was the NLF, perceived by PSD as a 'deconstructed organization structure' of 'undercover agents and saboteurs' and 'VC guerillas' that presented particular challenges. First, pacification required enough manpower to hold 'decontaminated areas', but committing sufficient military assets to static defense meant the risk of losing the initiative and the ability to react to large-scale NLF operations. Second, the very nature of the insurgency exposed a missing link in the military-NP defense chain that protected pacified areas.[34] In contested zones, an ARVN presence and on-going clearing operations could ensure a degree of security. However, upon the redeployment of these units and the transfer of responsibility to local territorial units, security rapidly deteriorated, threatening efforts at holding and building.[35] To remedy the perceived security gap and empower pacification, the GVN created the NPFF in January 1965.

In late 1964, PSD laid out its vision for the NPFF.[36] Initially, US planners favored a 'militant police force' comprised largely of local recruits from cleared areas. Intended to act as a deterrent and to provide immediate response to low-level threats, the force

33 Ibid., p. 2. See also OPS, 'Public Safety Program', pp. 29-30. The first provincial NPFF Company deployed to Long An on 28 November 1965. NARA: 'Vietnam National Police Field Force: History, Role and Mission'.

34 NARA: RG 286 A1 E32, Box 76, IPS 12, Police Administration, 1973 through 1974, IPS 12 Field Police History Key Details, 1965-1972, 'PIOCC/DIOCC Coordinator Briefing', p. 1. The "Armed Forces" were understood as ARVN but also included "the RF and PF and PSDF" while the NP were defined as the "ordinary National Police." See also OPS, 'Public Safety Program', pp. 29-30.

35 OPS, 'The Public Safety Program', pp. 15-16, 28-34. See also Records of the Virtual Vietnam Center Archive, Texas Tech University (TTVN), John Haseman Collection, Civil Operations Rural Development Support, MACV, 'The Vietnamese Village: Handbook for Advisors', <http://www.vietnam.ttu.edu/, Item 14040103001>.

36 The PSD push for a civil-policing option was based on two key factors. First, experience in fighting insurgencies in Malaya and the Philippines provided models of a paramilitary force designed as an action of police intelligence assets. USAID-PSD noted the particular success of the Philippines Constabulary as an effective paramilitary police force. NARA: 'Republic of South Vietnam National Police Field Force', p. 1. Frank E. Walton, a former deputy chief of the Los Angeles Police Department before his retirement and employment with USAID where he acted as Chief, Public Safety Directorate Vietnam, held a particular interest in policing the Philippines. See Walton, Frank (ed.), *Survey of Philippine Law Enforcement*, (Washington: Department of State, Agency for International Development, Office of Public Safety, 1966). See also OPS, 'Public Safety Program', p. 29. Second, consideration was given to the necessity of establishing a force that would serve as the foundation for the post-hostility transfer of military capabilities to a civil organization. NARA: 'PIOCC/DIOCC Coordinator Briefing', p. 2. For early CIA interest in the NPFF project see Ahern, Thomas, *Vietnam Declassified: The CIA and Counterinsurgency* (Lexington: University of Kentucky Press, 2010), pp. 258, 428.

was to be 'well trained, armed...disciplined and reasonably paid'. As local policemen rather than soldiers, they could more readily identify with their fellow citizens and, over time, 'win the respect and eventually the confidence, loyalty and cooperation' of the population.[37] Indeed, should sustained pacification be achieved, local units would remain in place and 'revert to and perform normal police functions and duties'. From the outset, the NPFF were intended as policemen rather than soldiers and were expected over time to help defeat the insurgency in essence working themselves out of a job.[38]

In the early stages of planning, the NPFF's primary policing role was for the 'rapid, small scale application of force' intended to assist both military and civilian police efforts at suppressing 'residual Viet Cong subversion', chiefly through resource and population control operations.[39] In carrying out these missions, the NPPF would be capable of static, 'semi-static', and mobile operations ranging from fixed checkpoints, to control points, to 'surprise check points, area patrols, raids, and ambushes'.

Defeating the NLF in newly pacified and contested areas also entailed offensive operations. Indeed, PSD intended that the NPFF develop its own intelligence and carry out a variety of missions independently. Working from local knowledge, small units would observe communication, courier, and supply routes to generate actionable intelligence with an eye to choking-off the 'continuing flow of resources to the VC from sympathizers in the already pacified areas'. Further, units would enforce curfews, carry out 'well executed ambush operations', launch raids on insurgent camps, gather

37 NARA: RG 286 A1 E32, Box 76, IPS 12, Police Administration, 1973 through 1974, IPS 12 Field Police History Key Details, 1965-1972, FY 72/73, 'National Police Field Force', 9 December 1964, p. 3.

38 For the significance of the civil rather than military orientation see NARA: RG 286 A1 E32 Box 7, IPS 1: General Policy, Guidelines and Background, 1969 through 1971, IPS 1: Territorial Security, National Police Territorial Forces Local Security, 1967-1971, 'David Lazar, Deputy for CORDS to PSD, Utilization of National Police Field Forces', 14 October, 1970.

39 NARA: RG 286 A1 E32, Box 76, IPS 12, Police Administration, 1973 through 1974, IPS 12 Field Police History Key Details, 1965-1972, FY 72/73, 'National Police Field Force', 9 December, 1964, pp. 4-5. Further, the NPFF were to provide security and assistance to NP units for Resource Control operations as well as carrying out raids in their support. In regards to interagency cooperation, the NPFF were not supplemental but rather charged most broadly with assisting 'ARVN, Regional Forces, and Popular Forces operations as needed.' PSD perceptions of resources and population control is best articulated in Adkins, E.D., 'Police and Resources Control in Counterinsurgency', (Saigon: Department of State, Agency for International Development, Office of Public Safety, 1964). For the significance of the manual see Records of the Virtual Vietnam Center Archive, Texas Tech University (TTVN), Vladimir Lehovich Collection, 'Memo from Jack E. Ryan, Chief, Public Safety Division, USOM Vietnam, Re: Distribution of the Manual, The Police and Resources Control in Counterinsurgency, 24 June 1964', <http://www.vietnam.ttu.edu>, Item 12050208001 and OPS, 'Public Safety Program', pp. 39-48.

intelligence, and provide security for the national highway system.[40] In short, PSD perceived proper deployment as 'forward-based' and proactive, engaging 'hardcore VC units'.

1965-1966: Growing Pains

As the first NPFF companies began to deploy in late 1965, PSD's early ambitious vision was significantly scaled back. Specifically, the NPFF initial function was threefold: to maintain the presence of GVN 'strength and security' and to provide protection to villages and hamlets, to contain and to suppress civil unrest in urban areas, and to maintain security in and near the northern Demilitarized Zone.[41] To that end, in early December 1965, the NP specifically directed the NPFF to extend police services and GVN influence into cleared yet still contested areas by doing the following:

1. Extensive police patrolling of the assigned area of operation (primary mission).
2. Elimination of local VC guerillas and VCI infrastructure in conjunction with the Special Branch Police.
3. Conducting resource control operations.
4. Conducting civic action programs.[42]

Theoretically the NPFF would in time provide security in pacified areas thereby freeing up the ARVN and RF for offensive operations. Importantly, though paramilitary, the NPFF were not envisioned as yet another combat arm for direct action. Further, units were not to be deployed in static defense missions or for personal security duties.[43] In contrast, the new force was intended to proactively engage in pacification efforts such as resources and population control. To this end, the NPFF was intended to 'go on the offensive' as 'small, mobile, armed tactical police units capable of observing, controlling, patrolling, ambushing or otherwise interdicting the movement of VC supplies, couriers, explosives, recruiters, etc'.[44] Indeed, in cleared areas, platoons were

40 NARA: 'National Police Field Force', 9 December, 1964, pp. 4-5. The goal of such operations was to 'obtain VC intelligence by captured documents, personnel, equipment etc.'

41 NARA: RG 286 A1 E31, Box 67, IPS #12, Police Administration 1955 through 1967, IPS 12, 'NPFF Organization and Function Manual, 1965', p. 1. See also NARA: RG 286 A1 E32, Box 76, IPS 12, Police Administration, 1973 through 1974, IPS 12 Field Police History Key Details, 1965-1972, 'FY 72/73 Program Narrative'. NARA: RG 286 A1 E32, Box 71, IPS 12 Police Administration, 1971, IPS 12, 'The Role and Mission of the NPFF'.

42 NARA: 'FY 72/73 Program Narrative'. See also NARA: 'The Role and Mission of the NPFF', p. 1.

43 NARA: 'Briefing on GVN National Police and Public Safety Division', p. 8. OPS, 'Public Safety Program', p. 35.

44 NARA: 'National Police Field Force'.

even expected to initiate and maintain civic action programs either on their own or in collaboration with other civilian agencies.[45] In essence, the NPFF was tasked primarily with extensive patrolling, extending a police presence into the countryside, and improving the government's image. Eliminating residual insurgent elements was only a secondary mission and conducted in conjunction with PSB.[46]

PSD envisioned a force of 15,000, rising to about 30,000 should conditions warrant.[47] Organizationally, overall command of the new force rested with the Director General of the National Police (DGNP) in Saigon.[48] Direct control of the NPFF branch, however, belonged to the Assistant to the Director General of National Police.[49] Officially titled Assistant DGNP for NPFF, the position consisted of both staff (as assistant to the DGNP) and command roles (as NPFF Commander). In this position the ADGNP-NPFF directed the force through a twelve position command staff.[50]

In the field, NPFF organization began at the Corps Tactical Zone (CTZ) level with an Assistant to the Director of NP serving as the regional NPFF headquarters. This regional NPFF commander also acted as an assistant to the NPFF Commander and Battalion Commander, a unit consisting of six field companies and a service company.[51] At the Provincial level, the NPFF Company operated with a headquarters element of 24 men and four platoons under a commander who served as the Assistant for NPFF to the Provincial NP Chief through his company headquarters.[52] In the provinces, the operational command of all police, including the NPFF, flowed from

45 OPS, 'Public Safety Program', p. 34.

46 NARA: RG 286 A1 E31, Box 280, IPS 13, Field Police, 1971, 'Fact Sheet: The Change in Roles and Missions of the Field Police, 13 August 1971'.

47 NARA: RG 286 A1 E32, Box 67, IPS 12, Police Administration 1955 through 1967, IPS 12, NPFF/Organization and Functions Manual, 1965, Field Force Division, Office of Public Safety, USAID, Vietnam, 'Organization and Functions Manual and Staffing Patterns', p. 1.

48 NARA: 'PIOCC/DIOCC Coordinator Briefing', p. 5. At the DGNP level, a six man US Advisory team was also deployed.

49 ADG for NPFF included Lieutenant Colonel Pham Huy Sanh and in June 1968 Lieutenant Colonel Nguyen Van Dai. See NARA: RG 286 A1 E31, Box 53, IPS 3-1, Assessment National Police Performance, 1968-1971, 'Memorandum of Conversation', p. 4.

50 See NARA: 'DGNP Organization and Administration Assessment 6 September 1968'.

51 These companies assisted 'regional area NPFF companies for logistics support, administration, personnel recruiting etc.' See NARA: 'PIOCC/DIOCC Coordinator Briefing', p. 5. In the NPFF Province Company HQ, the commander acted also as the Assistant Province Chief of Police 'responsible for discipline, command, personnel and their equipment'. See ibid., p. 5.

52 Beginning in 1968, provinces with five or more districts were assigned two companies. NARA: 'Republic of South Vietnam National Police Field Force 1971', p. 3. Such arrangements however could lead to disagreements and rivalries arising between company commanders. In most cases Chiefs of Police were reluctant to correct the problem by attaching one company to the other based on command seniority. See NARA: RG 286 A1 E32, Box 46, IPS 2-3 Program Review Book II NPFF Information, 1969, 'Memorandum from Chief NPFF Advisor William Grieves to Director–PSD Frank Walton, Analysis

the Province Chief to his Province police chief and finally to the NPFF company commander.[53] In the districts, the structure was replicated with lines of command passing from district chief, to police chief, to platoon commander. At this level, the NPFF deployed as a platoon consisting of a four man headquarters and three 'combat squads' of 12 men and it was here that PSD expected them to carry out missions.[54]

1967-1968: From Shotgun to Rifle

The publication of NPFF Standard Operating Procedures (SOP) in 1966 broadly confirmed the role and missions established the previous year.[55] However, throughout 1967, the first in a series of US initiated adaptations began that significantly altered the NPFF's operations and deployment. By December 1966, concern over the NPFF's proper and effective utilization had reached the highest levels of the US Mission.[56] For PSD planners, the problem had little to do with capability, but rather utilization. The structure of civil policing consisted of two lines of command. In terms of administrative matters, orders ran from the Prime Minister, to the Ministry of the Interior, to the DGNP, Corps NP Director, and finally to the Province Police Chief. In operational matters, however, orders passed from the Prime Minister, to Corps Commander, to Province Chief, to Provincial Police Chief. While the DGNP commanded the NP, Province Chiefs, responsible for law and order, controlled specific deployment and operations themselves, outside the police command structure. The problem then was one of lines of command and authority; in essence the NP was national in name only.[57]

of NPFF-1969, 15 January 1970'. See also Andrade, Dale, *Ashes to Ashes: The Phoenix Program and the Vietnam War* (Lexington: Lexington Books, 1990), p. 156.

53 Administratively, NP, including the NPFF, received 'technical guidance and support from the DGNP.' Operationally, individual Province Chiefs 'who are responsible for law enforcement in their own areas' controlled all NP assets. NARA: RG 286 A1 E32, Box 24, IPS 2-1 Staff Reports, 1966-1968, IPS 2-1, Action Programs, 1967-1968, MACCORDS-PS Briefing, 'Briefing on GVN National Police and Public Safety Division', p. 2.

54 NARA: 'PIOCC/DIOCC Coordinator Briefing', pp. 5-6.

55 The 1966 SOP added the mission of civil disturbance control. See NARA: RG 286 A1 E32, Box 76, IPS 12, Police Administration, 1973 through 1974, IPS 12 Field Police History Key Details, 1965-1972, 'FY 72/73 Program Narrative'. See also RG 286 A1 E32, Box 71, IPS 12 Police Administration, 1971, IPS 12, 'Role and Mission of the Field Police; Responsibilities of Province and District Chiefs of Police', 9 August 1971, p. 2. Additionally, the 1967 SOP changed neither role nor missions other than dropping the civic action mission. See NARA: 'The Role and Mission of the NPFF', p. 1.

56 Beginning in December 1966, the PSD NPFF advisory branch began providing BG Nguyen Ngoc Loan, the National Police Director General, with 'recommendations for the correction of any company misuse.' NARA: 'Briefing on GVN National Police and Public Safety Division', p. 10. See also TTVN, Central Intelligence Agency, Intelligence Report, 'The Situation in South Vietnam (Weekly)', 30 January 1967, p. II-2, Central Intelligence Agency Collection, http://www.vietnam.ttu.edu, Item 04108118006.

57 NARA: 'Briefing on GVN National Police and Public Safety Division', p. 2.

Consequently, in the provinces and districts, NPFF commanders were simultaneously responsible to both the DGNP and their specific, local Chief, ensuring that leaders 'often find it difficult to comply with the instructions...opposed by the Province Chief'.[58] For his part, a Province and District Chief, could, as was often the case, 'ignore the orders of the DGNP on their [NPFF] proper use and deployment'.[59]

The reality at the provincial and district level was that NPFF units rarely patrolled at all, as Province and District Chiefs often favored their deployment for urban defense, and generally in a provincial or district capital rather than in villages and hamlets. The negative outcomes of deploying the NPFF as static guards were not only a violation of standard operating procedures but rather had short and long-term implications for the success of the force. In the short run, static duty simply negated the significant efforts already made to train and deploy the Field Force to both attack the NLF and conduct rural patrols. In the long-term, static duty undercut not only planned operations against the NLF but also meant that previously secured areas were exposed to re-infiltration, renewed attacks, and destabilization.[60] As a result, unchallenged in the rural areas, resurgent NLF forces could 'terrorize the villages and hamlets undisturbed' and prevent the 'final phases of pacification and social development'.[61] From the US perspective, the time had come to force the NPFF into the field. How this would be accomplished and for what purpose would evolve throughout the remainder of the American intervention in Vietnam.

At a meeting on 1 February 1967 Deputy Ambassador William J. Porter pressed DGNP General Nguyen Ngoc Loan on the improper use of the NPFF units. While Loan did remind Porter that it was the Province Chief's prerogative to deploy police assets as he saw fit, he was sensitive to the Deputy Ambassador's concerns. Porter indicated that given their extensive support for the NP, the US wished to see the NPFF adhering to its 'agreed upon mission...in rural areas undergoing pacification'. Specifically, Porter suggested that the NPFF be linked to the Revolutionary Development program, the principal mechanism for pacification in rural Vietnam. In response, Loan candidly detailed his inability to secure 'across the board cooperation from many of the Province Chiefs'.[62]

58 Ibid., pp. 2, 9-10. See also NARA: 'Republic of South Vietnam National Police Field Force 1971', p. 1.
59 NARA: 'Briefing on GVN National Police and Public Safety Division', pp. 9-10.
60 For specific examples of improper deployment at the provincial level see NARA: RG 286 A1 E31, Box 53, IPS 3, 'Vietnam Inspection Tour Report of Frank Walton Chief, Vietnam Division, Office of Public Safety October 1967', pp. 7, 22.
61 NARA: 'PIOCC/DIOCC Coordinator Briefing', p. 1. See also NARA: 'Republic of South Vietnam National Police Field Force 1971', p.1 and OPS, 'Public Safety Program', p. 34.
62 NARA: RG 286 A1 E32, Box 24, IPS 2-1 Staff Reports, 1966-1968, IPS 2-1 Correspondence, 1967, 'National Police Field Force Support for Revolutionary Development', pp. 1-2.

Initially, with Loan's endorsement, Porter suggested that the Office of Civil Operations directly approach the Minister of Revolutionary Development, General Nguyen Duc Thang.[63] The goal was to get the NPFF into the field and the means to do so would be support for Revolutionary Development, a program widely endorsed and engaged with by the National Police, Province and District Chiefs, and US agencies. However, this initiative proved short-lived, as by the spring of 1967, Revolutionary Development as the program of choice for re-focusing the NPFF had been overshadowed.[64]

On 9 May 1967 CORDS assumed responsibility for coordinating US pacification efforts from the national to village levels.[65] By mid-June, the Deputy for CORDS (DEPCORDS), Ambassador Robert Komer, was already beginning his push to re-target paramilitary policing. In a memorandum to MACV Commander General William Westmoreland, he clearly laid out his intention to recast the structure, roles, and missions of the NPFF to reflect his own notions of counterinsurgency.[66]

63 The Office of Civil Operations (OCO) as established in November 1966 with a civilian leadership in an effort to coordinate civilian pacification programs. OCO would be unable to achieve its aim but did reinforce Robert Komer's view that a successful pacification program would necessarily require the resources of MACV. See Hunt, *Pacification*, pp. 71-85.

64 By April 1967, PSD understood that ARVN, in particular territorial RF/PF units, would now take the lead role in RD thus allowing the 'NPFF...to play a more significant role in the attack on the VC political cadres and not to overly concern itself with security in heavily contested areas.' NARA: RG 286 A1 E32, Box 24, IPS 2-1 Staff Reports, 1966-1968, IPS 2-1, Action Programs, 1967-1968, 'Letter from John F. Manopoli, Chief PSD-CORDS to Director Byron Engle, OPS-AID 6 July 1967'. See also NARA: RG 286 A1 E32, Box 7, IPS 1 Territorial Security, Local Security, 1969-1971, MACCORDS-PS, 'Standing Operating Procedures for NPFF', 29 September 1967.

65 For an excellent study of CORDS see Hunt, *Pacification*. See also Clarke, Jeffrey, *Advice and Support: The Final Years, 1965-1973* (Washington, DC: Center for Military History, 1988). For a briefer outline see Andrade, Dale and Willbanks, James H., 'CORDS/Phoenix: Counterinsurgency Lessons from Vietnam for the Future', *Military Review*, March-April 2006, pp. 9-23. Contemporary studies are found in: Office of Public Safety, AID, Department of State, 'Background on US MACCORDS', Washington, DC, 23 January 1969; Office of Public Safety, AID, Department of State, Joseph Mendenhall, 'US Government, USAID; and, US CORDS Objectives and Organization in Vietnam', Washington, DC, 22 July 1969 and Office of Public Safety, AID, Department of State, G.D. Jacobson, 'Organization and function: Assistant Chief of Staff for Civil Operation and Rural Development Support', Washington, DC, 25 November 1970.

66 Komer, Robert, 'Memorandum From the Deputy for Civil Operations and Revolutionary Development (Komer) to the Commander, Military Assistance Command, Vietnam (Westmoreland)', in Sieg, Kent (ed.), *Foreign Relations of the United States, 1964–1968, Vietnam, 1967*, Vol. V (Washington, DC: United States Government Printing Office, 2002), Document 199. See also NARA: RG 286 A1 E32, Box 24, IPS 2-1 Staff Reports, 1966-1968, IPS 2-1, Action Programs, 1967-1968, 'Public Safety Division Action Program: FY 1968', p. 1.

For Komer, destroying the Vietcong Infrastructure (VCI) was the essential element of pacification and its prosecution primarily a 'police type matter'.[67] Consequently, he proposed that the Police Special Branch (PSB), the GVN agency with 'the greatest intelligence capability in this field', be paired with a refocused NPFF. The force would act as PSB's 'chief exploitation arm' to locate and eradicate the VCI in areas undergoing pacification.[68] Komer's initiatives were welcome news to PSD. Indeed, as early as April 1967, PSD Chief John Manopoli had ordered a 'complete re-evaluation of the NPFF' and shared the Ambassador's belief that 'the civil police have a major role to play in pacification, particularly as the most potent weapon to be directed against the VC infrastructure'.[69] The overall program, a means to coordinate NP units and Province and District Chiefs, would be the Intelligence Coordination and Exploitation Program (ICEX) and, in time, Phung Hoang (PHOENIX).

Komer did realize that by creating a police-run intelligence network he risked establishing two 'intelligence chains', one military (tactical) and the other civil (anti-infrastructure), but he argued duplication would be minimal. Further, he assured Westmoreland of his intention to 'personally monitor and if necessary manage this experiment'.[70] Convinced of the centrality of anti-VCI operations as key to pacification, Komer had sought assistance from the Central Intelligence Agency (CIA) on 'how to mount a more effective attack, especially at the critical district and provincial levels'. After consultation with the CIA, he set about 're-vamping' and redeploying the

67 Ibid. Komer stated: 'In my judgment, attack on the infrastructure is—in both its intelligence and exploitation aspects—primarily a police-type measure.' See Andrade, *Ashes to Ashes*, pp. 1-14 for an excellent overview of the Vietcong Infrastructure.

68 Komer, 'Memorandum from the Deputy for Civil Operations and Revolutionary Development'. CORDS-PSD understood that pacification was carried out in three stages and that not all areas were in the same stage. The problem is to create and enforce a SOP applicable in all stages and nation-wide. For the three stages see NARA: RG 286 A1 E32, Box 24, IPS 2-1 Staff Reports, 1966-1968, IPS 2-1, Action Programs, 1967-1968, 'Major Police Problems: Retargeting the NPFF', 5 July 1967, TAB A. Initially, the NPFF acted on intelligence collected, collated and evaluated by PSB supported by a Province Interrogation Center (PIC), the precursor of the PIOCC/DIOCC. See NARA RG 286 A1 E32, Box 24, IPS 2-1 Staff Reports, 1966-1968, IPS 2-1 Correspondence, 1967, 'Annex J: Attack on the VC Infrastructure to Combined Campaign Plan, 1968, AB 143', p. J-3. Komer also included the use of Provincial Reconnaissance Units (PRU) as an additional action arm.

69 NARA: 'Letter from John F. Manopoli, Chief PSD-CORDS to Director Byron Engle, OPS-AID'. See also NARA: RG 286 A1 E32, Box 24, IPS 2-1 Staff Reports, 1966-1968, IPS 2-1, Action Programs, 1967-1968, 'Letter from John F. Manopoli, Chief PSD-CORDS to Frank E. Walton, Chief Vietnam Division, OPS-AID 10 July 1967' and Hunt, *Pacification*, pp. 112-113, 116.

70 Komer, 'Memorandum from the Deputy for Civil Operations and Revolutionary Development'. In a 1970 reflection a largely unapologetic Robert Komer 'pled guilty to over-managing' but maintained that it helped create a 'sense of dynamism' within CORDS. See Komer, Robert, *Organization and Management of the 'New Model' Pacification Program, 1966-1969* (Santa Monica: RAND, 1970), pp. 239-240.

NPFF, even if it this set him at odds with the DGNP for NPFF, Lieutenant Colonel Pham Huy Sanh.[71]

In Komer's view the real struggle for 'hearts and minds', and thus the battlefield of pacification, was at the district level. Previously, he argued districts had been overlooked or ignored, and operations on the whole followed a 'shotgun approach', centered on cordon and search operations.[72] To effectively combat the VCI, he maintained, an 'operational concept at the cutting edge…analogous to a 'rifle shot' should be adopted'. PSB developed intelligence would engender 'quick reaction operations aimed at individual cadre or at most small groups' thereby allowing the NPFF to '[Cut] off the heads of the infrastructure at local levels' and to ultimately 'degrade the whole structure'.[73] To that end, Komer proposed a three-stage plan: concept approval, program development, and presentation of the new plan to the GVN.

On 24 July 1967 Komer had reached the second stage as he unveiled his new action program, dubbed Project TAKEOFF.[74] This plan reflected the Ambassador's belief

71 Komer noted: 'Therefore, I had CIA in Washington do a study for me on how to mount a more effective attack on VC infrastructure, especially at the critical district and province levels. I have since personally revised the study with CORDS and OSA help'. Komer also sought the expertise of the Office of Strategic Analysis (OSI): OSA: Office of systems analysis: 'I think this sound, because anti-infrastructure intelligence and operations are primarily a police-type matter, and OSA has extensive expertise. Thus, on the principle of choosing the best project manager, I chose OSA. But at each level the operation will come under the relevant commander.' Memorandum from the Deputy for Civil Operations and Revolutionary Development (Komer) to the Commander, Military Assistance Command, Vietnam (Westmoreland), Attachment, Saigon, 14 June 1967, https://history.state.gov/historicaldocuments/frus1964-68v05/d199. See also Komer, *Organization and Management*, p. 64.

72 For a detailed narrative of one such combined operation see Blake, Philip, 'Cordon and Search' in *Infantry Magazine* (ed.), *A Distant Challenge: The US Infantryman in Vietnam, 1967-1972* (Nashville: The Battery Press, 1983), pp. 39-43.

73 While Komer did acknowledge the significance of the provincial level, he argued the need to work at both levels. To that end, he called for the creation of 'pilot DIOCC in all corps areas and revitalize the PICC (sic) and target them at the VC infrastructure.' Records of the Virtual Vietnam Center Archive, Texas Tech University, US Marine Corps Division Vietnam War Documents Collection, 'Project TAKEOFF, Vol. II', http://www.virtualarchive.vietnam.ttu.edu/, Item 1201065024, pp. VII-13. See also Komer, *Organization and Management*, pp. 64-70.

74 In mid-June, Komer had already informed Westmoreland of his intention of focusing part of the new plan on 'rooting out' the VCI remarking 'I propose to make it part of Project TAKEOFF.' See Komer, 'Memorandum From the Deputy for Civil Operations and Revolutionary Development'. In 1970 Komer claimed that the program 'was the guideline directive for the new pacification program and priorities. It was the bible for what pressed on the Vietnamese all up and down the line. It unified our key advisory guidance from Saigon level to district.' Komer, *Organization and Management*, p. 64. For their part, the GVN in general expressed a 'lukewarm' response to TAKEOFF. However, in mid-August 1967 at meeting involving Westmoreland, Bunker, Komer, Ky, Vien, and Thang, the

that GVN leadership, at all levels, had proven incapable of managing the war effort, and highlighted eight priority programs to receive particular attention and support from CORDS.[75] The end result, Komer argued, was to 'give pacification a new thrust' and push the GVN to develop its own plans in accordance with the project's principles.[76] While TAKEOFF specifically detailed a need to overhaul the NP, the Ambassador recognized that the project would need to focus initially on three rather than eight areas: local security, Revolutionary Development, and eradicating the VCI.[77] For Komer, the tip of the spear would be the NPFF.[78]

As part of Project TAKEOFF, Komer insisted that the NPFF be expanded and reorganized and that changes in both force structure and standard operating procedures should focus solely on improving VCI neutralization.[79] Further, deployment would be largely fixed at the provincial level where adjustments to meet local challenges could most effectively be made.[80] Almost immediately, he felt challenged by the very organization he looked to transform.

On 12 August, new NP authored standard operating procedures circulated that seemingly showed a very different view of the NPFF than that envisioned by TAKEOFF. The new program did contain similar language but with key differences in expectations and application. The standard operating procedures stated that the eventual objective was to extend police activities into all rural areas and laid out the NPFF's missions as:

Vietnamese leadership indicated that they were 'also contemplating some reorganization of its pacification program' that included a 'more direct attack on the VCI along the lines outlined by Ambassador Komer.' See Bunker, Ellsworth, 'Telegram from the Embassy in Vietnam to the Department of State, 3243 16 August 1967', in Sieg, Kent (ed.), *Foreign Relations of the United States, 1964–1968, Vietnam, 1967*, Vol. V (Washington, DC: United States Government Printing Office, 2002), Document 280. For the 'lukewarm' response see TTVN: 'Project TAKEOFF', p. 2.

75 Ibid., pp. XII-2. See also Hunt, *Pacification*, p. 113.

76 TTVN: 'Project TAKEOFF, Briefing on Project TAKEOFF', Slide A.

77 See Jones, Frank, *Blowtorch: Robert Komer, Vietnam, and American Cold War Strategy* (Annapolis: Naval Institute Press, 2013). See also Carafano, James Jay and Richard Weitz, *Mismanaging Mayhem: How Washington Responds to Crisis* (Westport: Praeger, 2007), pp. 451-481.

78 NARA: RG 286 A1 E32, Box 45, IPS 2-2 Program Surveys, 1966-1969, IPS 2-3 NPFI Survey and Reorganization of NPFF, 1967, 'Project TAKEOFF Action Program to Revamp Police and NPFF: Retarget the NPFF Towards the VC Infrastructure'. He also included the PRU. See also Komer, *Organization and Management*, p. 67, and Hunt, *Pacification*, p. 104.

79 The NPFF component of TAKEOFF called for 22,500 policemen deployed as 110 companies by the end of 1968. RG 286 A1 E32, Box 45, IPS 2-2 Program Surveys, 1966-1969, IPS 2-3 NPFI Survey and Reorganization of NPFF, 1967, 'Re-organization of NPFF', 9 December 1967, p.2. See also NARA: 'Project TAKEOFF Action Program to Revamp Police and NPFF' and TTVN: 'Project TAKEOFF', p. 3.

80 NARA: 'Letter from John F. Manopoli, Chief PSD-CORDS to Frank E. Walton, Chief Vietnam Division, OPS-AID', p. 2.

1. The action arm of the Special Police Branch, locate and eliminate the VC infrastructure.
2. To operate as the search element in joint FW/ARVN/NPFF cordon and search operations.
3. To provide area security…through continuous day patrols and night ambushes.
4. To operate mobile checkpoints.
5. To perform all possible civil police functions.[81]

Ambassador Komer immediately rejected the proposed standard operating procedures as out of step with Project TAKEOFF, both in terms of prioritizing anti-VCI operations and achieving the reorganization necessary to do so. In effect, Komer believed that responsibility for multiple missions would lead to overall paralysis. While acknowledging that it was 'better than the previous SOP' he rejected it as failing to clearly target the VCI. Further, Komer ordered Manopili to begin reworking the Standard Operating Procedures so 'that the entire NPFF organization, as well as province and district chiefs, understands that the new primary mission of the NPFF was to be the action arm of the PSB'.[82]

Manopili quickly responded to Komer's criticism by pointing out that indeed, this is precisely what the new standard operating procedures did do, but that the translation of the document from Vietnamese appeared less 'forceful and…complete to an English speaker'. Despite the GVN's general 'lukewarm reaction' to Project TAKEOFF, the PSD Chief assured his boss that the NPFF leadership was fully behind the program. He concluded by predicting that the impending reorganization to facilitate the emphasis on anti-VCI operations would reinforce this.[83] By year's end, however, both men would be disappointed.[84]

81 The newly expanded SOP was circulated 12 August 1967 as NPFF #SO: 5.6.1 /TCSQG/CSDC/VP, 12 August 1967. See Records of the Virtual Vietnam Center Archive, Texas Tech University (TTVN), Douglas Pike Collection: Unit 06, Democratic Republic of Vietnam, 'MACCORDS-PS, Letter to MACV VII B, CORDS 'C', PSD/NPFF from MG Walter Kerwin, Chief of Staff, 'Guidelines for Advice of National Police Field Forces 18 April 1968', <http://www.virtualarchive.vietnam.ttu.edu/>, Item 2321601008, p. 1. The SOP is also clearly detailed in NARA: RG 286 A1 E32, Box 45, IPS 2-2 Program Surveys, 1966-1969, IPS 2-3, NPFI Survey and Reorganization of NPFF, 1967, 'Reorganization of NPFF 9 December 1967', p. 1.

82 NARA: RG 286 A1 E32, Box 7, IPS 1 Territorial Security, Local Security, 1969-1971, 'Letter from R.W. Komer to John Manopoli 26 September 1967'.

83 Manopoli pointed out that translation problems were also at the heart of the 1965 NPFF Concept. The problem he stated was that the translation from English to Vietnamese did not convey in strong enough terms the proper use of the NPFF. Consequently, an interpretative 'loop-hole' existed in which a Province/District Chief might prioritize the use of NPFF assets that amounted to static defense and, in PSD view, misuse. See NARA: 'Standing Operating Procedures for NPFF'

84 Interestingly, in October, DGNP General Nguyen Ngoc Loan met with top PSD officials Frank Walton and John Manopoli in Saigon. During the meeting, Loan detailed his

At an ICEX conference on 5 December 1967, Lieutenant Colonel Sanh unveiled his new force deployment scheme intended to accompany his earlier standard operating procedures. With an eye to eventually extending police activities into all rural areas, Sanh proposed 'layering' the NPFF from district to corps, with the bulk of forces at the provincial and corps level. The proposal maintained that to best ensure overall control and prevent misuse, district platoons were to be organic elements of provincial companies and assigned to areas 'considered suitable by the Special Branch for their primary mission of eliminating the VC infrastructure'. However, while anti-VCI operations were placed at the fore, Sanh made it clear that with the majority of units held at provincial and corps level, the NPFF's other missions would not be overlooked. Importantly, Sanh contended that NPFF missions varied in importance depending upon the intensity of insurgent activity in a particular area. Consequently, establishing a range of missions ensured that the NPFF did 'not sit idle when not employed as the Special Branch action arm, but must perform its other missions if total pacification is to be realized'.[85] To carry out their missions, Sanh proposed an NPFF initially consisting of 25,920 personnel and increasing to 30,000 by 1969. The plan envisioned a one platoon per district scheme covering 249 districts (249 platoons of 44 men), 47 provincial companies (at 185 men), four battalions at the corps level, and a single battalion in the Capital Military District (five battalions of 1,314).

Despite PSD's view that the new scheme was 'completely unrealistic' in terms of manpower, no objections were raised at the meeting. A response from DEPCORDS came quickly. After receiving a report from Manopoli a few days later summarizing Sanh's plan, Komer's response was blistering: 'Disapproved. I do <u>not</u> like Sanh's plan at all and won't support it'. He continued: 'If DGNP insists on retaining the area security mission the least we can do is...make it clear that area security is undertaken only as an adjunct to performance of police functions'.[86] By this he meant neutralizing the VCI. In terms of both missions and the organization, CORDS/PSD and the NPFF command were very far apart.

For PSD, more critical than the particulars of the reorganization plan was that Sahn had 'packaged' standard operating procedures with it. Their concern was that an overhaul would lose sight of the NPFF's real job, anti-VCI operations, and

view that the NPFF's function remained twofold: supporting the uniformed police and exploiting intelligence gathered by the Special Branch. In essence, the NPFF would continue its mission of extending GVN influence into the countryside by providing area security and would also continue on offensive, targeting the VCI in collaboration with the PSB. NARA: 'Vietnam Inspection Tour Report of Frank Walton Chief, Vietnam Division, Office of Public Safety October 1967', p. 2. For lukewarm reaction more generally see Project TAKEOFF, p. 2.

85 NARA: 'Re-organization of NPFF 9 December 1967', p. 1.

86 NARA: RG 286 A1 E32, Box 45, IPS 2-2 Program Surveys, 1966-1969, IPS 2-3 NPFI Survey and Reorganization of NPFF, 1967, R.W. Komer, 'Re-organization of NPFF 28 December 1967'.

remove the most effective means of doing this, namely units deployed selectively in relation to the intensity of insurgent activity.[87] Sanh's scheme proposed three levels of police deployment: district platoons, provincial companies, and corps battalions, effectively ensuring diffused rather than centralized control. Citing the need to retain a straightforward chain of command from corps battalion to provincial battalion to company, PSD feared that without it the NPFF 'would be continuously misused'.[88] Only with a chain of command that linked commanders from province to corps could proper utilization be assured.

Komer's central objection was to the 'one size fits all' deployment. While he agreed with Sanh that the NPFF could not effectively attack the VCI in company strength, he maintained that every district did not require a platoon nor did provinces need both company and district platoons. Rather than a universal layering scheme, deployment should be flexible and justified functionally.[89] To that end, PSD proposed a 'more realistic approach to the district platoon concept' in which platoons would be assigned to a province company dependent on the number of 'sufficiently pacified districts to permit NPFF operations'.[90] In early January, despite reservations on the reorganization plan, Komer indicated that he was open to discussing a modified solution with Sanh.[91] However, no new 1968 standard operating procedures were forthcoming and by year's end, both he and Sanh had been replaced.

In the absence of specific anti-VCI focused standard operating procedures, PSD turned to advisors as the only viable mechanism for refocusing efforts, approving objectives, and achieving the necessary interagency coordination. In April, PSD circulated to its advisors 'Guidelines for Advice of National Police Field Forces' to address the ongoing problem of the misuse of the NPFF, particularly at the hands of Province Chiefs.[92] The NPFF's function was clearly and directly stated: 'eliminate the VC infrastructure in districts, villages and hamlets' as the primary PHOENIX

87 NARA: 'Project TAKEOFF Action Program to Revamp Police and NPFF'.

88 NARA: RG 286 A1 E32, Box 45, IPS 2-2 Program Surveys, 1966-1969, IPS 2-3 NPFI Survey and Reorganization of NPFF, 1967, 'Draft: Re-organization of NPFF 6 December 1967', p. 4.

89 NARA: 'Re-organization of NPFF 28 December 1967'. For Komer and his CORDS and PSD staff this meant the force structure detailed in TAKEOFF.

90 NARA: 'Draft: Re-organization of NPFF 6 December 1967', p. 3.

91 NARA: RG 286 A1 E32, Box 45, IPS 2-2 Program Surveys, 1966-1969, IPS 2-3 NPFI Survey and Reorganization of NPFF, 1967, 'Re-organization of NPFF 8 January 1968'.

92 TTVN: 'Guidelines for Advice of National Police Field Forces'. The Guidelines covered ten areas: Purpose, Concept, Organization, Responsibilities, Relationships, Recruiting, Training, Operational Procedures, Logistics and Construction. See also NARA: 'DGNP Organization and Administration Assessment 6 September 1968', p. 2 and NARA: RG 286 A1 E32 Box 76 IPS 12 Police Administration 1973 through 1974, IPS 12 FP History Key Details 1965-1972, 'Fact Sheet: National Police and Police Field Forces 31 May, 1967', p. 2.

exploitation force, even at the expense of other police duties.[93] It argued that only once the insurgents were neutralized, could the NPFF carry out 'continuous day and night patrols and ambushes' to prevent a NLF resurgence and safeguard the extension of a uniformed NP presence into the countryside.[94] Advisors were also reminded of their primary responsibility to insure that the Province Chiefs properly utilized NPFF units to that end. By April 1968, PSD's efforts to re-target the NPFF were largely in place and Manopoli quickly moved to settle the outstanding issue of force levels and deployment levels and locations.

In mid-June, DGNP Colonel Tran Van Hai met with Manopoli to discuss the ongoing 'problems of organization, administration, operation and training' that PSD 'continually signaled in writing'.[95] During the meeting, the PSD Chief suggested he provide a corrective action plan, an offer Hai accepted. One such plan focused specifically on the NPFF and offered a remedy to the earlier Sanh-Komer exchange. While initially presented as recommendations, the plan called for a reexamination of NPFF deployment to better facilitate anti-VCI operations. By September PSD had resolved to push for the assignment of at least one company per province to target the VCI at district level and below.[96] Further, PSD also advocated that platoons be required to carry out missions regularly at the district level and below based on intelligence developed by PSB in the District Intelligence and Operations Coordinating Centers (DIOCC). In sum, the goal was to ensure proper utilization and reduce 'inappropriate missions' such as static defense.[97]

By mid-summer 1968, Komer and PSD had institutionalized the primacy of anti-VCI operations by linking the NPFF to the PHOENIX program.[98] Proper

93 NARA: RG 286 A1 E32 Box 7, IPS 1: General Policy, Guidelines and Background, 1969 through 1971, IPS 1, 'Public Safety Sector Analysis 13 September 1968', p. 1. A fuller study of Phung Hoang can be found in Andrade, *Ashes to Ashes*, and Moyar, Mark, *Phoenix and the Birds of Prey* (Lincoln: University of Nebraska Press, 1997).

94 TTVN: 'Guidelines for Advice of National Police Field Forces', pp. 1-8. Providing a reserve for riot control and civil disturbances was also included in the list of functions.

95 NARA: RG 286 A1 E32, Box 45, IPS 2-2, Program Surveys, 1966-1969, 'Letter from John F. Manopoli, Chief, PSD-CORDS to DGNP Colonel Tran Van Hai 28 June 1968', p. 1.

96 NARA: 'Public Safety Sector Analysis 13 September 1968', p. 26. Further, deployment of additional units in the Province was seen as contingent on the pacification status and the established priority of a province.

97 NARA: RG 286 A1 E32, Box 45, IPS 2-2, Program Surveys, 1966-1969, 'Public Safety Division Action Programs: National Police Field Force', p. 2.

98 Decree No. 161 SL/AN, Republic of Vietnam, Office of the Central Executive Committee, date 30 October 1967 and Decree No. 280-a/TT/SL, Republic of Vietnam, Office of the President, date 1 July 1968, SECRET. A translation of the decree was filed with NARA: 'DGNP Organization and Administration Assessment 6 September 1968'. The NPPF function of providing 'armed support of Special Police in the operational destruction of armed terrorists and enemy saboteurs' was specified by the GVN's Central Executive Committee NP Decree in October 1967 and linked to establishment

utilization now had a single definition: 'armed terrorists', the VCI would be specifically targeted by PHOENIX with the NPFF acting as the exploitation force. All 'additional functions' would now be considered as extensions of this. In terms of overall anti-VCI doctrine, Komer had realized his vision of a civil police force as the centerpiece of his 'New Model' pacification, and he used a GVN decree to do it. In short order, PSD had incorporated both PHOENIX and the need to re-target the NPFF as its action arm as key program priorities going forward. For both PSD and the NPFF hierarchy, however, the issue of misuse and the absence of a means to enforce doctrinal compliance remained unresolved issues.[99] At the lowest levels, province and district Chiefs continued to ignore orders, ensuring persistent misuse of the NPFF. Yet again, to enforce conformity PSD was forced to rely on the only tools available to US agencies: increased use of advisors and the rewriting of policies.[100]

1969-1971: Full Circle

The February 1968 Tet Offensive shattered General Westmoreland's assessment that victory was within reach. Simultaneously, however, Tet also proved disastrous for the NLF and their northern compatriots. Indeed, despite the initial shock of the offensive (and attendant media coverage in the United States), communist forces

of PHOENIX established by Presidential Decree 1 July 1968. In essence, the 'armed terrorists' detailed in 1967 would be the VCI specifically targeted by the program, establishing the NPFF as the exploitation force for PSB and PHOENIX. All 'additional functions' would now be considered as extensions of this function. See also Hunt, *Pacification*, p. 113.

99 NARA: RG 286 A1 E32 Box 7, IPS 1: General Policy, Guidelines and Background, 1969 through 1971, IPS 1: Public Safety Sector Analysis, 1969, 'Public Safety Program – II Corps 13 September 1968', p. 11.

100 PSD understood that at 'present US influence on Vietnamese performance is dependent on our ability to persuade, cajole, suggest or plead.' NARA: Project TAKEOFF, p. XI-1. The challenge of prioritizing anti-VCI operations could, in some cases, also extend very high into the top leadership of the GVN. For example, Ambassador William Colby, Komer's replacement, reported to his new boss General Abrams that: 'The Police Field Force 'is targeted specifically at the infrastructure.' He continued: 'The thing is that frankly, six months to a year ago the police were operating in their world and the military in the military and there was very little attention to the political command structure of the VC.' He stated: 'The major effort on our side to date has been organizational, to try to get this accepted as an important target. It wasn't, frankly, for a long time.' Abrams added: 'Several months ago I attended a quarterly review with General Vien. When it was all over he asked if I had any remarks to make, so I got up and made what I thought was a very stirring speech about eliminating the infrastructure. Then he got up and made a speech about Cambodia. So I realized there really wasn't a meshing of the gears.' Sorley, Lewis (ed.), *Vietnam Chronicles: The Abrams Tapes, 1968-1972* (Lubbock: Texas Tech University Press, 2004), pp. 60-61. Abrams also referred to NPFF in I CTZ conducting combined operations with ARVN and RF/PF stating: 'and that's the people [NPFF] that can really root these people [infrastructure] out.' Ibid., p. 71.

failed to hold military objectives or foment an anticipated general uprising. As early as March 1968 Komer argued that the NLF had failed to ensure 'pacification's demise' and that losses had created a 'vacuum' that severely weakened their position in the countryside.[101] Sensing an opportunity to consolidate and extend GVN influence into contested and communist controlled areas Komer pushed throughout the summer for new 'political-pacification program'.[102] Despite initially facing significant resistance in both Washington and Saigon, his efforts resulted in a comprehensive pacification plan: Accelerated Pacification Campaign (APC).[103]

Beginning on 1 November 1968 with the launching of the APC and the National Pacification Development Plan (NPDP), PSD embraced the programs and undertook a concerted effort to find an answer to the execution problem.[104] The solution would overturn the 1968 decision to deploy one company per province to carry out 'priority tasks against the VCI at district level and below'.[105]

The ambitious post-Tet NPDP asserted that the war had reached a turning point in which the GVN was 'now stronger then we have ever been, and the enemy is at his weakest period'. For Saigon, the way forward was to secure 90 percent of the population at the hamlet and village level, establish local government and defense, and encourage rural development. Unsurprisingly, eliminating the VCI through PHOENIX and military operations remained a critical prerequisite for pacification.[106]

Along with the NPDP, in 1969 the primacy of anti-VCI operations, already in practice, was finally enshrined in new standard operating procedures.[107] While the role of the NPFF remained essentially unchanged, missions were prioritized as:

101 Komer's full assessment of Tet and the APC is best expressed in Komer, *Organization and Management*, pp. 76-93. See also Hunt, *Pacification*, pp. 136-143.

102 For an in-depth study of pacification and the APC see Hunt, *Pacification*, pp. 144-207.

103 For General Abrams' initial reticence see ibid., pp. 149-152, and for the Vietnamese view see pp. 156-159.

104 See Jones, *Blowtorch*, pp. 190-214, and Komer, *Organization and Management*, pp.76-93. See also Sorley, Lewis, *A Better War: The Unexamined Victories and Final Tragedy of America's Last Years in Vietnam* (Orlando: Harcourt, 1999), p. 65-69, 72-79, 193.

105 NARA: 'Public Safety Sector Analysis 13 September 1968', pp. 25-26.

106 Republic of Vietnam Central Pacification and Development Council, 'Guidelines for Pacification Campaign', 15 December 1968, pp. 1-7. The NPDP specially called for the elimination of 33,000 VCI 'under the Phoenix Program and other joint operations conducted by Police and Army units.' An excellent analysis of the Accelerated Pacification Campaign is found in Hunt, *Pacification*, pp. 157-159, 172, 197-207.

107 NARA: 'The Role and Mission of the NPFF', p. 5. More generally, 1969 marked a turning in the GVN's views on the NP and pacification. After 'years of neglect...the GVN has made concerted efforts to provide the police a more proper balance in share of the nation's manpower and financial resources.' Further, a series of Presidential decrees worked to redesign and reorganize the police structure to promote increased prestige, more effective operations, coordination and manpower. The NPFF was certainly a key part of this shift. Finally, after years in planning by both the NP and PSD, the Prime Minister pushed forward a National Police Statute to 'formalize the NPC and its relationships with other

1. To support and cooperate with the Special Police Branch collecting, compiling, exploiting intelligence and destroying VC Infrastructure (the primary mission).
2. To support resource control operations.
3. To support the pacification program.
4. To control riots and other civil disturbances.[108]

In order to fully carry out their operations, and in line with the broader 'district and below' focus, the NPDP called for NPFF redeployment. In essence, the rigid company per province model failed, as there were not enough platoons to allow for full coverage of all districts. At best, a single company could supply enough men for only three districts. Further, as mobile provincial forces rather than district elements, they were unaccustomed to working consistently with a specific district chief, DIOCC, or other allied units.[109] To align deployment with the overall 'village war' focus, the plan mandated that each District (and therefore DIOCC) receive a NPFF platoon. Given that there were 47 Provinces and 263 Districts with 50 NPFF companies assigned at the Provincial level, the DGNP dissolved PFF battalions in CTZ I and III to reinforce units 'at the district level and below'.[110]

Significantly, while the overall NPDP was a GVN initiative, the redeployment and placement of 'one platoon per district in support of the DIOCC' was wholly a US idea and implemented 'after urging by MACCORDS and the Director, PHOENIX'. Certainly, the shift bore some similarity to Sanh's 1967 plan, but

government agencies' and decouple it from the 'lethargic Vietnamese Civil Service'. Such changes, PSD believed, would both empower a clear NP mandate and put an end to the shifts in 'management and operation' that accompanied changes in the GVN administration. NARA: RG 286 A1 E31, Box 230, IPS 1-1: Briefing Materials, 1971-1972, IPS 1-1 Historical References Miscellaneous Folder I, 1970-1971, 'Fact Sheet: Public Safety Program—Vietnam', pp. 1-8.

108 NARA: 'The Role and Mission of the NPFF', p. 2. For a full explanation and examples resource control operations see 'The Role of Public Safety', pp. 7-8.

109 Republic of Vietnam Central Pacification and Development Council, *Guidelines for Pacification Campaign* (Saigon: 15 December 1968), Annex II, pp. 1-2. This also meant that the Provincial Chief could more readily continue the pattern of misuse or improper deployment as had long been noted.

110 Ibid., pp. 1-2. The problem of proper utilization was, by late 1968, compounded by a NP (and NPFF) manpower shortage and PSD acknowledged that the plan was a 'calculated risk' and required 'that all assets were spread thinly.' NARA: RG 286 A1 E32 Box 19, IPS 2 Audit Reports January-August 1971, Pacification Research Report NPFF 1969-1971, MACCORDS-PS, 'National Police 5 February 1969'. The program called for the NPFF manpower shortage to be addressed in the short term with the transfer to policemen aged 18-20. In the longer term, the plan vaguely called for the creation of thirteen new units in 1969. See NARA: RG 286 A1 E32 Box 19, IPS 2 Audit Reports 13 January-August 1971, Pacification Research Report NPFF 1969-1971, MACCORDS-PS, 'Letter from CORDS-PSD Chief John Manopoli to DGNP Colonel Tran Van Hai 13 February 1969', p. 2.

Komer's stamp is clearly in evidence as the new deployment scheme was intended to work in conjunction with the newly established PHOENIX program centered on the DIOCC. For its part, the DGNP and Assistant DGNP for NPFF 'aggressively and enthusiastically supported and implemented the 1969 Pacification Plan as written'.[111] All that remained was the necessary 'refinement' to coordinate managerial planning with operational realities.

In early January 1969, Komer's DEPCORDS successor William Colby noted that while the US mandated DIOCC-focused redeployment marked an important step forward, it also proved a 'further example of our tendency...to divide the war into neat little geographic pieces'.[112] For Colby, the plan failed to take into account a district's size, population, or the level of insurgent activity. He urged PSD to propose modifications to the scheme that empowered the 'NPFF...to do its real job against the VCI' in areas most important to overall pacification and under the most threat from insurgents.[113]

PSD's response to Colby's request revealed an even deeper concern over the gap between planning and application than that expressed by the DEPCORDS. Operational analysis, Manopoli reported, produced three key findings. First, virtually all NPFF operations targeting the VCI and based on DIOCC/PSB intelligence were conducted by platoon-sized units or smaller, regardless of an area's pacification priority. Second, again regardless of a district's priority, DIOCC's failed to generate sufficient, specific targets to 'keep more than one platoon occupied on its primary mission'. Third, there was little relation between an area's priority and VCI 'yield', or between population and neutralizations.[114] Consequently, PSD feared that the 1969 redeployment, while in line with both the NPDP and PHOENIX's district focus, would simply replicate the problem of NPFF misuse. Their fears were almost immediately proven correct.

PSD's policy decisions had determined the NPFF's primary target was the VCI and moved them into the firing line in the districts.[115] The problem, however, remained operational and interagency coordination, not whether or where targets existed but rather whether DIOCC and PSB could accurately identify them and pass actionable

111 NARA: 'National Police 5 February 1969'.
112 NARA: RG 286 A1 E32 Box 19, IPS 2 Audit Reports January-August 1971, Pacification Research Report NPFF 1969-1971, DEPCORDS-MACV W.E. Colby, 'Memorandum to ACofS, CORDS: National Police', 20 January 1969. Komer noted that he had groomed Colby as his 'hand-picked successor', a move supported by both Ambassador Bunker and General Abrams. See R. Komer, *Organization and Management*, p. 92.
113 Komer, *Organization and Management*, p. 92.
114 NARA: 'National Police 5 February 1969'.
115 NARA: RG 286 A1 E32, Box 71, IPS 12 Police Administration, 1971, IPS 12, Field Police Briefing, 'Phoenix Coordinators Orientation Course', p. 5. NARA: 'Republic of South Vietnam National Police Field Force 1971', pp. 5-6.

intelligence on to the NPFF.[116] For PSD the problem was twofold. First, PSD worried that deploying to 'districts in excess of the demonstrated capability of the DIOCC to utilize them' risked returning units to static defense of a district town rather than provincial city. Second, at both the provincial (company) and district (platoon) level, many advisors maintained that the significant reason for the perceived NPFF's poor performance rested with the DIOCC and PSB's 'poor, slow or non-existent intelligence and targeting'.[117] Essentially, NPFF units proved valuable and effective if those 'responsible for targeting...started doing their job'.[118] In the absence of specific targets, platoons were largely tasked from the provincial (company) level with extended cordon and search operations that only marginally impacted the VCI while producing the perception (and complaints) that they were 'doing nothing' else. For some District PSD advisors, the solution was straightforward: follow the already established standard operating procedures of acting on PSB developed intelligence while carrying out independent operations that did not require orders from the province chief. These district advisors encouraged platoons to conduct a range of missions up to four days in duration, thereby sidestepping the need to clear operations at the provincial level.

116 Throughout 1968 poor DIOCC and PSB intelligence and targeting continued to effect the volume and effectiveness of NPFF operations. Further, in some cases assigned units failed to receive regular missions at all and could wait up three months without a specific target. NARA: 'Memorandum from Chief NPFF Advisor William Grieves to Director –PSD Frank Walton', p. 2. A lack of adequate, reliable and timely actionable intelligence was a primary complaint from NPFF advisors. See NARA: RG 286 A1 E32, Box 76, IPS 12, Police Administration, 1973 through 1974, IPS 12 Field Police History Key Details, 1965-1972, 'NPPF History, Part II', p. 5. As late as November 1970 the Quang Nam Province PHOENIX Briefing noted 'the apparatus of the PHOENIX (PIOCC and DIOCC'S) had not achieved the goal that its name implies...to be an intelligence and operations coordinating center for the attack on the Infrastructure. In most cases, the formal organizations...have become repositories of information, useful for studies, much like an archive. Often there is a failure to react to intelligence, or to develop the systematic pursuit of the VCI that the program invisions [sic].' The Briefing concluded by recommending that the NPFF be placed directly under the DIOCC rather than having orders channeled through the District Police Chief. Records of the Virtual Vietnam Center Archive, Texas Tech University, US Marine Corps Division Vietnam War Documents Collection, 'Quang Nam Province PHOENIX Briefing November 1970', <http://www.virtualarchive.vietnam.ttu.edu/>, Item 1201065048.

117 NARA: RG 286 A1 E32 Box 76 IPS 12 Police Administration 1973 through 1974, IPS 12 FP History Key Details 1965-1972, 'Input for 2b, Enclosure 1, Accomplishments and Problems for 1969'. See also NARA: RG 286 A1 E32 Box 76 IPS 12 Police Administration 1973 through 1974, IPS 12 FP History Key Details, 1965-1972, 'In-Depth Review of all Program Activities 15 January 1970', p. 1. NARA: 'PIOCC/DIOCC Coordinator Briefing', p. 5. NARA: RG 286 A1 E32 Box 76 IPS 12 Police Administration 1973 through 1974, IPS 12 FP History Key Details, 1965-1972, 'Fact Sheet: National Police Field Forces' 20 January 1970', pp. 2-3.

118 NARA: RG 472 Advisory Team Reports, Advisory Team 90, Box 1612, 1601-11A, NPFF File, 1970, 'NPFF Mission at District Level 18 May 1970', p. 1.

Their answer was more missions, even if shorter; thereby getting the FP into the field rather than waiting on PSB intelligence that might never arrive.[119]

Yet, PSD officials and NPFF advisors also understood that the problem was more than simply improper utilization. Getting police units 'out in the field as much as possible' was easier said than done. In some cases, insurgent activity in contested areas made it difficult for even better trained and equipped US units to operate effectively. Further, even when supplied by PHOENIX with targets, simply 'mounting up and moving out and making an arrest' proved impossible. Rather, operations required a time-consuming process of joint briefings and coordination to assure the necessary military assets were in place and friendly-fire incidents avoided.[120] In effect, anti-VCI operations were governed by broader military realities. Whatever the desires of PSD, the NPFF faced an inescapable situation in which their *raison d'être*, anti-VCI operations, were necessarily 'militarized', and the standard operating procedures trumped by insurgent action and ARVN responses. In many cases the reality was not that the NPFF failed to carry out their missions as mandated, but rather that they could not.[121]

As an immediate fix, PSD directed provincial advisors to coordinate with US personnel attached to allied agencies and, in the districts, report deficiencies to their superiors who, in turn, would take it up with the relevant agencies in Saigon.[122] By the end of 1969, despite PSD efforts and a resulting flow of directives from Saigon and CTZ authorities, problems with compliance persisted, particularly at the province and district levels. However pointed the directives, outside the capital and corps headquarters, many were simply ignored. By the beginning of 1970 PSD realized that any substantial improvement could only be achieved by increasing the number of advisors in the field rather than by issuing official directives. In short, effective interagency coordination required one US advisor with the DIOCC coordinating with another with the NPFF.[123] Over the longer term, PSD's remedy was again

119 The range of possible missions included 'day and night patrols, ambushes, cordon and search, mobile check points, riverine operations, US and Vietnamese operations, mini cav operations, refugee program and as a last resort rather than have them do nothing mobile patrols through villages and hamlets.' NARA: 'NPFF Mission at District Level 18 May 1970', p. 1.

120 NARA: RG 286 A1 E32 Box 76 IPS 12 Police Administration 1973 through 1974, IPS 12 PSD/National Field Force Police Log Frame, 1970-1975, 'Evaluation Report, National Police Field Force Thua Thien, I Corps Tactical Zone 2 October 1968'.

121 In the specific case of the NPFF in Thua Thien, the PSD evaluator rejected the claim that the companies were not properly utilized. Rather he praised their good work declaring: 'the record of VC KIA, WIA, VCI captured...more than attest to this fact.' See ibid.

122 NARA: 'Input for 2b, Enclosure 1, Accomplishments and Problems for 1969.' An excellent example of such an effort is found in NARA: 'PIOCC/DIOCC Coordinator Briefing'. For reporting to Saigon security agencies see NARA: 'In-Depth Review of all Program Activities 15 January 1970', p. 2.

123 NARA: 'In-Depth Review of all Program Activities 15 January 1970', pp. 3-4.

managerial; to 'fix' the platoon per district formula on a (provincial) case-by-case basis to fit specific 'field conditions' and an area's demonstrated ability to employ the NPFF properly. This solution, again, was broadly in line with Komer's 1967 views. Significantly, neither DEPCORDS nor PSD considered modifying the primacy of the anti-VCI focus, a turn they had worked so hard to institute. Rather, as evidenced in a congratulatory letter from Manopoli to DGNP Colonel Hai, PSD urged flexibility of deployment not mission. Indeed, despite his earlier report to Colby, the PSD Chief advised that platoons be prioritized for 'areas of maximum importance to pacification where there is a large VCI problem'.[124]

Accompanying the prioritizing of the anti-VCI mission, the NPFF structure was simplified beginning in late January 1969. To best facilitate the 'district and below' focus, 87 operational companies were formed that encompassed all provinces, four Regional Headquarters and service companies, two battalion headquarters companies, a National Headquarters, a National Service Company, and the National Training Center.[125] This restructuring abandoned the four platoons per provincial company scheme in favor of a cellular structure with a 14-man provincial headquarters and a 40-man platoon assigned to each district.[126]

The move simultaneously addressed four concerns. First, deploying platoons at the district level projected a police presence and offered security in villages. Second, moving units out of a Province Chief's immediate control reduced the possibility for misuse.[127] Third, with NPFF elements on hand, any intelligence generated by PSB

124 NARA: 'Letter from CORDS-PSD Chief John Manopoli to DGNP Colonel Tran Van Hai 13 February 1969', p. 2. In closing, Manopoli also noted that a number of ambitious province Police Chiefs had already embraced the idea by dividing platoons, with larger sub-units deployed in more prioritized areas.

125 NARA: RG 286 A1 E32, Box 76, IPS 12, Police Administration, 1973 through 1974, IPS 12 National Field Police Program, FY1973-1974, 'FY-73/74 Program Narrative', pp. 1-2.

126 NARA: RG 286 A1 E32, Box 76, IPS 12, Police Administration, 1973 through 1974, IPS 12 Field Police History Key Details, 1965-1972, FY 72/73 'Salient Budgeting Facts and Considerations'. Companies assigned to NPFF Battalions (222 Bn. and 5th Bn.) consisted of four platoons per company. NARA: RG 286 A1 E32, Box 76, IPS 12, Police Administration, 1973 through 1974, IPS 12 Field Police History Key Details, 1965-1972, FY 72/73, 'National Police Field Force Historical Summary'. Whatever the official complement, NPFF units were, almost universally, chronically understrength. See NARA: RG 286 A1 E32, Box 71, IPS 12 Police Administration, 1971, IPS 12, Field Police Briefing, 'Briefing Field Police, Vietnam', p. 5.

127 See NARA: 'NPFF History, Part II, p. 7, NARA: RG 286 A1 E32 Box 7, IPS 1: General Policy, Guidelines and Background, 1969 through 1971, IPS 1: Public Safety Sector Analysis, 1969, 'Public Safety Program—II Corps 16 September, 1968', p. 2 and NARA: RG 286 A1 E32 Box 7, IPS 1: General Policy, Guidelines and Background, 1969 through 1971, IPS 1: Public Safety Sector Analysis, 1969, 'Public Safety Program—IV Corps 16 September, 1968', p. 2. NARA: 'Republic of South Vietnam National Police Field Force 1971', p. 4.

and the DIOCC could be acted on rapidly.[128] Fourth, PSD understood that district level deployment meant a greater possibly of US advisors enjoying regular contact and opportunities to influence their proper use.[129] The effect of these changes would have a profound impact on NPFF operations.

The anti-VCI focus was the NPFF's only mission to be fully 'spelled out' and emphasized as the priority focus in both standard operating procedures and directives.[130] In short order, however, PSD quickly understood that the changes had lessened rather than increased their overall effectiveness.[131] Indeed, by 1970 an alarmed PSD noted that the central problem had shifted from misuse to very little use at all as 'many Vietnamese and US officials lost sight of the other police mission of the NPFF' as Sanh feared in 1967.[132] At the district level, police, local officials, and even some US advisors largely ignored tasking platoons with operations other than anti-VCI actions, interpreting priority of mission to mean exclusivity.[133]

Simultaneously PHOENIX consistently failed to produce sufficient operational intelligence to keep assigned security assets, including NPFF units, fully occupied with missions targeting the VCI.[134] Indeed, some platoons waited up to three months for a specific target and remained in static positions, their patrol effectiveness largely negated.[135] Further even when units did carry out missions other than anti-VCI

128 NARA: RG 286 A1 E32, Box 76, IPS 12, Police Administration, 1973 through 1974, IPS 12 Field Police History Key Details, 1965-1972, 'NPFF Summary Presentation', p. 3 and NARA: 'NPPF History, Part II', p. 5.

129 NARA: RG 286 A1 E32 Box 76 IPS 12 Police Administration 1973 through 1974, IPS 12 FP History Key Details 1965-1972, 'Police Field Forces'.

130 NARA: 'Briefing Field Police, Vietnam', p. 6.

131 NARA: 'Fact Sheet: The Change in Roles and Missions of the Field Police'.

132 NARA: 'The Role and Mission of the NPFF', p. 2. See also NARA: 'Fact Sheet: The Change in Roles and Missions of the Field Police' and NARA: 'Republic of South Vietnam National Police Field Force 1971', p. 9. In a scathing 1970 memorandum to all District Senior Advisors, Tay Ninh District NPFF Advisor Matthew Dettloff voiced his concern over the negative consequences of the 'VCI only' mission priority and noted PSB's consistent failure to provide targets. He asserted that the only way of 'eliminating the complaints that the NPFF are doing nothing' was for units to carry out the range of missions for which they were authorized. He concluded by reminding District advisors that 'district has authority to send NPFF out on three and four day missions' and that 'as a last resort rather than have them do nothing, mobile patrols through the villages and hamlets' should be conducted. NARA: 'NPFF Mission at District Level 18 May 1970', pp. 1-2.

133 The danger of this outcome had already been predicted by PSD in late 1967. See NARA: 'Draft: Re-organization of NPFF 6 December 1967', p. 2.

134 NARA: RG 286 A1 E31, Box 280, IPS 13, Field Police, 1971, 'Fact Sheet: Use of NPFF 20 January 1971'. PSD reported that in 1971 DIOCC's developed only 2.5 missions per month per available platoon. NARA: 'Briefing Field Police, Vietnam', p. 16.

135 NARA: 'Fact Sheet: The Change in Roles and Missions of the Field Police'. For the three month wait time see NARA: 'Briefing Field Police, Vietnam', p. 6. In an April 1971 report to DEPCORDS Colby, the new PSD Director Michael McCann noted that the 'great

operations yet fully in line with standard operating procedures, such actions were regularly reported as misuse.[136] The cumulative result was that in the field the NPFF were seen as police in name only and chronically underutilized.

By mid-1971, 75 percent of all platoon-size units operated at the district level or below.[137] Consequently, PSD targeted Province and District Chiefs of Police, by way of their US advisors, as the most direct and capable means to ensure proper use.[138] In August, Police Chiefs received a directive restating the NPFF's proper missions. To correct the problem of underutilization and fulfill its role of providing 'police services and police security in areas where conditions limit the ability of the…[uniformed] National Police', the primary missions were reordered to 'constant and extensive police patrolling' and away from 'conducting raids…against the VCI'. Further, the briefing specifically addressed mission priorities. While noting that priorities differed according to local conditions, intra-village and hamlet patrolling would henceforth 'constitute the normal day–to-day work of an FP unit'.[139] Only when developed intelligence provided specific targets would anti-VCI operations take priority.[140] In effect, the NPFF had come full circle to its original 1965 mission.[141]

The final shift in mission priority was also accompanied by a growing sense among PSD advisors that the perceived problems with the NPFF were a function of metrics and mission. From 1965 on, the primary metric for NPFF effectiveness employed by PSD was a straightforward equation: 'number of VC killed and captured per NPFF policeman per year'. By 1970, some advisors working in the districts noted the seemingly obvious, that performance could vary widely among provinces and was often dependent on factors external to the NPFF. Such factors could range from a province or district administration's (including the Police Chief's) compliance with directives to the effectiveness of the DIOCC and the quality and timeliness of PSB actionable intelligence.[142] As one PSD assessor candidly remarked in a 1970 report:

majority of PHOENIX operations' were Cordon and Search and lacked specific individual VCI targets. NARA: RG 286 A1 E31, Box 280, IPS 13, Field Police, 1971, 'Fact Sheet: Proper Utilization of the NPFF in the PHOENIX Program 28 April 1971'.

136 NARA: 'Briefing Field Police, Vietnam', p. 6. See also NARA: 'Fact Sheet: The Change in Roles and Missions of the Field Police'.

137 NARA: 'Fact Sheet: Public Safety Program—Vietnam', p. 4.

138 NARA: 'Fact Sheet: Use of NPFF 20 January 1971', p. 2.

139 NARA: 'Role and Mission of the Field Police; Responsibilities of Province and District Chiefs of Police 9 August 1971', pp. 1-2.

140 NARA: RG 286 A1 E31, Box 280, IPS 13, Field Police, 1971, 'The Change in Roles and Missions of the Field Police 10 August 1971'. The re-emphasis on day-to-day duties was broadly in line with the recommendations of Sir Robert Thompson. At the a March 1971 conference held to discuss his findings regarding the NPFF in his extensive study on the National Police, Thompson specifically addressed daily as well as anti-VCI missions. NARA: 'The Role and Mission of the NPFF', pp. 3-4.

141 NARA: 'Briefing Field Police, Vietnam', p. 8 and NARA: 'Role and Mission of the Field Police; Responsibilities of Province and District Chiefs of Police 9 August 1971', p. 1.

142 NARA: 'Vietnam National Police Field Force: History, Role and Mission', pp. 2-3.

> I cannot subscribe to this method of measuring effectiveness of any type of police organization, no matter how unique the situation is in Vietnam. That it is carrying out its basic mission of allowing the NP to operate effectively with the rural areas is a more important indication of how effective the NPFF has been in performing its duties.[143]

The reason for the success, he added, was increased willingness to deploy at the district level and below.[144] While this view was certainly not shared throughout PSD, the 1970 shift in mission prioritization certainly was in line with it.

Full utilization, however, could not be achieved solely by issuing a mission restatement. Indeed, PSD understood a link between the primacy of anti-VCI operations and a broader sense that the NPFF were a force separate from the NPC. The way forward was managerial and involved a restatement of the mission with a re-structuring of the NPFF command. Through 1971 a reorganization shifted the NPFF from the Support Division of DGNP to a Bureau of the Operations Bloc DGNP, while regional and national FP Headquarters as separate units were eliminated and the size and function of provincial headquarters greatly reduced with duties absorbed by appropriate NP Headquarters.[145]

Placing the NPFF firmly within the NPC structure emphasized the responsibility of NP commanders for their field police units, thereby limiting misuse and underutilization.[146] Further, by reinforcing that the NPFF were an organic component of the NP, the 'separate force myth' could be dispelled and a range of missions more readily embraced. In essence, force integration promoted increased and more effective use of the NPFF on a day-to-day basis (Mission 1) while ensuring that they still remained available for PHOENIX operations (Mission 2).[147] Unsurprisingly, PSD turned again to their advisors to play a key role in helping to implement the

143 Ibid., p. 3.

144 The report also offered an alternate 'much more complex index system' to evaluate NPFF effectiveness. The report marks an important shift in which the role of the NPFF 'comes full circle' and the primary function of the NPFF shifted 'to safe guard the country' rather than 'kill or capture VC.' Ibid., p. 3.

145 NARA: 'Briefing Field Police, Vietnam', p. 8 and NARA: RG 286 A1 E32, Box 76, IPS 12, National Field Police Program FY 1973-1974, 'FY 73/74 Program Narrative: National Field Police', pp. 1-2. The re-organization also established a FP staff service with the Operations Bloc of the NPC; a Regional FP staff Bureau within the Operations Service of each of the four Regional Police Commands; a FP staff Section/Company Headquarters assigned to the Operations Bureau of each Provincial Police Command; and a platoon assigned to the Provincial District Police Command. NARA: RG 286 A1 E31, Box 280, IPS 13, Field Police, 1971, 'An Overview of the Field Police Service; Guidance for the Field Police Service for the Public Safety Advisor', p. 1.

146 Ibid., p. 6. In 1971, the NPFF was re-designated Field Police.

147 NARA: 'Briefing Field Police, Vietnam', pp. 8-9.

problem-solving changes.[148] The 1971 modifications marked the last significant PSD-inspired policy development for the NPFF as US intervention reached the eleventh hour. In short order, Public Safety, like all other advisory programs, began to pack up and go home.[149]

Conclusion

Beginning in 1961, Public Safety Division prosecuted the 'other war'. However, to do so effectively required close collaboration, not just with other US agencies but also the Vietnamese themselves. At its core, PSD was composed of managers who understood that effectiveness or ineffectiveness, success or failure was determined by objective metrics. Developing a credible policy and program was therefore largely a 'numbers game' in which quantifiable problems required quantifiable solutions.

This chapter considers some of the ways in which PSD-NPFF collaboration evolved and GVN and US officials wrestled with the core problem of utilization. As we have seen, utilization assumed a binary definition namely proper or improper and determined largely by measureable formulas such as number of platoons per district, patrols per month and neutralizations per policeman. The NPFF fell short of expectations, at best deemed 'ineffective' and at worst 'lousy'.[150] Unsurprisingly, this verdict is largely supported by the limited historiography that considers the National Police. While this chapter does little to overturn such conclusions, it does highlight two little researched areas: PSD's long-standing awareness of its internal problems and the significant efforts to correct them. Public Safety continuously refined procedures and pushed policies, attempting to effect change with the only means at their disposal: a relationship with the NPC. Whether engaging the command level in Saigon or advising in the provinces and districts, PSD moved from the background, as they had intended, and assumed a role center stage.

Public Safety faced a central disconnect related to the very nature of the Vietnamese state. To create, build, and adapt a field police program, PSD necessarily worked from the 'top down' while paramilitary policing itself was carried out in the field from the 'bottom up'. Indeed, support from the upper echelons of the NPC did not inevitably translate to effective implementation. The limitations of collaboration proved straightforward: there simply was no way for PSD to ensure that plans were carried out. Any efforts to do so meant reliance on US advisors and undercut the very reason for collaboration in the first place, namely to 'prime the pump' and prepare the

148 TTVN: 'Guidelines for Advice of National Police Field Forces', p. 1. See also NARA: 'Public Safety Program—II Corps 16 September, 1968', p. 2, and OPS, 'Public Safety Program Information Handbook', pp. 34-35.

149 Office of Public Safety, AID, Department of State, 'Phaseout of US assistance to South Vietnam in support of police organizations, law enforcement, and public safety related programs', Washington, DC, February 1975.

150 For Komer's harsh critique see Komer, *Organization and Management*, pp. 170-172.

Vietnamese to police their own state. Try as they might, systemic strains and demands undercut PSD's efforts to meet goals and overcome challenges.

That the NPFF proved ineffective is an incomplete answer without considering the ways in which policies, problems, and solutions evolved over time. Why, when, and how development occurred remain important considerations. If effectiveness can be measured by effort and not solely result, PSD can claim some measure of success. Core problems were not simply identified but a series of remedies continually offered. Despite their inability to ensure that the NPFF played an effective role in pacification, the program developed and evolved, highlighting an ability and willingness to make changes. Importantly, to simply deem the Public Safety-NPFF project a failure risks ignoring the decisions and debates that made it so. Of course, not everything evolved. In the end, what is most striking about their management and problem solving was that PSD consistently clung to the notion that it was indeed possible to manage their way to pacification.

Office of Public Safety, 1966

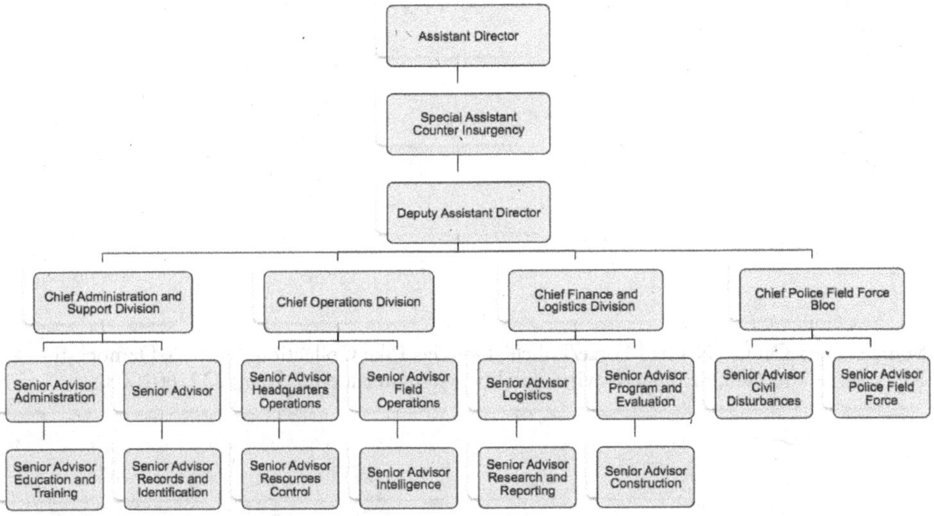

Source: Office of Public Safety, AID, Department of State, 'The Public Safety Program Vietnam', Saigon, April 1966, p.20.

Public Safety Directorate, 1972

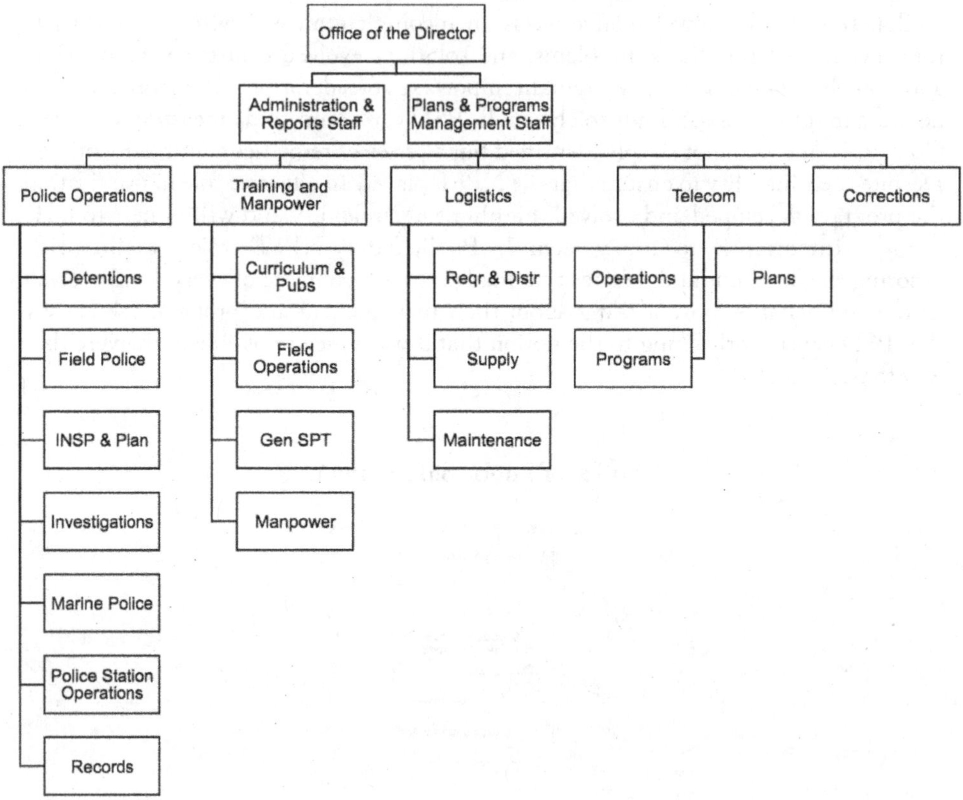

Source: 'Data On GVN Field Force/Police', Douglas Pike Collection: Unit 06, Democratic Republic of Vietnam, http://www.virtualarchive.vietnam.ttu.edu/, Item: 2321601008.

Organizational Chart of the National Police of Vietnam, 1968

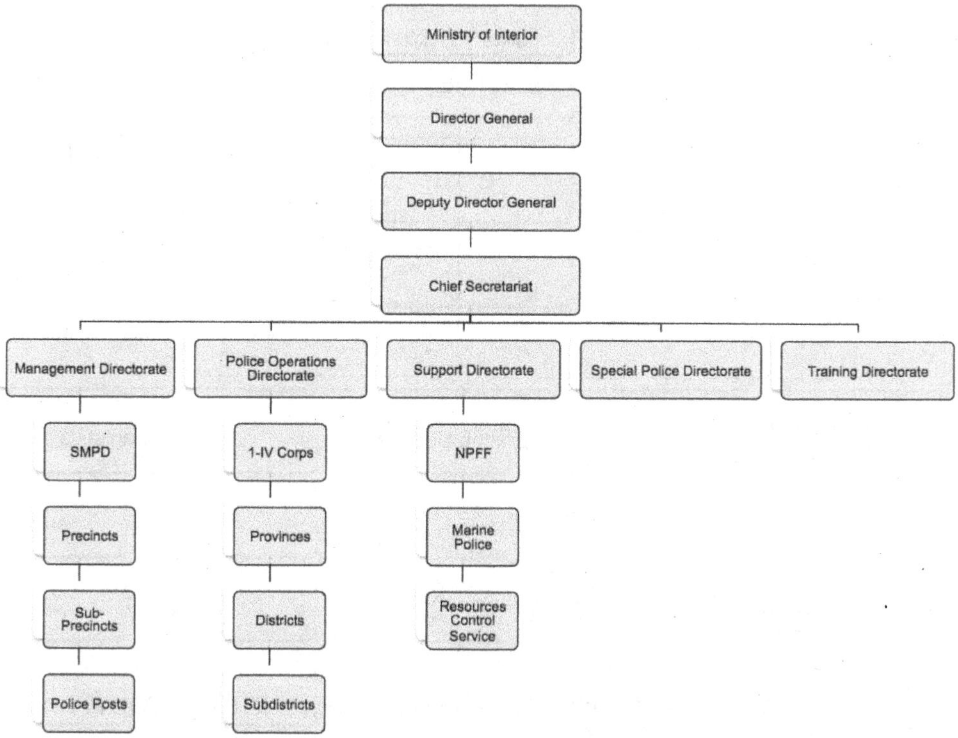

Source: Office of Public Safety, AID, Department of State, 'The Role of Public Safety in Support of the National Police of Vietnam', Washington, DC, April 1969, Chart B.

Organization of Armed Support Bloc, 1968

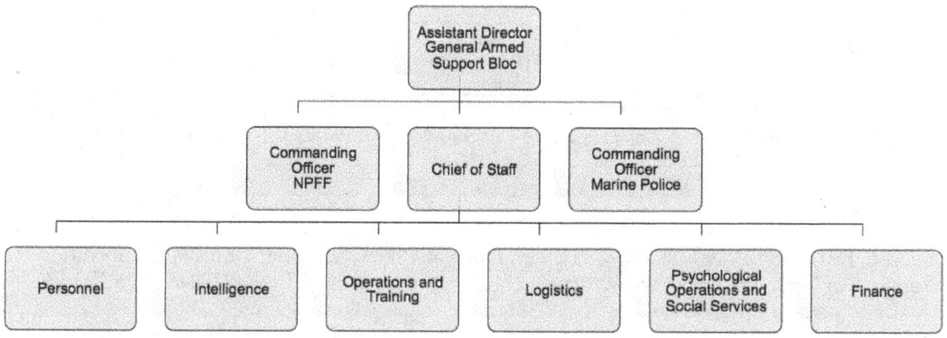

Source: 'Data On GVN Field Force/Police', Douglas Pike Collection: Unit 06, Democratic Republic of Vietnam, http://www.virtualarchive.vietnam.ttu.edu/, Item: 2321601008, Tab A.

Organization of National Police Field Force Headquarters, 1971

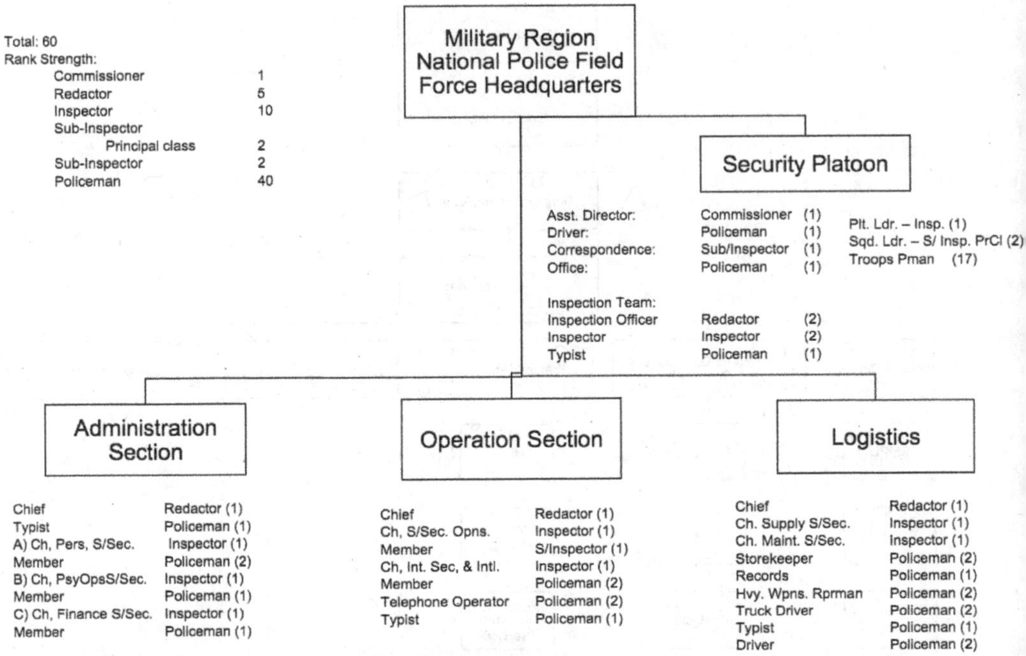

Source: RG 286 A1 E32, Box 71, IPS 12 Police Administration, 1971, IPS 12, 'TOE FFP-1-71/1', p.21.

Organizational Chart of National Police Field Forces Battalion, 1968

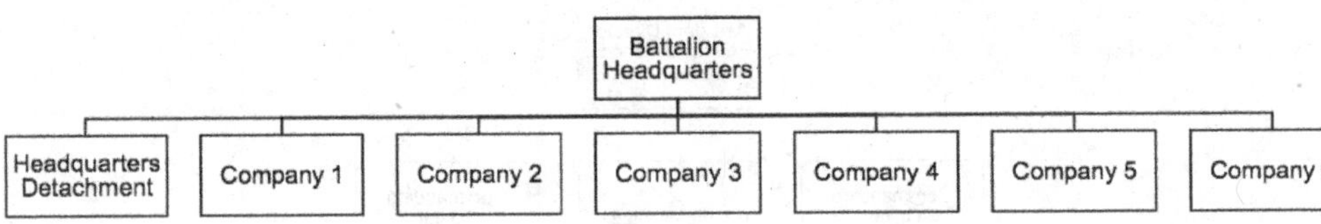

Source: 'Data On GVN Field Force/Police', Douglas Pike Collection: Unit 06, Democratic Republic of Vietnam, http://www.virtualarchive.vietnam.ttu.edu/, Item: 2321601008, Tab B.

Organization of National Police Field Force Company (Battalion/City), 1971

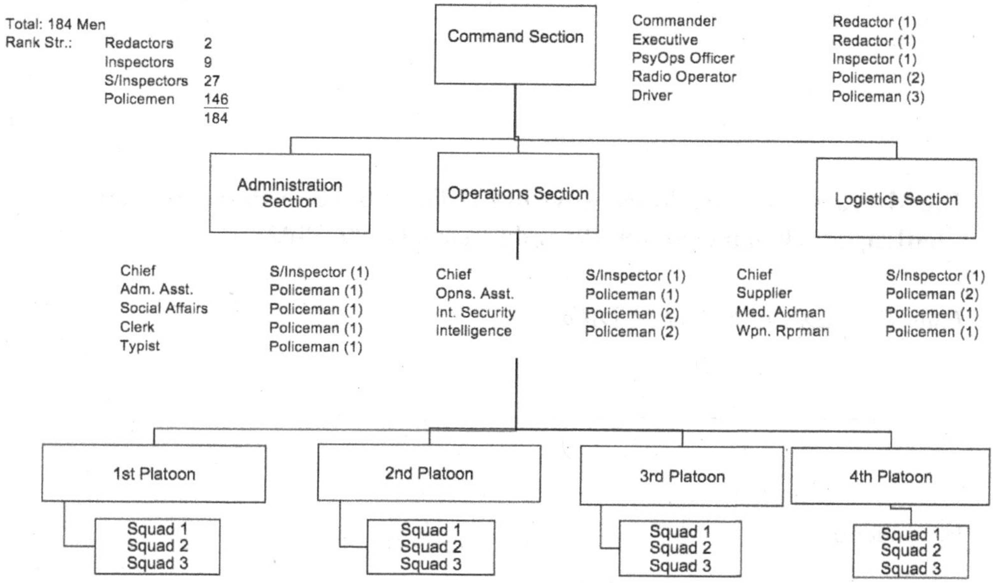

Source: RG 286 A1 E32, Box 71, IPS 12 Police Administration, 1971, IPS 12, 'TOE FFP-1-71/1', p.14.

Organization of National Police Field Force Platoon, 1971

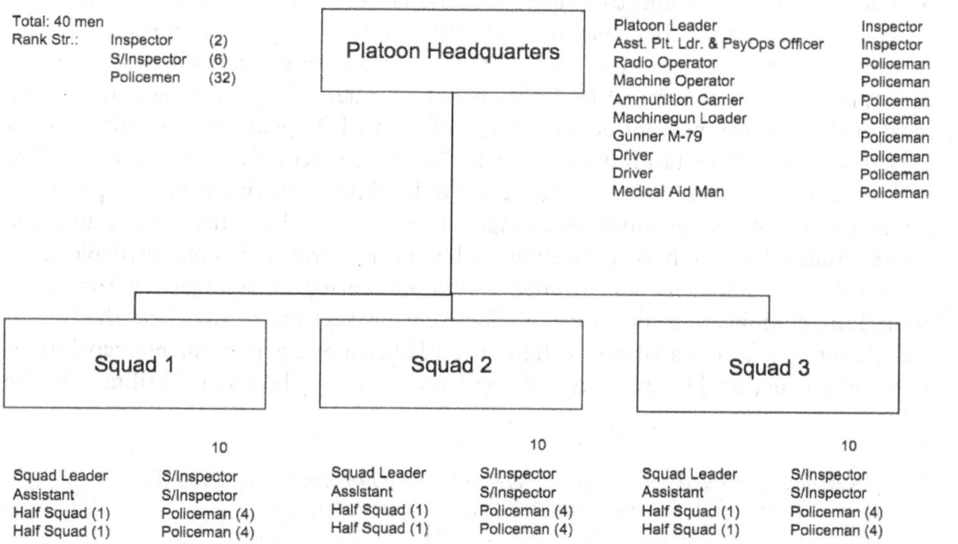

Source: RG 286 A1 E32, Box 71, IPS 12 Police Administration, 1971, IPS 12, 'TOE FFP-1-71/1', p.1.

6

The Military Police as Police Advisors: A Potential Solution with Many Challenges—Panama (1989-99) and Kosovo (1999-2002)

Jason E. Fritz and Robert N. Dillon

Introduction

The US Department of Defense defines foreign internal defense (FID) as 'participation by civilian and military agencies of a government in any of the action programs taken by another government or other designated organization to free and protect its society from subversion, lawlessness, insurgency, terrorism, and other threats to its security'.[1] This definition covers a multitude of types of civilian and military operations, including peacekeeping, post-conflict, shaping, stability, counter-narcotic, and normal bilateral relations. Excepting the latter, each of these scenarios are reactions to a changing social, political, or security order in the recipient state. While advising and training local civilian police may not be an element of each FID operation the United States undertakes, it will certainly be present in many—particularly during post-conflict and peacekeeping operations—as the nature of local police institutions and operations are major factors during times of change.[2] However, unlike many other states, the United States does not have a standing civilian police force that is readily deployable, logistically self-sufficient, and trained and equipped for high-threat environments, something complicating its ability to effectively conduct police advising. The lack of a civilian police force capable of conducting FID creates a gap in current capabilities required to further US interests. We will now explore the use of Military Police

1 US Army, *Joint Publication JP 3-22 Foreign Internal Defense, 12 July 2010* (Fort Leavenworth, KS: US Army Combined Arms Center, 2012), p. ix.

2 Marenin, Otwin, 'Policing Change, Changing Police: Some Thematic Questions' in Marenin, Otwin (ed.), *Policing Change, Changing Police: International Perspectives* (New York: Routledge, 1996), p. 5.

through historical case studies to see if they can fill that capability gap, and their ultimate suitability for performing the mission.

First, we must examine the environments in which FID operations often occur as this affects police advising in many ways. We then examine the options available to and constraints upon policymakers to execute police advising. Following this, we describe the positive and negative aspects of using military police as police advisors, including deployment capabilities, suitability, current doctrine and training of military police, and potential outcomes of this solution on local police institutions. Before providing concluding observations and recommendations on the use of military police as police advisors, we explore two operational cases during which military police were used as police advisors: Panama and Kosovo.

The Environment

The nature of FID requires intervening forces to operate in complex environments in which a number of trade-offs must be considered. Before discussing these trade-offs, we will attempt to describe the challenges presented by the environments during FID operations. By definition, FID is conducted in states with threats to the security of the citizens and the state through state failure, insurgency, terrorism, or more general lawlessness. Often, these states are entering or attempting to recover from civil conflict. There may still be organized non-state armed groups that need to be demobilized or dealt with. Political, economic, and educational systems may be dysfunctional. The host-nation police force may be a remnant of a corrupt regime, ineffectual, or even non-existent, requiring intervening states to establish forces from scratch. Each of these factors affect police advising, as advisors assist host-nations in molding their police forces into the right organization to address their needs; policing cannot be disentangled from the security, social, or political conditions of the state.[3]

Regardless of the challenges involved, in the view of US policymakers police assistance and advising should be designed to accomplish two overarching objectives: to create a safe and secure environment and to ensure host-nation police contribute to democracy strengthening. The former is the fundamental purpose of police and can be achieved by multiple paths with varying degrees of adherence to democratic principles, which include 'policing that uses minimal force, is relatively incorrupt, and provides reasonably impartial assistance and known Western-style criminal justice framework'.[4] Indeed, US law requires all assistance to foreign police forces in a FID context to 'include training in internationally recognized standards of human rights, the rule of law, anti-corruption, and the promotion of civilian police roles that support

3 Hills, Alice, *Policing Africa: Internal Security and the Limits of Liberalization* (Boulder, CO: Lynne Rienner Publishers, 2000), p. 62.
4 Hills, Alice, *Policing Post-Conflict Cities* (New York: Zed Books, 2008), p. 67.

democracy'.[5] Police advisors play a major role in achieving both objectives and in providing host-nation police with examples of good policing and how good policing contributes to strengthening democracy.[6]

From these considerations, host-nation police forces must make a number of decisions that balance the achievement of long- and short-term objectives which will ultimately determine the role of the police force within that society. These decisions occur at the tactical and strategic levels, and many are decided at political levels outside the purview of the police force itself. These include but are not limited to: balancing the integration of former rebels into the police force toward long-term cohesiveness versus the immediacy of ethnically homogeneous forces;[7] dealing with politically connected officers that may impede professionalization of the force;[8] lowering recruiting standards in areas of low education and literacy to grow the force in the near future;[9] pushing for police professionalization and reform while the courts and corrections systems lag (as they tend to);[10] and determining how to eradicate pervasive corruption to prevent the police from becoming predatory to the population.[11]

Police advisors play a major role in helping their host-nation counterparts navigate these issues, either through direct advice and mentoring, or through emulation. They must do so through every level of the organization, ranging from the ministerial to patrol units. However, these big-picture issues are not the advisors' sole concerns. They still must train, mentor, and advise host-nation police so that they can function as: (1) core patrol police; (2) criminal investigators; (3) public order units responding to civil unrest; (4) armed units combating high-end threats; (5) intelligence gatherers; and (6) border controllers.[12] As the preponderance of police in any state belong to the first two categories, this chapter applies mostly to them. Beyond their prevalence, the officers in these roles have contact with the public more often than the others and 'can make the greatest impact on governmental legitimacy'.[13]

5 '22 US Code § 2420 - Police Training Prohibition', LII, *Legal Information Institute*, <https://www.law.cornell.edu/uscode/text/22/2420> (accessed 27 June 2016).
6 Bayley, David H., *Changing the Guard: Developing Democratic Police Abroad* (New York: Oxford University Press, 2005), p. 62.
7 McFate, Sean, *The Link between DDR and SSR in Conflict-Affected Countries* (Washington, DC: United States Institute of Peace, 2010), p. 12.
8 Bayley, *Changing the Guard*, p. 12.
9 Wade, David, 'Afghan Civilian Police: Police Instead of Soldiers', in Finkenbinder, Karen, and Paul M. Sangrey (eds), *Social Capital, Policing and the Rule-of-Law: Keys to Stabilization* (Carlisle, PA: Peacekeeping and Stability Operations Institute, 2013), p. 129.
10 Bayley, *Changing the Guard*, p. 66.
11 Keller, Dennis E., *US Military Forces and Police Assistance in Stability Operations: The Least-Worst Option to Fill the US Capacity Gap*, PKSOI Papers (Carlisle, PA: Strategic Studies Institute, 2010), p. 23.
12 Bayley, David H., and Robert M. Perito, *The Police in War: Fighting Insurgency, Terrorism, and Violent Crime* (Boulder, CO: Lynne Rienner Pub, 2010), p. 73.
13 Ibid.

Due to the nature of the environment and their mission, police advisors in FID operations must possess three attributes: they must be easily deployable, able to protect themselves in hostile conditions, and be experts in the policing profession. The United States, however, does not have a dedicated agency to support police advising during FID operations. Despite having over 750,000 sworn officers nationwide, civilian American police are dispersed over 18,000 federal, state, and local agencies, and not one of these agencies has a unit dedicated to supporting police-building activities outside of the United States.[14] When federal officers do contribute to police advising missions, they are taken from their operational roles, which contrary to the host-forces' needs, is primarily criminal investigation and not community patrolling or problem-oriented policing.[15] The United States has relied on contractor support to fill this deployable need—from Haiti to Kosovo to Iraq and Afghanistan—with mixed results.[16]

Without a dedicated civilian police solution, and the less than ideal option of using contractors, police advising has usually been taken on by the US military. Within the US Army, the Military Police Corps is often considered the most appropriate tool for police advising in FID; it is a relatively large organization designed to deploy quickly to hostile areas to conduct law enforcement operations in support of larger missions. Further, the use of military police as police advisors, particularly in a post-conflict setting, could smooth the transition from military to civilian control of operations.[17] However, recent scholarship has noted potential adverse consequences of using military police to train civilian police.[18] To explore these pros and cons of using US Army Military Police for police advising in FID,[19] we examine two cases where they were used in such a role: Panama (1989-99) and Kosovo (1999-2).

14 Banks, Duren, et al., *National Sources of Law Enforcement Employment Data*, Program Report (Bureau of Justice Statistics, 2016), pp. 1–2, <http://www.bjs.gov/content/pub/pdf/nsleed.pdf> (accessed 27 June 2016).

15 Bayley, *Changing the Guard*, p. 104. Many federal law enforcement agencies do operate internationally, but their primary objectives are to support US justice issues and not the development of foreign agencies.

16 Jayamaha, Dilshika, et al., *Lessons Learned from US Government Law Enforcement in International Operations* (Carlisle, PA: Strategic Studies Institute, 2010), p. 26; Dillon, Robert, *Putting the Police Back into the Military Police* (Washington, DC: US Army Office of the Provost Marshal General, 2011), p. 10; Rosenau, William, *'Low-Cost Trigger-Pullers': The Politics of Policing in the Context of Contemporary 'State Building' and Counterinsurgency* (Santa Monica, CA: RAND, 2008), p. 16.

17 Dillon, *Putting the Police Back into the Military Police*, p. 30.

18 Friesendorf, Cornelius and Jörg, Krempel, *Militarized Versus Civilian Policing: Problems of Reforming the Afghan National Police*, PRIF Report No. 102 (Frankfurt am Main: Peace Research Institute Frankfurt (PRIF), 2011), p. 43.

19 Hereafter, we refer to the institution of the US Army Military Police Corps as Military Police, the capitalization denoting it is a formal functional title within the US Army.

Panama (1989-99)

The US intervention in Panama had antecedents in the early and mid-1980s, but the events of February 1988 were integral to the decision to depose the regime of Manuel Noriega. First, two grand juries in Florida indicted Noriega on drug trafficking charges that month.[20] Then on the 26th Noriega—then chief of staff of the Panamanian Defense Force (PDF)—deposed the elected president, Eric Arturo Delvalle.[21] The US military immediately began planning for operations to depose Noriega and on 18 December 1989, President George H.W. Bush made the decision to invade Panama and capture Noriega.[22] The military operation, later named Operation Just Cause, consisted of offensive operations against the PDF and its command and control networks, as well as defensive operations to protect US interests, including the Panama Canal.[23] However, the detailed planning of the invasion did not include plans for the stabilization phase. After six days of operations, by 26 December the PDF was defeated, but the PDF's defeat meant that no organization was effectively policing the country, and this was so in spite of the US military's half-hearted attempts to do so with combat units.[24]

With some overlap, the combat operations of Operation Just Cause morphed into the stability operations of Operation Promote Liberty, which was initially headed by a Civil Military Operations Task Force (CMOTF). However, the CMOTF was manned mostly by Civil Affairs organizations and did not plan for law enforcement responsibilities, including the training of the new Panamanian internal security organization.[25] Nearly a month after the invasion, the Military Support Group (MSG) took control over all the disparate groups tasked with filling in for or training host nations (such as the CMOTF), including the establishment and building of

20 Fishel, John T., *The Fog of Peace: Planning and Executing the Restoration of Panama* (Carlisle, PA: Strategic Studies Institute, 1992), p. 2, <http://oai.dtic.mil/oai/oai?verb=getRecord&metadataPrefix=html&identifier=ADA251124> (accessed 17 June 2016).

21 Gray, Anthony, and Maxwell Manwaring, 'Panama: Operation Just Cause' in Oakley, Robert B., Michael J. Dziedzic, and Eliot M. Goldberg (eds), *Policing the New World Disorder: Peace Operations and Public Security* (Washington, DC: NDU Press, 1998), pp. 41–68.

22 Taw, Jennifer M., *Operation Just Cause: Lessons for Operations Other than War* (Santa Monica, CA: Rand, 1996), p. 6.

23 Ibid., pp. 6–7.

24 Conley Jr, William J., *Operations 'Just Cause' and 'Promote Liberty': The Implications of Military Operations Other Than War* (US Marine Corps Command and Staff College, 2001), p. 18, <http://oai.dtic.mil/oai/oai?verb=getRecord&metadataPrefix=html&identifier=ADA401263> (accessed 27 June 2016).

25 Jayamaha, et al., *Lessons Learned from US Government Law Enforcement in International Operations*, p. 20.

Panamanian police capabilities.[26] To generate the newly minted Panamanian National Police (PNP), the MSG was given a Military Police brigade. This brigade provided informal training through joint patrolling with the PNP and formal training by way of a 20-hour basic police training course.[27]

In early 1990, the US Congress reiterated its prohibition on police training—specifically by the US military—in its allocation of assistance funds to rebuild Panamanian institutions. In this legislation, Congress authorized the International Criminal Investigative Training Assistance Program (ICITAP) to develop a training program for the PNP, a civilian agency within the US Department of Justice that at the time had no previous experience providing training in basic police skills to foreign governments.[28] Because ICITAP needed time to develop the training program, the US ambassador in Panama allowed the US military to continue its mentorship activities with the PNP until ICITAP was able to take over this responsibility. Further, US Army reservists who were police officers in their civilian jobs provided a stop-gap measure by conducting a short training course for the PNP. While this training seems to have been effective, the ambassador expressed concern that the military was influencing the PNP to organize itself too much like a military force instead of a law enforcement organization.[29] By the end of 1990, the initial training of recruits for the PNP had passed to ICITAP, which maintained its operations until 1999.[30]

The use of US Army Military Police in Operations Just Cause and Promote Liberty produced both successes and failures. The use of Military Police to conduct joint patrols with the PNP set a precedent for the use of Military Police during the tense times in the aftermath of a conflict. While an ad hoc arrangement, their use in this regard leveraged the most appropriate asset the United States had in Panama at the time. The Military Police were able to adapt to the changing security and political environment to assist in the achievement of strategic goals, specifically the establishment of a Panamanian police service.

There were, however, problems with using Military Police to advise the newly formed PNP. First, there are distinct differences between military and civilian police. In the case of Panama, this concern was expressed by the US ambassador when he allowed US forces to continue to train the PNP until ICITAP was fully operational

26 Cole, Ronald H., *Operation Just Cause: The Planning and Execution of Joint Operations in Panama February 1988—January 1990* (Washington, DC: Joint History Office, Office of the Chairman of the Joint Chiefs of Staff, 1995), p. 43, <http://www.dtic.mil/doctrine/doctrine/history/justcaus.pdf> (accessed 27 June 2016).

27 Gray and Manwaring, 'Panama: Operation Just Cause', p. 60; Jayamaha, et al., *Lessons Learned from US Government Law Enforcement in International Operations*, p. 24.

28 *Urgent Assistance for Democracy in Panama Act of 1990, Section 101.b*, <http://thomas.loc.gov/cgi-bin/query/z?c101:H.R.3952.ENR:>.

29 Gray and Manwaring, 'Panama: Operation Just Cause', p. 60.

30 Ibid., p. 61; Jayamaha, et al., *Lessons Learned from US Government Law Enforcement in International Operations*, p. 27.

in spite of his observation that US military forces had organized the PNP according to a military instead of a police model.[31] While Military Police are simultaneously military and police, they are organized and equipped to police the military, which is strikingly different from typical civilian agencies. This works well for the Military Police, but when advising civilian police forces those civilians may attempt to emulate the military aspects of Military Police that are inappropriate for civilian policing, such as strict hierarchical structures or enemy-centric operations.

Another problem was that the military planning for the post-combat phases of US operations were wholly inadequate with respect to the Panamanian police. US Army Military Police stepped in to fill a capability gap in building an indigenous police force, a mission for which they were neither trained, equipped, nor legally authorized. The fits and starts in the establishment of the PNP began with the failure to plan for its development and interagency confusion on designating a responsible body. But the reaction of the Military Police units deployed to Panama to fill a void that was not previously identified, and to execute this ad hoc mission at a high standard, provides one example of the effective use of Military Police as police advisors in FID.

Kosovo (1999-2002)

Following the collapse of Yugoslavia in 1991, Kosovo became part of the Republic of Serbia, to which it had been joined following the First World War. Kosovo is 92 percent ethnic Albanians, with the remainder of the population consisting primarily of ethnic Serbians who have a different religion, language, and culture.[32] After the collapse of the Yugoslav state, Kosovars put pressure on Serbia to give Kosovo its freedom. Serbia's response was a massive crackdown, the eviction of Albanian Kosovars from jobs and positions of power, and the installation of Serbian Kosovars in their place. The subsequent war was brutal, with Serbian Kosovars conducting ethnic cleansing and Albanian Kosovars committing their own reprisals. The North Atlantic Treaty Organization (NATO) conducted an air campaign against Serbian forces in Kosovo from March until June 1999. At that point UN Security Council Resolution (UNSCR) 1244 passed, creating an authority for international assistance to administer Kosovo and help build its institutions. Included among these was an authority for NATO to ensure public safety and to build local police forces.[33]

The implementation of UNSCR 1244 was executed by KFOR—NATO's Kosovo Force—under the auspices of Operation Joint Guardian. KFOR consisted of some 50,000 troops from 30 countries, divided into five multinational brigade areas of

31 Gray and Manwaring, 'Panama: Operation Just Cause', p. 60.

32 'The World Factbook', <https://www.cia.gov/library/publications/the-world-factbook/geos/kv.html> (accessed 30 June 2016).

33 Security Council resolution 1244 (1999), *On the Deployment of International Civil and Security Presences in Kosovo*, S/RES/1244, <https://documents-dds-ny.un.org/doc/UNDOC/GEN/N99/172/89/PDF/N9917289.pdf?OpenElement> (10 June 1999).

operation.[34] The US contingent, Task Force Falcon, was made up of 7,000 troops and had responsibility for the south eastern sector of Kosovo.[35] Establishing the rule of law was a slow process as the Yugoslav police had withdrawn and UN civilian police were slow to deploy. Throughout 1999, the UN Mission in Kosovo (UNMIK) was unable to field even a third of the 6,000 officers they requested.[36] Based on lessons learned from the intervention in Bosnia, where the lack of public security caused general unrest in the aftermath of the initial incursion, KFOR included some law enforcement personnel with their forces in the initial phase of operations. For its contingent, the United States deployed a military police battalion of over 300 soldiers and 10 criminal investigators.[37]

Before UNMIK civilian police were fully deployed and the Kosovo Police were formed, this Military Police battalion was the primary law enforcement organization in the US sector. However, the soldiers' lack of basic investigator skills, rarely used on military posts, proved problematic in a real-world law enforcement setting.[38] As local and international civilian police arrived, US Military Police were placed in police stations with their civilian counterparts, often to provide security for the stations. While Military Police had no official role in training the Kosovo Police, they often provided informal training as part of their advisory duties.

However, as UNMIK civilian police and the Kosovar police were stood-up, US Military Police took less of a role outside of detention operations and the policing of US forces. As Kosovar criminal justice systems developed, the military ceded its detention operations to Kosovo's courts and prisons. With military forces still in the country, the provost marshal at Camp Bondsteel, the primary US military facility in Kosovo, oversaw law enforcement in the camp and liaised with the police headquarters near the camp.[39] But the provost marshal had no formal role in conducting or overseeing police advising for Kosovo's police.

The precedent of using military police as police advisors set in Panama was seen again a decade later in Kosovo. US Army Military Police deployed with the initial forces and were able to fill the gap in law enforcement capability between the dissolution of the previous government's police force and the establishment of the post-intervention

34 Perito, Robert M., *Where Is the Lone Ranger When We Need Him?: America's Search for a Postconflict Stability Force* (Washington, DC: United States Institute of Peace, 2004), p. 184.
35 Nardulli, Bruce R., et al., *Disjointed War: Military Operations in Kosovo, 1999* (Santa Monica, CA: Rand, 2002), p. 103.
36 Ibid., p. 107.
37 Jayamaha, et al., *Lessons Learned from US Government Law Enforcement in International Operations*, p. 115.
38 Swengros, 'Military Police Functions in Kosovo', *Military Police*, 19:1 (2000).
39 Author interview with Camp Bondsteel Provost Marshal Office leader at Camp Bondsteel, August 2009.

force. Once the new police force was operational, Military Police soldiers conducted some joint patrolling with and informal training for their indigenous colleagues.

Just as in Panama, these acts were ad hoc and decided after operations had begun. Operational planners at NATO had thought to include Military Police units with each of the multinational brigades, but had not considered their use beyond the typical wartime responsibilities of military police: detention operations, policing friendly forces, and responding to civil unrest. They did not foresee the need to use these soldiers and Marines as law enforcement officers or as advisors to the nascent Kosovo police, in essence failing to use Military Police units to their fullest potential in a dangerous and uncertain environment. Because of the widespread, if late deployed and often too small UNMIK civilian police presence, US Military Police had a short-lived role in advising the Kosovo police force, a force which reflected their civilian advisors in training, equipment, organization, and interaction with the local population.

Military Police as Police Advisors in FID

US Army and Marine Corps Military Police have served as police advisors in FID operations, although primarily in an ad hoc manner. After operations in Panama, war planners recognized the importance of law enforcement in developing long-term peace and stability, and yet planning for the establishment and development of indigenous police forces was never well conceived, as seen during operations in Kosovo. Military Police forces seem the obvious choice for police advising in FID, particularly in the immediate aftermath of high-intensity combat operations. Military police units are usually embedded in major military organizations, are quickly deployable, well equipped, highly trained to survive in hostile environments, support the principles of unity of effort and command, and leverage what should be their greatest attribute: expertise in enforcing the rule of law.

There are, however, downsides to using them as police advisors for nascent host-nation law enforcement agencies. As is clearly seen in the cases of US forces in Panama and Kosovo, the Military Police differ from civilian police because of their dual roles as policemen and as soldiers. Also, legal limits on police development under the Foreign Assistance Act have created challenges in leveraging Military Police to build civilian police capabilities, while simultaneously dampening the Military Police's willingness as an institution to train and equip its forces for a mission it is permitted to execute only under exceptions to the law. Finally, recent scholarship suggests that using military forces to develop police forces results in local police that are partially competent in police tasks and partially competent in military tasks, but not fully competent in either. This issue is addressed below.

Readily Deployable

As mentioned above, the United States does not keep a standing capability to conduct police advising during FID operations. No single federal law enforcement agency does so and the dispersed model of state and local policing within the US precludes the ability of these agencies to maintain such a capability. Unlike other countries, the United States does not have a national uniformed police force from which it could draw law enforcement professionals to deploy as police advisors. Countries such as France, Spain, Italy, and Australia not only have federal forces, but these forces typically work with both ministries of justice and defense and therefore have the training and equipment to survive in the hostile environments in which FID typically occurs. Even when these nations' specialist paramilitary police units are deployed to FID environments, they are most often deployed in small numbers and kept in reserve for situations involving acute public disorder.

Military Police units have been able to fill this gap in past operations, as evidenced by operations in Panama and Kosovo. While their distribution within the US Army has shifted over time, they have been regularly embedded at least at the division level with the increasing emphasis on FID and stability operations. As of this writing, Military Police are not part of brigade combat teams, typically the smallest deployable command, but US Army planning allocates a Military Police company to brigades based on operational need. Military Police were able to act as ad hoc police advisors in Panama and Kosovo because they were part and parcel of the combat formations that initiated those operations. Even when augmented with separate Military Police battalions, military commands are adept at absorbing additional units and integrating them into their operations.[40] In addition to having internal and augmented Military Police capacity, every command staff at brigade level and above has at least one Military Police officer to serve as the planner for rule-of-law operations. The previous case studies demonstrate that planning for building and advising host-nation police has been, on the whole, poor. However, the ability to plan properly exists, and the capability of Military Police to lead police advising and reform efforts should be emphasized as senior service colleges seek to standardize planning for these missions instead of relying on ad hoc procedures and assignments.

Military Police are readily available for immediate use as police advisors in FID, but are they trained and equipped to effectively meet this mission? We return to the question of training specific to police advising in the next section, but Military Police certainly possess the training necessary to survive in a hostile FID environment. As opposed to contracted civilian police advisors, Military Police personnel spend innumerable hours training for security scenarios such as those they might find as police advisors performing FID operations. Indeed, the primary doctrine for

40 Kelly, Terrence K., et al., *A Stability Police Force for the United States: Justification and Options for Creating US Capabilities* (Santa Monica, CA: RAND Arroyo Center, 2009), p. 119.

company-level Military Police leaders has no less than four times as many pages on combat operations than policing operations.[41]

Military Police are equally well equipped for these environments. Even without authorization from the host nation, Military Police will have an assortment of weapons for self-defense purely because of their military status, including even anti-armor missiles. They also possess body armor and armored vehicles that increase the likelihood of their survival when they are attacked by forces with capabilities exceeding those of typical criminal organizations. Military Police equipment would include mine-resistant vehicles that are highly survivable against both improvised explosive device attacks and mines. Particularly in the early days of the FID mission in the aftermath of high-intensity conflict, the ability of Military Police to fight and survive give them a great advantage over contracted civilian advisors.

The most powerful argument that Military Police are the best solution for police advising in FID—especially in the immediate aftermath of a conflict—is that they will already be on the ground to conduct the mission. Even when the Military Police element in the initial force does not have the capacity to conduct its military and police missions, they are readily deployable and can arrive in large formations as needed. Further, they are trained and equipped to work in hostile environments. Coupled with the organic logistical support that the Army maintains, Military Police provide an ideal choice as police advisors after the end of a major conflict.

The Civilian Policing Expertise Gap

Military Police straddle two professional realms, as indicated by the term *military police* itself. Because of their important military roles—detention operations, area security, and policing the military force—Military Police have had challenges demonstrating their ability to conduct traditional civil police functions. Operations in Iraq and Afghanistan have shown that 'the Military Police struggled with a fundamental lack of understanding [of] the role of civilian police in a whole of government approach, police management at the large organizational level, and the expertise to design a long-term, coherent plan of development and reform'.[42] This contradicts the observation that advisors should 'know first-hand what it is like to accommodate simultaneously the stipulations of law, the directives of elected politicians, and the needs of a diverse public'.[43]

Joint and Army doctrine have reflected this history. *Joint Publication 3-22 (Foreign Internal Defense)* suggests using the US Departments of Justice and State to train

41 US Army, *Field Manual 3-19.4 (Military Police Leaders' Handbook)* (Fort Leavenworth, KS: Combined Arms Center, 2002), <http://usacac.army.mil/sites/default/files/misc/doctrine/CDG/cdg_resources/manuals/fm/fm3_19x4.pdf> (accessed 9 August 2016).

42 Dillon, *Putting the Police Back into the Military Police*, p. 19.

43 Bayley, *Changing the Guard*, p. 104.

and advise host-nation police forces, without mentioning Military Police, as 'police are best trained by other [civilian] police'.[44] Even within the Joint Force, Military Police are not the police advisor of choice. US Army doctrine recognizes its own role in filling the gap between the need for civilian expertise and when it can arrive: 'Although the military may be involved in developing the justice and law enforcement forces, this task should be assumed by other agencies as soon as possible'.[45] However, this doctrine does not specify that the Military Police should fill this gap, but rather assumes that *any* ground forces could serve as interim police advisors. The Military Police are caught in a trap of not being considered qualified for the job, yet not being able to develop the professionalization needed to be qualified for the job.[46] Meanwhile, the need for quickly deployable and competent police advisors remains.

Legal Limitations on Military Police and their Effect

Section 660 of the Foreign Assistance Act has had a significant affect on Military Police acting in a police advisory role. Section 660, officially known as 22 US Code § 2420, consists of four subsections. The first subsection is the prohibition on the use of US government funds to 'provide training or advice, or provide any financial support, for police, prisons, or other law enforcement forces for any foreign government'.[47] The other three subsections provide exceptions to the first. Subsection (c) provides an exception to the prohibition for states with 'a longstanding democratic tradition' that 'does not have standing armed forces, and does not engage in a consistent pattern of gross violations of internationally recognized human rights'.[48] This certainly is not a description of a state that requires assistance for FID. Subsection (d) provides exceptions specifically and uniquely for Honduras and El Salvador. Subsection (b) provides seven exceptions to the police training prohibition. These include in the direct interest of US law, contracts existing prior to the enactment of Section 660, maritime law enforcement, regional security in the Eastern Caribbean, sanctions enforcement, and customs enforcement. It also includes an exception for:

> assistance provided to reconstitute civilian police authority and capability in the post-conflict restoration of host nation infrastructure for the purposes of supporting a nation emerging from instability, and the provision of professional public safety training, to include training in internationally recognized standards

44 US Army, *Joint Publication JP 3-22 Foreign Internal Defense, 12 July 2010*, p. 87.
45 US Army, *Field Manual 3-07 (Stability Operations)* (Fort Leavenworth, KS: Combined Arms Center, 2008), pp. 6–13, <http://41pylqn86jp37e3n04us8vqq.wpengine.netdna-cdn.com/wp-content/uploads/2014/06/FM3-07.-Stability-Operations.pdf> (accessed 7 August 2016).
46 Dillon, *Putting the Police Back into the Military Police*, p. 21.
47 '22 US Code § 2420 - Police Training Prohibition.'
48 Ibid.

> of human rights, the rule of law, anti-corruption, and the promotion of civilian police roles that support democracy.[49]

This clause—the most pertinent to police advising in FID—immediately poses concerns for Military Police. Historically, this has confined police advising to post-conflict environments and prevented the use of police advisors to prevent conflict. However, there have been some recent changes to this practice worthy of further discussion.

The greatest impact of Section 660, however, is that it has had the effect of dampening the institutionalization of police advising as a primary skillset for Military Police much as it has in civilian US federal agencies. A blanket prohibition on training foreign police telegraphs to the military leadership that police training and advising will not be regularly funded, and that rather 'there is no positive institutional mandate for foreign police assistance'.[50] If it is not regularly funded, then US government organizations will not maintain the capability to conduct the mission *at the institutional level*. This results in a cycle where Military Police units train for police advising only after they have been given the order to be police advisors, or because junior to mid-grade officers make a personal point to train for these tasks. In cases, this has happened only after the advisors arrived in the theater. Even for long duration missions, police assistance funding is provided only in yearly funding authorizations. There is no commitment from national decision-makers for maintaining an institutional capability for the Military Police to conduct police advising.

Concerns with Military Forces Training Civilian Police

There is a greater philosophical concern with using Military Police as police advisors for civilian police. One with real effect over time is that the civilian police would look and act more like the military than a police force needed to enforce the rule of law. There are two routes by which civilian police eventually become full or partially militarized, meaning organized, trained, and equipped like military forces: their advisors lead them in that direction, or they choose to follow that path.

In typical democratic societies, the police force is the arm of the government most citizens interact with on any given day. Counterinsurgency theory aligns with this idea, with references to the importance of civilian police being found in the writings of early counterinsurgency theorists such as Roger Trinquier, David Galula, and Robert Thompson.[51] The US counterinsurgency doctrine developed soon after the

49 Ibid.

50 Keller, *US Military Forces and Police Assistance in Stability Operations*, p. 21.

51 Trinquier, Roger, *Modern Warfare: A French View of Counterinsurgency* (Westport, CT: Praeger, 2006), p. 17; Galula, David, *Counterinsurgency Warfare: Theory and Practice* (Westport, CT: Praeger, 1965), p. 87; Thompson, Robert Grainger Ker, *Defeating Communist Insurgency: The Lessons of Malaya and Vietnam* (Westport, CT: Praeger, 1966), p. 85.

beginning of operations in Iraq and Afghanistan suggested a situationally-dependent minimum counterinsurgents-to-inhabitants ratio of 20 to 25 per 1,000 inhabitants for success, a formula taken from a then decade-old article whose intent was not to proscribe force ratios.[52] From reading counterinsurgency doctrine—both old and new—advisors in Iraq and Afghanistan pushed local authorities to create a police force of substantial size in order to increase the force ratio and satisfy the doctrinal need for police in these environments.

Conceptualizing the host-nation police as part of a 'force ratio' defines the organization in terms of its counter-guerilla mission instead of its law enforcement mission. Military officers, including Military Police officers, 'often define security exclusively in terms of defeating the guerrillas, and under this conception, the police are expected to function as war-fighting auxiliaries to the armed forces'.[53] The mixing of military and police roles in high-violence, post-conflict environments results in police forces unsuited for the conduct of routine policing. Paramilitary police forces in states in a post-conflict environment tend to be poor police because of their emphasis on traditional military tasks (such as counterinsurgency), and are also poor substitutes for better trained and equipped military forces.[54] Given the general ineffectiveness of the Afghan police and their tendency to abuse the population,[55] the push for a greater number of counterinsurgents is 'an over-emphasis on outputs over outcomes and this causes dysfunction within policing'.[56]

Beyond the concern of military units advising civilian police toward military instead of law enforcement ends, using Military Police to advise civilian police for extensive periods could trigger isomorphic tendencies in the police force. In states where the police are poorly trained, paid, and equipped, have been ineffectual, and where violence is high, the local police may look to other organizations as models.[57] When US Military Police are closely attached to such civilian police units, the latter may attempt to emulate the former. This emulation could exist at the tactical or strategic levels, whereby local civilian police increasingly ask for more military equipment

52 US Army, *Field Manual 3-24 (Counterinsurgency)* (Fort Leavenworth, KS: Combined Arms Center, 2006), pp. 1–13, <http://usacac.army.mil/cac2/Repository/Materials/COIN-FM3-24.pdf> (accessed 8 August 2016); Quinlivan, James T., 'Force Requirements in Stability Operations', *Parameters*, 24:4 (1996), pp. 59–69.

53 Rosenau, *'Low-Cost Trigger-Pullers': The Politics of Policing in the Context of Contemporary 'State Building' and Counterinsurgency'*, p. 27.

54 Friesendorf and Krempel, *Militarized versus Civilian Policing*, pp. 29–31; Rosenau, *'Low-Cost Trigger-Pullers': The Politics of Policing in the Context of Contemporary 'State Building' and Counterinsurgency'*, pp. 26–27.

55 Inspectors General, US Department of State and US Department of Defense, *Interagency Assessment of Afghanistan Police Training and Readiness*, (Washington, DC: US Department of State and US Department of Defense, 2006), p. 1.

56 Dillon, *Putting the Police Back into the Military Police*, p. 11.

57 Cooper, Jonathon A., *In Search of Police Legitimacy: Territoriality, Isomorphism, and Changes in Policing Practices* (El Paso, TX: Lfb Scholarly Publications Llc, 2014), p. 5.

and training. This is not to negate a very real local concern of their survival on a battlefield, but militarization need not be the only method by which civilian police protect themselves in violent environments.[58]

Some militarization of the police is inevitable in unstable states with high levels of violence where FID missions are needed. Survivability is imperative, but militarization crosses a line when police units focus their efforts on defeating military threats, usually the purview of their army counterparts, instead of enforcing the rule of law. This shift in policing focus changes the role of police from an institution purportedly existing to protect the population, to one that in effect exists to protect the state. This type of police militarization stands in stark contrast with the principles of democratic policing.[59]

As discussed previously, there are two paths by which civilian police under advisors assume a military character: they are pushed to do so or they choose to do so. In Panama the US ambassador was concerned that the PNP were being pushed towards militarization, and in Kosovo the police did not militarize. While there are many good reasons to use Military Police as police advisors in FID, doing so creates a challenge in that they are likely—both purposefully and by example—helping to create a militarized police that stands at odds with their desired outcome of building effective police that support the democratization of the state.[60] As the US Army Military Police School modifies its curriculum to better meet future needs, instruction on this challenge would increase awareness concerning the potential pitfalls involved with the militarization of civilian police by Military Police.

Conclusion

Foreign Internal Defense is typically conducted in austere and hostile environments, requiring an asset with the capability of doing police advising that can get to the recipient country quickly and operate in an unstable or high risk security environment. Police advising is usually done with indigenous territorial and investigative police units, requiring expertise in these two facets of policing. US police advisors must also perform their jobs while including considerations for human rights, the rule of law, anti-corruption measures, and the principles of democratic policing.

The ideal police advisor would be able to effectively perform all of these missions, but as we have shown here, such a civilian police advisor does not exist. Civilian police advisors from the United States are generally contractors because the United States does not have a federal, uniformed law enforcement agency from which to second

58 Friesendorf and Krempel, *Militarized Versus Civilian Policing*, p. 31.

59 Hills, Alice, 'The Inherent Limits of Military Forces in Policing Peace Operations', *International Peacekeeping*, 8:3 (2001), p. 92; Hill, Stephen, and Randall Berger, 'A Paramilitary Policing Juggernaut', *Social Justice*, 36:1 (2009), pp. 32–34.

60 Beede, Benjamin R., 'The Roles of Paramilitary and Militarized Police', *Journal of Political and Military Sociology*, 36:1 (2008), pp. 59–60.

personnel for advisor duty. This stands in stark contrast to other developed states that not only have such a capability, but (like Australia) maintain the organizational capability to deploy their national police on such missions. The United States' contracted solution for police advising means that the US government is most often not able to get police advisors into a country for months. Once they are there, they depend on other agencies for the logistical support and security they need as they possess no organic sustainment capabilities.

In most late- and post-conflict FID operations, the US military has filled the void left by the lack of civilian capacity for police advising. From operations in Panama to Kosovo, and every operation in between and since, US Army and Marine Corps Military Police have been embedded with the initial intervention forces. Military Police units are by design quickly deployable and can survive in hostile environments. However, as exhibited here, military planners, even when aware of the challenge, have failed to adequately plan for police advising immediately after the end of major hostilities. Military Police have served as police advisors in an ad hoc manner without a plan, often until and after civilian advisors have been fielded.

Military Police have a proven capability to serve as police advisors and should be able to do so in future FID operations. The US Army Military Police Corps has taken steps that will codify the skills it needs to maintain a standing capability for police advising.[61] While this strategic plan covers three lines of effort, the two most pertinent to police advising in FID are a 'Ready and Professional MP' and 'Shape the Security Environment'. The former intends to focus the Military Police force toward professionalization in the sense of industry standards in the civilian world, better making Military Police capable of advising civilian police.[62] This includes working more closely with civilian federal law enforcement agencies and other joint and multinational partners to foster closer relationships with other organizations and give individual Military Police personnel experiences that improve traditional policing skills.[63]

Included in the US Army Military Police Corps' 'Shape the Security Environment' line of effort is a focus on enhancing the Corps' ability to build partner capacity, including in police advising.[64] As advising continues to gain in importance throughout the US Army, this focus reflects the police element and suggests a future review of Joint and Army doctrine to account for codified capabilities. This effort to institutionalize police advising indicates that the Army Military Police have overcome the barrier to codification presented by Section 660. Indeed, the *Strategic Plan* exceeds post-conflict FID and states that Military Police will be involved in pre-conflict and bilateral

61 US Army Office of the Provost Marshal General, *2025 Military Police Force Strategic Plan* (Washington, DC: US Army, 2016).
62 Ibid., p. 31.
63 Ibid., p. 33.
64 Ibid., p. 39.

efforts, including the Regional Alignment of Forces and the Military Police Security Force Assistance Team that is designed to embed with Special Operations Forces during FID operations.[65]

While the US Army Military Police Corps takes the steps to establish itself as the police advising solution of choice, fully leveraging this capability requires other individuals and institutions to also take action. Senior service and planning schools should institutionalize police reform and advising into their curricula. As shown in the two case studies examined here, having Military Police on the ground when needed for police advising did not translate into their use as such. The entirety of Army and Joint forces should better prepare for the planning of this vital task so that planning for police advising becomes a standard and regular aspect of war planning. Planning for the use of Military Police as police advisors in FID requires institutionalization beyond the Joint and Army force. Relevant civilian agencies, including law enforcement arms and the Department of State, should realize that as no civilian solution exists, and considering the mixed record of using civilian contractors, that Military Police are currently the best tool for police advising and that it is organizationally preparing to improve this capability. As Military Police personnel begin to work more closely with their interagency partners, these agencies should recognize the asset that Military Police provide and future policy should reflect this.

More research is needed on the role of Military Police as police advisors to foreign civilian police. In spite of decades of serving in this role, very little concerning these activities has been recorded from the individuals involved. Until that definitive account is written, we are able to glean some tentative lessons from past FID operations where Military Police personnel served as police advisors. Despite pressures to the contrary, Military Police should institutionalize the capability to be police advisors, and they should be provided the ability to build the skillsets that would make them better advisors—steps the Military Police Corps is already undertaking. Their role as advisors should be better planned before their deployment, and Military Police should be considered a short-term but effective solution for the police advising problem during FID.

65 For a comprehensive review of Regionally Aligned Forces see Cantwell, Gregory L., Tarn D., Warren, and Mark E. Orwat (eds), *Regionally Aligned Forces: Concept Viability and Implementation* (Carlisle, PA: US Army War College Student Publications, 2015).

7

The Street Cop Fallacy: Effectively Targeting Local Police Reform in Kosovo Since 2008 and Bosnia, 2003-2012

Birte Julia Gippert

Introduction

International intervention in post-conflict states has over the past decades increased in intrusiveness, scope, and ambition. External support for police reforms comes into play in situations where local police capacities are absent or so dysfunctional and biased they cannot effectively carry out the core responsibilities of a police force.[1] Reforming police after conflict is hence not a technical exercise aimed at strengthening an apolitical institution, but a social and political task that goes to the heart of local power balances and perceptions of internal security.[2] Consequently, local organizational structures and power hierarchies influence how police reform is carried out most efficiently. That means local structures and hierarchies determine which level of the police needs to be targeted to be most effective.

Many authors, however, observe that whenever international police officers fail to find the practical nitty-gritty guidance they require in order to implement 'European and international best practices', these officers fall back on their national guidelines and procedures. In a similar vein, police reform specialists have started to recommend national policing models and experience as guidance for post-conflict police reform. One such example is the recommendation to include into all reforms the so-called 'street cops'. This recommendation is based on the idea that these lower ranking officers have broad discretion in implementing laws and police procedures on the

1 Hansen, Annika, *From Congo to Kosovo: Civilian Police in Peace Operations*, Adelphi Paper 343, International Institute for Strategic Studies (London: Routledge, 2002).

2 Eide, Espen Barth and Tor Tanke Holm (eds), *Peacebuilding and Police Reform* (London: Routledge, 2000).

street. To fit their preferred style and mode of policing, they tend to change or adapt reforms from above (from the 'management cops'). If street cops do not buy into the reforms, this tendency to modify reforms can mean they will not get implemented in full or as intended.[3] As a result, scholars working in this field have recommended a bottom-up approach to police reforms to ensure proper implementation.

While this advice at face value sounds reasonable, it presents three interrelated problems. First, the scholars who originally made these recommendations drew them from observations of 1970s and 1980s policing problems in the United Kingdom (UK) and the United States (US). The noted divide between street cops and management cops was the consequence of the beginning of institutionalizing policing procedures to cut down on ingrained police secrecy, graft, and corruption.[4] As such this scholarship represented a very particular moment in time and reflected a policing situation prior to these changes. In this particular time and context street cops had a very large degree of discretion and leeway in how to interpret the laws and which jobs to 'crime' (meaning to recognise that an offense has been committed and formally start an investigation, which means it will show up in the crime statistics) and which to 'cuff' (meaning getting rid of it to avoid investigating its appearance in the crime statistics). Second, and consequentially, modern day policing in the UK (used as an example here) bears little resemblance to the policing practices and cultures of discretion described in this earlier scholarship. The modern street cop in the UK is monitored nearly completely, from Closed Circuit Television (CCTV) on the streets and in all public areas of the police stations, to body-worn cameras by officers, trackers in police cars, and recording of all internal radio communications and 999 calls, not to mention members of the public with smartphones. Discretion to 'cuff' jobs, let off offenders, and bend or break policies and laws to fit their convenience has hence become very limited. Third, if policing in the UK has moved so far away from the days of Life on Mars,[5] why does

3 Merlingen, Michael and Rasa Ostrauskaite, 'ESDP Police Missions: Meaning Context and Operational Challenges', *European Foreign Affairs Review*, 10 (2005), pp. 215-235; Peake, Gordon and Otwin Marenin, 'Their Reports Are Not Read and Their Recommendations Are Resisted: The Challange for the Global Police Policy Community', *Police Practice and Research*, 9:11 (2008), pp. 59-69; Wood, Jennifer, 'Cultural Change in the Governance of Security', *Policing and Society*, 14:1 (2004), pp. 31-48; Marenin, Otwin, 'Implementing Police Reforms: The Role of the Transnational Policy Community', in Goldsmith, Andrew and James Sheptycki (eds), *Crafting Transnational Policing: Police Capacity-Building and Global Policing Reform* (Oxford: Hart Publishing, 2007), pp. 177-201.

4 Ianni, Francis and Elizabeth Reuss-Ianni, 'Street Cops and Management Cops: The Two Cultures of Policing', in Punch, Maurice (ed.), *Control in the Police Organization* (Cambridge MA: MIT Press, 1983); Holdaway, Simon, 'Recruitment, Race, and the Police Subculture', in Stephens, Mike and Paul Becker (eds), *Police Force, Police Service: Care and Control in Britain* (Basingstoke: Macmillan, 1994); Waddington, Tank, *Policing Citizens* (London: UCL Press, 1999).

5 *Life on Mars* is a 2006-2007 BBC TV series in which a modern day copper from Manchester wakes up after an accident to find himself in 1973 Manchester. The series is

this outdated reality serve to inform international peacebuilding practices today? While some post-conflict environments may resemble 1970s British policing more than its modern equivalent, the uncritical import of the assumptions of unlimited police discretion and reform slippage—what I term the 'street cop fallacy'—hinders the proper understanding of post-conflict policing realities. This chapter argues that such an understanding is required to allow for effective targeting of police reforms.

Based on these problems with the scholarship, this chapter has three objectives. First, it presents and analyzes the original scholarship's arguments about street and management cops to understand the assumptions and context that spawned them. From this, it draws a comparison with modern day British policing, which constitutes the actual national background British police officers fall back on in an international police reform operation. Second, this chapter shows that the street cop fallacy misunderstands post-conflict police reform contexts. Its application to international peacebuilding has clouded rather than supported our approach to effectively targeting police reform as the insistence on bottom-up reforms does not consider the particular local organization of the police. Empirical evidence from the EU's two largest police support operations, the EU Rule of Law Mission in Kosovo (EULEX) and the EU Police Mission (EUPM) in Bosnia-Herzegovina (BiH) demonstrates that police reform in both countries needs to follow a top-down approach due to the rigid hierarchy of the local polices forces' chain of command, which negates any attempt to target reforms at lower level police officers. Lower ranks have no discretion whatsoever, not because of a high degree of institutionalization and surveillance as in Britain, but because the rigid hierarchy forbids delegation of power and decision-making to lower ranks. International police reforms in Kosovo and Bosnia therefore need to target the highest ranks and then rely on senior leaders to effect the changes throughout the local police. Hence, they require a top-down rather than a bottom-up approach to police reform. Third, drawing on the different realities of policing (1970s-1980s UK, modern day UK, Kosovo/BiH) this chapter constructs a matrix of the two principles which determine these different realities, the degree of institutionalization, and the degree of hierarchy. A matrix along these two axes helps visualize the differences and understand the principles and assumptions at play in each, and can serve to locate other post-conflict cases which divert from all three cases discussed here. This matrix hence allows for clearly depicting the real context of local police reform rather than 'borrowing' that of other countries and times, and assists in targeting police reforms to the level of the police where they will be most effective. The following section presents the two determinants of policing styles and then analyzes the policing models of Britain and the US before the 1970s and today, as those are the cases discussed in the scholarship that inform the peacebuilding recommendations regarding street cops.

about how he struggles to adapt to their realities of policing. See BBC, <http://www.bbc.co.uk/programmes/b006t85s>.

Life on Mars vs. Surveillance Culture

This chapter focuses on the effective targeting of international police reforms. It shows that the level at which reforms are best targeted depends on two determinants: the level of hierarchy and the level of institutionalization. Both concepts are not binary but matters of degree. The position of each force on the spectra of hierarchy and institutionalization tell us where international police reforms need to be targeted, at the top or at the bottom.

Institutionalization is understood here as behavior and actions of the police being guided and limited by laws, policies, rules, and formal guidelines of the police organization. A high degree of institutionalization means that officer conduct is determined strongly by such laws and policies and that consequently the degree of discretion they can exercise is very limited. A low degree of institutionalization means that officers are only roughly guided by laws and policies; they can exercise a high degree of discretion and autonomy in deciding how to apply laws and policies.

Hierarchy is understood here as an indicator of the internal coherence of a police organization and refers to the strength of the chain of command. A high degree of hierarchy means that officers are guided unquestioningly by the orders of their superiors, and as long as they do so are protected by them in turn. A low degree of hierarchy means officers have a high degree of personal autonomy and may follow orders of their superiors as long as these do not contravene any important code of conduct (formal or informal). Likewise, in this case the strength of the relationship between the ranks is quite loose.

With this conceptual understanding in mind, the following section analyzes policing in the UK before and after the reforms of the 1970s and 1980s and shows how their position on the spectra of institutionalization and hierarchy changed as a result of these reforms.

Policing in the 1960s and 1970s in both Britain and the US was based on the laws of the state and the professional judgement of the officer in interpreting and applying them. Police officers hence had a large degree of discretion in how and when to apply these laws. Waddington captures this spirit very well: 'police officers do not mechanically enforce the law: they pay attention to some incidents and not to others; they invoke their formal powers against some suspects while allowing others to go with a warning; they pay more attention to some people than to others. In other words, discretion is the pivot upon which the exercise of authority revolves'.[6] Discretion was aided by the low degree of external accountability and high ethos of solidarity in which officers, even if they made a mistake, could often rely on their line managers or peers to help them cover it up.

It is this solidarity and cohesion of the police, including the higher ranks, that street cops in 1980s New York lamented to have lost, according to the observational work of

6 Waddington, 'Policing Citizens', p. 31.

Francis Ianni and Elizabeth Reuss-Ianni.[7] Their work captures a point in time in the US in which this ethos and style of policing was in the process of being reformed due to the downsides of solidarity, namely corruption and graft. The authors found that as a result of this top-down reform process, which aimed at greater accountability of the police, the police became divided into what they call 'street cops' and 'management cops'.[8] Street cops are lower ranking officers who exercised a large degree of autonomy in their style of policing. They were disgruntled about the reforms that centralized decision-making at the higher levels, thus reducing their autonomy. Hence a split was observed by the authors in which street cops started to view the 'management cops' as being separate and more closely aligned with politics, and holding a different ethos of policing. Street cops preferred the 'good old days' of policing using their gut-level and professional experience to guide them rather than implementing the policies of 'management'.[9] Essentially, senior leaders were aiming to cut-down the discretion of officers and make policing more coherent and accountable by instituting standardized policies and guidelines. Lower level officers viewed these attempts with suspicion as they preferred to keep their discretion and autonomy rather than have their 'hands tied' by such reforms.

The divergence in policing cultures between the street cops and the management cops led to reforms and programs introduced by management being adjusted and changed by street cops to fit their preferred style and ethos of policing. Simon Holdaway, a policing scholar, gives several examples of how management reforms to cut down on street robberies were changed by street cops to the degree that the original intent of the changes was no longer recognizable.[10] Such reform or project slippage and adjustment is what Ianni and Reuss-Ianni also highlight with regard to the division between the two policing cultures, suggesting that any reform needs to be bought into by street cops to ensure it actually gets implemented as intended. Nigel Fielding and Tank Waddington, British policing scholars, come to the same conclusion based on their work with the British police in the 1970s and 1980s.[11] It is important to note that these works observed and explained a temporary and dynamic process particular to the late 1970s and 1980s (and to a degree in the 1990s) in both Britain and the US. This process was characterized by the clash of the 'Life on Mars' style of policing (high discretion and autonomy) and the beginning of surveillance policing that sought to eradicate both in the name of institutionalization and accountability. Although this scholarship captures a time in which top-down reforms were harder to enforce due

7 Ianni and Reuss-Ianni, 'Street Cops and Management Cops: The Two Cultures of Policing', p. 253.
8 Ibid., p. 254.
9 Ibid.
10 Holdaway, 'Recruitment, Race, and the Police Subculture'.
11 Fielding, Nigel, *Community Policing* (Oxford: Claredon Press, 1995); Waddington, 'Policing Citizens'; Fielding, Nigel, *Joining Forces: Police Training, Socialization, and Occupational Competence* (London: Routledge, 1988).

to the insistence of street cops on their autonomy, it finally did succeed in regulating street cop conduct.

Consequently, reading the police scholarship of the 1980s and 1990s today (2016) makes it sound as though it was describing a different planet, especially if one had not lived through those times. Policing in Britain today is no longer characterized by high levels of discretion and autonomy, but rather by the comprehensive surveillance and accountability the police are subject to by their internal Police Standards Department, the Police and Crime Commissioner, the Independent Police Complaints Commission, and of course the media and general public. While this does not exclude the possibility of leeway in certain instances, Waddington's dictum that 'police do not mechanically enforce the law' no longer rings true today as the web of policies, laws, and guidelines has become so dense as to leave little discretion for the officers and actually makes their policing-style resemble that of a bureaucratic machine. In that sense, the top-down reforms succeeded.[12]

To visualize policing in 2016 Britain, compared to the 1970s and 1980s, one can simply follow the trail of any incoming 999 call. The initial call and the reply of the control room are recorded as are all radio-communications between officers, including units being sent to the address of the caller. The time it takes a supervisor to pick up the new job created by the call and dispatch a unit is recorded ('dispatch time'). Trackers in the police cars give supervisors the chance to monitor where the unit is at any point in time. The response time of the unit is recorded and becomes part of the force's statistics on service delivery. At the scene, the body-worn cameras of the officers record their entire encounter with the caller and their dealing with the situation.[13] If the scene of the incident is in a public place, CCTV footage will record the police officer's actions and often individual members of the public do the same on their smartphones, especially if force is used. If anyone is arrested at the scene, the arrest is also captured on the body-worn cameras of the officers. All public areas of police stations, including the custody block, to which the arrested person is then brought, are monitored by CCTV with audio, including interview rooms and holding cells. The interviews are recorded and strict rules apply as to how long all custody records have to be stored. All detained individuals have the right to make a phone call, speak to their solicitor at any time, be served meals and drinks, and have a period of eight hours of rest in the 24 hours the police can hold them.[14]

What this illustration shows is the limited opportunities police officers today have to exercise the kind of discretion the scholarship on the 1980s and 1990s discusses. Police conduct is not only monitored on the streets, in public places, and private

12 Waddington, 'Policing Citizens', p. 31.

13 Police standard operating procedures now dictate that any encounter with a member of the public is recorded on body-worn camera. This is to ensure accountability as well as correct police conduct.

14 House of Commons, *Police and Criminal Evidence Act*; interviews with UK Police officers, April 2016.

homes, but also in the police station. All conduct is furthermore subject to internal and external investigations. This serves to discourage the form of solidarity that in the past led officers to help colleagues cover up mistakes or policy breaches.[15] Such cover-ups are also made harder by the institutionalization of Victim Satisfaction Call-Backs, a policy introduced by all forces around the late 2000s, in which supervisors randomly call up victims of investigated crimes to ask whether they were satisfied with the police service provided.[16] Further, a formal policy on handling domestic violence, an area in which previously discretion was broad, was brought in as of 2009. This policy requires officers to fill in a DASH (domestic abuse, stalking, honor-based violence) form, essentially a tick list of whether the severity of a case is to be graded 'standard', 'medium', or 'high', which then determines the police response. This has closed off the possibility of officers accepting threadbare accounts of victims claiming to have 'fallen down' or 'having run into an open door' because they are scared of the perpetrator's reaction or the lack of interest and action by the police. At the same time 'positive action' policies were introduced, meaning the police had to act, at the very least, to remove one party from the dispute scene or put future safeguards into place. The possibility to 'cuff' jobs, has hence been further limited.[17]

The essential difference between policing in the 1970s and before and policing in 2016 is the degree of institutionalization and accountability; an ongoing process the above policy changes show. While policing scholars Gordon Peake and Otwin Marenin rightly point out that the police reform community tends to re-invent the wheel rather than read the lessons provided by their predecessors, this comparison does highlight the absurdity of recommending post-conflict police reform lessons based on a UK and US policing reality that no longer exists.[18] Rather than follow the street cop fallacy, the following sections show the realities of police reform in Kosovo and Bosnia-Herzegovina and highlight how these realities determine where to focus police reforms most effectively.

15 See the website of the IPCC for their powers: <https://www.ipcc.gov.uk/>.
16 Thames Valley Police, Freedom of Information Request to Thames Valley Police, 25 June 2016, on file with the author; Metropolitan Police Service, Freedom of Information Request to the Metropolitan Police Service, 17 June 2016, on file with the author. There is a rather stark example of the need for such checks in Thames Valley Police. The investigating officer kept a log of his checks on the victim which turned out to be entirely fabricated when supervisors realised the victim had actually passed away months prior, <http://www.bbc.co.uk/news/uk-england-berkshire-35776843>.
17 Interview with PSD Inspector of Thames Valley Police, March 2013.
18 Peake and Marenin, 'Their Reports Are Not Read'.

International Police Reform

The question of what policing is has filled many books.[19] A useful definition is provided by Waddington, who considers policing 'the exercise of the authority of [the] state over the civil population. That authority is based on the monopoly of legitimate coercion. How this is done and the way that policing is organized reflects the relationship between the civil population and the state'.[20] This definition draws attention to several features that make policing such an important task. First, the police are the most visible arm of the state. As the primary internal security instrument, police are tasked with maintaining civil law and order in the state, as opposed to the military who are in charge of external security. Second, the police embody the state's legitimate right to the use force. In the Weberian understanding, a state's sovereignty is defined precisely by this monopoly of the use of force.[21] How police are used and structured is therefore a key political concern for the state and its citizens. Finally, the police's organizational culture mirrors the state's approach to its own citizens. The police can, at extreme ends, either serve the state and protect it against its population, or it can serve the citizens and ensure their security.[22] The police therefore play a key role in the organizational structure of a state.

In civil wars, law and order breaks down or is enforced by military rather than civilian means. This confounds the traditional internal and external security roles of the police and military.[23] Additionally, the police itself often become embroiled in the conflict, and lose their civilian nature and neutrality. In many cases the police become or have traditionally been tools of oppression in the hands of elites, and used against the population or parts of the population.[24] In order to ensure lasting peace, conditions have to be created in which the police maintain law and order, protect all civilians, and are accountable to comprehensive civilian controls.[25]

Ideally, each society can create these conditions internally. However, after conflict the resources and capabilities of states and the ties that hold together society are often

19 Fielding, 'Community Policing'; Morash, Merry and J. Kevin Ford, 'Transforming Police Organizations', in Morash, Merry and J. Kevin Ford (eds), *The Move to Community Policing* (Thousand Oaks, CA: SAGE Publications, 2002); Eide and Holm (eds), *Peacebuilding and Police Reform.*

20 Waddington, 'Policing Citizens', p. 13.

21 Weber, Max, *Economy and Society*, Guenther Roth and Claus Wittich (eds) (Berkeley, CA: University of California Press, 1978).

22 Fielding, 'Community Policing'.

23 Eide and Holm (eds), *Peacebuilding and Police Reform.*

24 Collantes-Celador, Gemma, 'Police Reform: Peacebuilding through "Democratic Policing"?', *International Peacekeeping*, 12:3 (2005), pp. 364–376; Charley, Joseph P. Chris and Freida Ibiduni M'Cormack, 'A "Force for Good"? Police Reform in Post-Conflict Sierra Leone', *IDS Bulletin*, 43:4 (2012), pp. 49–62.

25 Call, Charles and Michael Barnett, 'Looking for a Few Good Cops: Peacekeeping, Peacebuilding, and CIVPOL', in Eide and Holm (eds), *Peacebuilding and Police Reform.*

shattered. External support for police reforms comes into play in such situations where either police capacities are absent, or so dysfunctional and biased they cannot effectively carry out the core responsibilities listed above.[26] Reforming police after conflict is hence not a technical exercise aimed at strengthening an apolitical institution, but a social and political task that goes to the heart of local power balances and perceptions of internal security.[27] Consequently, local organizational structures and power hierarchies influence how police reform is carried out most efficiently and which level of the police it needs to target to be most effective. The following case studies show that unless the organizational structures of the local police are the subject of reform, it is most effective to work with them rather than against them.

EU Police Building

Throughout the Yugoslav wars in the 1990s, the EU witnessed its dependence on US warfighting ability. The militaries of the member states were unprepared for anything but territorial defense, lacked force projection capabilities, and a common strategic culture.[28] In reaction, France and Britain signed what became known as the St Malo Declaration in December 1998, which states that 'the Union must have the capacity for autonomous action, backed up by credible military forces, the means to decide to use them, and a readiness to do so, in order to respond to international crises'.[29] The outcome was the Common Security and Defence Policy (CSDP), inaugurated in 1999, with which the EU equipped itself with the mechanisms for conducting independent military and civilian crisis management. While the development of military means had been prioritized and made headlines both internationally and in the member states, it was the civilian crisis management capacities which have grown fastest and from which the vast majority of missions have been deployed so far.[30] Civilian Crisis Management, which includes police reform, is the EU equivalent of United Nations peacebuilding. Both can potentially apply to pre- and post-conflict

26 Hansen, *From Congo to Kosovo: Civilian Police in Peace Operations.*

27 Eide and Holm (eds), *Peacebuilding and Police Reform*; Hansen, *From Congo to Kosovo: Civilian Police in Peace Operations.*

28 Freire, Maria Raquel, 'The European Security and Defence Policy', in Merlingen, Michael and Rasa Ostrauskaite (eds), *European Security and Defence Policy: An Implementation Perspective* (London: Routledge, 2008).

29 Rutten, Maartje, 'From St Malo to Nice. European Defence–Core Documents', Chaillot Paper 47 (Paris: Institute for Security Studies, Western European Union, May 2001).

30 Merand, Frederic, *European Defence Policy: Beyond the Nation State* (Abingdon: Oxford University Press, 2008); Howorth, Joylon, 'The EU's Security and Defence Policy: Towards a Strategic Approach', in Hill, Christopher and Michael Smith (eds), *International Relations and the European Union* (Abingdon: Oxford University Press, 2011); The International Institute for Strategic Studies, *European Military Capabilities: Building Armed Forces for Modern Operations* (London: International Institute for Strategic Studies, 2008).

situations in which non-military tools are required to secure peace and stability. The EU deployed its first peacebuilding mission on 1 January 2003, the EU Police Mission in Bosnia-Herzegovina.

The Yugoslav Legacy

This section analyses police reform efforts by the EU in Kosovo and Bosnia and illustrates on the basis of empirical data where on the spectra of hierarchy and institutionalization these forces can be found, and how this position determines their policing styles. As argued above, the organizational style of any police force determines at which level police reforms are targeted most effectively.

Kosovo and Bosnia had both been part of the communist state of Yugoslavia since 1945, and emerged in their current form after the protracted and violent struggles known as the Yugoslav wars.[31] Bosnia had been a republic within Yugoslavia and hence one of its constituent units with the theoretical right to secede. Just how theoretical this right was became obvious when the government declared Bosnia's independence from Yugoslavia in 1992 and was subsequently invaded by troops from Serbia and Croatia fighting to retain the territory of 'their' ethnic groups. In the four years of civil war, Bosnia was torn apart and the Bosnian police, divided into ethnically coherent units, turned into paramilitary troops that were involved in some of the worst atrocities committed during the war.[32]

Kosovo had been an autonomous province of the Republic of Serbia despite its ethnic Albanian majority and was thus considered part of Serbia even after the war. Serbia, under Slobodan Milosevic, instituted an effective 'apartheid regime' in Kosovo from 1989 onwards, banning Albanians from holding public office and other jobs, or being taught in their own language.[33] The Kosovo conflict became militarized in 1997-98 when Kosovo-Albanians saw the international community resolving the Bosnian war without considering the situation of Kosovo-Albanians. The Kosovo Liberation Army started an armed insurgency against the Serbian regime that controlled Kosovo that lasted until March 1999 when NATO decided to stop what was amounting to ethnic cleansing by the Serbian Army in Kosovo.[34] However, after the withdrawal

31 Woodward, Susan L., *The Balkan Tragedy* (Washington, DC: The Brookings Institute, 1995); Crnobrnja, Mihaljo, *The Yugoslav Drama* (London: I.B. Tauris, 1994); Silber, Laura and Allan Little, *The Death of Yugoslavia* (London: Penguin, 1996).

32 Collantes-Celador, Gemma, 'Becoming "European" through Police Reform: A Successful Strategy in Bosnia and Herzegovina?', *Crime, Law and Social Change*, 51:2 (2008), pp. 231-242.

33 Weller, Marc, *The Crisis in Kosovo 1989–1999. International Documents and Analysis*, Vol. I (London: Documents and Analysis Pub., 1999).

34 Judah, Tim, *Kosovo: War and Revenge* (New Haven, CT: Yale University Press, 2002); King, Iain and Whit Mason, *Peace at Any Price: How the World Failed Kosovo* (Ithaca: Cornell University Press, 2006).

of Serbian troops, the Serbian controlled administration broke down, necessitating a UN administration of Kosovo.[35] Kosovo-Albanians declared independence from Serbia unilaterally in 2008 and remain to this date (2016) in legal limbo as Serbia and Russia block their acceptance into the UN to deny them international legitimacy. The Kosovo police, controlled and staffed mainly by Serbs, disintegrated after the NATO bombings.

While the approach of the international community to police reform in the two countries was as different as their respective situations after the wars, their local background of police styles was remarkably similar, being shaped by existing and traditional Yugoslav policing mentalities. Beginning in 1996, Bosnian police reform was carried out by the International Police Training Force (IPTF), mandated by the United Nations. It was mandated to vet all officers for war crimes and significantly reduce the size of the police force, which had swelled during the war. Despite criticisms and drawbacks, IPTF succeeded in demilitarizing the Bosnian police, reasserting its role and self-understanding as a civilian law and order enforcer, and starting to create the mindset of public service.[36] The European Union Police Mission in Bosnia-Herzegovina took over from IPTF in January 2003 with the mandate to bring the local police 'closer to European standards'.[37]

In Kosovo, however, the decision was taken by the UN mission to build up a new police force from scratch and takeover executive policing of the country in the meantime. The Kosovo Police (KP) started acting as an independent police force in charge of the territory after the country's declaration of independence in 2008 as local politicians refused to respect the UN mission's right and legitimacy in governing and policing.[38] The Kosovo government did, however, accept the EU Rule of Law Mission (EULEX) for advising and monitoring the local police.[39] As Kosovo is not recognized as an independent state by the UN and some EU member states, EULEX officially continues the UN policy of not recognizing Kosovo's independence and treating Kosovo's status as unresolved. This is, however, only diplomatic window-dressing to

35 The Security Council, 'Security Council Resolution 1244' (S/RES/1244), (10 June 1999).
36 Palmer, Kendall, 'Police Reforms in Bosnia-Herzegovina: External Pressure and Internal Resistance', in Caparini, Marina and Otwin Marenin (eds), *Transforming Police in Central and Eastern Europe* (Geneva: DCAF, 2004), pp. 169-193; The International Crisis Group, 'Policing the Police in Bosnia: A Further Reform Agenda' (Sarajevo: The International Crisis Group, 2002).
37 The Council of the European Union, 'Joint Action 2002/210/CFSP' (1 March 2002), OJ L 70, 2002.
38 Harris, Frank, 'Police Reform in Kosovo: A Case Study', unpublished, copy with author, 2009.
39 The Council of the European Union, 'Council of the European Union Joint Action, 2008/124/CFSP', O.J. (L42) 92, 2008.

maintain Russian and Serbian support for the operation as much of EULEX's work is based on Kosovo state laws.[40]

Both Bosnia and Kosovo hence have featured two of the largest and most comprehensive EU police missions to date; EUPM closed down in June 2012 after nine years on the ground, while EULEX is still ongoing. There are excellent works on both missions and the impact they have or have not had on the local police, but this chapter focuses on the structures and hierarchies of the two police forces in order to explore how international reforms can be best targeted.[41]

Hierarchy Trumps All

Despite their different experiences during and after the Yugoslav wars, both Kosovo and Bosnia share the legacy of Yugoslav policing, which remains visible and strong in both 'new' forces. The police in the former Yugoslavia was a highly professional force whose aim was to protect the state from internal threats. Policing was therefore directed against controlling the behavior and action of the population and ensuring their support to the state. The police adhered to a very strict understanding of hierarchy within the command structure, which made decision-making rigid and consequently slow.[42] This organizational legacy of Yugoslav times has persisted despite the reforms in Bosnia and the creation of the Kosovo Police. Both forces display a very strict command structure characterized by little to no delegation of power to middle-management or lower ranks, centralization of decision-making at the top (no matter how small the decision) and consequently very little discretion for lower

40 de Wet, Erika, 'The International Constitutional Order', *International and Comparative Law Quarterly*, 55:1 (2006), pp. 51-76; Muharremi, Robert, 'The European Union Rule of Law Mission in Kosovo (EULEX) from the Perspective of Kosovo Constitunional Law', *Zeitschrift für Ausländisches Öffentliches Recht und Völkerrecht*, 70 (2010), pp. 357-379.

41 Richter, Solveig, 'Promoting Rule of Law without State-Building: Can EULEX Square the Circle in Kosovo?', in Asseburg, Muriel and Ronja Kempin (eds), *The EU as a Strategic Actor in the Realm of Security and Defence?* (Berlin: German Institute for International and Security Affairs, 2009), pp. 30–45; Grevi, Giovanni, 'The EU Rule-of-Law Mission in Kosovo (EULEX Kosovo)', in Grevi, Helly and Dan Keohane (eds), *European Security and Defence Policy: The First 10 Years* (Paris: European Union Institute for Security Studies, 2009); Mühlmann, Thomas, 'Police Restructuring in Bosnia-Herzegovina: Problems of Internationally-Led Security Sector Reform', *Journal of Intervention and Statebuilding*, 2:1 (2007), pp. 37–65; Mühlmann, Thomas, 'The Police Mission EUPM in Bosnia 2003-05', in Merlingen and Ostrauskaite (eds), *European Security and Defence Policy*, pp. 43–59; Gippert, Birte Julia, 'Exploring Local Compliance with Peacebuilding Reforms: Legitimacy, Coercion and Reward-Seeking in Police Reform in Kosovo', *International Peacekeeping*, 23:1 (2016), pp. 52–78; Keukeleire, Stephan and Robin Thiers, *EULEX Kosovo: Walking a Thin Line, Aiming for the Rule of Law* (Leuven: Asser Press, 2010).

42 Dziedzic, Michael, 'Introduction', in Oakley, Robert B., Micheal J. Dziedzic, and Eliot M. Goldberg (eds), *Policing The New World Disorder: Peace Operations and Public Security* (Washington, DC: National Defense Univeristy Press, 1998), pp. 3-18.

ranking officers. Any changes or reforms need to follow this top-down organizational structure. Diversion from this command structure is penalized swiftly and harshly and the weakness of the local police federations mean officers know better than to argue with their superiors.[43] A local cultural tradition of respect for authority figures and elders further compounds this absolute hierarchy.

It is this reality of policing in Bosnia and Kosovo in which the reforms of EULEX and EUPM haven been taking place. For both operations, no reform of the police structure and organization was envisioned, which means any reforms have to occur with the consent of the existing leadership. Both operations employed co-location as a means of delivering reforms. Co-location means placing international officers alongside their local counterparts to monitor, mentor, and advise them in accordance with the mandates of the two missions.

In Bosnia, the first of the two missions, co-location was only effected at the middle- and senior ranks of the local police as the EU wanted to exercise a small footprint and not be too intrusive.[44] EUPM therefore did not work with 'street cops' but focused their reforms on the higher ranks. Michael Merlingen and Rasa Ostrauskaite criticize this lack of involvement with lower ranks, quoting the 1980s and 1990s scholarship which highlights the danger of not including street cops into the reform process. For these authors, EUPM's organizational approach to reform was therefore a direct explanation for the mission's failure to implement reforms in a meaningful way.[45]

However, my own field work in Bosnia, combined with an examination of EUPM's monthly reports, show a different picture. While EUPM was clearly struggling to implement reforms and to obtain local support beyond rhetoric and empty gestures, this was not because of their organizational approach but because of the content of the reforms. The Dayton Peace Agreement of 1995 established a Bosnian state that comprised two strong (ethnically-based) entities: the Bosniak-Croat Federation and the Serb-majority but ethnically mixed Republika Srpska (RS), hence achieving peace by separating the warring parties.[46] Policing is an entity right, which, in the Republika Srpska is conducted by one centralized force and in the Federation by 10 cantonal forces.[47] EUPM's mandate and reform program aimed at strengthening the central level of the state and support the Office of the High Representative's project

43 International Crisis Group, 'The Rule of Law in Independent Kosovo', Europe Report No. 204 (Prishtina/Brussels, May 2010); The International Crisis Group, 'Bosnia's Stalled Police Reform: No Progress, No EU', Europe Report No. 164 (6 September 2005).

44 Merlingen and Ostrauskaite, 'ESDP Police Missions: Meaning Context and Operational Challenges', p. 231.

45 Ibid., pp. 231-323.

46 GFAP, 'The General Framework Agreement for Peace in Bosnia and Herzegovina', Dayton, Ohio, November 1995.

47 In addition, there is one Federal police force, a separate force for the Brcko District which joins the Federation to the Republika Srpska in the north, and two state-wide forces tasked with border control and serious crimes.

to centralize the police, abolishing the decentralized system of police.[48] These reform projects threatened the established local power structures in the RS and the delicate balance of power between the ethnic groups in mixed Federation cantons such as Mostar.

The RS vehemently opposed any reforms that would take policing rights away from the entities, arguing that policing is a vital security guarantee for Serbs in the Bosniak-majority Bosnian state, and that such a change would contravene the constitution; a valid assertion.[49] In the mixed Federation cantons like Mostar the police became a tool for ethnic power plays in which the two groups, Bosniaks and Croats, asserted their dominance and ensured protection of their own respective group. While now in one Federation, Mostar is the stark reminder that these two groups were initially enemies that fought a very bitter war in and around Mostar. They only allied in February 1994 to face the greater threat of the Serbian military.[50] Interviews with local police officers and former EUPM staff show the entrenched nature of these power struggles in Mostar. At the time of my field work, the position of police commissioner had been vacant for over three months as the two groups could not agree on a candidate. The fact that there was a 'neutral' board that was meant to make the appointment (introduced by IPTF reforms) was literally laughed at by one interviewee, a high ranking Mostar police officer.[51] Politics and ethnic power struggles pervade policing in Bosnia and the following statement of the International Crisis Group rings as true today as it did at the time of the report:

> The role of the police is not seen as being to 'serve and protect' everyone, but to serve and protect 'one's own kind', whether they be co-nationals, colleagues or political master. The communist-era doctrine that the police exist to defend the regime persists, except that the working class has been replaced by the nation as the ostensible beneficiary. Even 'moderate' politicians expect—and are often allowed—to influence investigations, recruitment, and budgetary allocations.[52]

The police are linked directly to politics, usually through the senior police ranks. While this link is institutionalized through the oversight of the Ministry of Interior

48 The Office of the High Representative is an international institution responsible for overseeing the implementation of the civilian aspects of the General Framework Agreement for Peace that ended the Bosnian civil war in 1995. The High Representative has the power to remove public officials including police officers, who violate the Dayton Agreement and to impose laws if the elected officials fail to do so.

49 Mühlmann, 'Police Restructuring in Bosnia-Herzegovina: Problems of Internationally-Led Security Sector Reform'.

50 Woodward, *The Balkan Tragedy*; Donia, Robert and John Fine Jr., *Bosnia and Hercegovina: A Tradition Betrayed* (London: Hurst and Company, 1994).

51 Interviews, Bosnian police, Mostar, October 2013.

52 International Crisis Group, 'Policing the Police in Bosnia: A Further Reform Agenda', p. i.

it is abused to take direct influence in the running and operations of the police. Both EUPM reports and interviewees tell tales of aborted investigations, lost evidence, or unwilling investigators in cases related to well-connected individuals or politicians.[53] The years-long struggle with the RS to persuade them to 'find' former Bosnian-Serb leaders wanted by The Hague for war crimes, including Radovan Karadzic, illustrates this problem.[54]

The abuse of power, in which the police is an important tool, also has considerable influence on the way policing is conducted and the chain of command. EUPM's struggle to implement community policing as a new approach in which the community serves as a partner and reference point for policing priorities, was characteristic for the content of the reforms being the problem, not their organizational approach.[55] Community policing was meant to heal the broken trust between the population (particularly ethnic minorities living in a majority area) and the police that had become militarized and actively participated in the atrocities committed during the war.[56] These reforms entail by definition a delegation of power from the higher ranks to lower ranked community police officers and to the community.

EUPM's community policing reforms were introduced into the Federation cantons and the RS in May 2004.[57] Implementation consisted of four different stages through which all Federation cantons worked without major problems. In the RS, however, the Ministry of Interior, responsible for the police, refused pointblank to introduce the reforms.[58] Only after considerable pressure was put on the RS leadership by EUPM and the OHR (including threatening to fire recalcitrant officers) were the reforms slowly started in November 2004. They were reported as finished in 2005.[59] Speaking to officers of the RS police and members of the Ministry of Interior (MOI) reveals that these reforms were resisted because they threatened the tight grip the MOI holds over the police. Delegation of power was equated with 'loss of power', which was resisted at all costs.[60] In the ethnically mixed canton of Mostar, where implementation had worked fine, community policing was abandoned the minute the

53 EUPM, 'Monthly Assessment Report November 2004', Council of the European Union 16241/04 (17 December 2004); interviews with Bosnian Police, October 2013.
54 International Crisis Group, 'Policing the Police in Bosnia: A Further Reform Agenda'.
55 Morash and Ford, 'Transforming Police Organizations'.
56 Collantes-Celador, 'Becoming "European" through Police Reform: A Successful Strategy in Bosnia and Herzegovina?'
57 EUPM, 'Project Implementation Plan 5.5. Implementation of Community Policing' (15 January 2004). Copy with the author.
58 EUPM, 'EUPM Monthly Assessment Report November 2004', Council of the European Union 16241/04 (17 December 2004). Copy with the author.
59 EUPM, 'Cover Letter PIP 5.5. Implementation of Community Policing', Programme Development and Coordination Department (4 November, 2005). Copy with the author.
60 Interviews, Bosnian police and MoI (October 2013).

EUPM co-locators left. Mostar today does not have a community policing concept for the same reasons as the RS.[61]

These examples showcase that the problems EUPM faced in implementing their reforms were due to local resistance to the content and consequences of reform, rather than the fact they did not consult street cops. Indeed, EUPM learned very quickly, as did I with regard to obtaining permission for my interviews, that in Bosnia all policing decisions are taken by senior leaders. There is consequently no point whatsoever in consulting street cops about reforms, or indeed trying to interview them without senior rank permission. The Yugoslav legacy in Bosnia entails an almost absolute chain of command without delegation of power to lower ranks. As these reform examples show, the slightest indication that a delegation of power would be required was resisted greatly.[62]

The scholarship on post-conflict police reform uses Kosovo as an example of how the EU has learned from its mistakes, as in Kosovo co-location was effected throughout all ranks of the police.[63] International officers accompanied their counterparts ranging from lower ranking officers to the general director of the police. Speaking to EULEX staff, however, reveals that this was simply window-dressing as working with lower ranks was 'incredibly frustrating' and 'pointless'.[64] All interviewees confirmed the same story. Lower ranking officers were friendly and interested in the reforms, but would refuse to implement anything without the direct order of their line manager. If problems of cooperation or with details of the reforms occurred with a lower ranking officer, the EULEX member of staff would have to speak to his EULEX superior to get him to speak to his local counterpart and make him order his lower ranked officer to comply with the reform. Lower ranked officers showed no flexibility in making decisions even if they were officially within their remit but always consulted with their line manager, who usually then consulted his, all the way up to the senior management. This was a time-consuming exercise that frustrated EULEX officers who told me they were simply not used to such a lack of delegation of power.[65] The same was true for middle-management ranks, who were also unwilling to make decisions. One long-serving EULEX officer observed 'this is not a chain of command

61 EUPM, 'EUPM Monthly Assessment Report, July 2004', Council of the European Union, 11917/04 (24 August 2004). Copy with the author. Interviews Bosnian Police, Mostar, October 2013.

62 There was less resistance in the ethnically more homogenous cantons as the delegation there did not threaten the chain of command's power and the political grasp over the police as there were no power struggles ongoing.

63 Merlingen, Michael and Rasa Ostrauskaite (eds), *European Union Peacebuilding and Policing: Governance and the European Security and Defence Policy* (London: Taylor and Francis, 2006); Merlingen, Michael, 'The EU Police Mission in Bosnia and Hezegovina (EUPM)', in Grevi, Helly and Dan Keohane (eds), *European Security and Defence Policy: The First 10 Years* (European Union Institute for Security Studies, 2009), pp. 161–171.

64 Interviews, EULEX staff, Kosovo, April 2013.

65 Ibid.

they have here. There is flexibility in any chain, between the links, you know. This here is a rod of command'.[66]

While politicization of the police is less of a problem in Kosovo's day-to-day policing, it does permeate the senior ranks. This is facilitated by the Law on Police, which makes the general director appointable by the Prime Minister for terms as short as six weeks.[67] This ensures political control of the direction of the police and is used to cut short investigations into well-connected individuals or members of government.[68] This also could be seen in the reaction of local officers when co-located with EULEX officers during investigations into organized crime or in cases of alleged corruption. In many cases, the local officers would simply admit they did not feel comfortable investigating the case as they feared the consequences. The same is true for local judges, many of whom refused to try certain individuals.[69] EULEX reforms that targeted the interface between the police and the prosecution were never started on the local side for nontransparent reasons including 'lack of resources'.[70] That is the reason EULEX was granted executive powers in investigating and trying individuals for war-crimes, serious financial crimes, as well as corruption and organized crime. However, their track-record is, for different reasons, not much better.[71]

The Yugoslav legacy of a strict command structure, no delegation of power, and little discretion for lower ranking officers is hence as present in Kosovo as it is in Bosnia. EULEX staff equally had to learn quickly that targeting the senior ranks of the police was the only effective way of getting anything done. This comparative analysis of Bosnia and Kosovo shows that despite the different approaches to police reform taken by the international community, vetting versus recreating the police, and the difference between EUPM and EULEX with regard to co-location, the result was similar in both cases. In both countries, the local police judged police reforms on their content and the danger they posed to entrenched authorities rather than on whether they targeted lower ranked officers. Whenever the local police had a general director who was supportive of international reforms, their reform implementation increased

66 Ibid.
67 The Assembly of Kosovo, *Law on Police*, Law Nr. 03/L-035, 2008.
68 International Crisis Group, 'The Rule of Law in Independent Kosovo'.
69 Interviews, EULEX staff (April, 2012); International Crisis Group, 'The Rule of Law in Independent Kosovo'.
70 EULEX, *Monitoring, Mentoring and Advising Tracking Mechanism* (February 2011); EULEX, *Programme Report 2011* (2011).
71 KIPRED, 'A Comprehensive Analysis of EULEX: What next?', Policy Paper No. 1/13 (January 2013); Gippert, Birte Julia, 'The Sum of Its Parts? Sources of Local Legitimacy', *Cooperation and Conflict*, <http://cac.sagepub.com/cgi/reprint/0010836716652426v1.pdf?ijkey=hPvLudDrTtQQj6Xandkeytype=finite>; EULEX, *Programme Report 2010* (2010).

in speed and ease, whereas general directors who were suspicious of international influence slowed down reforms.[72]

The absolute power of the chain of command in Kosovo and Bosnia means that any reforms that have senior management backing will be enforced through the chain and implemented correctly. This was shown during many of my interviews at police stations across Kosovo, which were implementing EULEX's reforms. The station managers often did not know that these reforms were not police chain of command reforms because that was who ordered them to be implemented. Once the reforms become part of the local chain of command, implementation is almost guaranteed as, like in Bosnia, the hierarchy of the police trumps all other considerations of lower ranking officers, even if they doubt the merit of the reforms. A bottom-up approach to police reform that targets street cops is hence ineffective and impractical in both Kosovo and Bosnia.

A Policing Matrix

This chapter deals with several different fields of policing scholarship and concepts. This section draws these diverse issues together and highlights the determinants that underlie the different policing cultures that have been discussed. This section shows that all these styles work on the spectra of two policing principles: institutionalization and hierarchy. As elaborated above, the position on each spectrum determines the ensuing policing style and tells us how to approach reforms. The different styles of policing this chapter has explored all fall at different points on the matrix constructed by these two policing principles. The following graph is a visualization of the matrix and the approximate positions the different policing styles take.

This graph illustrates the different degrees of institutionalization and hierarchy that determine the policing style of the forces analyzed here: the UK before the late 1970s, the UK in 2016, and Kosovo and Bosnia pre- and post-conflict. The graph shows the result of the process of reforms the countries went through and how it changed their place in the matrix. Kosovo and Bosnia retained a very high degree of hierarchy in which orders are obeyed without question. However, the reforms did have an impact on the degree of institutionalization of the local police forces. Writing and implementing policies for the forces was a large part of the reform agenda of both EUPM and EULEX, and while some of the more controversial policies and standard operating procedures (SOPs) have only ended up in senior leaders' drawers, many others are being implemented and have led to a more coherent approach to policing. Examples of this include a more coherent approach to traffic policing in Kosovo where officers only issue penalty notices, but to deter corruption they do not collect fines on the spot. Also, the public complaints procedure in both countries has

72 EULEX, 'EULEX Programme—Final Report on MMA Action PSD 14/2009–Annual Patrol Plan/Stations' (25 March 2012).

Matrix of Hierarchy and Institutionalization

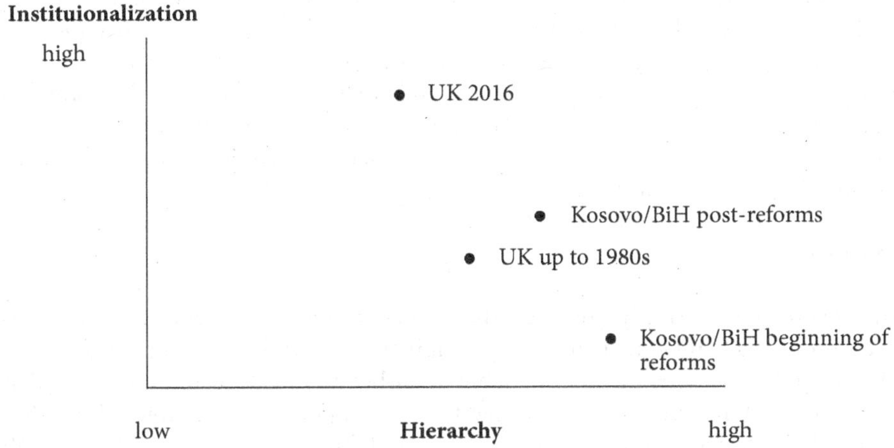

been regulated to ensure a systematic collection and response to complaints about officers rather than burying them. This is mirrored in Kosovo by the high approval ratings of the population for their local police, crucial documents that do not exist in this form for Bosnia.[73]

Policing in the UK changed from a position in which hierarchy trumped institutionalization (the 1960s and 1970s) to a position in which institutionalization is so strong that officers will no longer unquestioningly follow orders they know to breach policy. This does of course still happen, but only in minor cases, and it is more often that officers report incidents they have witnessed, including examples of arresting a colleague for drunk driving, inappropriate sexual relations with victims, or breach of data protection.[74] Hierarchy still matters of course; an order is binding for officers unless it breaches policies or law.

The police are an inherently hierarchical organization, but the style of policing nevertheless fluctuates between the ends of these two spectra. In police forces that are located on the higher end of the hierarchy spectrum, it is unlikely that lower ranking police officers will have much discretion beyond what they are granted from the chain of command. The same is true for officers of police forces that are located high on the

73 Saferworld, 'Still Time to Act' (Prishtina, October 2012); Saferworld, 'A Matter of Trust' (Prishtina, October 2010); Bennett, Christine, 'Public Perceptions of Safety and Security in Kosovo: Time to Act' (October 2011); UNDP, 'Public Pulse Poll' (August 2012).

74 Interviews with UK officers, March 2016.

institutionalization spectrum, but for the different reason that their actions are guided and limited by existing policies and laws, rather than their line managers.

Understanding these determinants of policing styles and how they align can provide a guide for successful police reforms. Street cops will have discretion in some forces and in those cases making sure they are on board with the reforms will have an impact on how successfully they are implemented and adhered to. However, there are many forces, post-conflict or not, where for different reasons targeting reforms at street cops is a waste of time and may in the worst case alienate the senior management, further limiting the chance of success.

Conclusion

This chapter has critically analyzed the scholarship and the context in which the writings on street and management cops originated. It has found that the very specific time and policing context this scholarship describes no longer corresponds to policing realities in the UK. That means first, that the current policing background UK officers seconded to international police operations would fall back on is very different to that described in the street cop scholarship dating from the 1980s and 1990s. Second, if many Western states have overcome this state of policing that underlies the street cop scholarship, why would we apply it to post-conflict police reforms? While it is certainly useful to learn lessons from past scholars and practitioners as Peake and Marenin point out, it is absurd to apply lessons based on a UK and US policing reality that no longer exists (and with good reason).

Underlying the street cop fallacy is a useful distinction between targeting police reforms at the top or at the bottom level of the organization. However, as this chapter has demonstrated, which level is targeted needs to be informed by the policing realities of the country the mission operates in and not simply by a wholesale import of recommendations from (potentially outdated) academic scholarship. The final section of this chapter has drawn-out the operating principles that determine the policing style of any police force: the position a force takes on the matrix of hierarchy and institutionalization. Understanding this position assists in targeting police reforms to the level they can operate at most effectively. Police forces that are strictly hierarchical like the ones in Kosovo and Bosnia will adopt a top-down approach to reforms and this needs to be recognized by the implementing international agencies—unless it is the organizational approach that is subject to reform. In addition to technical expertise, successful reform requires knowledge of the local context, culture, and police organization, something few international operations have recognized.[75]

Targeting police reforms to the right level of the police means utilizing the local organizational power for its own benefit. In Kosovo and Bosnia, the absolute

75 Autesserre, Severine, *Peaceland. Conflict Resolution and the Everyday Politics of International Intervention* (New York: Cambridge University Press, 2014).

power of the chain of command meant that once reforms had been accepted by the senior management, implementation and adherence were almost guaranteed. Given the increasingly tight budgets of international operations, especially since the last economic downturn, operations and their sending organizations are under pressure to deliver results and show success.[76] Finally, donors and practitioners have increasingly understood the importance of winning local legitimacy and support for their projects and reforms as legitimacy can ensure local compliance and support for reforms, which in turn increases the likelihood of the reforms becoming sustainable.[77] Targeting reforms to the right level of the police means working 'with the grain', utilizing the power of the local organization, and ideally winning their legitimacy and respect for showing knowledge and consideration to local organizational practices.

76 Jones, Bruce, Richard Gowan, and Jake Sherman, 'Building on Brahimi: Peacekeeping in an Era of Strategic Uncertainty' (New York: NYU Center on International Cooperation, 2009).

77 Whalan, Jeni, *How Peace Operations Work: Power, Legitimacy and Effectiveness* (Abingdon: Oxford University Press, 2013); Gippert, 'Exploring Local Compliance with Peacebuilding Reforms'; Department for International Development, 'State-Building, Peace-Building, and Service Delivery in Fragile and Conflict-Affected States' (London: GSDRC, 2012); OECD-DAC, 'The State's Legitimacy in Fragile Situations: Unpacking Complexity' (Vienna: OECD, 2010).

8

Challenges in Police Development: Insights from the War in Afghanistan, 2001-2011

Brian Erickson

Introduction

This chapter examines the role of police advising and development in counterinsurgency (COIN) environments and the varying approaches to police advising that were represented in recent experiences in Afghanistan. First, by establishing the premise that the purpose of policing is fundamentally different from the role of the military, it examines the full spectrum of police capabilities that are required and the core principles that guide police training and development. Examining police training philosophies, it explores the frictions and tensions that exist in balancing immediate imperatives for security against the proper role, force structure, and quality of police. Using recent operations and international training approaches in Afghanistan, this chapter highlights the challenges that exist in developing a sufficiently robust police presence while attempting to establish the conditions for the longer-term establishment of the rule of law. Finally, by evaluating the varying approaches to police advising it offers some insights concerning the advantages and disadvantages in developing a para-militarised police force or working towards developing police that understand and uphold the principles of democratic policing traditions.

The Role of Police

According to Antonio Giustozzi, 'policing is a specific strategy for consolidating the monopoly on violence'.[1] Towards that end, policing fulfills a vital role within societies that links the population to the government and is often the visible embodiment of the rule of law. Essentially, policemen and policewomen are citizens in uniform who are empowered to conduct their duties by the lawfully established government. Effectively, there are two broad types of police and constabulary forces that exist around the world; those that serve the regime/government and act to preserve the existing power structure; and police that serve with the consent of the population and uphold the existing order to establish the rule of law. In the 'Western' democratic policing tradition there are many types of police including:[2] '(1) uniformed general duties police who patrol and respond to calls for citizen assistance; (2) nonuniformed [*sic*] criminal investigators; (3) stability police units to control incidents of collective disorder such as strikes and demonstrations, as well as to protect police installations and personnel; (4) armed units that undertake offensive operations against insurgents, terrorists, criminal gangs, and violent criminals; (5) covert intelligence agents and analysts; and (6) border police'.[3] Effectively, these broad categories of police functions describe and categorize the full spectrum of policing capability that is required to identify criminality through the generation of criminal intelligence, enforcement of the law, prevention of civil disorder, control of access to sovereign borders, and assistance to the population in the resolution of minor infractions and grievances. Further, this definition exemplifies the broad variations of actual capabilities that are needed in order to make the police effective. When compared to military organizations, the police operate within a less strict chain of command and it is often the individual policeman, or small teams of police forces, who are relied upon to interpret and respond to criminal activity to enforce the law.[4] A critical assumption within the aforementioned categories of police is that they are empowered to operate

1 Giustozzi, Antonio, *The Art of Coercion: The Primitive Accumulation and Management of Coercive Power* (New York: Columbia University Press, 2011), pp. 12-15, 227.

2 The use of democratic policing is preferred for this paper as it reflects the perspective of the Western world of what a police force or police service should represent. An alternate term that effectively captures a similar perspective is referred to as 'community policing'. Whilst not synonymous, there are subtle differences within these terms that are useful for academic debate but do not substantially change the nature or composition of police forces.

3 Bayley, David H. and Robert M. Perito, *The Police in War: Fighting Insurgency, Terrorism, and Violent Crime* (London: Lynne Rienner, 2010), p. 73.

4 In most Western nations, individual police officers on patrol are often the norm as they have freedom of movement within the society and must use their personal discretion and judgement to enforce the laws based on their individual observations. Soldiers, by comparison, rarely operate independently, and follow the orders received and manoeuvre as part of a combat team (section, platoon, company, etc.).

within their mandates because they are active participants in the community have the trust and consent of the population that they are policing.[5]

The philosophical principles that guide Anglo-American policing are neatly summarised in the words of Sir Robert Peel who established the conditions for the London Metropolitan Police Force in 1829. Occasionally referred to as 'Peelian Principles', Sir Robert Peel argued that a police force should be guided by the following nine principles (italics and emphasis added):

1. To prevent crime and disorder, as an alternative to their repression by military force and severity of legal punishment (*The basic mission for which the police exist is to* ***prevent crime and disorder).***
2. To recognise always that the power of the police to fulfil their functions and duties is dependent on public approval of their existence, actions and behaviour and on their ability to secure and maintain public respect. (*The ability of the police to perform their duties* ***is dependent upon public approval*** *of police actions; Principle of Consent*).
3. To recognise always that to secure and maintain the respect and approval of the public means also the securing of the willing co-operation of the public in the task of securing observance of laws. (***Police must secure the willing co-operation of the public in voluntary observance of the law to be able to secure and maintain the respect of the public.***).
4. To recognise always that the extent to which the co-operation of the public can be secured diminishes proportionately the necessity of the use of physical force and compulsion for achieving police objectives (*The degree of co-operation of the public that can be secured* ***diminishes proportionately to the necessity of the use of physical force****; Principle of Discretion*).
5. To seek and preserve public favour, not by pandering to public opinion; but by constantly demonstrating absolutely impartial service to law, in complete independence of policy, and without regard to the justice or injustice of the substance of individual laws, by ready offering of individual service and friendship to all members of the public without regard to their wealth or social standing, by ready exercise of courtesy and friendly good humour; and by ready offering of individual sacrifice in protecting and preserving life. (*Police seek and preserve public favour not by catering to public opinion but by constantly demonstrating absolute* ***impartial service to the law****; Principle of Impartiality*).
6. To use physical force only when the exercise of persuasion, advice and warning is found to be insufficient to obtain public co-operation to an extent necessary to secure observance of law or to restore order, and to use only the minimum degree of physical force which is necessary on any particular occasion for achieving a police objective. (*Police use physical force to the extent necessary to*

5 Giustozzi, *The Art of Coercion*, pp. 210-211.

secure observance of the law or to restore order only when the ***exercise of persuasion, advice, and warning is found to be insufficient****; Principle of Minimum Force*).

7. To maintain at all times a relationship with the public that gives reality to the historic tradition that the police are the public and that the public are the police, the police being only members of the public who are paid to give full time attention to duties which are incumbent on every citizen in the interests of community welfare and existence. (***The police are the public and the public are the police****; Principle of Civilianization*).
8. To recognise always the need for strict adherence to police-executive functions, and to refrain from even seeming to usurp the powers of the judiciary of avenging individuals or the State, and of authoritatively judging guilt and punishing the guilty. (*Police should always direct their action strictly towards their functions and never appear to usurp the powers of the judiciary;* ***Principle of Adherence to the Law***).
9. To recognise always that the test of police efficiency is the absence of crime and disorder, and not the visible evidence of police action in dealing with them. (***Principle of Police Effectiveness***).[6]

If policing is indeed a deliberate strategy governments use to gain the monopoly on the legitimate use of violence, then it holds true that the population derives justice and security from its representative government (or is beholden to the system provided by the regime); the interface of the government at the local level is, therefore, the police; the police, in turn, derive their mandate from the laws of the land (determined by the government) but acquire their ability to effectively police from the consent of the population that they are serving. The police almost always have a jurisdictional mandate that exclusively rests within the internal geographical boundaries of the state and often have no authority to conduct activities outside of their country. The ultimate goal of policing then becomes the government gaining a monopoly on the legitimate use of force within its territorial boundaries and maintaining the capability and the capacity to remove criminal elements who oppose this monopoly (clearly contested environments such as conflict or post-conflict areas present unique challenges in gaining and sustaining control over legitimate violence).

The Role of the Military

By contrast, the role of a military is generally the protection of national interests in the international context.[7] While the composition of militaries can vary greatly from state

6 'Policing by Consent', UK Home Office, published 10 Dec. 2012, <https://www.gov.uk/government/publications/policing-by-consent> (accessed 6 Sept. 2015).

7 The guiding intellectual principles for US Military are still, arguably, heavily influenced by the classic logic of Clausewitz's *On War*, which prescribes that all warfare is ultimately an

to state, militaries exist to defeat the military capabilities of an adversary and seek to attain political ends through the deliberate application of violence. Armies the world over are specifically designed and equipped based on the capabilities of the state and the perception of threats to national interests. Less esoterically, militaries seek decision through the threat of violence (deterrence) and the deliberate, often overwhelming, use of force to disarm, attrite, exhaust, or annihilate an opposing military. The military mandate is often the specific application of violence to gain decision through battle.[8] Clearly, the fundamental purposes of the military and police forces are different, yet in recent conflicts the development and training of indigenous forces has been conflated in the term 'security forces', which complicates the understanding of what type of force is being developed. Moreover, while both armies and police have a role to play in protecting non-combatants or the civilian population, their respective approaches to achieving security are fundamentally different.

The dominant perspective and purpose for military power (and the subsequent culture of most armies) is based on the premise that an adversary can be defeated on the battlefield and be held to the terms of said defeat. This perspective, informed largely by the varying interpretations of Clausewitz's *On War* tends to bias the military's perspective towards preparing for the decisive defeat of an adversary through attrition, exhaustion, or annihilation. From a Western military doctrinal perspective, United States Joint Publication 5.0, Operational Planning, clearly highlights the perceived missions of a military, expressed in five operational phases (Shape, Deter, Seize the Initiative, Dominate, Stabilize, and Enable Civil Authority). The US military emphasizes conventional military campaigns that reinforce the culture of military superiority and the decisive defeat of the adversary (Figure 1). While it is accepted that these notional phases of a military campaign may overlap and should be viewed as conditions based versus linear or sequential activities, this approach presupposes clear lines of transition between phases of a military operation and that the final phases of a campaign occur only after the adversary has been 'dominated' (i.e., defeated on the battlefield).

extension of politics. For a concise summary see Freedman, Lawrence, *Strategy: A History* (New York: Oxford University Press, 2013), pp. 82-95.

8 Ibid.

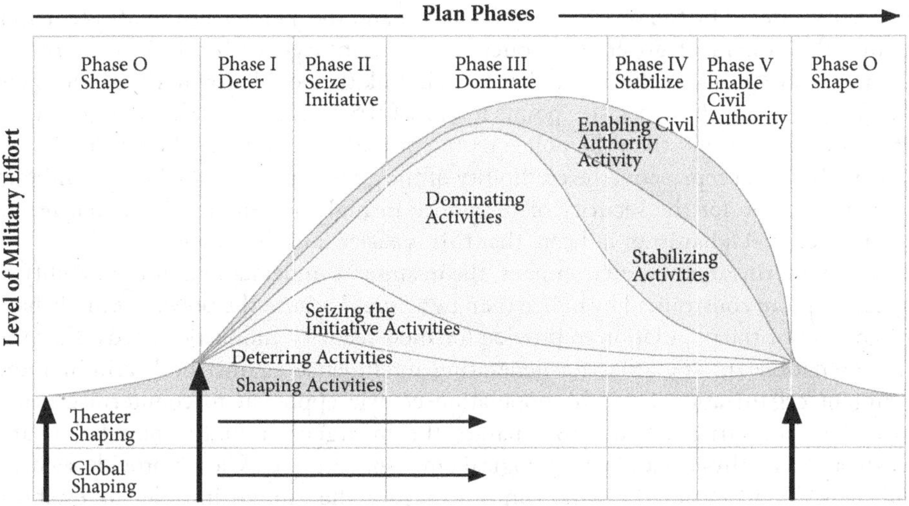

Figure 1: Notional Operation Plan Phases[9]

There have been recent efforts within the US military to address this doctrinal deficiency through the development of population-centric COIN doctrine but the fundamental role and purpose of the military is still perceived as an organization that must be able to defeat an adversary on the battlefield. Moreover, militaries often view the threat posed by a peer nation-state as far greater than that posed by an insurgency and are often ill-prepared to address the specific challenges posed by non-state actors in small wars. This presents specific challenges to the later phases of an operation when the adversary chooses irregular means to achieve its goals.

Framing the Problem: Criminality and Insurgent Operations

The military's doctrinal approach to countering insurgency has historically either adopted an enemy-centric or population-centric approach.[10] In either approach, the military tends to view insurgents as an enemy to be defeated or destroyed or, at a minimum, separated from the population. Conversely, the police tend towards a view that anyone who violates the accepted laws, including bearing arms against the legitimate government (such as insurgents), are criminals who should be apprehended and dealt with through the government's legal and judicial processes. Both perspectives lead to the argument that counterinsurgency is, in effect, a struggle for governance;

9 Department of Defense, Joint Publication 5.0, pp. III-39, <http://www.dtic.mil/doctrine/new_pubs/jp5_0.pdf>.

10 Galula, David, *Counterinsurgency Warfare* (Westport, CT: Praeger Security International, 2006), pp. 44-74.

the system offered by the legitimate government and the counterinsurgents is battling against the system of governance offered by the insurgent. The legitimacy of the government requires an effective police force to link the population to the government at all levels. If one of the decisive points for all COIN operations is the achievement of effective governance,[11] then the police represent both a critical capability and critical vulnerability that represents the credibility of the government. Arguably, the military exists to provide for the security of the police in high risk environments but recent experiences in Afghanistan indicate that this is easier said than done.

In a counterinsurgency environment, the insurgents understand that their ability to operate is more constrained by police than by armies because the police normally have the consent of the population to provide for their security and justice needs. Further, the population are key allies for generating intelligence against both criminal and insurgent organizations. As the population-centric approach to counterinsurgency prescribes, militaries attempt to separate the insurgent from the population and 'create a secure physical and psychological environment' (i.e., Clear); provide security and deny the adversary the opportunity to regain the ground in order to 'establish firm government control of the populace and area' (i.e., Hold); and then connect the population to the legitimate government and 'gain the populace's support' (i.e., Build).[12] Here, again, the phases of the operation are presented in linear and sequential terms, presupposing that gaining popular support occurs only after the clear and hold phases are complete. From a military perspective, this makes sense as this sequential approach is the norm for conventional operations and, as Conrad Crane has observed, 'who controls the ground controls the message'.[13]

For the police, however, in order to be credible in the eyes of the population they serve they must provide a full-spectrum of policing capability at all times and in all phases of the counterinsurgency. Their inability to provide for the justice and security needs of the population cannot wait for the clear and hold phases to be complete; the inability of the police to provide the population with access to justice may give rise to additional grievances and inadvertently create support for the insurgent cause. Herein lays a potential critical flaw within currently accepted counterinsurgency approaches. If the police are poorly armed and poorly trained, they are highly vulnerable to attack from the adversary and present a lucrative target for discrediting the government. One approach to addressing this vulnerability is to create a police force with paramilitary

11 Lessons from Iraq and Afghanistan indicate that there are at least seven decisive points in any COIN campaign, namely: Governance, Rule of Law, Local Security, Provision of Services, Denial of Sanctuary, Control of the Strategic Narrative, and Development of Indigenous Forces. From discussions with Dr. Jeffrey Reilly and Colonel (USAF, Retired) Richard Perry, United States Air Command and Staff College.

12 FM 3-24/MCWP 3-33.5, *Counterinsurgency*, US Department of Defense, 15 Dec. 2006, pp. 5-18.

13 Crane, Conrad, 'Observation on the Long War', <http://warontherocks.com/2014/09/observations-on-the-long-war/> (accessed 27 Sept. 2015).

capabilities by providing them with basic soldiering skills to enhance their self-protection capabilities. The intuitive solution would be to have highly trained police who are able to address the justice and security needs of the population. This solution, however, takes a significant amount of time to implement which may not be feasible while the conditions on the ground are insecure.

From the insurgent's perspective, they must attempt to separate the police from their communities through direct (attacking) and indirect (discrediting) methods. In so doing, they are better positioned to further their own drive toward achieving their governance objective and can offer an alternative security model based on their desired political objectives. The police present a much more valuable target for insurgents because the uniformed police are the visible representatives of the government that is being challenged. Further, the ability to show the inherent vulnerability of the police sends a powerful message and creates the narrative that if the police cannot protect themselves, then how can they protect the population? In general police are more lightly armed than conventional military forces and, with the possible exception of gendarmerie forces, often lack the heavy weapons and enablers possessed by the military.[14] Well-trained and well-equipped military forces present a much more difficult tactical challenge to insurgents and ultimately represent a less lucrative target in terms of the over-arching strategic objective of establishing their own system of justice and security. Unless the situation is overwhelmingly favorable, insurgents often prefer to avoid direct action against trained military forces; rather, they will normally limit their efforts against equally well armed military forces to indirect attacks, ambushes, or other means of guerilla warfighting to preserve their forces whilst doing enough to sufficiently harass or disrupt their conventional opponents.[15] When the conditions are not favorable, the insurgents often simply blend back into the local population and retain the initiative to engage at a time of their choosing in the future.

Ultimately, the perspectives of the police and the military, and their international advisors, towards the insurgents themselves shapes and defines how the campaign will be planned and executed; whether criminals to be apprehended and brought to justice or enemy combatants that must be separated from the people, captured, or killed, an active insurgency presents a real and direct challenge to the security of the population and the legitimacy of the government.

Case Study: Developing Policing in Afghanistan

There is an inherent challenge with assigning military professionals to advise civilian police as there is a natural tendency to fall back on the known; an indirect or oftentimes deliberate result may be a paramilitarization of the police development effort. This point was exemplified in the recent police development efforts in Afghanistan where

14 Giustozzi, *The Art of Coercion*, pp. 18-21.
15 Galula, *Counterinsurgency Warfare*.

the military represented the vast majority of police trainers and advisors. The re is a balance that must be struck between the security and force protection requirements of the operation and the ability of the mentored force to actually develop into a credible police 'force' or police 'service' that links the population to the justice system. The conflation of soldiering skills with police training creates the dilemma wherein the emphasis is placed on the primacy of security at the expense of traditional policing duties. Accordingly, this creates a necessity at some point in the future for an element of police reform and retraining to emphasize the community-based policing approach that addresses traditional, core policing functions. Western police forces often cite the motto '*To Serve and Protect*', which captures the dual agendas of protecting the population but highlights the primacy of service to the legitimate authority and the law. Moreover, the very idea that western militaries would be used to 'police' their population is abhorrent and is legislatively prohibited from occurring in many countries.[16]

The formal establishment of the current Afghanistan National Police began with the signing of the Bonn treaty in December 2001. Afghanistan's recent history, from the Soviet occupation in 1979 to the rise and the fall of the Taliban regime resulted in decades of conflict where the national police force were unable to establish the rule of law outside of the major population centers.[17] The international effort to develop an effective police force in Afghanistan was immediately challenged by the conditions on the ground and the fact that there was no modern memory of anything that resembled democratic policing, nor a population that had the human capital to rapidly establish the conditions for policing. As Robert M. Perito notes, '[b]y 2002, there were, however, an estimated 50,000 men working as police, but they were untrained, ill-equipped, illiterate (70–90 percent), and owed their allegiance to warlords and local commanders and not the central government. Many were former mujahedeen whose experience of acting with impunity prepared them poorly to serve as police in a democratic society'.[18]

The approach that the international community took in developing police forces in Afghanistan was one of lead nations and donors, with Italy taking the lead in regard to Rule of Law, assisting the Ministry of Justice, developing the Afghan courts and judges, and Germany taking the lead in training the Afghan National Police.[19] The

16 In Canada, for example, there is specific legislation detailing the circumstances where and when the Canadian Armed Forces can be used to assist Law Enforcement or Aid to the Civil Power are codified in the National Defence Act and the Queen's Regulations and Orders (Volume 1, Chapter 23) and can be accessed here: <http://www.forces.gc.ca/en/about-policies-standards-queens-regulations-orders-vol-01/ch-23.page>.

17 Giustozzi, Antonio and Mohammad Isaqadeh, *Policing Afghanistan: The Politics of the Lame Leviathan* (London: Hurst & Company, 2013), pp. 13-34.

18 Perito, Robert M., 'Afghanistan's Police: The Weak Link in Security Sector Reform', Special Report, *The United States Institute for Peace*, 12 Aug. 2009, <http://www.usip.org/sites/default/files/afghanistan_police_0.pdf>, (accessed 11 Aug. 2015).

19 For more on Italy's role as the lead nation in rule of law reform see: Tondini, Matteo, *Statebuilding and Justice Reform: Post Conflict Reconstruction in Afghanistan* (London:

challenge of this initial approach was captured in a 2011 NATO Training Mission-Afghanistan (NTM-A) White Paper which indicates that '[s]tarting in 2002, the introduction of multiple bilateral police training initiatives created a lack of unity of effort in the police training function. German, US State Department, US Department of Defense, European Union (EU) and other contributing nations conducted various forms of police training. The result lacked a coherent strategy, unity of effort and defined leadership. Each nation brought their own funding, national standards and techniques, and national caveats resulting in a confusing array of training initiatives for the Afghan National Police'.[20] As a further complication, the sub-elements of the Afghan National Police were established under various internationally sponsored programs into police organizations, departments, or 'pillars', each of which often relied on a different sponsor or donor nation for advising and assistance, each of whom had a unique perspective on how the Afghan National Police should be trained and developed. Over the course of more than a decade, international advising and assistance in Afghanistan has evolved and includes efforts to develop the following police capabilities and organizations:

1. Afghan Uniformed Police (AUP) which was renamed to Afghan National Police (ANP));
2. Afghan Anti-Crime Police (AACP);
3. Afghan National Civil Order Police (ANCOP);
4. Afghan Border Police (ABP);
5. Afghan Highway Police (AHP);
6. Afghan National Police Auxiliary (ANPA) from 2006-2008;
7. Afghan Public Protection Force (APPF) from 2009 onwards;
8. Afghan Local Police (ALP);
9. Afghan Traffic Police (ATP);
10. Criminal Investigation Division;
11. General Directorate of Police Special Units (GDPSU) including the Afghan Special Police—Crisis Response Units (CRU); and
12. Counter-Narcotics Police of Afghanistan (CNPA).[21]

Taylor and Francis, 2010) and for details on the police reform see Holt, Victoria K., 'Peace and Stability in Afghanistan: US Goals Challenged by Security Gap', *The Stimson Center*, June 2002, <http://www.stimson.org/images/uploads/research-pdfs/AfghanSecurityGapfactsheet_063102.pdf>, (accessed 22 Aug 2015), and Cordesman, Anthony, Adam Mausner, and David Kasten, *Winning in Afghanistan: Creating Effective Afghan Security Forces* (Washington, DC: Center for Strategic & International Studies, May 2009).

20 White Paper, 'EUPOL: Partnering for Civil Police', Office of the Deputy to the Commanding General, 8 Aug. 2011, p. 5.

21 Various sources, primarily the Official Website of the Ministry of Interior, Afghanistan <http://moi.gov.af/en>.

The 'pillarization' of the Afghan police organization and the further devolvement of training partnering to 'donor' countries exacerbated the inability to gain uniformity of approach. Nations often trained the Afghan police in their image and based on their national approaches rather than on what was the appropriate fit for Afghanistan. The French and Italian trainers were focused on developing the police along the lines of *Carabineiri* and *Gendarmerie* with civil order police as the model; the German trainers were focused on highly trained, low numbers of police officers and the Border police; and the NATO focus was on large numbers of 'little soldiers' or 'security forces' that could be used to fill perceived security gaps created by the insurgents across the country.[22] Moreover, the international community could never truly agree on whether the Afghan National Police should be a police force or a police service or even how many police were needed.[23] The simplest conceptual differentiation between a police 'force' and a police 'service' is that a police is force is built with a perspective to enforce the law, and a police 'service' is one that exists to serve and protect the population. Many in the international community argued for a smaller police force (no more than 50,000) and a scalable army that would protect the police during the insurgency. This approach was based on the philosophy that a small number of highly trained and effective police was much more consistent with the principles of policing. Determining how many police are needed is a complex formula, more art than science, which is based not only on the security needs but on the ability of the police to uphold and enforce the law, address criminality, and deal with the low-level disputes of the population. Here, as with population-centric counterinsurgency strategy, the support of the population is key, and the population must participate in its own security by allowing themselves to be held accountable for breaking the laws established by the central government. The principle of consent is critical because if the population is 'law-abiding' and sees the police as a credible entity, then the overall number of police needed decreases and larger areas can be policed by fewer police. If the population does not support the police, then a larger number are required to enforce the government's laws. Alternatively, a small number of trained police reinforced and supported by a trained and capable army would help ensure that the state maintained the monopoly on the lawful use of force. The argument for a smaller number of highly trained police was a constant refrain from the international donors in Afghanistan where human capital was at a premium and the development of qualified, literate, and un-corruptible police was a constant challenge. Further, the challenge of getting the Afghan Army and the Afghan police to work together was often very real and the competition for resources

22 Cordesman, Anthony H., *Afghan National Security Forces: What It Will Take to Implement the ISAF Strategy* (Washington, DC: Center for Strategic and International Studies, 2010), pp. 123-131.

23 The debate on whether to refer to police as a force or service exemplifies the challenge that the international community faced, primarily between the US government's desire for a robust counterinsurgent and counterterrorist force and the European donors' desire for a police service that was focused on democratic policing.

from the international community exacerbated the development of both entities. The scale of the task of developing even 50,000 qualified police was daunting and, despite the best of intentions from all international actors and the Afghan Government, was quickly overtaken by the difficulties associated with actually recruiting, properly training and equipping both the Afghan Army and Police.[24]

By 2006 the largest donor for police and army training became the United States and the majority of partnering was delivered by the US Army through either bilateral efforts or through the Combined Security Transition Command–Afghanistan (CSTC-A) organization. In 2007, a European Union Police (EUPOL) mission in Afghanistan authorised the deployment of 400 police advisors but due to the uneven security situation across Afghanistan, there were only 218 police advisors in the country.[25] By contrast, by November 2009, the International Security Assistance Force (ISAF), which included CSTC-A, the NATO-Training Mission-Afghanistan, and the ISAF Joint Command was by far the largest contributor to the training of Afghan Army, Police, and Air Forces with, at its peak, over 130,000 military personnel from 51 NATO and partner nations.[26]

Despite the vast numerical and financial superiority of ISAF, successive commanders, including Generals Stanley A. McChrystal (2009-2011), David H. Petraeus (2011-2012), and John R. Allan (2011-2013), all struggled to differentiate security from policing and to establish distinct roles and missions between the Afghan Army and the Afghan police. As evidence, the term Afghan National Security Forces (ANSF) was coined and used almost exclusively when either discussing police or army development. The conflation of police and army into security forces caused much confusion amongst the ISAF trainers with little understanding or experience in police development. Further, ISAF failed to truly develop a coherent police training approach and its focus ranged from developing the counterinsurgency forces, to counterterrorism forces, to civil-order police, and included multiple efforts to develop institutional capacity and ministerial reform with the Ministry of the Interior and Ministry of Defense. Though a named NATO organization, the US military perspective (and US funding) was dominant among the varying approaches to police development and the focus became training basic 'soldier skills' within the police. The ISAF training approach for the police was often expressed by the need to improve the police's ability to 'shoot, move, and communicate'.[27] This decision was, arguably, directly linked to the perception, and oftentimes the reality, that the Afghan police were generally corrupt, poorly trained, poorly equipped, and or generally ineffective against an adversary that was better armed and prepared for 'combat'.

24 Cordesman, *Afghan National Security Forces*, p. 127.
25 Perito and Bayley, *The Police in War*, pp. 30-31.
26 <http://www.nato.int/cps/en/natolive/topics_8189.htm> (accessed 27 Sept. 2015).
27 Jones, Seth G., *In the Graveyard of Empires: America's War in Afghanistan* (New York: W.W. Norton, 2009).

By 2009, the overall international focus of developing a national police force shifted towards rapid expansion, accepting that increased quantity was more pressing than overall quality given the levels of violence in Afghanistan. This change in approach was driven primarily by a 2010 US Center for Army Analysis study on the number of 'security forces' that would be required to enable coalition redeployment in order to allow for the transition of security responsibilities to the Afghans with a reasonable chance of success in neutralizing the insurgency. The United States secured presidential approval to increase the size of the Afghan Army, Air Force, and Police from a planned total of 305,600 to an end-strength of 357,000 (157,000 Police). This growth, however, did not differentiate between soldier and police skills and was focused on the ANP's ability to conduct counterinsurgency based in Western military doctrine. Effectively, this shift in training methodology established the police as a paramilitary force in Afghanistan, accepting that there would be large numbers of poorly trained police (often referred to as 'little soldiers') and that democratic policing would be an aspirational goal and developed only later through police reform and only after the insurgency had been defeated. Here again, the conflation of police and army into the 'Afghanistan National Security Forces (ANSF)'—which also included the rarely considered Afghan National Directorate of Security (NDS)—further complicated the division of responsibilities between the role of the Afghan National Army and the Afghan National Police.

This deliberate shift towards quantity over quality effectively established two armies in Afghanistan: a well-equipped, well-trained, well-funded, well-partnered–Afghan National Army (in the image of the contributing ISAF nations), and another well-equipped, well-funded, marginally-trained, and marginally-partnered Afghan National Police. Most military planners and advisors from ISAF had no idea that, according to Afghan law, the Afghan Army had no authority to act on its own within Afghanistan and that by law their operations against insurgents were only legal when they were conducted in support of the police. Moreover, the NDS and MOI were the only ministries able to act independently to detain and arrest suspected terrorists and suspected insurgents. Fundamentally, ISAF saw the Afghan army and police as nothing more than a counterinsurgency force; almost all lines of development were based upon this premise.

Conversely, EUPOL and many other donor nations saw the primacy of police who served with the consent of the population and worked to establish the 'Rule of Law' as fundamental. The emphasis on democratic policing and the EUPOL approach did not mean that the police do not have a role in counterinsurgency, quite the contrary; their approach was one based on the primacy of police as the key instrument of securing and protecting the population. As illustrated in *The Police in War*, the police must have primacy in COIN and the insurgency itself is fundamentally a political struggle.[28]

28 Bayley and Perito, *The Police in War*.

Democratic police advocates see counterinsurgency not as a battlefield or a 'COIN fight' but as criminal activity that must be addressed within the legal system.

The almost incompatible approaches of EUPOL and NTM-A (with NTM-A having a much larger advisor presence and funding) led to the near inevitable paramilitarization of the police in Afghanistan. While efforts were made to ensure that the police and the army worked together, it was often easier to work within the Ministry of the Interior to up-arm the police or to develop a *Gendarmerie*-like force than it was to get the Ministry of Defence to support and protect the police. In the short-term, the paramilitarization of the police is the reality in Afghanistan, although there is some continuing effort to reform and develop democratic policing and to make the police less focused on counterinsurgency and more focused on the approach outlined by the 'Peelian Principles'.

The EUPOL approach did, however, have its own challenges. Whilst espousing the need for greater quality and a community-based approach to developing the police, the requisite international police trainers failed to appear in sufficient numbers to make this vision a reality. Many small programs were established (primarily in Kabul or in Northern Afghanistan) that focused on areas of donor interest such as gender equality and judicial reform amongst other niche programs. Further, outside of the US many nations failed to back up their vision with significant financial contributions that would have contributed to furthering their interests and styles of policing. Contributing further to the challenge of generating police advisors was the fact that the rate of casualties sustained by the Afghan National Police was often many-times greater than those sustained by the Afghan National Army (as indicated by the Brookings Institute summary below) further challenged the international community to generate sufficient numbers of civilian police advisors from donor countries who would operate in a high-threat environment outside of the safer urban centers.

	2007	2008	2009	2010	2011	2012	Estimated Total
ANA	209	226	282	519	550	1,200	2,986
ANP	803	880	646	961	1,400	2,200	6,890

Afghan National Army (ANA) and Afghan National Police (ANP) Personnel Fatalities, January 2007-2012[29]

A brief summary of the advantages and disadvantages of the aforementioned approaches which appears in the table below. While not exhaustive, it should serve

29 Livingston, Ian S., and Michael O'Hanlon, *Afghanistan Index*, Brookings Institute, 31 Mar. 2016, <http://www.brookings.edu/~/media/Programs/foreign-policy/afghanistan-index/index20160330.pdf?la=en> (accessed 6 June 2016).

to inform the discussion on which approach is optimal for future police development and reform efforts.

	Advantages	Disadvantages
Democratic (Community) Policing	• Solid foundation for enduring policing in the affected nation-state • Fundamentally civilian in nature • Consent of the Population; people are part of their own security • Connects the population with the government; gains trust and confidence • Emphasizes quality over quantity • Addresses criminality (source of many grievances) • Facilitates the establishment of the Rule of Law • Police intelligence focuses on criminal activity, evidence collection and prosecution • Use of force approach is more consistent with policing principles	• Higher vulnerability • Requires significant time to train and knowledge of the Law • Requires higher levels of literacy • Requires significant International police trainers (proven difficult to generate in insecure environments) • Lack of international consensus over the approach to training • Requires equal, parallel development in the judiciary and penal systems to be fully effective • Requires enduring donor support • Requires generational change and relative local security
Paramilitarized Police (COIN focused)	• Security Focus, addresses immediate, short term security challenges • High number of adequately trained personnel can be generated rapidly • Primary training can be delivered by military trainers • Police intelligence focused on countering insurgent threats • Does not require high levels of literacy (more 'hands-on')	• Skills primarily based on soldiering (Shoot, Move, Communicate) • Significant reformation and additional training to make them 'police' • Often poorly trained and only able to conduct security tasks • Fails to adequately address criminality; can further disenfranchise the population • Use of force approach often inconsistent with policing principles • Requires significant infrastructure • Logistics and sustainment

Conclusion

Considering the fact that the effort to develop the Afghan National Police was an international undertaking that involved a coalition of 28 NATO and 10 non-NATO nations that formed ISAF, a European Police training mission, and numerous bilateral police training programs, it was, arguably, an effort on a scale that previously had never been attempted by the international community. The desire to establish a functioning, credible, centrally controlled police force was highly influenced by the donor nations and the net result was a paramilitary police. The police in Afghanistan were used as 'little soldiers' in furtherance of the international coalition's interest in stabilizing Afghanistan and expediting their exit. The recognized need to reform and professionalize the Afghan Police was understood but fell victim to the expedience of developing a large number of 'boots on the ground' that would eventually replace the ISAF presence. The conflation of police and army into the ANSF not only blurred the lines between the role of the soldier and that of the policeman but adds to the difficulty in determining what real lessons can be learned from the effort. The experiences in Afghanistan lead to the observation that a large number of poorly armed and poorly trained police is counterproductive for achieving the objectives of the overall counterinsurgency campaign; they are highly vulnerable to attack from the adversary which, in turn, undermines the credibility of the government's ability to provide security. Moreover, one of the key lessons from Afghanistan is that while the international community was heavily involved in the development of the ANP, the lack of consensus on the role of the police, the intense focus of developing the ANA (at the expense of the ANP), and the competing national agendas for police training, compounded the challenges of developing an effective national police enterprise. The philosophical differences between the key donors with respect to democratic policing and counterinsurgency were, ultimately, never reconciled and serve to illustrate that when consensus cannot be gained nations will revert to what they know as the model for indigenous force development. Further, the fact that donor nations are funding the initiatives leads to the not unreasonable expectation that the execution of training and development will be in accordance with the donor nations' interests and desired outcomes.

In conflict environments there must be sufficient emphasis placed on training the police with individual survival skills and training conducted in the areas of weapons handling, communication, and self-defense skills. This is critical to ensure that the police can protect themselves but should not be the model for future efforts as it leads, ultimately, to the need for substantial reform and retraining to fulfill the primary role of policing the population. Consistent with military population-centric approaches to counterinsurgency, the police should have primacy in gaining the consent of the population to be policed, and by ensuring that the population contributes to its own security, the complimentary ends of connecting the population to the government and establishing the rule of law can be met.

Counterinsurgency dogma and doctrine is still widely debated and the various camps are split as to the best method to establish security and justice in conflict zones. Insurgents seeking changes to the political governance of a nation usually cannot be defeated solely by physical means. The counterinsurgents must win if not the support, at least the compliance of the population, and must present a credible alternative to the insurgent. In Afghanistan, this means that the police must be seen as the more capable security and justice provider than the main insurgent group, the Taliban. Insurgent and subversive (terrorist) acts must be seen as crimes and treated in accordance with Afghan law. While not a panacea for police development and reform, considering the 'Peelian Principles' for policing is an excellent foundation from which to consider methodologies and approaches to developing police in the future.

9

Village Stability Operations and the Afghan Local Police, 2010-2015

Mark Moyar

Introduction

Following the 9/11 attacks, the US government sent its special operations forces to Afghanistan to help the Northern Alliance resistance movement comprised of non-Pashtun ethnic groups that had been waging an insurgency against the Taliban since 1996. American advice and firepower enabled the Northern Alliance to drive the Taliban from all of Afghanistan's major population centers within two months. An interim Afghan government, led by Hamid Karzai, and the US-led coalition of nations that backed it decided to establish security in the countryside by parceling out large chunks of territory to regional warlords, who were the only Afghans readily capable of securing large areas. These warlords commanded militias of 10,000 men or more, giving them influence across multiple provinces.

Within six months, the warlords had enrolled 200,000 fighters in what were called the Afghan Militia Forces. These militias quickly solidified control over the population and wiped out Taliban remnants. They proved, however, to be highly abusive in their treatment of the population, committing criminal acts of violence and stealing property or land from other groups, particularly those who had been friendly to the Taliban. Their behavior tarnished the image of the Karzai government and spawned resentment that insurgents would exploit in future years.[1]

1 Hodes, Cyrus and Mark Sedra, *The Search for Security in Post-Taliban Afghanistan* (Abingdon: Routledge, 2007), pp. 11-12; Gannon, Kathy, 'Afghanistan Unbound', *Foreign Affairs,* 83:3 (May/June 2004); Sinno, Andulkader H., *Organizations at War in Afghanistan and Beyond* (Ithaca: Cornell University Press, 2008), p. 273; Millen, Raymond A., *Afghanistan: Reconstituting a Collapsed State* (Carlisle, Pennsylvania: Strategic Studies

After the fall of the Taliban, US special operations forces established bases near the Afghan border with Pakistan, manned by both US SOF and Afghan Militia Forces. The Americans used the bases to lead raids against suspected extremists, with the Afghan Militia Forces accompanying them in some cases.[2] From 2002 through 2004, the Taliban and other extremist groups were largely inactive in Afghanistan's interior, which some observers cited as evidence that the raiding approach was effective in suppressing these groups.

The primary reason for the inactivity of hostile forces inside Afghanistan from 2002 to 2004, however, was a strategic decision on the part of the Taliban to rest and regroup inside Pakistan during that period. In 2005, the Taliban and affiliated extremist groups, most notably the Haqqani Network and Hezb-e-Islami Gulbuddin, began mobilizing rural Afghans against the Karzai government. They carried out attacks on pro-government militias, proving themselves superior combatants on numerous occasions. In eastern and southern Afghanistan, where the Taliban had always derived most of their support because of the concentration of ethnic Pashtuns, villages and districts fell under insurgent domination.

The international community, which by this time had already soured on decentralized security and regional militias for humanitarian reasons, seized on this insurgent resurgence as proof that revamping Afghanistan's security forces was imperative for reasons of security as well as human rights. Over the course of 2005, the United States and other foreign powers convinced Karzai to disarm some of the militiamen, and to incorporate others into the Afghan National Police. Militia commanders became chiefs of police. To strengthen the central government's control over rural security, Karzai sent additional National Police and National Army soldiers to the provinces.

The United States and its NATO partners also pressed Karzai to centralize and modernize the civil administration. They advocated bureaucratization, institutionalization of the rule of law, and transparency. Instead of allowing provincial governors to make patronage payments to villages in return for their support as governors of the past had done, the NATO countries called for the channeling of developmental and other governmental funding through official, transparent pathways.

During the shift from regional militias to national security forces, objections from NATO officials over the involvement of militia commanders in corruption, drug trafficking, or human rights violations resulted in the dismissal of some commanders. But these dismissals removed some of the most tactically competent, experienced, and charismatic leaders, and the individuals who took their places often did not possess comparable talents. Thus, while abuses of power declined, so did military

Institute, 2005), pp. 2-3, 11; Jalali, Ali A., 'Rebuilding Afghanistan's National Army', *Parameters*, 32:3 (Autumn 2002), pp. 167-170.

2 Robinson, Linda, *One Hundred Victories: Special Ops and the Future of American Warfare* (New York: Public Affairs, 2013), pp. 9-11.

effectiveness, which facilitated large insurgent gains.[3] In addition, the demobilization of militia units and the collapse of others due to poor leadership or enemy advances left large numbers of experienced and armed fighters without employment, many of whom chose to sign on with the insurgents when offered well-paying jobs.[4]

For the next several years, neither the rebranded Afghan National Police nor the Afghan National Army were able to prevent the Taliban and other insurgent groups from increasing their control over territory and population. The misbehavior and ineptitude of the Afghan National Security Forces made the insurgents more and more attractive to the populace. Afghanistan's foreign allies had too few troops to compensate for the deficiencies of the Afghan security forces as the US military had concentrated its combat power in Iraq and its NATO partners had provided only enough troops to assist Afghanistan under pre-insurgency conditions.

During the early years of the insurgency, the Afghan National Army made significant qualitative improvements, thanks to effective ministerial leadership and extensive support from the US military. The Afghan National Police, however, foundered because of poor leadership at all levels and low-quality training and leadership development. When Afghan National Army forces and NATO forces cleared areas of insurgents with overwhelming force, they attempted to turn them over to the police so that they could move on to other missions, but the police usually lacked the capabilities to prevent the insurgents from coming back.[5]

The poor showing of the national security forces led to a resurgence in interest in local security forces. In 2006, the US Combined Joint Special Operations Task Force-Afghanistan (CJSOTF-A) supported the creation of an Afghan government program called the Afghan National Auxiliary Police, which was intended to recruit local men to secure their home areas. It also supported the development of Afghan army special operations forces, which would eventually form the Afghan National Army Special Operations Command and its two main ground components, the Commandos and the Special Forces. The Afghan National Auxiliary Police program expanded rapidly to a strength of 11,000 by offering good salaries to prospective members and giving

3 Much of Helmand province, for instance, fell under Taliban sway as the result of the replacement of provincial leaders and the ensuing collapse of the security forces. Coghlan, Tom, 'The Taliban in Helmand: An Oral History', in Giustozzi, Antonio (ed.), *Decoding the New Taliban* (New York: Columbia University Press, 2009), pp. 137-138.

4 Elias, Mohammad Osman Tariq, 'The Resurgence of the Taliban in Kabul', in Giustozzi (ed.), *Decoding the New Taliban*, p. 53.

5 Jones, Seth G., 'The Rise of Afghanistan's Insurgency: State Failure and Jihad', *International Security*, 32:4 (Spring 2008), p. 23; International Crisis Group, 'Reforming Afghanistan's Police', Asia Report No. 138 (30 August 2007); Patel, Seema and Steven Ross, 'Breaking Point: Measuring Progress in Afghanistan', Center for Strategic and International Studies (March 2007), <http://www.csis.org>, pp. 36-37; Wilder, Andrew, 'Cops or Robbers? The Struggle to Reform the Afghan National Police', Afghanistan Research and Evaluation Unit (July 2007), <http://areu.org.af/Uploads/EditionPdfs/717E-Cops%20or%20Robbers-IP-print.pdf>.

recruits just three weeks of training before sending them into the field.[6] The formation of new units proved too rapid to ensure that these units had adequate leadership, and external supervision of fielded units was insufficient to identify and correct leadership problems. The majority of these policemen either deserted or defected. As a result, the program was terminated in September 2008, at which time the remaining 3,200 members were merged into the Afghan National Police.[7]

The failure of the Afghan National Auxiliary Police program rekindled Afghan and NATO opposition to local security forces. From 2007 to 2009, the Afghan government increased the centralization of police recruitment and training. To eliminate the temptations to abuse power arising from deployment in an officer's home district, the Afghan National Police became more systematic in sending policemen to serve in districts other than their native ones. But this swing of the pendulum was no more effective than previous ones in halting the momentum of the insurgents.[8]

Meanwhile, US counterinsurgency successes in Iraq during 2007 and 2008 enabled and encouraged the United States to move tens of thousands of additional troops to Afghanistan for use in counterinsurgency during 2009. Within the US government, advocates of counterinsurgency contended that village security was necessary to deny sanctuaries to terrorists and collect information on them, and to prevent insurgents from toppling the Afghan central government. During the first year of the Obama administration, they prevailed in White House debates with advocates of counterterrorism, who maintained that the United States could keep the terrorists at bay with drones and a small number of special operations forces at a few major bases. Consequently, the US military became much more involved in conducting population security operations and supporting Afghan population security operations.

The Creation of VSO/ALP

In 2009, the concept of community self-defense attracted the attention of the newly created Combined Forces Special Operations Component Command-Afghanistan (CFSOCC-A). A one-star command located in Kabul, CFSOCC-A had been established to put a higher, strategic level headquarters above the Combined Joint

6 Hulslander, Robert and Jake Spivey, 'Village Stability Operations and Afghan Local Police', *PRISM,* 3:3 (June 2012), p. 127.

7 Lefèvre, Matthew, 'Local Defence in Afghanistan: A review of Government-Backed Initiatives', Afghanistan Analysis Network (May 2010), <http://aan-afghanistan.com/uploads/20100525MLefevre-LDIpaper.pdf>; Royal United Services Institute and Foreign Policy Research Institute, 'Reforming the Afghan National Police' (November 2009), <http://www.rusi.org/downloads/assets/ANP_Nov09.pdf>, p. 102.

8 Perito, Robert M., *Afghanistan's Police: The Weak Link in Security Sector Reform* (Washington: DC: US Institute of Peace, August 2009), <http://www.usip.org/sites/default/files/afghanistan_police.pdf>; From, James A. and Joseph D. Keefe, 'Policing in Afghanistan: Reform that Respects Tradition: Need for a Strategic Shift', Institute for Defense Analyses (May 2010).

Special Operations Task Force-Afghanistan. The first CFSOCC-A commander, Brigadier General Edward Reeder, had already spent three tours in Afghanistan, including one as CJSOTF-A commander in 2006-2007. During those tours, he had been impressed by the inability of highly successful direct-action missions to halt the growth of the Afghan insurgency. To provide local security that would thwart the insurgents over the long term, Reeder was now convinced, some fraction of US SOF had to be devoted to population security, with an emphasis on building Afghan capabilities.[9]

During 2009, General Reeder's command organized local security forces under two programs, the Afghan Public Protection Program and the Community Defense Initiative. The Afghan Public Protection Program did not live up to expectations, owing to Afghan leadership problems and coalition conflicts over supervisory responsibilities. It would not be expanded beyond its pilot location in Wardak province. The Community Defense Initiative, on the other hand, showed real promise in mobilizing communities against the insurgents. Focusing on local security, US special operations forces organized Afghan militia units in villages scattered around the country. The program was rechristened the Local Defense Initiative at the beginning of 2010, but without significant changes. Two months later, CFSOCC-A changed the name again, to Village Stability Operations, or VSO, but this time made major changes. The SOF teams assigned to Village Stability Operations now had responsibility for promoting governance and social and economic development as well as security.

The early successes caught the attention of General Stanley McChrystal. He became so impressed with VSO and ALP by the middle of 2010 that he came out in favor of a dramatic expansion of the VSO program. US ambassador Karl Eikenberry, however, opposed expansion because of concerns that the local self-defense forces would turn into predatory militias. Eikenberry's objection received reinforcement from an even more powerful source, President Karzai. 'We have to make sure that we don't develop militias or any other kinds of forces that might undermine the government and become another kind of instability', said Karzai's spokesman, Waheed Omar. 'Our concern comes from what we experienced in our history where governments in the 1980s developed local militias that then became a source of problems for law and order in the country'.[10] Hekmat Karzai, a cousin of President Karzai who directed the Centre for Conflict and Peace Studies in Kabul, wrote in an essay, 'Afghans are worried about the strategy because previous experience shows that such efforts offer only short-term solutions and will not provide lasting peace or security'. Previous attempts to recruit

9 Robinson, *One Hundred Victories*, pp. 10-14.

10 Rubin, Alissa J. and Richard A. Oppel Jr., 'US And Afghanistan Debate More Village Forces', *New York Times* (13 July 2010).

local security forces, he observed, 'ran into serious challenges of vetting, command and control, and, most important of all, secured only questionable loyalty'.[11]

The arrival of General David Petraeus as the new ISAF commander in July 2010 altered the dynamics of the debate. Having recently helped rescue the United States from military doom in Iraq, he enjoyed extraordinary prestige within the US government and around the world. Petraeus had overseen the growth of highly effective local security forces in Iraq, and he believed that VSO could achieve comparable successes in Afghanistan. During his first ten days in Afghanistan, Petraeus met nearly every day with Karzai, and each time he urged Karzai to approve a village security force program under the auspices of CFSOCC-A. Karzai gave the matter serious consideration, while Eikenberry's opposition ebbed.

On 14 July 2010, Karzai offered to authorize local security forces, but only on the condition that they be placed under the control of the Afghan National Police and the Ministry of Interior. Karzai added that he wanted to call them the Afghan Local Police, because the term police had a more favorable connotation in Afghan minds than the other leading option—militia—which was popularly associated with the rapacious militias of the 1990s. Petraeus accepted Karzai's stipulations, and the deal was sealed.[12] The program was scheduled to last two to five years, after which time the Afghan Local Police would be incorporated into the Afghan National Police. Karzai agreed to a strength of 10,000 local policemen, a figure that a senior US official said could be reached within 14 months. Some senior US officers talked about expanding the program to 50,000 or 100,000, the type of numbers that would be needed to make a dramatic strategic impact like that of the Sons of Iraq. CFSOCC-A was named the program's executive agent, a mission it held until 1 July 2012, when CFSOCC-A was subsumed by Special Operations Joint Task Force-Afghanistan (SOJTF-A), a two-star command encompassing all coalition special operations forces.[13]

SOF team members provided three weeks of training to ALP guardians in subjects such as weapons training, improvised explosive device (IED) detection, first aid, human rights, and the rule of law. The duration of training was kept short by design. Given the historical propensity of Afghan militia to switch sides opportunistically, American and Afghan organizers did not want to create forces so capable that they could pose a future threat to governmental control. In addition, most potential ALP

11 Dreazen, Yochi J., 'Going Native', *National Journal* (13 November 2010).

12 American deference to Karzai's insistence on subordinating ALP to the Afghan district-level government leadership provoked mixed reactions on the American side. Some viewed it as positive, because they deemed it crucial for the villages to develop loyalty to the central government and for the central government to develop the capacity to administer village programs. Others viewed it as negative, because the district governments were often weak or predatory and thus could spoil or subvert the program.

13 Naylor, Sean D., 'Program has Afghans as First Line of Defense', *Army Times* (21 July 2010).

recruits had day jobs and would be reluctant to join a program requiring longer training.

Early experiments with village self-defense forces had shown that villages in the vicinity of the original site often became eager to participate in the program after seeing it bring security and resources to a neighboring village. To establish a prolonged presence in multiple villages, SOF teams split into smaller groups. Over time, the ALP presence might expand outward along major roads, with one or two dozen ALP manning checkpoints under the command of an Afghan checkpoint commander.

In the first months of VSO and ALP, American participation was restricted to Special Operations Forces. But the ALP growth targets set by General Petraeus and President Karzai demanded more Americans than SOF could provide. One team of Americans could cover at best ten villages, with a total of about 300 ALP guardians. While the US Special Operations Command Central had more SOF operators than any other theater special operations command, it had numerous other requirements and thus could not provide enough teams to meet even the initial target of 10,000.

Petraeus therefore decided to augment CFSOCC-A with general-purpose forces. In January 2011, he assigned the 1-16 US Army Infantry Battalion to CSOCC-A for use in expanding VSO. Squad and platoon sized elements of the battalion were integrated into SOF teams conducting Village Stability Operations, while the battalion headquarters became VSCC-North. In April 2011, the 1-505th battalion of the 82nd Airborne Division was chosen as the second general-purpose-force battalion to support VSO.[14] As VSO and ALP evolved, some of the general-purpose forces continued to serve as augmentees to US SOF teams, while others received responsibility for advising ALP without SOF participation.[15]

The effectiveness of the GPF in VSO varied widely. The attitudes and capabilities of company and battalion commanders were leading determinants of GPF effectiveness in mission accomplishment. The extent of pre-deployment training also had a substantial bearing on initial preparedness. Light infantry units assigned to VSO generally performed better than the mechanized infantry units assigned because of their greater familiarity with and suitability to the light-infantry tasks associated with VSO. General-purpose troops often did not have the same levels of maturity or physical fitness as the SOF personnel, though some units took care to remove the least-qualified personnel from their deployment rosters.[16]

14 Madden, Dan, 'The Evolution of Precision Counterinsurgency: A History of Village Stability Operations and the Afghan Local Police', CFSOCC-A Commander's Initiative Group (June 30, 2011).

15 Inspector General, United States Department of Defense, 'Assessment of US Government and Coalition Efforts to Develop the Afghan Local Police' (July 9, 2012), p. 20. Some of the general-force units received SOF 'advisors' to fill positions in their staffs.

16 Robins, Damon, 'Special Operations Forces and Conventional Forces Integration: Lessons Learned in Village Stability Operations' (22 May 2012).

Selecting Communities and Leaders

Decisions on which villages to support, and which elites within those villages to support, had an enormous impact on the effectiveness of Village Stability Operations. Most of the first sites for VSO and its predecessor programs were chosen because the village had evidenced a strong popular desire for local self-defense forces. As the program expanded, ISAF directed the addition of sites in strategically important villages, such as those astride critical lines of communication or in districts of high priority in the ISAF campaign plan, which meant that the popular desire was not necessarily so strong.

After the Afghan government sanctioned the ALP program, it became actively involved in selecting sites for VSO and ALP, which inserted new factors into the selection process. At times, the Afghan government sought to establish sites in areas based on the personal or political interests of individuals or groups with strong influence in Kabul. Most momentous was the insistence of Tajik leaders, inside and outside the government, for VSO and ALP in predominantly Tajik provinces. The insurgents were weak in most of these areas, but the Tajiks argued that VSO and ALP belonged there nonetheless because the Tajik communities deserved resources as much as Pashtun communities did, if not more so, owing to their loyalty to the government and the obligation of the national government to divide resources equitably. An unspoken rationale for expanding VSO and ALP into these areas was the desire of ethnic minorities for preparedness for a potential ethnic civil war against Pashtuns. The United States resisted efforts to use VSO and ALP for purposes besides countering the existing insurgents, but as a foreign ally it was not always able to overrule the Afghan leadership.[17]

Gauging local interest in Village Stability Operations and the Afghan Local Police was easy in communities where the elites pushed aggressively for ALP. Where such local drive was lacking, on the other hand, determining the level of interest could be highly difficult, owing to Afghans' survivalist predilection for exaggerating their support for whichever powerful people were interviewing them. Even more difficult to discern were the local political dynamics that could affect long-term effectiveness, particularly divisions within the community. Rarely did VSO teams arrive at a village with much information on the human terrain. US intelligence resources in Afghanistan had for years been concentrated on red (enemy) targets and not on white (population) or green (Afghan government), and they largely remained so from 2010 onwards.

In order to understand the power, social status, and motives of local elites and institutions, therefore, newly arrived SOF teams could rely on no human terrain model for analytical guidance, and instead had to start on the premise that no social structure could be taken for granted. Prior to forming an ALP unit, most of the VSO teams spent months on human terrain analysis. They obtained information

17 Author interviews during research trips to Afghanistan, 2010-2013.

from Afghan officials at the district and provincial levels, Afghan security forces, and Afghan and coalition intelligence organizations, as well as from village residents themselves. According to numerous VSO participants, the time and effort expended on analyzing the human terrain were well worth it.[18]

Warlords and insurgents frequently strong-armed community councils, known as *shuras*, behind the scenes. Some communities could not agree on which elders belonged in the *shura*, because of internal feuds or accusations of complicity with the insurgents, and thus ALP units could be created only by forming a *shura* beholden to select factions or bypassing the *shura* process. Even if the *shura* did represent the entire population adequately, it could still create an ALP unit that imposed a tyranny of the majority. Divided by three decades of violent internecine conflict, Afghan ethnic groups, tribes, and extended families often used the power of the majority to oppress minorities, particularly in areas with diverse populations.[19]

The coalition was rightfully worried that empowering groups to fight their tribal or ethnic rivals would cause those rivals to side with the insurgents. The risks of creating a new armed force or supporting an existing armed force in an area beset by ethnic, tribal, or familial infighting were high enough to dissuade the Americans from conducting VSO and organizing ALP in some villages. In other cases, the locals themselves decided that fractiousness made ALP unwise.[20]

Yet the villages that expressed a desire for local security forces were so often driven by a desire to avenge offenses committed by rival tribes or ethnic groups that some Americans concluded that tribal and ethnic motives were the only way to mobilize the population *en masse* against the insurgents. Lieutenant Colonel Brian Petit, who commanded Special Operations Task Force South (2nd Battalion, 1st Special Forces Group) in southern Afghanistan in 2010, wrote, 'Among the villages engaged in southern Afghanistan, groups supporting village stability initiatives fell into two categories: 1) a dominant tribe or group strong enough to endure insurgent attacks, or 2) a disenfranchised tribe or group seeking to ascend in the power structure by aligning itself with powerful Afghan or coalition partners. A third group was present, although rarely: those committed to combating the Taliban for ideological or personal reasons'.[21]

Some VSO participants did believe it possible to mitigate tribal and ethnic antagonisms by emphasizing the engagement of villages, since village identity tended to be strong even in villages with diverse populations. 'We should place community kinships above tribal kinships', Petit wrote. 'Community kinships are less divisive in

18 Young, Neiman C., '4th and Long: The Role of Civil Affairs in Village Stability Operations', *Special Warfare*, 24:3 (July-September 2011), p. 19.

19 Brown, Drew, 'US Encouraged By Afghans Banding Together To Protect Villages', *Stars and Stripes* (10 July 2010).

20 Hodge, Amanda, 'Afghanistan's Ragtag Militia, a Mixed Blessing of High Risk', *The Weekend Australian* (7 April 2012).

21 Petit, Brian, 'The Fight for the Village', *Military Review*, 91:3 (May-June 2011), pp. 30-31.

binding villages to their districts and their local leaders. Ideally, tribal engagement is a means to progress into community engagement'.[22] Appeals to village solidarity helped ease tensions and at times convinced different groups to work together, but tribal and ethnic animosity often ran too deep to be overcome by community kinship.

Another formidable obstacle to establishment of viable ALP units was a lack of popular receptivity to ALP. At the early VSO sites, 60 percent of the SOF teams encountered serious difficulties in recruiting ALP guardians, despite an emphasis on establishing sites in locations considered favorable to ALP. Enemy intimidation often accounted for the unwillingness of seemingly auspicious communities to participate. Insurgents frequently threatened or killed community leaders who were seen cooperating with the VSO teams, causing individuals and communities who had initially been receptive to give a cold shoulder to VSO and ALP.

From the outset, VSO teams encountered villages that were unwilling to participate because of the perception that the Afghan government was going to lose the war in the end. Insurgent propagandists used US announcements of troop withdrawal dates to persuade citizens that the disappearance of American support would cause the Afghan government to succumb in the end to the insurgents, whose leaders and backers in Pakistan were in for the long haul. Insurgent military successes conveyed an air of ultimate superiority, in addition to enabling the insurgents to intimidate and kill would-be opponents.[23]

The Americans themselves ruled out a large number of villages for VSO and ALP because of lack of public interest. They excluded a good deal more because the ravages of war had left villages bereft of men with strong leadership skills. When added to the villages omitted because of tribal or ethnic divisions, these exclusions amounted to a clear recognition that the ALP could not solve the insurgency problem across the whole country by itself. This reality undercut the argument of some US observers that the program should become the primary force for rural security. Karzai's preference for national security forces over local security forces would, in any event, almost certainly have prevented massive expansion even had the initial expansion been easier. Securing and governing the bulk of Afghanistan's villages would have to be left to the Afghan National Security Forces, coalition general-purpose forces, and the Afghan civil administration.

The official directive that community self-defense be established only where a strong community elite existed was at times disregarded, either because an area was considered strategically crucial, or coalition officials wanted to see rapid growth in community security programs, or Afghan political leaders wanted additional security forces there for their own reasons. Local police forces created under these conditions generally did not fare well. Some of the coalition teams assigned to such areas spent their entire tours fighting and were unable to recruit any self-defense forces at all.

22 Ibid., p. 27.
23 Author interviews, 2010-2013.

Except in the minority of cases where a community had already organized itself against the insurgents, the coalition SOF had to provide much of the leadership in the initial stages of VSO. Hence, the mobilization of the people in these villages depended heavily on the actions of the VSO personnel, especially the VSO team leader. Most of the team leaders were competent military commanders, having already passed through rigorous screening processes that assigned high priority to the attributes of combat leadership. But some were considerably better than others at convincing villagers to support VSO and ALP, leading Afghan policemen, and organizing governance and development. These activities required non-military competencies for which it was more difficult to screen officers, and which were not necessarily high priorities in officer selection and promotion within the US SOF community. Among these competencies were the comprehension of foreign operational environments, the influencing of foreigners through interpersonal communications, and the solving of complex and ambiguous problems through creativity, flexibility, intuition, and judgment.

Security

Establishing a modicum of security was an essential first step in village stability operations, for two main reasons. The first was the behavior of the citizenry. Security was the top priority of rural Afghans, as it is for most any people living in an insecure environment. Fearing for their lives, Afghans tended to support the side that seemed to have a more pervasive armed presence in their village and was more successful in battle than its adversaries. The local population would not turn against the insurgents unless a formidable intervening force could provide protection from insurgent reprisals.[24]

The second reason for the preeminence of security was the dependence of governance and development on security. Without security, the government seldom made progress in governance and development as insurgents would kill or coerce government officials and development workers. Unfortunately, the coalition learned this lesson the hard way on a number of occasions in Afghanistan.[25]

Some of the high-profile ALP successes originated with the conversion of preexisting local militias into ALP units. More often than not, though, the ALP were built from scratch. Because newly formed units needed time to gel, the VSO teams typically devoted much of their time in the shaping phase to the establishment of security, patrolling in and around the village and executing targeted strikes against the insurgents, at times with the help of other coalition SOF units or the Afghan National Army Special Forces or Commandos.[26]

24 Ibid.

25 Moyar, Mark, 'Development in Afghanistan's Counterinsurgency: A New Guide', *Orbis Operations* (March 2011), <http://smallwarsjournal.com/documents/development-in-afghanistan-coinmoyar.pdf>.

26 Author interviews, 2010-2013.

Once the VSO team and the village elites agreed to form an ALP unit, the VSO teams organized *shuras* at which elders designated ALP guardians and vouched for their good conduct. The names and other background information of the prospective ALP went to coalition and Afghan intelligence personnel and Afghan Ministry of Interior personnel, who reviewed each individual and investigated those who seemed suspicious.[27] The vetting procedures included biometric screening.[28]

Vetting often proved controversial. Some local communities and officials excluded from the ALP during the vetting process viewed it as a smoke screen that masked sinister motives. Some seemingly virtuous volunteers were turned down, while shady characters gained admittance. In the Shindand district of Herat province, the district governor attributed ALP misbehavior to the improper screening of the ALP, which had been done without input from the district leadership. 'These people who have been recruited up to this point, they are not good people', the district governor, Lal Mohammad, Omerzai, told Heidi Vogt of the Associated Press. 'They have criminal backgrounds'.[29]

Yet in other parts of the country, local Afghan officials and citizens were very positive about the vetting process. Travelling to other provinces, Vogt heard praise of the vetting from some Afghans. 'It's like a filter three times over', local councilor Abdul Habib said of the ALP vetting in Farah province. 'The elders filter, the council filters and the chief of police filters'.[30]

Once admitted into the ALP, the local policemen received a salary of $120 per month, two thirds of the salary of the Afghan National Policemen. The decision to pay salaries to ALP was based on the experiences of the Community Defense Initiative (CDI) program, a forerunner of Village Stability Operations. When CDI began, US SOF did not pay the members of the local security forces, based on the assertions of some village leaders that funding local development projects would be sufficient compensation for the community, and based on concerns within the SOF community that paying personnel would make the program too expensive to sustain in the long term. This approach worked in some villages, but it failed to obtain enough recruits for the self-defense forces on a large scale, particularly in areas where the social structure had been decimated by decades of war. In order to obtain recruits in sufficient quantities, the ODA teams assigned to CDI started paying individuals.[31]

27 US Department of Defense, 'Report on Progress Toward Security and Stability in Afghanistan', p. 79.
28 Hulslander and Spivey, 'Village Stability Operations and Afghan Local Police.'
29 Vogt, Heidi, 'Afghans See Warlord Footprints in New Police Force', *Associated Press* (21 February 2011).
30 Ibid.
31 The ODA teams did not pay specifically for service in the self-defense forces, because they did not have funds authorized for funding local security forces. Instead, they relied on a method that had been widely used in Iraq, using CERP funds to pay individuals for work on development projects with a tacit understanding that these individuals

Service in the ALP was originally intended to be a part-time job. Many ALP, however, found themselves working full-time as ALP and living at their checkpoints. ALP guardians frequently expressed a desire for greater pay, pointing out that they worked as much or more than ANP and were often engaged in combat more frequently. Some complained that low pay compelled them to demand food from citizens. Independent experts, however, contended that ALP salaries were still well above the salary of an average Afghan, leading the US leadership to resist requests for ALP salary increases. Afghans who wished to obtain higher salaries, it was said, could join the ANP.[32]

The ALP, like other homegrown security forces, enjoyed the great advantage of familiarity with the terrain, both physical and human. They knew where the enemy was most likely to operate and most likely to hide if under pressure. They could easily identify homegrown insurgents and newcomers to the area, who would have appeared no different from other villagers in the eyes of foreign forces or Afghans from other parts of the country. 'All of my men are from our village, and we can easily spot anyone who doesn't belong here', one commander explained.[33]

Local roots also afforded the ALP much better access to information from the population than national or international security forces. Afghan villagers were understandably reluctant to provide information to the counterinsurgents for fear that their assistance would become known to the insurgents and they would face severe retribution. Policemen or soldiers who came from elsewhere, about whom the citizens knew little and with whom the citizens did not have longstanding relationships, might be willing to betray their informants to the insurgents for money or out of secret sympathy for the insurgents. Villagers were much more likely to give sensitive information to ALP guardians because of their common kinship or decades of neighborly familiarity.

Villagers provided the ALP with information on the movements and activities of insurgents and other suspicious individuals. They reported where the insurgents placed improvised explosive devices (IEDs), which were the biggest single threat to coalition forces. Individuals who would feign ignorance of the location of IEDs when confronted by strange Afghan or foreign troops would often divulge the location to friends or relatives in the ALP. An ALP unit in the village of Siah Choy, for instance, disarmed 150 IEDs in the space of a few months.[34]

The insurgents were quick to recognize the strengths of the ALP program. To counter it, they relied heavily on violence and intimidation, making local ALP leaders

would participate in security operations aimed at protecting development work and the community more generally.

32 Author interviews, 2010-2013.

33 Trofimov, Yaroslav, 'US Enlists New Afghan Village Forces', *Wall Street Journal* (1 July 2010).

34 Gentile, Carmen, 'Afghan Self-Defense Groups Give Communities Freedom', *USA Today* (16 August 2012).

and their elite backers their foremost targets. Intercepted Taliban communications asserted, 'If you can kill an ALP commander, it's worth 10 coalition soldiers'.[35] The insurgents also employed propaganda against the ALP, including the broadcasting of false reports of ALP atrocities. Force, however, was their most effective countermeasure.

The most spectacular insurgent attack on SOF-supported local defense forces came in June 2010, just prior to the transition from the Local Defense Initiative to the Afghan Local Police. In June 2010, a Taliban suicide bomber blew himself up at a wedding in Kandahar province attended by numerous members of a local self-defense force, killing 40 people and wounding 80.[36] The number of civilian bystanders killed in that attack created enormous revulsion in Afghan society, which was most probably why the insurgents thereafter restricted their attacks on the ALP to more discriminate strikes, involving ground assaults and suicide bombings aimed at ALP commanders. Some of the strikes claimed the lives of their targets and other ALP guardians, but the ALP thwarted a considerable number of others, benefitting from their ability to identify insurgents approaching their villages.[37]

Initially, most ALP guardians possessed AK-47 assault rifles that belonged to them or their relatives. The United States provided vehicles, radios, and other equipment.[38] The Afghan government and the coalition chose not to give the ALP heavy weapons, for fear that those weapons might one day be turned against the government. The insurgents quickly discerned this limitation, and began engaging the ALP with heavy weapons from ranges beyond the effective range of the AK-47.

To foil this tactic, US military officers proposed the distribution of Kalashnikov PKM machine guns to the ALP. In response, the Afghan Ministry of Interior laid out a process for requesting medium crew-served weapons for ALP use. The ministry announced the process in July 2011, but in the months that followed, few ALP received machine guns. Provincial and district governors and police chiefs obstructed the distribution of the weapons because of persistent fears that the ALP or insurgents might use them against the government in the future. Many of these officials, furthermore, considered ALP a lower priority than ANP and thus gave the latter the lion's share of weapons and other resources.[39]

Through the concerted efforts of CFSOCC-A and the NATO Training Mission-Afghanistan (NTM-A), the machine guns began flowing in early 2012. Adhering to a policy of providing one PKM for every six guardians, NTM-A distributed 1,745 of

35 Hodge, 'Afghanistan's Ragtag Militia, a Mixed Blessing of High Risk'.
36 Rodriguez, Alex, 'Anti-Taliban Tribal Militias Come With Baggage', *Los Angeles Times* (19 June 2010).
37 Nissenbaum, Dion, 'Insurgents Hit Ex-Taliban Leader's Police Unit', *Wall Street Journal* (6 April 2012).
38 Michaels, Jim, 'Officials Tripling Afghan Defense Forces', *USA Today* (30 June 2011).
39 Inspector General, United States Department of Defense, 'Assessment of US Government and Coalition Efforts to Develop the Afghan Local Police', pp. 31-34.

the weapons to the ALP by the end of April 2012.[40] Once the ALP had the capability to return fire at longer ranges, their losses to enemy machine guns and other heavy weapons declined sharply.

Governance and Development

In the counterinsurgency environment of rural Afghanistan, governance ranked second in importance to security, in terms of both the population's preferences and the practical necessities of the conflict. Afghans valued good governance more than social and economic development and were more likely to side with the insurgents because of bad governance rather than underdevelopment. The counterinsurgents had to establish governance of a certain quality before they could achieve meaningful development, for the quality of governance determined whether developmental resources were spent on items that promoted support for the government or were diverted into the pockets of government officials or businessmen.[41]

Although the coalition divided security, governance, and development into distinct lines of operations, they were not independent of each other. Gains or setbacks in one often led to gains or setbacks in another. For instance, providing developmental aid to a tribe in conjunction with a shift in local military conditions could cause the tribe to discontinue support for the insurgents and improve security further, whereas that aid would have achieved little without the change in military conditions. The replacement of an effective district governor with a corrupt one could lead villagers to take up arms against the government and hence diminish security, or it could result in pilferage from health programs by the governor and his subordinates and hence undermine development.

Because of President Karzai's insistence on subordinating the ALP to the district administration, official VSO policy emphasized the strengthening of ties between the district government and the villages. In practice, strengthening these connections often proved highly difficult, and at times was impossible. The district government was virtually nonexistent in some of the districts where coalition forces were engaged in VSO, owing to lack of staff or the inability of staff to travel to villages for reasons of distance or insecurity. In other districts, the district leadership was so oppressive that villages had no desire to have any connection to it. In fact, poor district governance ranked among the top reasons why certain villages were selected for VSO in the first place. Even where the district leadership was reasonably capable, some villages wanted nothing to do with it because of a traditional preference for autonomy.

40 Ibid., p. 97.

41 Wilder, Andrew, 'Losing Hearts and Minds in Afghanistan', Middle East Institute (December 2009); Moyar, 'Development in Afghanistan's Counterinsurgency'; Thompson, Edwina, Report on Wilton Park Conference 1022 (1 April 2010), <http://www.wiltonpark.org.uk/resources/en/pdf/22290903/22291297/wp1022-report>.

The typical district had a governor and police chief who had been appointed by the central government in Kabul. Although district governors were considered the chief executives in a district, they had no official authority over the district police chiefs, whose official responsibilities included the ALP as well as the ANP.[42] Actual authority was often different from formal authority; the most powerful individual in a district could be the district governor, the district police chief, or a power broker with no formal position in the government. Some of the governors and police chiefs were socially influential individuals native to the district, which gave them a base of supporters and informants, but also inclined them to take sides in local feuds. The majority came from other parts of the country, which meant that they had neither a local support base nor a stake in local squabbles.[43]

SOF teams found that VSO and ALP most often made considerable progress where the Afghan government's district leaders were capable and approved of the programs. Such officials cooperated on the governance and developmental measures advocated by the SOF personnel, and effectively supervised the ALP. Such officials were vital for sustaining the ALP and good governance after the coalition personnel departed. They were also vital to promoting harmony between the groups that were well represented in the ALP and those that were not.

When the district-level leadership was very weak or resistant to VSO and ALP, progress remained localized at the village level, and chances for sustainability were low since the VSO teams would ultimately turn the ALP and their other programs over to the district government. 'A successful village stability program such as the Khas Oruzgan effort will have limited effects when the district level governance is not capable or willing to continue the forward progress', observed Brian Petit. 'When villages seek aid from a dysfunctional, undermanned, or corrupt district center, progress becomes tenuous, and islands of security become vulnerable to anti-government influence'.[44]

At times, VSO teams implemented programs aimed at reducing the excesses of district leaders. One Civil Affairs team leader noted that his team sought to ease villager concerns about corrupt district leadership by creating a program that made district finances public and required use of local contractors on projects.[45] In a sovereign country, however, such reforms could make little headway in the face of active resistance from the local leadership.

The most effective way to combat bad leadership at the district level was to convince higher Afghan authorities to replace individuals. Coalition officials frequently lobbied the Afghan government to replace bad district governors and police chiefs, largely

42 From time to time, coalition experts recommended elections for district officials, but the concept never gained traction, leaving Karzai and his inner circle with the final say on appointments.
43 Author interviews, 2010-2013.
44 Petit, 'The Fight for the Village', p. 30.
45 Young, '4th and Long', p. 20.

based on reporting from coalition personnel working at the local level, such as the VSO teams. The ability of coalition personnel to advocate worthy replacements was constrained by their limited knowledge of individual leaders and human terrain, and by a scarcity of high-quality Afghan human capital with which ineffectual or malign leaders could be replaced. It was further circumscribed by the quality of US-Afghan relations at the national level, which varied over time based on personal relationships and international developments.

Developmental aid could be very effective as a means of building community support for the ALP and coalition forces, if spent astutely and in concert with security and governance initiatives. It was generally most effective when used to secure the support of local elites. The most effective aid programs were those that concentrated on influencing the small number of rural elites who had the status and capabilities necessary to organize opposition to the insurgents. Accustomed to bargaining, these individuals were generally willing to accept developmental aid in return for actions against the insurgents, provided that the insurgents were not so strong that they could easily kill those who opposed them. The rest of the population would follow their lead.[46]

Abuses of Power

Throughout human history, the abuse of power has been a leading cause of insurgency, and overcoming it has been a critical challenge of counterinsurgency. Some of the Afghans who had authority over the ALP abused that authority for the benefit of themselves or their families, tribes, or ethnic groups. The real source of this misconduct was not the ALP program, but rather the disintegration of the Afghan social order dating back to the late 1970s. Every organization and program run by Afghans was susceptible to the same malfeasance as the ALP. But the role of American SOF in organizing the ALP gave the US government considerable responsibility for their conduct, and culpability for their misdeeds.

Both critics and defenders of the ALP agreed that abuses of power stemmed largely from problems within the Afghan leadership. For the first years of the ALP program, the perpetrators of abuses were usually ALP commanders, while district police chiefs became more prominent as their authority over the ALP increased. Some of the culprits were relatives or friends of high officials in the national government and had been given their jobs for the purpose of enriching themselves and their highly placed connections. Others had paid large sums for their appointments and were intent on recouping their investments by extorting money from international aid programs, commercial enterprises, and private citizens. Still others had been put into these

46 Author interviews, 2010-2013.

leadership positions because of their military prowess or charisma, with little regard for their integrity or concern for the general population.[47]

Verifying alleged acts of wrongdoing was often as difficult as it was important. The insurgents were known to plant bogus accusations of human rights violations against the ALP in order to undermine the program. Following a September 2011 report in which Human Rights Watch enumerated 32 claims that Afghan Local Policemen were guilty of human rights abuses, the US government conducted an official investigation and determined that some of the 32 allegations, including the most serious ones, could not be substantiated, and that some of the others had been committed by individuals or groups who falsely purported to belong to the ALP. The investigators determined that only a small number of the alleged actions had definitely been committed by the Afghan Local Police. Among those pinned on the ALP were the stabbing of an ALP guardian by two individuals from a different ALP unit and the detention of Afghan National Police officers by ALP units.[48]

Some of the most problematic ALP sites were reformed during 2012, as the United Nations Mission in Afghanistan (UNAMA) observed. The ANP increased its control over unruly ALP in Baghlan and Herat provinces, resulting in reductions in abuses. The US SOF demobilized 258 of 770 ALP in Wardak province because of misbehavior.[49] The ALP commander who had been accused of the most crimes, Hakeem Shujayee in Oruzgan, was arrested in the summer of 2012 on charges of murder and rape.[50] ALP commanders fired numerous individuals who were considered inadequate, some of whom had to stand trial for their abuses.[51] As one prosecutor noted, the fact that the

47 Noor Ul Haq, the widely publicized ALP commander in Baghlan province, exemplified the commander selected for military achievements without concern for how he might treat the population. In early 2011, coalition officials acknowledged that Haq had been accused of more than 100 crimes, and that his militiamen were shaking down passersby at checkpoints. Partlow, Joshua, 'US Effort to Arm Afghan Villagers Carries Some Risks', *Washington Post* (7 February 2011). For another report on complaints of demands for bribes at ALP checkpoints, in Helmand province, see Gannon, Kathy, 'Police Test Afghanistan's Fragile Ethnic Balance', *Associated Press* (14 November 2012).

48 Inspector General, United States Department of Defense, 'Assessment of US Government and Coalition Efforts to Develop the Afghan Local Police', p. 28; Londono, Ernesto, 'US Cites Local Afghan Police Abuses', *Washington Post* (16 December 2011). A United Nations report stated, 'UNAMA documented some allegations of human rights abuses which had been falsely attributed to ALP and had been actually committed by Pro-Government militia groups who call themselves ALP.' Human Rights Unit of the United Nations Assistance Mission in Afghanistan, 'Afghanistan Mid-Year Report 2012', pp. 47-48.

49 Human Rights Unit of the United Nations Assistance Mission in Afghanistan, 'Afghanistan Mid-Year Report 2012', p. 48.

50 Cloud, David S., and Shashank Bengali, 'Afghan Police With A Past', *Los Angeles Times* (11 February 2013).

51 Robinson, Linda, 'Is There Hope For Afghanistan?', *ForeignPolicy.com* (29 November 2011).

ALP fell under the Ministry of Interior made it considerably easier to prosecute its members than would be true of non-governmental armed groups.[52] In addition, ALP training was modified to incorporate additional coverage of human rights issues, at the recommendation of village leaders.[53] The vigorous combating of abuses led not only to a decline in human rights violations but also in negative media stories about the ALP and negative local perceptions of the ALP.

Assessing Effectiveness

Although no single metric conclusively demonstrated effectiveness in securing the population, some valuable insights could be derived from the most common metrics, as well as some less common ones, when taken in the proper context. The substantial levels of violence in many areas where the ALP had been present for a year or more indicated that the program was not achieving security gains as rapidly as its source of inspiration, the Sons of Iraq program. The casualty levels of the ALP, together with qualitative accounts of ALP performance, showed that many ALP were willing to fight and that the insurgents were intent on fighting them.

A valuable statistic less often cited was the number of VSO sites overrun by the enemy. At the start of VSO and ALP, there had been considerable concern that dispersing coalition forces and ALP guardians in remote areas risked the overrunning of entire units. Yet no VSO or ALP sites were completely overrun in the first years of the program. Some observers attributed this outcome to effective Afghan and coalition leadership and to robust coalition combat support. That explanation is correct, but it is also incomplete. The lack of devastating attacks on VSO and ALP sites was also the result of decisions to avoid establishing ALP sites in some of the most dangerous areas on account of inhospitable terrain, lack of community interest, or enemy strength.[54]

A large amount of the most valuable evidence on ALP effectiveness came from purely qualitative sources. Foremost among these were insurgent sources, which were very reliable when they testified to counterinsurgent successes since the insurgents had nothing to gain from exaggerating ALP effectiveness, whereas coalition and Afghan officials stood to benefit from evidence of effectiveness and thus had to be viewed more skeptically. Numerous insurgent sources acknowledged that the ALP were increasing the government's control of the population and hence impeding insurgent activities.[55]

52 Rubin, Alissa J., 'Afghan Rape Case Turns Focus on Local Police', *New York Times* (27 June 2012).

53 Human Rights Unit of the United Nations Assistance Mission in Afghanistan, 'Afghanistan Mid-Year Report 2012', pp. 45-46.

54 In Regional Command East, for instance, ALP had few sites in areas where the enemy had the capability to operate in company strength or larger.

55 Cloud, David S. and Laura King, 'Report Faults Afghan Police', *Los Angeles Times* (14 May 2012).

Human rights organizations also supplied highly credible qualitative data. Distrustful of the ALP because of past human rights violations by Afghan militias, the human rights organizations had no interest in exaggerating ALP successes or otherwise reporting information that could be used to justify expanding or extending the program. Thus, human rights organizations that attributed security improvements to the ALP enjoyed especial credibility. In July 2012, for instance, a United Nations human rights report on 51 Afghan districts stated, 'Many communities reported improvement in the security environment in areas with ALP presence and a reduced presence of Anti-Government Elements'.[56]

Transition

From the outset, the VSO and ALP programs emphasized the development of Afghan capacity and the transition of duties from coalition forces to Afghans. In December 2009, President Barack Obama announced that ISAF would transition security responsibility to Afghan security forces by the end of 2014, and CFSOCC-A based its planning on that timeline. In 2010, CFSOCC-A initiated extensive transition planning, and in 2011 it added 'transition' as a fifth phase to VSO's 'clear-hold-build-expand' sequence.

Transition received further impetus in the middle of 2011, when the Obama administration aborted plans for a counterinsurgency campaign in eastern Afghanistan similar to the one that had been executed in southern and southwestern Afghanistan. Under a new strategy, US conventional forces would be withdrawn more quickly and greater emphasis was to be put on swift transitioning of responsibilities to Afghans. Direct-action missions against the Taliban and other hostile groups were expected to compensate for the reduced US participation in population security operations.

The challenges of transitioning VSO in this relatively short time were multiplied by plans for rapid growth of the ALP program. In June 2011, when the ALP had 6,500 guardians at 41 sites, Afghan and coalition officials agreed to a plan that increased authorized ALP strength from 10,000 to 30,000.[57] The force size was projected to reach 17,000 in December 2012, 22,000 in July 2013, and 30,000 in December 2015.[58] The program ended up meeting the December 2012 and July 2013 targets on time, and it met the December 2015 goal well ahead of schedule in late 2013.

Transition was further constrained by the size of US forces assigned to VSO. Most of the ALP development fell upon their shoulders, for only a few Afghan units

56 Human Rights Unit of the United Nations Assistance Mission in Afghanistan, 'Afghanistan Mid-Year Report 2012', p. 7. See also Afghanistan Independent Human Rights Commission, 'From *Arbaki* to Local Police: Today's Challenges and Tomorrow's Concerns' (Spring 2012).

57 Michaels, 'Officials Tripling Afghan Defense Forces'.

58 US Department of Defense, 'Report on Progress Toward Security and Stability in Afghanistan', p. 78.

were deemed capable of performing the mission.[59] In mid-2012, when the ALP had a strength of roughly 13,000, two US conventional infantry battalions and 80 SOF teams were attached to ALP and the number of US troops began to decline thereafter.[60] The more thinly that coalition forces were spread, the less influence they had on ALP development.

While ALP training was itself only three weeks in duration, building successful ALP units demanded a much longer presence by the coalition SOF team, GPF unit, or other supporting force. In villages that had not already organized a militia force, the shaping phase alone typically took three to four months during the warm months, when the enemy resistance was strongest, and two to three months during the colder months when fighting subsided. Teams that attempted to accelerate this phase were often unable to gain adequate comprehension of the human terrain or to establish relationships with influential members of the community, and hence made mistakes in enlisting community assistance and selecting ALP guardians.

Early on, VSO teams found that the coalition presence had to be maintained at least for two years to ensure that the ALP remained viable after the coalition forces departed. That amount of time was needed to develop able Afghan leadership and instill confidence in the community that the ALP could resist the insurgents without suffering annihilation. The desires of coalition policymakers to withdraw their forces from Afghanistan sooner rather than later created much consternation among Afghan civilians that coalition SOF would depart too soon, and hence ALP units would be overrun or compelled into submission through insurgent threats. In January 2013, a Rand Corporation report warned of a collapse of the ALP if the United States phased out its support too rapidly.[61]

The most difficult facet of transition for the ALP and the rest of the Afghan government was logistics. During the early stages of VSO, the SOF teams provided logistical support to the ALP, but as part of transition the ALP's logistics were supposed to be transferred to the logistical system of the Afghan National Police, which belonged to the Ministry of Interior, because the ALP also fell bureaucratically under the Ministry of Interior. The ANP logistical system was mentored primarily by the NATO Training Mission-Afghanistan, and the system made significant advances during 2010 and 2011. By 2012, nevertheless, it was still hampered by corruption, illiteracy, and indifference.[62] Coalition partners often had to perform logistical

59 ANA Special Forces were training ALP at eight sites, and the ANP were not involved in ALP training at all. Human Rights Unit of the United Nations Assistance Mission in Afghanistan, 'Afghanistan Mid-Year Report 2012', p. 46.

60 Inspector General, United States Department of Defense, 'Assessment of US Government and Coalition Efforts to Develop the Afghan Local Police', p. 15.

61 Hodge, Nathan, 'New Threat Seen In Afghan Pullout', *Wall Street Journal* (23 January 2013).

62 US Department of Defense, 'Report on Progress Toward Security and Stability in Afghanistan', p. 79.

functions themselves, or escort Afghan officials to Afghan logistical facilities to ensure that items were received. A July 2012 report by the Department of Defense Inspector General noted that it had heard from many coalition and ALP personnel that equipment and supplies often failed to reach ALP units because of provincial or district governors or police chiefs who did not support the ALP or 'diverted equipment to other than the designated ALP unit or for non-official use by others'.[63] The authors concluded that the ALP could not be sustained if the coalition's logistical support came to an end.[64]

Transition of ALP units began in earnest in 2012. VSO teams that had been located in villages pulled back to more central locations, often near district capitals where they could spend more time working with district officials. Some teams, in fact, had already been concentrating their efforts at the district level, in awareness that the program's ultimate fate hinged on the performance of district officials. By late 2012, SOJTF-A had transitioned primary responsibility for supervising the ALP to the Afghan National Security Forces in 21 districts. Adherence to the stringent criteria for transition ensured that chances for maintaining effective ALP in these districts were good. Only in one case, in Badghis province during the middle of 2012, did a transitioned ALP unit defect to the Taliban.[65]

The other 73 districts where ALP were active at the end of 2012 were considerably more problematic, as most of them were deficient in many or all of the five key criteria for initiating transition. At the start of 2013, JSOTF-A faced the task of bolstering these units while at the same time it was notified of further ALP growth and more rapid US SOF withdrawal.[66] In February 2013, however, US officials announced that they had gained the support of Afghan officials in extending the ALP for five more years and increasing it in size from the current 19,600 to 45,000.[67] That same month, President Obama announced in the State of the Union Address that he would remove 34,000 US troops by the end of 2013. The number was expected to be reduced below

63 Inspector General, United States Department of Defense, 'Assessment of US Government and Coalition Efforts to Develop the Afghan Local Police', p. 53.

64 Ibid., pp. 47-50.

65 Salahuddin, Sayed, 'Afghan Local Police Group Deserts to Taliban-Led Insurgents', *Washington Post* (4 July 2012).

66 In early 2012, COMISAF had directed CFSOCC-A to conduct a study on making ALP an 'enduring program' beyond 2014. For much of 2012, Ministry of Interior officials and provincial governors favored ending the program within five years of inception as stated in the official decree, though the majority of village elders favored making the ALP permanent because they were more accountable to their elders and extended families. Inspector General, United States Department of Defense, 'Assessment of US Government and Coalition Efforts to Develop the Afghan Local Police', p. 12. Karzai reportedly did not view the ALP as a long-term solution because of the number of complaints received from Afghan citizens that ALP members were abusing their power. Sieff, Kevin, 'US, Afghanistan Differ Over Local Police', *Washington Post* (15 January 2013).

67 Cloud and Bengali, 'Afghan Police With A Past'.

10,000 by the end of 2014.[68] With 5,509 CJSOTF-A personnel assigned to VSO/ALP as of late 2012, the size of the US commitment would have to be far smaller by the end of 2014. While the 34,000 scheduled for withdrawal in 2013 would not include many SOF, they did constitute more than one third of ISAF, whose contributions in security, logistics, and other areas facilitated VSO and ALP.[69]

The transition of resource authority to the Afghan National Police leadership and the withdrawal of US influence solidified the control of both the National Police and its parent ministry, the Ministry of Interior, over the Afghan Local Police. Giving the National Police and Ministry of Interior complete ownership of the ALP units increased the likelihood that powerful officials would become patrons of the ALP, instead of viewing the ALP as an American program of little benefit to them as had often been true. In a country where patronage networks remained strong despite more than a decade of Western efforts to break the patronage culture, the existence of patronage was critical to the long-term logistical sustainability of any security force.

Patrons also had the ability to use other security forces to support the ALP. The strengthening of ALP ties to the National Police and Ministry of Interior led district and provincial police chiefs to use their ANP forces to provide area security where ALP were located, to protect supply lines to ALP checkpoints, and to provide quick-reaction forces to ALP areas under attack. With ANP concentrated at district headquarters, they were better situated to assist the ALP than most other armed forces were. Some ANP even served with the ALP at checkpoints, all but guaranteeing that the ALP received as much support from the police leadership as the ANP.

In early 2013, when reductions in troop numbers and enabler support made time-based transition of the ALP imperative, districts had to be transitioned regardless of the conditions in which the ALP program found itself. Some districts that clearly did not meet the criteria of sustainable ALP nonetheless were handed over to the Afghans. In several of these areas, the enemy was able to overrun ALP checkpoints.

The accelerated pace of transition deprived many districts of the extended SOF mentorship that originally had been central to the ALP. Instead of receiving the desired two years of SOF mentorship, many ALP received less than one year prior to transition. In response to the curtailment of SOF mentorship, SOJTF-A extended ALP training from three weeks to four weeks in early 2013. As SOF on-the-job training of ALP disappeared, that amount of training might still have sufficed for regular patrolmen, but it was not nearly enough for inexperienced Afghans holding leadership positions.

68 Chandrasekaran, Rajiv, 'Obama To Cut Troop Level In Half Over Next Year', *Washington Post* (13 February 2013).

69 US Department of Defense, 'Report on Progress Toward Security and Stability in Afghanistan', p. 80; Katzman, Kenneth, 'Afghanistan: Post-Taliban Governance, Security, and US Policy', Congressional Research Service (8 March 2013), p. 80.

The combination of the drawdown in US SOF and the plans to expand the ALP to 45,000 necessitated greater involvement from the Afghan central government in organizing new ALP units. Some district and provincial Afghan officials proved capable of carrying out this task effectively, but others did not. In certain districts, Afghan officials selected communities and leaders without the extensive human terrain analysis employed in prior efforts, or made choices based exclusively on their personal, tribal, or ethnic agendas. Some officials skipped the vetting of recruits, hiring anyone who turned up at recruiting sites. The ALP units created under such conditions encountered numerous problems.[70]

Conclusions

The VSO and ALP programs offer important lessons for community mobilization programs in other countries, and for counterinsurgency and foreign assistance more broadly. The size and duration of these programs, along with the availability of voluminous information on their implementation, make them especially valuable subjects of inquiry for those seeking lessons that may have practical value in the future. This section highlights key lessons and discusses their applicability in other settings, emphasizing which aspects are likely to be universally applicable and which are likely to be suitable only under certain conditions.

The US special operations command in Afghanistan created the community mobilization programs that evolved into VSO and ALP only after a detailed inquiry into whether conditions in Afghanistan were suitable. Experts from inside and outside the command determined that the conditions were favorable in enough villages to merit a sizable program, but that they were not favorable in many others, which necessitated careful selections of sites. Such an initial inquiry is imperative for future community mobilization initiatives. In other parts of the world, conditions may be unsuitable in so many villages that community mobilization is not worth attempting. Alternatively, the number of villages with potential for community mobilization may be so high as to warrant a program of larger scale than VSO and ALP. A program of that magnitude would almost certainly entail participation from general-purpose forces, given that two battalions of general-purpose forces were required for VSO and ALP.

The effectiveness of VSO teams in mobilizing specific communities and forming ALP units depended heavily on the quality of the human terrain analysis employed prior to engagement. The irregular and informal power structures resulting from decades of violent conflict and rivalries among ethnicities, tribes, and families demanded a detailed understanding of political relationships and political personalities. Developing this understanding required several months of information gathering, much of it provided by partner-nation government personnel and US interagency

70 Author interviews, 2010-2013.

partners. The elimination or shortening of the human terrain analysis often led to mistakes in site selection or ALP recruitment, which empowered malign individuals or inflamed tensions between different population groups. A similar period of time is likely to be required in counterinsurgency situations in other countries where the human terrain is so varied and divided. Some countries, it should be noted, have considerably less diversity and division within their populations than Afghanistan.

Community opinion, as embodied in the *shura*, was supposed to guide the formation and oversight of ALP units. But *shuras* proved susceptible to manipulation by powerful figures, inside and outside the government. At times, social divisions prevented *shuras* from reaching compromises acceptable to all major groups in the community. Consequently, VSO teams sometimes had to intervene in the *shura* process, or bypass it. In some villages, they had to pick sides. The difficulties of developing community consensus deserve consideration in any population mobilization program, particularly since Westerners often underestimate the complexities and complications of reaching consensus.

The viability of VSO and ALP in an area was heavily dependent on the composition of the civilian elites in that area. Chances for success were much higher in areas where traditional tribal elites retained influence, as they had vested interests in local security and good governance, and could convince large numbers of locals to join the ALP or contribute in other ways. Where such elites were absent, locals of lesser social standing or individuals from other areas held sway, but without the same degree of respect from the population. They faced more difficulty in obtaining support, and were more liable to prey on the population, undermining VSO, ALP, and the government cause more generally. Few countries have seen their rural elites devastated to the same extent as Afghanistan's over the past four decades, but in conflict-prone countries practitioners must be attuned to the possibility that past events may have displaced traditional rural elites. With urban insurgency also a major concern in certain countries, the migration of elites from rural to urban areas and the power structures of urban communities are also deserving of intensive study.

In Afghanistan, VSO and ALP served as supplements to, not substitutes for, governmental and coalition efforts in security, governance, and development. Early on, some US planners advocated making the ALP large enough to assume responsibility for population security in much of the country, but Afghan governmental resistance prevented the program from reaching such proportions. The limitations on size ensured that the ALP would not have a decisive strategic impact, though they also allowed the cherry-picking of sites most conducive to the program, which raised the probability of success for the average VSO team and ALP unit. Those considering community mobilization on a larger scale must bear in mind that the larger the program, the lower the degree of selectivity in choosing communities and hence the lower the frequency of success.

As a lightly armed and static force, the ALP were often highly effective at controlling populous areas and resisting small-scale insurgent encroachment. They could not, however, withstand large attacks or conduct mobile offensive operations, tasks that were also critical in this war and in most other counterinsurgencies. Dispersed into small groups of 10 or 20 men, they occupied fixed checkpoints where enemy forces could readily mass, and when they travelled outside checkpoints they were even fewer in number. In areas where the enemy was incapable of assembling in strength, these vulnerabilities did not matter very much, but in those places where the insurgents could attack in platoon size or larger, the ALP needed military and police forces with greater firepower and mobility to provide area security and serve as quick-reaction forces. ALP units were used as mobile strike forces on occasion, but the US and Afghan governments preferred to leave such operations to national forces, and the same is likely to be true in future conflicts.

The case of VSO and ALP highlighted the need for the cooperation of partner-nation leadership in undertaking large-scale community mobilization. Partner-nation leaders do not necessarily share the interests or the worldview of their allies, and therefore may object to community mobilization of the sort envisioned by Americans. The Afghan government obstructed community mobilization on terms other than its own, which compelled the United States to alter its proposals for the ALP program in substantial ways, to include the capping of its size and the subordination of its personnel to the Ministry of Interior. Other partner nations will likely drive an even harder bargain, since they are usually less reliant on the United States for survival than Afghanistan was in 2010.

Ownership by the host-nation government deprived the United States of the latitude it had in Iraq, where the Sons of Iraq program initially fell under the authority of the US military. It also left the program subject to the whims of ineffective or predatory Afghan leaders. In future endeavors, the value of host-nation ownership will depend on the quality of host-nation leadership, which is likely to be less than stellar, for nations with high-quality leadership usually do not need foreign help in securing their own territory.

Host-nation ownership did have some large advantages for the ALP. It encouraged the national leadership to support the program and develop the self-sufficiency required for long-term sustainability. As SOJTF-A transferred support responsibilities to the Afghan Ministry of Interior, powerful Afghan leaders showed greater interest in the success of the ALP and took positive actions to advance the ALP cause, such as ensuring that units received supplies and providing quick-reaction forces in the event of attacks.

Ownership was especially important in Afghanistan because of the persistence of patronage networks, which maintained informal channels of power in the government that were often stronger than the official lines of authority. The United States and other Western nations prodded the Afghan leadership to replace patronage networks with formal bureaucratic structures, as they have in numerous other countries. The fact that patronage politics continued to thrive after ten years of massive foreign involvement in Afghanistan suggests that progress in reforming governance will be slow in other countries with patronage cultures, a club that includes most countries of the Third World.

Initially, some ALP units depended on American air assets for supplies and reinforcement, as no Afghan or coalition forces were nearby. A substantial number of ALP sites had been established in remote areas for the express purpose of denying the enemy sanctuary in distant or mountainous regions. As American air disappeared, these sites could no longer receive logistical support or military reinforcement, leaving them highly vulnerable to insurgent encirclement. It is not clear how these ALP sites have fared since the American aircraft stopped coming, but the outlook does not seem very promising. In future efforts, American planners should consider the long-term viability of supporting indigenous forces in remote areas before training and arming them.

The experiences of VSO and ALP demonstrated large variations in the effectiveness of US SOF personnel in community mobilization. VSO and ALP often demanded skills beyond those required in an individual's prior assignments, such as the ability to persuade and lead people from a very different culture and the ability to organize governance and development activities. The effectiveness of VSO team leaders depended on their adaptability and complex problem-solving abilities, which can be scarce talents even in special operations forces. Because SOF can be expected to participate in community mobilization in the future, SOF force providers should examine their personnel selection and promotion practices for opportunities to enhance the aptitude of their human capital in these areas.

Screening indigenous personnel for the ALP presented different challenges. Basic attributes such as work ethic and loyalty to the government that were commonplace among US personnel could not be taken for granted with Afghans. Therefore, the selection criteria for ALP guardians, and especially ALP leaders, had to include these elemental traits, which necessarily meant less emphasis on higher order skills. Local *shuras* were supposed to select members of the community for the ALP, but coalition and Afghan governmental personnel sometimes played a major role in the selection process, as well as in ongoing monitoring to detect those who might be sympathetic to the insurgents or otherwise unsuitable for the program. Even with the use of advanced intelligence capabilities, a number of malign individuals slipped through the filters and committed crimes against the population or perpetrated violence against other ALP or coalition SOF. Future adversaries of the United States will likely be aware of the insider attacks committed by members of Afghanistan's security forces and will seek to replicate them in partner-nation forces, necessitating continued vigilance in personnel screening.

The implementation of VSO and ALP amply illustrated the pros and cons of relying on local rural populations to secure and govern themselves. Because the ALP were native to their areas of operation, they had intimate familiarity with the human terrain as well as personal ties that encouraged the population to provide information. Consequently, they could collect large amounts of intelligence information even though they did not possess specialized intelligence training or assets. Their inherent intelligence capabilities gave them an enormous cost advantage over the national security forces and coalition forces that expended lavish amounts on intelligence, and a great advantage overall against Afghan National Security Forces that could not afford such expenditures. The ALP also benefited from Afghan traditions of village self-defense and the general tendency of individuals to prize the security of their families, which made local Afghans more resolute than Afghans from outside in combating insurgents. The superiority of the ALP to the Afghan National Security Forces in these respects strengthens the case that local policemen should play a lasting role in Afghanistan, and in other countries with similar human terrain.

In Afghanistan, the chief disadvantage of local security forces was the risk of inflaming social divisions that the enemy could exploit. The perception of governmental favoritism toward the recruited group and the misbehavior of the resultant forces could give the insurgents powerful recruiting tools. When SOF recruitment of local forces spurs violent tribal or ethnic strife, in Afghanistan or any other country with a weak national identity, it deepens blood feuds and thereby undermines the prospects for long-term stability. On the other hand, tribal or ethnic rivalries might be so pronounced already that they cannot be made much worse, as was the case in parts of Afghanistan.

The advantages of employing local personnel generally outweighed the disadvantages. In mid-2013, the ALP study group was impressed that nearly every observer they encountered, including many who had been skeptical about the program at the time of its inception, acknowledged that the ALP program was, in a considerable number of areas, effective in providing security and setting the conditions for governance and development. The weight of evidence, of which the most credible was qualitative and came from sources outside the Afghan and coalition governments, indicated that the ALP on the whole improved security and weakened the insurgents more effectively than the Afghan National Security Forces. The ability of VSO and ALP to handpick sites, it should be remembered, gave the ALP advantages over national security forces, as did the support provided to the ALP sites by highly capable coalition SOF. Had the ALP program been implemented nationwide, it undoubtedly would have been less successful in some areas than the national forces. Nevertheless, the inherent advantages of local security forces were clear, undeniable, and powerful. In any future counterinsurgency, recruiting locals into community self-defense forces is an option that deserves serious consideration.

The successes of VSO and ALP, limited though they were by program size and Afghan human terrain, had strategic benefits out of proportion to their costs, even when one includes the large investment of SOF personnel into the program. According to enemy sources, insurgent leaders generally viewed the ALP as the foremost obstacle to the success of the insurgency. For that reason, they concentrated much of their offensive activity against the ALP, reducing their ability to act elsewhere. The ALP's prominence in guarding their own villages also undermined the enemy narrative that the insurgents were waging a war against foreign infidels, which sapped the enthusiasm of Afghans and foreign Islamists who had seen the war as a defense of the Islamic faith.

Whether the ALP's short-term security gains will translate into long-term stability remains to be seen. The future of the ALP depends on the ability of the Afghan government, at the district level and above, to manage the ALP units, curb social divisions, and integrate local and national security forces. It also depends on Afghan perceptions of which side is likely to win the war, and on the extent of Pakistani support to Afghan insurgents. If the right conditions prevail, the ALP will have contributed meaningfully to Afghanistan's long-term stability. If not, then some or all of the ALP will disband or go over to the enemy side.

VSO and ALP were most effective when they exploited the interrelationships among security, governance, and development. The establishment of security could facilitate governance and development, and good governance could promote development. When used astutely and in tandem with security activities, governance and development could improve security and weaken the insurgents. SOF Civil Affairs provided valuable expertise in governance and development, but nearly all of the SOF personnel assigned to VSO participated in governance and development in one way or another. Future community mobilization efforts, in Afghanistan and elsewhere, will similarly immerse SOF in governance and development, and thus these subjects deserve to be taught in depth to SOF beyond the Civil Affairs community.

While improvements in the quality of governance led directly to greater popular support for the Afghan government, advances in development did not necessarily affect support levels. Development aid was most effective in altering community allegiance when it was provided to local elites in return for their assistance, rather than as a philanthropic donation to the whole village. The former indicated that the Americans were savvy players, and it concentrated resources on the individuals who had the greatest influence and capability, while the latter indicated that the Americans were suckers and it diffused power. This lesson is likely applicable in other traditional rural societies. Another lesson, applicable mainly to highly heterogeneous and fractious societies like Afghanistan's, is that aid runs the risk of inadvertently generating internecine resentments because groups may view anything given to another group as unjustifiable favoritism.

The subordination of the ALP to the Afghan government led the US SOF command to make the connection of villages to district governance a central feature of Village Stability Operations. Connecting villages to districts proved one of the foremost challenges to VSO, because the district government was often weak, nonexistent, malign, or unwanted. While coalition SOF personnel could make up for some of the deficiencies of the district government, their presence was only temporary, leaving the long-term viability of district governance in the hands of the Afghan district leadership. VSO could contribute to the improvement of Afghan leadership quality by mentoring Afghan district leaders and convincing senior coalition officials to advise top Afghan officials that they should replace inferior Afghan district leaders. Such is likely to be the furthest possible extent of SOF governance assistance in future locales.

The experience of VSO and ALP highlighted the importance of indigenous leadership at all levels in waging a counterinsurgency. National-level leadership was crucial in gaining approval for the ALP and obtaining the support of other elements within the Afghan government. Provincial and district governors were critical for governance, wielding formal and informal authority in varying degrees. The performance of the ALP hinged on the police chiefs at the district and provincial levels, who had authority over the Afghan Local Police and could use the Afghan National Police to assist them, as well as the ALP commanders at the district level and at individual checkpoints.

Key US leaders, inside and outside the SOF community, recognized the importance of Afghan leadership to the success of the counterinsurgency effort, and some spent much of their time identifying problems and recommending solutions to their Afghan counterparts. The presence of US advisors with Afghan leaders supplied a steady stream of information about Afghans that could be used in assessing Afghan leaders. Their value in this regard alone made them a worthwhile asset. Advisors have provided this benefit in past conflicts, and should do so in future ones.

The ability of the United States to effect positive changes to Afghan leadership was heavily influenced by the political will at the top of the Afghan government, which was largely beyond the control of the highest SOF leadership. The power to appoint local officials was vested in the Afghan President and a few other top officials, as is also the case in numerous other countries. Influencing those appointments depended on high-level diplomacy and the priorities of those leaders. In Afghanistan, diplomatic discord and Afghan priorities that did not involve winning the war impeded efforts to effect changes. Nevertheless, some changes were made at American request, generally for the better.

Long-simmering conflicts and malign leadership resulted in abuses of power in a number of ALP units. Although relatively infrequent in comparison with those perpetrated by other Afghan security forces, these abuses attracted considerable media attention, which undermined support for the program among Afghan officials and civilians. Coalition personnel and the central Afghan leadership went to considerable lengths to curb such abuses. Firing and punishing offenders, especially those in positions of command, were the most effective means of stopping and discouraging offenses. Formal training and education, which SOF have used effectively in other countries to improve the behavior of security forces, were less valuable with the ALP because training was very short and education nonexistent. Prolonged partnering with Afghans, however, contributed to the overall decline in abuses of power. The exhortations of VSO teams to refrain from abusive behavior and their interventions to halt specific acts achieved immediate results, and likely had some affect on the mindsets of the Afghans who would lead the ALP after the Americans left.

Plans for large-scale US troop withdrawals from Afghanistan coincided with plans for expanding the ALP, which multiplied the burdens on coalition forces assigned to VSO and required accelerated transition of ALP sites to the Afghans. Experience showed that prolonged coalition presence, of at least two years, was usually required to build enough local capacity to ensure successful transition, yet the US withdrawal plans dictated that many sites be transitioned with much shorter periods of SOF mentorship.

During transition, the withdrawal of VSO teams from entire districts and provinces necessitated much greater involvement of Afghan officials in the selection of sites and the organization of units. The Afghans made the same mistakes as SOF, only more often, and they committed some mistakes that SOF had never committed. They often demonstrated carelessness, skipping over precautionary measures designed to minimize empowerment of malign actors. They injected their own personal, tribal, and ethnic agendas into the ALP, which led to discord and the squandering of resources. While some Afghan leaders did take over the organization of ALP effectively, the number who failed to do so is a cautionary note that should be considered when deciding how much responsibility to entrust to host-nation leaders in running programs of this type, and how soon that responsibility can be entrusted without precipitating collapse.

Logistical weaknesses, which were largely the result of Afghan leadership problems, posed grave threats to the success of transition. While Afghan deficiencies in literacy, technology, and technical knowledge impeded the development of Afghan logistical capabilities, these obstacles proved to be less formidable than the will of Afghan leaders in the Ministry of Interior's logistical system. For various reasons, of varying degrees of rectitude, Afghans at times prevented pay and materiel from flowing to the ALP because they did not want them to flow.

Coalition personnel long suspected that the willingness of the United States to meet logistical shortfalls caused the Afghans to avoid taking responsibility for meeting their own logistical needs. Some Afghans openly admitted that they did not feel a need to keep units supplied as long as the Americans were willing to do it. During transition, the coalition withdrew logistical support and vowed that it would not come to the rescue if the Afghans could not pay their policemen or keep them supplied with ammunition. In some instances, this approach caused the Afghans to make their system work. But in others, the Afghans were unable or unwilling to move the resources to the right places. Coalition commanders then faced a choice of whether to let the Afghans keep failing until they got their act together, which would involve significant political and military risks, or to provide emergency assistance in order to prevent political and military defeats, which would remove the incentives for the Afghans to become self-sufficient. In early 2013, the coalition leadership chose the latter option. But the withdrawal of US forces will ultimately leave the coalition with no choice but to leave the Afghans to sink or swim on their own.

Maintaining situational awareness proved to be another highly challenging part of transition. As SOF withdrew from villages and districts, they removed their own eyes and ears, and lost access to most of the Afghans who had helped keep them informed. Most other foreign personnel, including media and NGOs, had already withdrawn prior to SOF's departure, leaving Afghans as the only viable sources in most places. Few Afghans had strong incentives to continue providing information once SOF had left, but there was an important exception, the Afghan National Army Special Forces. Because the ANA SF maintained an enduring relationship with the

US special operations command and had their own reasons for maintaining contact with the ALP, they could serve as an ongoing source of information.

The achievements of VSO and ALP supported the view of counterinsurgency advocates that securing and mobilizing the rural Afghan population was critical to the security of Afghanistan and, less directly, the United States. These programs deprived the insurgents of recruits, information, and sanctuary areas, and consumed the attention of insurgent forces that could have caused other problems had there been no VSO and ALP. They gave international terrorists fewer places to hide.

The strengthening of the district government's control over the ALP did help improve stability in the remote areas. Whereas the Americans had been accepting of armed forces that were not beholden to the central government, the same could not be said of most district and provincial leaders, since they were the representatives of that central government. Good district and provincial governors and police chiefs could mediate conflicts among tribes and ethnic groups better than foreigners. They did not have the ability to visit remote locations on a moment's notice, as the Americans did, but they could still exert power in those places if they had the will to do so. The Taliban, after all, were able to exert power in the most remote valleys and mountains.

One of the most important lessons of VSO and ALP was that permanent village stability required building partner capacity beyond the village level. The Afghan government needed capacity at the district and provincial levels in order to sustain the ALP once the Americans departed, and it needed capacity at the regional and national levels to manage the provinces and direct national programs and resources. Recognition of the need for capacity at multiple levels, along with the imperatives of transition, caused VSO teams to shift attention from the village level to the district level during the latter stages of VSO. In 2013, SOJTF-A dedicated more resources to mentorship at the national level, and to training at the provincial and regional levels.

While an SOF presence at the village level was beneficial in many ways, SOF operators could cover only a small fraction of Afghanistan's villages even at the peak of VSO, when the program had more SOF manpower than any other program since the Vietnam War. In future scenarios, concentrating Americans at the village level will be most advisable when general-purpose forces can provide much of the manpower, since general-purpose forces have more manpower at their disposal. If the US military footprint is light, SOF must consider focusing its personnel at higher organizational levels, where the manpower demands are lower and the reach of partner-nation leaders greater. Training and education centers also provide excellent opportunities for small numbers of SOF to achieve large effects.

Despite their limitations, VSO and ALP showed clearly that SOF have much to contribute to community mobilization, counterinsurgency, and capacity building. VSO teams helped communities organize self-defense forces and they supported governance and development activities. By setting the security conditions required for nurturing the ALP and then helping the ALP maintain security, VSO affirmed the ability of SOF to secure environments in which enemies could otherwise hide and multiply. It did so very efficiently, causing considerably more harm to the insurgents than most other counterinsurgency initiatives. SOF mentorship and training enabled partner-nation personnel to sustain gains in security, governance, and development after all coalition personnel had left. In achieving stability and developing partner-nation human capital, VSO and ALP demonstrated convincingly the value of the indirect approach as a necessary complement to direct action.

10

Assessing the Dutch Integrated Police-Training Mission in Kunduz Province, Afghanistan, 2011-2013

Georg Frerks and Niels Terpstra

Introduction

In April 2010, the Dutch Parliament expressed its wish that after the withdrawal of the Dutch Task Force from Uruzgan, the Netherlands would remain actively involved in Afghanistan's reconstruction and asked the Dutch government to assess the need for a civilian police training and education program in Afghanistan. The resulting Integrated Police-Training Mission (IPM) was carried out in Kunduz Province, Afghanistan, from July 2011 until July 2013. The IPM aimed at strengthening the capacity of the Afghan civilian police, enhancing the cooperation between the police, prosecution and justice, and improving the awareness, acceptance, and access to the justice system among the local population. Parts of the mission were executed in the framework of the International Security Assistance Force (ISAF), especially the North Atlantic Treaty Organization's (NATO) Training Mission Afghanistan (NTM-A), and in cooperation with the European Union (EU) Police Mission in Afghanistan (EUPOL). The Dutch Parliament stipulated that policemen trained by Dutch nationals would not be allowed to engage in offensive tasks and it was also decided to only train policemen that would be deployed in Kunduz Province itself. To monitor this, the IPM operated a so-called track-and-trace system.

In order to study the IPM, we visited the mission in May 2013 and were able to interview both key civilian and military staff members of the Police Training Group-5 (PTG-5: the fifth rotation). In addition, the Afghan organization *Cooperation for Peace and Unity* (CPAU) interviewed Afghan police commanders, non-commissioned officers (NCOs), and patrolmen in Kunduz Province in May and June 2013 in accordance with a structured interview guide. A total of 30 police personnel were interviewed, among these were five policewomen. In early 2016 we went back to Afghanistan to interview several analysts residing in Kabul and Kunduz to establish a better first-hand insight into the changes that occurred in Kunduz after 2013. In addition, we studied relevant secondary public documentation and documents obtained from the TPG-5. We not only studied the curricula of the Initial Police Training Course (IPTC) and the Advanced Police Training Course (APTC), but also questioned the trainees themselves about their initial levels of competence and the progress made. We also tried to ascertain the actual use and sustainability of training outcomes, and what factors or processes promoted or inhibited the successful operational training results, including gender related issues, the institutional environment and the pressure of armed groups active in the area.

The Context of State-Building and Policing in Afghanistan

A well-functioning state should ideally possess a monopoly on the use of legitimate force over its territory under its governing institutions, and have the ability to ensure that laws are obeyed, and thereby guarantee security and peace for its population.[1] In order to do so, a legal system, army, and police force are deemed essential, as is a mechanism to ensure fair representation and the consent of the people. Even though this ideal may not completely reflect the decentralized, traditional power structures in Afghanistan, it forms the framework for foreign intervention policy and security sector reform in Afghanistan.[2] A professional and capable Afghan National Police (ANP), together with the Afghan National Army (ANA), was considered one of the key elements to enable the security transition and the drawdown of ISAF after 2014.[3] As Roland Paris and Timothy Sisk point out in *The Dilemmas of Statebuilding*, the provision of security and the rule of law with a reasonably effective police and justice system next to basic service provision and regulated budget plans with effective taxation could generally be seen as the 'core' statebuilding elements.[4]

Several observers have in this regard pointed out that the poor quality of the Afghan police force has been one of the main threats to legitimate state-building in Afghanistan.[5] The widely reported corruption, predatory activities, and other

1 Skinner, M., 'Counterinsurgency and State Building: An Assessment of the Role of the Afghan National Police', *Democracy and Security*, 4:3 (2008), pp. 290-311.
2 Ibid.
3 ISAF, *Declaration by the Heads of State and Government of the Nations contributing to the UN-Mandated, NATO-Led International Security Assistance Force (ISAF) in Afghanistan*, 20 November 2010.
4 Paris, R. and T.D. Sisk, *The Dilemmas of Statebuilding: Confronting the Contradictions of Postwar Peace Operations* (London and New York: Routledge, 2009), p. 15.
5 International Crisis Group (ICG), *Reforming Afghanistan's Police*, Asia Report No. 138 (30 August 2007); Skinner, M., 'Counterinsurgency and State Building', pp. 290-311; Ministry of Interior Affairs (MoI) of the Islamic Republic of Afghanistan, *Afghanistan National Police Strategy* (Kabul: Islamic Republic of Afghanistan, 2010); Max Planck Institute for Comparative Public Law and International Law (MPIL), *Provincial Needs*

misconduct in the ANP directly impacted the legitimacy of the state and the larger state-building project. The *Afghan National Police Strategy* of 2010 therefore emphasized the importance of improving the quality of relevant policing skills: 'The police recruitment and training processes have been focused on quantity rather than quality, [and] training at patrolmen level rather than leadership development, which resulted in a lack of professionalism. There is a need to improve the professional skills, leadership capability, and [to] raise the literacy rate within the police'.[6]

Improvement of police conduct became more urgent during the 'security transition' from 2011 to 2014 in preparation for the 'irreversible transition to full Afghan security responsibility and leadership'.[7] It became increasingly important to not only increase the number of policemen, but also to improve their professional conduct and capacities to stabilize regions such as Kunduz Province. Whereas previous US-led military-based police training often focused on fighting skills and counterinsurgency strategies, training based on principles of community policing and crime prevention were deemed equally relevant to the larger state-building efforts in Afghanistan. According to policing experts David Bayley and Robert Perito, 'the key contribution of local police forces…is to legitimate self-government by responding under law to the security needs of the individual citizens'.[8] Particularly in conflict-affected environments like Afghanistan, training should focus on 'core' policing ethics such as: being available, being helpful, and being fair and respectful.[9] Instead, the development of the ANP had largely been driven by immediate NATO counterinsurgency objectives.[10] According to the International Crisis Group (ICG), years of prioritizing counterinsurgency over community policing had also impeded the emergence of a police force that was able and willing to protect women's rights.[11]

A provincial needs assessment of Kunduz executed by the Max Planck Institute for Comparative Public Law and International Law (MPIL) in early 2011 identified widespread problems among the judicial institutions and the personnel working at those institutions in Kunduz Province:

Assessment: Criminal Justice in Kunduz Province (Heidelberg: Max Planck Institute, 2011); Giustozzi, A. and Mohammad Isaqzadeh, *Afghanistan's Paramilitary Policing in Context: The Risks of Expediency* (Kabul: Afghanistan Analysts Network, 2011); Sedra, M., 'The Hollowing-out of the Liberal Peace Project in Afghanistan: the Case of Security Sector Reform', *Central Asian Survey*, 32:3 (2013), pp. 371-387.

6 Ministry of Interior Affairs (MoI) of the Islamic Republic of Afghanistan, *Afghanistan National Police Strategy*, p. 9.

7 ISAF, *Declaration by the Heads of State and Government*, p. 2.

8 Bayley, D. H. and R. M. Perito, *The Police in War: Fighting Insurgency, Terrorism, and Violent Crime* (Boulder: Lynne Reinner, 2009), p. 3.

9 Bayley and Perito, *The Police in War*, pp. 83-86.

10 Sedra, M., 'The Hollowing-out of the Liberal Peace Project in Afghanistan', p. 373; Planty, J. and R. M. Perito, *Police Transition in Afghanistan* (Washington, DC: USIP, 2013).

11 International Crisis Group (ICG), *Women and Conflict in Afghanistan*, Asia Report No. 252, 14 October 2013.

> The situation of the judicial institutions in Kunduz Province has not sufficiently improved during the past years. They are not able to fulfill their tasks in an adequate manner. The main problems are (1) the poor education of law professionals; (2) widespread corruption; and (3) insufficient infrastructure and equipment of the judicial institutions especially on the district level.[12]

In other words, the problems were not limited to the police force only, but extended throughout the whole security-justice chain, necessitating improvements across various functional areas and increased educational efforts among law enforcement personnel, including prosecutors and lawyers. The EU had already focused on improving higher police structures, while NATO focused on lower police structures. Though the Dutch involvement in Kunduz was announced to cover the period from 2011 to 2014 and supported these efforts to build capacity in the civil police force and the judicial systems at different levels, the police training by Dutch trainers ended earlier than planned, in July 2013.

The Dutch Integrated Police-Training Mission

Drawing on the problems identified in Kunduz previous to the mission, four main themes were identified in the comprehensive mission design (CMD) of the Dutch IPM: 1) the reinforcement of the Afghan civilian police; 2) the improvement of cooperation between the Afghan civil police and the judicial system; 3) the improvement of the quality of the Afghan judicial system; and 4) the improvement of awareness and acceptance of the Afghan civil police and judicial systems by the Afghan people.[13]

The IPM worked to achieve the larger international objectives, but also formulated its own (national) goals. The mission consisted of efforts embedded within the structures of EUPOL and the NATO mission NTM-A, and a bilateral program on the rule of law. About 545 personnel in Kabul, Mazar-e-Sharif, and Kunduz participated in the mission, including civil and military trainers, military police, civil police, civil experts, and protection forces. The IPM collaborated with the UN mission UNAMA and the German Society for International Cooperation (GIZ).[14] The total cost for IPM operations from 2011 until the end of 2013 was approximately 215 million euros.[15]

12 Max Planck Institute for Comparative Public Law and International Law (MPIL), *Provincial Needs Assessment*, p. 3.

13 *Eindevaluatie geïntegreerde politietrainingsmissie*, attachment to file 27925, nr. 489 (Den Haag: Ministerie van Buitenlandse Zaken, Ministerie van Defensie, Ministerie van Veiligheid en Justitie, 29 januari 2014), p. 6.

14 Ibid., p. 5.

15 Per year the costs (in million euros) were: 69.2 in 2011; 98.8 in 2012; and 47.1 in 2013. See ibid., p. 32.

The IPM has been an 'integrated' police-training mission. This means that different Dutch ministries cooperated in the mission (Foreign Affairs; Defense; and Security and Justice) and the efforts were carried out through an array of different instruments under their purview. So, although—as the name of the mission indicates—training policemen was at its core, the IPM performed several other related activities, including conducting literacy courses, the education of female lawyers, the establishment of an Afghan Independent Bar Association (AIBA), mentoring aimed at improving organizational structures in the police departments and several 'hearts and mind projects'.[16] Additional activities by the EUPOL Field Office in Kunduz focused on middle and higher level cadre training, including train-the-trainer programs. EUPOL also mentored senior law police officers on specific themes relevant to their duties and professional development. At the national level Dutch trainers contributed to curricula development of the Kabul-based Police Staff College and the Criminal Investigation Department. The Police Staff College was set up in order to improve the management and leadership capacities of the Afghan police.[17] In this chapter, however, we will focus on the police training activities carried out in Kunduz Province.

The IPM can be considered an 'institution building' or 'capacity building' mission with a civil mandate. It was never intended to be, and has never been, a combat mission.[18] The Dutch government stressed in a letter to the Dutch Parliament that Dutch personnel would not get involved in offensive combat operations, even if their Afghan counterparts would.[19] The mission in Kunduz could arguably be characterized by the so called 'Dutch Approach'. As explained by the sociologist René Moelker:

> In contrast to the repellent instrument of forceful coercion this approach refrains from using an excess of violence; it is meant to display full professional military capacities whilst only using force in the last resort. It is meant to win over hearts and minds by reconstructing the society, by [the] method of 'smile and wave', and by enabling local authorities to take over public order issues themselves.[20]

In this view security is most effectively implemented whilst gaining or retaining legitimacy among the local population. In this view, coercive efforts are believed

16 As explained by IPM non-military staff on 9 and 10 May 2013, in interviews with the authors at the PRT in Kunduz.

17 *Eindevaluatie geïntegreerde politietrainingsmissie*, p. 22.

18 *Bestrijding internationaal terrorisme. Brief van de Ministers van Buitenlandse Zaken, van Defensie en van Veiligheid en Justitie en de Staatssecretaris Van Buitenlandse Zaken Aan de Voorzitter van de Tweede Kamer der Staten-Generaal Den Haag*, 27 januari 2011, Dossier 27 925 Nr. 419.

19 *Brief aan de Tweede Kamer n.a.v. het Algemeen Overleg over de geïntegreerde politietrainingsmissie in Afghanistan*, 27 januari 2011.

20 Moelker, R., 'The 'Dutch approach' and the Expeditionary Formula', in Hansen, F.S. (ed.), *The Comprehensive Approach: Challenges and Prospects* (Copenhagen: Royal Danish Defence College, 2009), pp. 86-87.

to frighten the population and drive them into the arms of anti-government armed groups.[21] In the IPM this Dutch approach was reflected in the emphasis on 'community policing'.[22] Finally, an overall important theme was the attention paid to gender issues both in training and practice, including community policing. Previous to the mission's start there were indications that the security situation in Kunduz was not stable enough to employ a mission with such a strict civil character. These considerations and hesitations were, however, downplayed by the government at the time due to the political support that was necessary in Parliament of a number of progressive parties who made their support conditional to a strict civil mandate to the mission.[23] In hindsight, but also with the indications at the time, one may therefore question whether this mandate was suitable to the security context at hand.

The major components of the IPM were the civilian police being trained in Kunduz by 20 Dutch police trainers (ultimately reduced to ten by the end of 2011) and six so called Police Operational Mentor and Liaison Teams (POMLTs) that provided support to the IPTC located at the German Police Training Centre (PTC) in Kunduz, and the APTC in several district capitals throughout the province. The IPM also trained Afghan trainers so that the ANP could educate its own staff in the future without relying on foreign guidance.

Based on the earlier six-week NTM-A basic course, Dutch instructors developed in cooperation with NTM-A and EUPOL an eight-week IPTC training course that was accredited by the Afghan Ministry of Interior Affairs (MoIA). As explained in the official curriculum, the IPTC was a 'basic police course, designed to give an entry level police recruit the necessary skills to be effective in the patrolman role'. It consisted of ten components: police basics; law, ethics and values; human rights and gender issues; duties at the police station; maintenance of public order; checkpoint duties; dealing with a common crime; dealing with terrorism; intelligence-led policing; and traffic policing. A total of 410 police personnel successfully completed the IPTC, including 15 policewomen.[24] In addition to new recruits, the training also included policemen that were already on duty but had never been trained before. Initially there were specific training modules for women, but beginning in mid-2012 these were replaced by a complete basic course designed especially for women. The IPM also trained 139 NCOs who had not participated in earlier training efforts. Forty-nine of these NCOs also attended the IPTC. At the end of 2012 the basic course and the NCO course were handed over to qualified Afghan police trainers, while the Dutch trainers restricted themselves to a mentoring role. Also, the PTC staff had been trained in order to fully function under Afghan control in the course of 2013.

21 Moelker, R., '"The 'Dutch Approach" and the Expeditionary Formula'.
22 *Artikel 100 Brief*, 2011, p. 2.
23 See for example the Green Left Party (Groenlinks), <https://groenlinks.nl/nieuws/brief-aan-leden-groenlinks-over-politiemissie-naar-kunduz>.
24 *Eindevaluatie geïntegreerde politietrainingsmissie*, pp. 17-18.

By the end of the mission, 385 policemen, officers, and NCOs successfully completed the APTC. The course was given not only in Kunduz town, but also in the Aliabad, Khanabad, and Imam Sahib districts in order to—as much as possible—reach the target group in their own working environment and avoid interrupting their normal duties. The POMLTs also delivered tailor-made courses to about 200 personnel. They provided the first APTC for policewomen in November 2012. Similarly to the IPTC, the POMLTs started training Afghan instructors to take over the APTC courses in the future under the supervision of the Provincial Police Commander.

Special attention has been paid to strengthening the contacts between the population at the village level and the police through community policing projects with an emphasis on improving the execution of police tasks, increasing police acceptance by the population, and strengthening mutual confidence. The German GIZ carried out some of the community policing projects. Among other activities, GIZ organized monthly meetings of 'neighborhood watch committees'. These committees enabled Afghan local communities to discuss police conduct and hold the police accountable if necessary.[25] In cooperation with EUPOL the *Police-e-Mardumi* (community policing) project was started. In this initiative local police contacted the population to explain their duties and responsibilities. The purpose was to create an environment in which Kunduz residents would more readily turn to the police and trust the police to take their cases seriously and to act professionally.

Early in 2013, the IPM started the Afghan Training and Mentoring Teams (ATMT) in order to secure the independent training of new recruits by the Afghan police itself. The ATMT is a program in which Afghan trainers are taught how to impart their knowledge and skills to other trainers. A total of eight Afghan mentoring trainers completed this training successfully.[26] A Police Advisory Group (PAG) was established to advise and assist the Afghan police on communication and information systems, personnel management, and logistics. Four advisors were deployed, respectively, in Kunduz city, Alia Bad, Imam Sahib, and Khanabad.

What Did the Trainees Learn?

This section is largely based on interviews held with a sample group of the trainees, both from the IPTC and the APTC. We have grouped the topics raised in the interviews in four broad categories: basic civic knowledge; practical policing skills; professional policing conduct; and community policing.

Basic civic knowledge here refers to understanding the basics of the Afghan constitution, fundamental human rights, and principles of good governance. With regard to Afghanistan's constitution most respondents claimed to have

25 Ibid., p. 20.

26 'Kunduz een terugblik', *KMAR Magazine*, 7 (July 2013), <http://www.116000.nl/uploads/PDF%20doc/KMarMagazine%207-2013_tcm4-1034108.pdf> (accessed 1 May 2015).

learned something about it, though perhaps quite superficially. As one respondent summarized: 'we learned that the Constitution is a national written agreement which has 12 chapters and 162 articles and that it is approved by the High Council of the people of Afghanistan and that we should protect all Articles of the Constitution'.[27] The IPTC trainees stated that they now know that every person has certain basic human rights and they as police officers should respect these rights. Several of them mentioned specifically that criminals also have rights. One respondent stressed that it is his *responsibility* to defend human rights.[28] Several respondents also referred to the Afghan constitution and to Allah. For example, one policeman stated: 'About human rights I have learned that the rights and privileges of a human are based on the Constitution and the Islamic right of freedom, education, and work. Human rights are equal for all, without discrimination, tribe and color'.[29] Another respondent said: 'Human rights is a gift from God'.[30] Several respondents also emphasized the equality of every human being, for example: 'I have learned that each person has rights from the moment he or she is brought into this world until he is dying, and no one can take these rights from him, like right of life, right of education, ownership, marriage, and freedom of choice'.[31] To sum up, it seems that among the respondents there is a certain level of awareness about human rights and human rights issues. Whether this is also commonly practiced is more difficult to determine on the basis of these interviews. Below we will therefore elaborate on the factors and processes that promote or inhibit the application of these more theoretical training aspects in practice.

With regard to women's rights, the IPTC respondents learned that violence against women is against the law and that they should protect women and try to prevent this violence from happening. In the words of one of the respondents: 'I have learned that violence against women is an illegal action and as police we have to prevent people from using violence against women and all those who committed violence should be dealt with by law enforcement'.[32] Moreover, several of the respondents said that 'We, as the police, are responsible to make men understand about women rights, to prevent violence against women. In the case of any violence, we will follow up the case legally'.[33] Another respondent explained that violence against women consists of different types like 'hitting a woman or giving a woman or girl as payment in a dispute [or] deal, compulsory sexual abuse, and marriage below [the age of] maturity...we condemn this and will punish those who are committing such violence'.[34] When discussing women's rights several respondents made references both to Islam and

27 Interview code: IPTC 11.
28 Interview code: IPTC 04.
29 Interview code: IPTC 13.
30 Interview code: IPTC 03.
31 Interview code: IPTC 11.
32 Interview code: IPTC 09.
33 Interview code: IPTC 02.
34 Interview code: IPTC 13.

Afghan law. For example, one respondent argued that sexual abuse towards women is 'an unlawful and illegal action in Islam and under the law of Afghanistan and that the police have the responsibility to arrest these people in order to stop other people from committing such actions'.[35]

The professional policing skills acquired vary from rather basic skills to more sophisticated competencies. We deal with them roughly in that order. One of the basic skills that the respondents mentioned were marching and saluting as a policeman. Most of them said they did not march before, but now they know how to march during ceremonies. One of the respondents pointed out that they learned how to be more disciplined in their professional conduct. With regard to dealing with Improvised Explosive Devices (IEDs), the responses varied among the respondents. Some of them stated that they did not learn anything about this, but others mentioned that they learned how to respond to a suspicious person and how they should act if somebody was wearing a suicide vest. These respondents had learned procedures for approaching such a person or shooting him in the leg, after which they would call the bomb disposal unit. They had learned also to secure an area where they suspected explosives, and wait for the bomb disposal unit.

With regard to the use of a radio the respondents' answers varied. Some stated that they had learned nothing about it, while others claim that they did. It is not clear from where that difference stems. Those who did learn about the radio pointed out that they now knew how to use it and that communicating with the commander is necessary in an operation or dangerous encounter and in the case of suspected IEDs. All IPTC respondents said they learned a great deal about self-defense. This is very important to them because they are now better able to protect themselves and better equipped to deal with criminals. With these skills they gained confidence and are better able to make arrests. All respondents stated that they learned about first aid. As one put it: 'In first aid we have learned different types of first aid assistance to the injured, like how to carry him to a safe place first, then stop bleeding of the wound, how to bandage the injury… and how to deliver him to the hospital'.[36] Most respondents have learned how to offer medical assistance to those in custody: 'Facing a wounded person in custody, we should apply a bandage properly, control the bleeding, and transport him to the nearest hospital'.[37]

In terms of providing and ensuring security as a police force, the respondents mentioned their newly acquired skills for manning traffic check points, traffic policing, and conducting house searches. Regarding their lessons about manning checkpoints the respondents said: 'We prepare ourselves for the checkpoint: one team from us maintains security of the checkpoint and another team identifies and stops vehicles

35 Interview code: IPTC 12.
36 Interview code: IPTC 16.
37 Interview code: IPTC 03.

that look suspicious. Then, we search the vehicles and people who are in the car'.[38] The necessity of policewomen in such cases was stressed by one of the female respondents: 'Policewomen are checking women and policemen are searching the men. In addition, we should be careful of suspicious behavior from suspected persons and be ready for self-defense'.[39] Several respondents showed their sensitivity to community policing practices (see below) while answering these questions. One respondent stated that the police should 'communicate in a good manner with drivers, and be polite. And then ask the driver and passengers to get out of the vehicle, and do body searching properly'.[40] Also for the APTC, vehicle checkpoints were one of the important components in the training. The respondents pointed out that they learned how to secure the checkpoint and search the vehicles at the same time, with one team checking and one team securing the area, keeping themselves safe. Several respondents mentioned that they learned to set up a checkpoint under different conditions: 'if we get a report about a suspect person... or if we get a report about drugs, these reports imply separate conditions to deal with'.[41]

With regard to traffic policing the respondents said they had learned to regulate traffic better than before the training. Several respondents said they now have the tools to order traffic flow, which may help them to prevent accidents. Also, some respondents said they learned how to adequately deal with a traffic accident. Some respondents added that they themselves as police officers should give a good example by driving carefully.

With regard to house searches most respondents mentioned the necessity of receiving a search warrant from the attorney's office. As one of the respondents said: 'When we receive a report, we should get a search warrant from the attorney. Then we are permitted to surround the house, and do not let anybody come close the house. Then we start the search process'.[42]

The IPM also paid particular attention to the professional procedures in a variety of situations that the AUP in Kunduz ought to follow. When asked how they learned to deal with theft for example, most respondents explicitly mentioned that they had to act within the boundaries of Afghan law and the formal procedures. Several respondents stressed that they had to capture the thief and 'surrender him according to the regulations of the law'. They also said they should not curse at the thief or beat him up. One of the respondents could exactly detail the correct procedures: 'When we see a person is stealing we should arrest him properly, search him correctly, report it by radio to the police station, observe human rights and not harm him, deliver him to the police station and report everything about the theft to the commander without any

38 Interview code: IPTC 10.
39 Interview code: IPTC 16.
40 Interview code: IPTC 03.
41 Interview code: APTC 02.
42 Interview code: IPTC 01.

partiality'.[43] Several other respondents mentioned that they learned the importance of collecting evidence, safeguarding relevant documents, and identifying witnesses at the place of the event.[44]

The respondents also mentioned what they learned with regard to handcuffing and making arrests. As one of the respondents explained: 'In making an arrest we should use police tactics in order to arrest the criminal without harm to us and to him; sometimes we should lay him on the ground and handcuff him. Sometimes we handcuff the person while he is standing or on his knees. After that we transport him to the police station'.[45] One of the respondents also mentioned the need for cooperation with the prosecutor: 'First, we plan if we want to arrest a criminal in a house. We take the prosecutor with us and an order from the court; then we are surrounding the area and entering into the house; then we very quickly arrest the criminal, handcuff him properly, and bring him to the police station'.[46] As several respondents pointed out, they are now better aware of the regulations under which they are allowed to handcuff or arrest somebody, and how the suspects should be treated according to the law.

When asked about how to deal with a dispute or conflict, several respondents stressed the need to try and prevent conflicts from worsening and not taking sides. Nearly all respondents asserted that it was their task to prevent further escalation in the community, to make both parties calm down, and try to settle the matter in a fair and objective way. One of the respondents declared:

> We should directly and tactfully interfere in the conflict, be careful of our own security and that of other civilian people, and act impartially as a police third party. If it's a small dispute we should separate them; if it's a larger dispute, which causes harm, we should arrest the disputants, search, and disarm them; we also have to handcuff and transport them to the police station and take reports from all the dispute witnesses in the police station.[47]

Other respondents also emphasized that they should act without any bias regarding the tribal affiliation of the disputants. Some mentioned the necessity of referring the case to the prosecutor if the case was more serious.

With regard to practices of corruption in the police force, all respondents pointed out that they learned about the negative effects of corruption and that they as police officers should not be involved in it. As one of the respondents put it: 'Corruption is destructive. It is bad for the police to [be] involve[d] in corruption. A police officer must be honest and fair. We should serve our country'.[48] Taking a broader perspective, one

43 Interview code: IPTC 18.
44 Interview code: IPTC 13.
45 Interview code: IPTC 13.
46 Interview code: IPTC 10.
47 Interview code: IPTC 12.
48 Interview code: IPTC 04.

of the respondents explained that: 'A country can make progress and develop upon the condition that corruption is eradicated there. If corruption exists inside the country, there will be no prosperity and development'.[49] Several respondents also remarked that they learned it was their responsibility to stop corruption in their institution: 'I have learned that corruption is a crime and illegal, and that the responsibility of the police is to remove corruption from their offices…the police have to be very strict in preventing corruption'.[50] The question, however, remains whether they genuinely believe this and whether they will put these lessons into practice. Prevailing structures may make it difficult for lower-ranking officers to stay out of corrupt practices as we will elaborate below when discussing the factors and processes that promote or inhibit the use and application of these anti-corruption training results in practice.

When examining community policing we deal with the respondents' answers on those topics that involve contacts with the public. As highlighted above, community policing—as one element of the so-called Dutch Approach—was an important aspect of the IPM. Several IPTC respondents said they learned to do policing in close communication with the communities. They patrolled in the communities to gather information and to establish more security. They learned how to resolve security problems and complaints from the people. As one of the respondents stated: 'We are sitting with the local representatives and looking at their problems. We get the people to understand that as police we are serving them and patrolling the area'.[51] Throughout all of the responses there seem to be lessons learned regarding their role as police officers serving within the community. With regard to their conduct in the police station, for example, most respondents pointed out that beyond securing the station effectively, they had learned to behave towards visitors in accordance with Afghan law and treat each of the visitors and those in custody with respect. As one of the respondents summed it up, they learned to: 'maintain security of the station, deal with visitors politely, get information from them, and ask them for which purpose they came'.[52] One of the female respondents added that body searches were particularly relevant to her tasks at the station as she had to do this for all women visitors.[53] This was also deemed particularly relevant for womens' representation during the then upcoming presidential and other elections.[54]

49 Interview code: IPTC 01.
50 Interview code: IPTC 16.
51 Interview code: IPTC 07.
52 Interview code: IPTC 09.
53 Interview code: IPTC 17.
54 The Independent Election Commission of Afghanistan pointed out in August 2013 that one of the inhibiting factors for women to be able to go and vote in 2014, would be the lack of trained female personnel doing body searches at the different voting sites. No presence of female personnel would make it impossible for women to vote. Source: *Volkskrant*, 'Tekort aan vrouwen voor fouilleren tijdens Afghaanse verkiezingen', 28 August 2013, <http://www.volkskrant.nl/buitenland/tekort-aan-vrouwen-voor-fouilleren-tijdens-afghaanse-verkiezingen~a3500052> (accessed 2 October 2015).

Whereas the IPTC training was done through theory and practice in a classroom setting, the APTC training was based in the police station or in the public area it covered. In other words, particularly in the APTC, community policing was put into actual practice in relation to the public. The APTC respondents pointed out that they learned different types of patrolling during their training, including single patrolling, double patrolling, and zigzag patrolling. They also said that during the patrol they had to find suspicious objects and be careful for their own security, and they explained how they could diminish security risks by having good contacts with the population, thus making the neighborhood safer. They learned foot patrolling and vehicle patrolling, and how to carry out patrolling during daytime and at night.

Factors Inhibiting the Implementation of the Training Lessons

Previous quantitative studies of CPAU showed that a large majority of police officers in Kunduz much appreciated their police training.[55] The respondents in this study also found their training courses very useful in executing their police work. Some skills were newly acquired; others skills improved or subsequently could be better applied in practice. However, some structural issues impeded them in fulfilling their duties fully, such as corruption, drug trafficking, skepticism within the community, and violence forced upon them by competing armed groups.

If we look at the police sector more broadly and through a structural perspective, one of the main impediments to a better-functioning police force in general is the corruption among the various levels of the Afghan state. In the *Afghan National Police Strategy* it is mentioned that corruption:

> erodes the trust and confidence of our people which the police must earn in order to be a valued institution. Also, corruption in the police force is a betrayal to the cause for which so many of our brave brothers and sisters in police uniform have made the ultimate sacrifice. The police, together with our judicial system, are responsible for the enforcement of the law and must set an example by eradicating all forms of corruption within the MoIA.[56]

This problem is obviously also directly tied to the larger relationship between the police and the public, a relationship that the community policing efforts addressed extensively. As Robert Perito points out:

55 Thiessen, C., *Assessment of the Dutch Integrated Police-Training Mission in Kunduz, Afghanistan: 2013 Progress Report,* CPAU policy report (Kabul: CPAU, 2014), p. 32.

56 Ministry of Interior Affairs (MoI) of the Islamic Republic of Afghanistan, *Afghanistan National Police Strategy,* p. 8.

> for many Afghans, the police were identified with demands for bribes, illegal taxes, and various kinds of human rights violations. They were also known to use house searches as an opportunity to shake down the occupants and steal their possessions. Corrupt police practices were felt most directly by the poorest members of society: taxi and truck drivers, traders, small businessmen and farmers. High levels of corruption and a culture of impunity severely undermined the legitimacy of the Afghan government and further eroded public support for the police.[57]

Fighting this corruption, in the eyes of the Afghan people, has also not been very effective. A national study by the UNDP found that only 57 percent of the Afghan population believes that the ANP is capable of dealing with corruption effectively. Additionally, 53 percent see the police as corrupt, compared to 79 percent for government employees in general and 73 percent for the court system.[58]

Questions can be raised regarding to what extent individual police officers are able to practice their newly acquired ideas in anti-corruption. Several authors have pointed out that corruption is a structural and endemic problem on which ISAF and EUPOL may not have much influence.[59] Rudra Chaudhuri and Theo Farrel from the War Studies Department at King's College argue that progress on anti-corruption is hindered by multiple tensions such as the fact that current Afghan politicians depend on well-entrenched patronage systems for their survival and their capacity to govern. Therefore, they argue that tackling corruption targets the bedrock of the Afghan government itself. Furthermore, they point out that ISAF itself often finds it expedient to work with corrupt power brokers.[60] In other words, it is questionable whether the learning achievements described previously can make a significant impact in such an environment.

Two other large structural problems closely related to corruption in the Afghan police force are drug use and drug trafficking among police officers. In 2013, opium production in Afghanistan showed an increase of 49 percent in comparison to the previous year—a total of 5,500 tons.[61] Next to funding anti-government groups and

57 Perito, R. M., *Afghanistan's Police: The Weak Link in Security Sector Reform*, Special Report 227 (Washington, DC: USIP, 2009), p. 7.
58 UNDP Afghanistan, *Police Perception Survey—2011: The Afghan Perspective* (Kabul: Aina Media, 2011), p. 5, <http://www.undp.org.af/Publications/KeyDocuments/2011/PPS-Eng%20Version-2011%20Final%20Lowest%20Res.pdf> (accessed 30 January 2014).
59 Chaudhuri, R. and T. Farrell, 'Campaign Disconnect: Operational Progress and Strategic Obstacles in Afghanistan, 2009-2011', *International Affairs*, 87:2 (2011), p. 287; Goodhand, J., 'Corrupting or Consolidating the Peace? The Drugs Economy and Post-Conflict Peacebuilding in Afghanistan', *International Peacekeeping*, 15:3 (2008), pp. 405-423.
60 Chaudhuri and Farrell, 'Campaign Disconnect', p. 287.
61 UNODC, *Afghanistan Opium Survey 2013*, <http://www.unodc.org/documents/crop-monitoring/Afghanistan/Afghan_report_Summary_Findings_2013.pdf> (accessed 8

operations,[62] Perito explains that the revenues obtained from opium production help spread and continue the large-scale corruption in the Afghan government.[63] Although, Kunduz has stayed a relatively poppy-free province when it comes to cultivation, it is a national northern hub—together with Takhar and Badakhshan—of trafficking narcotics and chemicals such as heroine and acetic anhydride.[64] These trafficking routes are supported by local warlords and non-state armed groups. Aside from the Afghan Taliban, elements of groups like the Hezb-i-Islami, are known to have been directly and indirectly involved in opiate trafficking for many years, particularly also in northeastern Afghanistan.[65] Corrupt government officials are also closely involved: according to some traffickers and couriers it is common practice to bribe government officials for about five percent of the value of the product. [66] Constituting a lucrative activity, drug trafficking is not likely to decrease much in the foreseeable future, and will continue to be a driver of corruption within the ANP.

Drug use within the ANP also continues to challenge its effectiveness. In 2010, nine percent of the 100,518 ANP officers evaluated, tested positive for drugs, 80 percent of these for THC and 15 percent for opiates.[67] Chuck Thiessen, Research Fellow at Coventry University, points out that a majority of the community members in Kunduz see drug use as a detriment to proper police functioning in the province.[68]

Following political scientist David Bayley and criminologist Clifford Shearing we define policing as 'the self-conscious process whereby societies designate and authorize people to create public safety'.[69] Additionally, we assume that those who are 'policing' require legitimacy from the communities they police.[70] In the case of Kunduz specifically, Thiessen explains that AUP police officers see local community

April 2014).

62 In *The Global Afghan Opium Trade: A threat assessment,* UNODC (2011), p. 9, finds that there is a strong link between insecurity and opium poppy cultivation and trafficking in Afghanistan. Anti-government elements are partly funding their operations from the opiate trade.

63 Perito, *Afghanistan's Police,* p. 7.

64 UNODC, *The Global Afghan Opium Trade: A Threat Assessment, 2011*, <http://www.unodc.org/documents/data-and analysis/Studies/Global_Afghan_Opium_Trade_2011-web.pdf> (accessed 8 April 2014).

65 Ibid., p. 31.

66 Ibid.

67 Arfsten, D.P., J.F. Moralez, L.L. Chester Jr., P. Mohamad, and T.H Weber, 'Drug Use among the Afghanistan National Police: A National Assessment', *Military Medicine*, 177:1 (2012), pp. 85-90. For clarification: THC, or tetrahydrocannabinol is usually referred to as the drug marijuana.

68 Thiessen, *Assessment of the Dutch Integrated Police-Training Mission.*

69 Bayley, D. and C. Shearing, 'The Future of Policing', *Law and Society Review*, 30 (1996), p. 586.

70 See for example: Dirkx, T., *At the Margins of the State: Intervention-Induced Opportunities for Arbakai Militias in the Context of the Dutch Integrated Police-Training Mission, in Kunduz Province, Afghanistan* (case study report) (Kabul: CPAU, 2013).

members as key to addressing a wide range of crimes, such as burglary, kidnapping, narcotics trading, and murder. Moreover, they mentioned the significant amount of intelligence that community members can provide.[71] Hence, it is essential for the AUP in Kunduz to establish good relationships with local communities.

Yet ANP members—in the perceptions of the Afghan population—are often seen as the opposite of good civil servants. Six in ten Afghans report a significant level of corruption among ANP members, a quarter report police favoritism on the basis of personal connections, and more than a quarter of Afghans identified ANP members as drug or narcotic users.[72] Moreover, the Afghan population shows a reluctance to engage with the ANP: approximately half of the population investigated by the UNDP in Afghanistan would take criminal matters elsewhere.[73] Also, the ICG described the ANP as an ill-behaving, drug-using, and abusive force acting with impunity.[74] Previous quantitative studies by CPAU showed that the police are—particularly for women—not the first ones to turn to in both civil and criminal cases: 'females will approach either a *shura* or the police for criminal cases, but strongly prefer to approach a *shura* in civil cases. For civil cases the police are virtually ignored by women according to female respondents'.[75] The respondents of this study, freshly trained police officers, clearly showed their intentions to work for the community and support local populations. As one of the respondents put it: 'In community policing a professional police has to gain trust and respect of the people, we should ask about problems and difficulties of the community and also prevent them from illegal and criminal activities by providing security'.[76] It remains, however, questionable to what extent these new recruits are able to improve police relationships with the communities. Similarly to issues of corruption, it is likely that new recruits only have a limited impact on the larger dynamics.

When female respondents in Kunduz were asked whether they would be able to join the police, Thiessen identified a small rise in the positive answers given by respondents when compared to previous survey results in 2011. In 2011, 25 percent of the women agreed, whereas in 2013 32 percent of the respondents agreed.[77] The evidence of this study also indicates some small improvements; the police training may have had a positive effect on certain challenges that women face. Nevertheless, these remain severe.

71 Thiessen, *Assessment of the Dutch Integrated Police-Training Mission*, p. 66.
72 UNDP Afghanistan, *Police Perception Survey—2010: The Afghan Perspective* (Kabul: Aina Media, 2010), pp. 5-6, <http://www.undp.org.af/publications/KeyDocuments/2011/Police%20Perception%20Survey%20Book%202010%20FINAL%20(6th%20Jan%202011).pdf> (accessed 30 January 2014).
73 UNDP Afghanistan, *Police Perception Survey—2010*, p. 6.
74 International Crisis Group (ICG) *Reforming Afghanistan's Police*, p. 16.
75 Thiessen, *Assessment of the Dutch Integrated Police-Training Mission*, p. 61.
76 Interview code: IPTC 15.
77 Thiessen, *Assessment of the Dutch Integrated Police-training Mission*, p. 55.

According to the UNDP national police perception survey in 2011, approximately 53 percent of the Afghan population believes it is a good idea to have female police officers in their community, whereas 42 percent think it is a bad idea.[78] On the provincial level in Kunduz women continue to be underrepresented in the police force and are not very well accepted by parts of the population. Of Kunduz community members investigated in 2013, just over half agreed or strongly agreed that a woman could get a job with the police.[79] Female respondents to this study mentioned opposition from communities towards their work as police officers. One of the female respondents said: 'when we are going to a community for searching houses, people threaten us saying to us that we are bad women because we became police'.[80] Police work is often still regarded as a job for men and not appropriate for women. Similarly, Louise Hancock, in a report for Oxfam Novib in Kabul, explains how communities often see policing as a disreputable job for Afghan women.[81]

Another challenge for female police officers is sexual assault and harassment by male police colleagues both within the police force and outside of it. A US National Public Radio report found allegations of systematic sexual coercion and rape of female police officers in Mazar-e-Sharif.[82] The report also claims that sexual favors were asked of female police officers in exchange for promotions. Women who try to report these issues are threatened and struggle to be heard. Also, one of the female respondents of this study referred to problems of sexual violence inside the police force: 'the police office itself is making trouble for the women because when they see that a woman is powerless and doesn't have support, police themselves also abuse her. So for all these reasons people don't let their women join the police'.[83] ICG also confirmed that policewomen are sexually assaulted and harassed by male colleagues.[84] From outside the police, female officers are targeted by insurgents. In July 2013, Lieutenant Islam Bibi, a senior female officer in southern Helmand province, was assassinated, while her successor, Lieutenant Nigar, was killed in September.[85] As the ICG points out: 'such attacks and threats undermine policewomens' ability to perform their duties and

78 UNDP Afghanistan, *Police Perception Survey—2011*, p. 5.
79 Thiessen, *Assessment of the Dutch Integrated Police-Training Mission*, p. 53.
80 Interview code: IPTC 17.
81 Hancock, L., *Women and the Afghan Police*, Oxfam Novib Policy Paper (The Hague: Oxfam Novib, 2013).
82 See: 'For Afghan Policewomen, Sex Abuse Is A Job Hazard', *US National Public Radio*, 8 March 2012.
83 Interview code: APTC 11.
84 International Crisis Group (ICG), *Women and Conflict in Afghanistan*, Asia Report No. 252, 14 October 2013, p. 18.
85 'Helmand's top female police officer shot dead', *The Telegraph* (4 July 2013); 'Top Afghan policewoman dies in gun attack', *Agence France-Presse* (17 September 2013). Top female police officer Lt. Nigar only used one name publicly. This is why she is referred to in the text as 'Nigar'.

deter women from joining the force, which in turn limits police protection for other women'.[86]

Another challenge for female police officers is that many provincial chiefs of police are reported as reluctant to hire women. Women are discriminated against, not supplied with uniforms, or only appointed to make tea and not conduct any core police tasks besides body searches.[87] According to Hancock's report, female involvement in the actual police investigations and police work is rare.[88] The responses in the authors' study, however, contradict these claims somewhat. Female respondents of this study explained that they regularly patrol, arrest and handcuff suspects, inspect crime scenes, and search houses.[89] They all emphasized that their bosses and male colleagues started to include them in important police tasks more extensively after finishing the training course. Although there is still a long way to go, these records could be seen as tentative signs of improvement for female officers that have received police-training in Kunduz province.

Evaluating the Mission

With regard to the course itself, some trainees pointed out that the training content was completely new to them. This was obviously the case for new recruits and those who had never received training. Most of the respondents already had learned about some parts of the curriculum in earlier training. Nearly all respondents said, however, that they learned many new skills during the IPTC or refreshed their existing skills. The IPCT trainees said that despite a variety of obstacles, the skills gained on manning checkpoints, vehicle, house and body searches, arrests, handcuffing, and patrolling were put into practice. They also mentioned knowledge and practice in saluting, first aid, self-defense, community policing, and 'fighting with the enemy', the latter being outside of the training mandate established by the Dutch Parliament. Also, the APCT trainees were able to put essential elements of the training into practice. They mostly used the skills gained in foot and vehicle patrolling, manning checkpoints, criminal case investigation, arrests and body searches, administering first aid, and also 'fighting with the enemy'.

In their evaluations of the Dutch trainers, the IPTC trainees were generally very positive. According to most of the trainees they were good trainers, very experienced, and with a clear way of teaching. Some of the respondents pointed out that they were surprised by their kind behavior and their positive interaction with the police recruits. The Dutch trainers were praised for their simple ways of teaching and their patience in

86 International Crisis Group (ICG), *Women and Conflict in Afghanistan*, p. 18.

87 Hancock, *Women and the Afghan Police;* International Crisis Group (ICG), *Women and Conflict in Afghanistan.*

88 Ibid.

89 Interview codes: APTC 11, IPTC 15,16,17,18.

repeating lessons until these were fully understood. Their politeness and their respect for the trainees was mentioned several times by respondents. With regard to the Dutch trainers, one of the respondents pointed out: 'They were good people, they were very good planners, they were on time. They were always sharing their opinions with the students, their experiences and stories from their country. That was a good method of teaching and kept students fresh and keen to learn the lessons'.[90] One respondent mentioned that the Dutch trainers followed the local social norms very well: 'They were very knowledgeable. They knew about everything. They were not Muslim but they respected our thoughts and values, and followed our social rules, principles, and norms very well'.[91] Another highlighted that the teaching was very well adapted to the level of the recruits: 'The teaching was based on our level and they were advising us to improve our work and performance. I was surprised how much they were thinking about us and supporting us'.[92]

All APTC respondents reported that they were very impressed by the APTC course and that they learned much, both in theory and practice. For several of the respondents it actually proved to be of greater value than they initially expected. One respondent stated: 'I was thinking that it would be a simple training and not much useful, but when I attended this course it was really very useful and effective'.[93] Another confirmed: 'I really learned lots of things which have improved my performance and skills as a police[man]'.[94] Several respondents especially liked the practical nature of the course.

There were also some points of criticism. Due to incomplete translations or their own language limitations the lessons were sometimes difficult to follow for the recruits. As one of the female respondents put it: 'We had some problems with the communication and translation. If experienced and educated Afghans were teaching us that would be better because they know how to teach and communicate [in our own language]. The translator can't transfer everything as good as they can actually teach us'.[95] Several respondents at the same time mentioned that they were looking forward to similar or more advanced training courses in the future because there would be much more for them to learn.

When asked about the prospect of the training being placed fully under Afghan authority and management, the respondents' opinions were mixed. Most supported a more prominent role for the Afghan trainers, but only with assistance from foreigners and continuing training of Afghan trainers. Several respondents stated that they do not believe that the Afghan trainers will be able to train with the same quality as the Dutch did as they will not have the same amount of knowledge and experience.

90 Interview code: IPTC 13.
91 Interview code: IPTC 01.
92 Interview code: IPTC 17.
93 Interview code: APTC 07.
94 Interview code: APTC 06.
95 Interview code: IPTC 18.

They think the best results would be achieved with continued Dutch participation. Others stressed that the Afghan trainers are in principle very capable of continuing the training, but that the Dutch should continue technical and professional training of those trainers in order to improve their quality. A female respondent was clearly against the transfer 'to Afghans because maybe they will be corrupt'.[96]

On the other hand, there are also respondents who believe in the complete transfer of training to Afghans. One of the respondents argues that the training could become longer and the training course itself could become more sustainable.[97] Moreover, it could be better tailored to the needs of students. According to one of the respondents: 'Afghans know the level of our education, and our cultural, societal, and environmental problems, so if they teach us it would be a very good fit'.[98] Another similarly states: 'The Afghans can better communicate with us and they know our problems and how to teach us'.[99] Several respondents mentioned that further actions should be taken to reinforce the Afghan police force in Kunduz. There is, for example, a need for more police equipment. The training could also be longer and more extensive, including more knowledge of Afghan law, forensic investigations, cartography, and the use of GPS. Finally, more literacy training was deemed necessary for the trainees, as too many Afghan police officers are illiterate or semi-literate.

After the withdrawal of the German Provincial Reconstruction Team (PRT) in Kunduz (where the Dutch trainers were stationed) and the handover of the responsibility over security to the Afghan counterparts, both the ANA and the ANP were increasingly feeling the heat of an offensive and successful Taliban insurgency throughout 2014 and 2015.[100] The ANA and ANP were eventually not able to fend off the insurgency that took over Kunduz city in September 2015, a significant and symbolic event we will come back to in the concluding section of this chapter.

Contributions to Achieving the Original IPM Objectives

As mentioned in the introduction, the objectives of the IPM were: 1) the reinforcement of the Afghan civilian police; 2) the improvement of cooperation between the Afghan civil police and the judicial system; 3) the improvement of the quality of the Afghan judicial system; and 4) the improvement of awareness and access to the Afghan civil

96 Interview code: APTC 11.
97 Interview code: APTC 06.
98 Interview code: APTC 05.
99 Interview code: APTC 06.
100 See for example in 2014: Cecchinel, L. *Taleban Closing in on the City: The Next Round of the Tug-of-War Over Kunduz* (Kabul: Afghan Analyst Network (AAN)), 2 September 2014), <https://www.afghanistan-analysts.org/the-next-round-of-the-tug-of-war-over-kunduz. See for developments in 2015: Ruttig, T. *ANSF Wrong-Footed: The Taleban Offensive in Kunduz* (Kabul: Afghan Analyst Network (AAN)), 3 May 2015), <https://www.afghanistan-analysts.org/ansf-wrong-footed-the-taleban-offensive-in-kunduz.

police and judicial systems by the Afghan people. The data enables us to assess the IPM's contribution to objectives one and two, and to a more limited extent, four. Below, we will discuss these three objectives in the same order and then place these observations within a broader perspective.

As mentioned earlier, the IPTC recruits pointed out that they use a variety of skills gained on a regular basis. The APTC recruits also mentioned that they use a number of skills on a regular basis. The opinions of the trainees themselves, both IPTC and APTC, are generally very positive, and most of the respondents would like additional training courses. In other words, one could argue that with the newly acquired skills and practices the Afghan Civilian Police force has been strengthened in its capacities.

The respondents also clearly refer to the cooperation between the Afghan civil police and the prosecutor when, for instance, making arrests and doing house searches. Several respondents further pointed out that they are now better aware of the regulations under which they are allowed to handcuff or arrest individuals and how the suspects should be treated according to the law. If the crime is more serious, they learned to refer it to the prosecutor.

Since the evidence for this study was only collected from IPTC and APTC recruits, the results are only from their perspective, and not from the community members themselves. Some respondents indicated that they have problems with certain communities as those communities do not respect them or are not aware of Afghan law and the role of the police. With regard to policewomen, there are continuing problems in entering local communities. Being a policewoman is still not well accepted throughout the province, though small gains have been reported. One of the respondents therefore pointed out that: 'we need to make people aware about the importance of policewomen; once they are aware, we can tell the communities that they need policewomen for a comfortable society'.[101]

We have seen what outputs the Dutch IPM has produced in terms of policemen and policewomen trained and what they have learned. The overall positive views of the trainees and their views on the usefulness of the training have also been established. It is, however, much more difficult to say anything meaningful about the final impact of the IPM in terms of the provincial population's security and improvements in the overall functioning of the police and judicial institutions. The CPAU 2014 *Final Assessment Report of the Dutch Integrated Police Training Mission in Kunduz* cautions that:

> building the capacity of rule of law institutions in Afghanistan is a long-term process requiring substantive national and international inputs that are beyond the scope and duration of the IPM....Furthermore, this change process is nonlinear and deterioration on a number of the indicators outlined in this 2014

101 Interview code: APTC 11.

> report may represent temporary setbacks rather than a diagnostic of terminal regression.[102]

The fall of Kunduz in September 2015 has proven to be more than a temporary setback. At the time of writing in 2016, the Taliban insurgency has taken firm control over most of the districts in the province and a Taliban judiciary exerts influence even in the city-center of Kunduz.[103]

According to CPAU's evaluation in 2014, the quality of the performance of the AUP in the perception of the population decreased in several areas (insufficient numbers, unwarranted outside influence, bribery), but increased in some others (literacy, drug abuse, and violence). The cooperation between the police and both formal and informal judicial authorities such as prosecutors, courts, *huqooq*, and *shura*, has been adequate or is improving.[104] The functioning of the judicial system, however, continued to show weaknesses in terms of unfair treatment, low quality, bribery, corruption, and influence peddling, while the role of the Taliban courts had increased in Kunduz Province. The access to police and justice has gone down, and trust and accountability levels decreased. There is also a perception of favoritism and patronage. Women's access to formal courts has decreased, but their access to informal systems improved. Overall, there is generally over the last two years a negative trend with a smaller number of positive developments.[105]

Putting the IPM results in a broader perspective, we must seriously consider the exogenous factors that impact the possibility of the police recruits executing their duties and doing their police work properly. As conflict analyst Toon Dirkx states: 'While the IPM may have had an influence on the endogenous factors within the mandate such as the training of the ANP officers, the influence on exogenous factors such as other

102 CPAU, *2014 Final Assessment Report of the Dutch Integrated Police Training Mission in Kunduz* (Kabul: CPAU, 2015), p. v.

103 See for example: Obaid, A., *The 2016 Insurgency in the North: Beyond Kunduz City—Lessons (Not Taken) from the Taleban Takeover* (Kabul: Afghan Analyst Network (AAN)), 30 January 2016), <https://www.afghanistan-analysts.org/the-2016-insurgency-in-the-north-beyond-kunduz-city-lessons-not-taken-from-the-taleban-takeover. See also: Interview code: 2016-KI07>.

104 The *Huqooq* literally means the rights of an individual under the law, commonly used to refer to the district level Civil Law Offices under the Department of Justice in Afghanistan. The *shura* is a gathering of elders to resolve a dispute. It is a Dari loanword from Arabic, often translated as 'council' or 'meeting'. Carter, L. and Connor, K., *A Preliminary Investigation of Contemporary Afghan Councils* (Peshawar: ACBAR, 1989), p. 9, explains that: 'a *shura* is a group of individuals which meets only in response to a specific need in order to decide how to meet the need. In most cases, this need is to resolve a conflict between individuals, families, groups of families, or whole tribes'. For elaboration on the *shura* see for example Coburn, N., *Informal Justice and the International Community in Afghanistan* (Washington, DC: United States Institute of Peace, 2013), <http://www.usip.org/publications/informal-justice-and-the-international-community-in-afghanistan>.

105 CPAU, *2014 Final Assessment Report of the Dutch Integrated Police Training Mission,* p. v-xi.

power holders in the province has been extremely limited'.[106] The Afghan Analyst Network came to similar conclusions with regard to the foreign involvement in Kunduz Province. The study points out that there is 'no single actor powerful enough to rule the largest part of the province'.[107] Subsequently, it concluded: 'local power structures in…Kunduz fluctuated, but as a whole remained largely unchanged over the course of the intervention'.[108] To further support that claim, two case studies conducted by CPAU and the journalistic accounts of Natalie Righton have also shown a continuing significant role for non-state (armed) actors throughout the province.[109] On top of that, several studies have pointed out that the number of militias in Kunduz has not decreased throughout the transitional years. For example, Gran Hewad, researcher at the Afghanistan Analysts Network, has pointed out that: 'the general trend is that the numbers of militias in Kunduz have been increasing, and the provincial security forces seem incapable of controlling them'.[110] Also, their 'exact number seems unknown… as diverging accounts from government officials and parliamentarians indicate'.[111] The limited ability to actually verify the official number of these militias could also be seen as yet another sign of limited control by the government institutions.

In parallel to the withdrawal of the coalition forces from Kunduz province, the security situation has deteriorated and stability declined. The ANSF was not been able to stop the Taliban from advancing in several of the districts in 2015. The upsurge of the Taliban eventually resulted in the fall of Kunduz to the Taliban in September 2015. It is reported that the ANA and ANP were not able—and in some instances not willing—to hold and defend the checkpoints.[112] Only after receiving support from the US Air Force and the Afghan Special Forces was Kunduz city brought back into government hands.[113]

At the time of this writing (May 2016) it is estimated that the Taliban controls more than 80 percent of the territory that constitutes Kunduz province.[114] The ANSF are now only present in the Kunduz city center, on some roads from the cities to

106 Dirkx, *At the Margins of the State*, p. 55.
107 Münch, P., *Local Afghan Power Structures and the International Military Intervention: A Review of Developments in Badakhshan and Kunduz Provinces* (Kabul: Afghan Analyst Network (AAN), 2013), p. 64.
108 Münch, *Local Afghan Power Structures*, p. 2.
109 Dirkx, *At the Margins of the State;* Terpstra, N., *The Dynamics of Justice Provision in the Context of Irregular Warfare and Legal Pluralism* (case study report), (Kabul: CPAU, 2013).
110 Hewad, G., *Legal, Illegal: Militia Recruitment and (Failed) Disarmament in Kunduz*, Afghanistan Analyst Network: Thematic Report (March 2013), p. 2.
111 Ibid., p. 2.
112 Interview code: 2016-KI07; interview code: 2016-KI03.
113 Interview code: 2016-KI03; see also: <http://www.nytimes.com/2015/10/14/world/asia/taliban-afghanistan-kunduz.html?_r=0> (accessed 8 November 2015).
114 Interview code: 2016-KI08. See also reporting by AAN in January 2016, stating the same, Obaid, *The 2016 Insurgency in the North.*

the districts, and in the district centers.[115] Due to overwhelming Taliban presence, the Afghan policemen and policewomen are limited in their movements. As one observer residing in Kunduz province pointed out: 'the police now only stay in the centers of the province and the district. They cannot walk the streets in the current situation....I used to see them every day, but after the fall they cannot walk around anymore'.[116] Despite the fact that we have not been able to get in touch with the interview respondents from 2013, it seems very likely that the Taliban takeover of most parts of the province has now made it impossible to implement everything that they have learned during the police training courses of the IPM. Moreover, it is very likely that some of them fled or left the police force as many of the ANP and ANA did around the fall of Kunduz.[117] Regarding the female police officers, one of the respondents pointed out that only those female police officers that have no families in the districts of Kunduz are now able to stay.[118] Those female police officers that have families in the districts will now be pressured by the Taliban to leave the police.

Conclusion

It is important to point out the difference between police patrolmen and NCOs learning skills on one hand, and actually being able *and* willing to put them to use in the larger context on the other. The recruits do know more about human rights and police responsibilities, but if the corps *per se* remains corrupt and abusive, and particularly their superiors and co-workers, this training may not have achieved the effect envisaged. The AUP has learned about professional police work, but they also operate in a context where different armed groups are fighting for territorial control and where other divisive forces are at work. For that matter, the capacities of the insurgency and other armed groups are also very much shaping the final effect of this training and even the possibility of implementing or applying it at all. Lastly, there is also the general fact that a change in perception or a lesson in human rights may not actually change behavior, and most certainly not transform a corrupt system or police corps.

The final conclusion must be that the IPM had planted some nice seedlings, but these have been overgrown by the larger causes of instability in the province. The trust of the population in the government and the police forces remains very low. Because of the large upsurge of the Taliban throughout the whole province the police have hardly any influence outside of the city center of Kunduz anymore. On top of that, several of the police officers have left the force due to their fear of the Taliban or for

115 Interview code: 2016-KI07; interview code: 2016-KI08; see also: Obaid, *The 2016 Insurgency in the North*.
116 Interview code: 2016-KI07.
117 Interview code: 2016-KI07; interview code: 2016-KI03.
118 Interview code: 2016-KI07.

other reasons. Taken all together, the police force of Kunduz is in a worse position than both at the beginning and the end of the IPM.

In more general terms we may conclude that 'community policing' in itself is very useful and important, but in a context with strong militias and a strong insurgency there must be a complementary show of force that is able to control the militias and the insurgency. Otherwise the civilian police are not able to perform their duties and it will be impossible to implement what they have learned. Building civilian trust—as an element of community policing—and military capabilities should go hand-in-hand. In this perspective, community policing is important in war settings like Afghanistan, but only if the army is realistically strong enough to maintain territorial control in the area where the policemen and women are deployed. The case of Kunduz shows that a very careful balance needs to be found between counter-insurgency efforts and investments in community policing during statebuilding operation like the one in Afghanistan.

11

The Thin Blue Line: Police Advising in Dynamic Environments, Iraq (2003-2014) and Afghanistan (2009-2015)

Nicholas Kramer and Craig Whiteside

Introduction

The study of policing is built upon a large body of work that supports expeditionary police advising in most situations, even in high conflict areas. The majority of this literature takes a task-oriented perspective on how to produce efficient and honest police in sufficient numbers to maintain the peace. Yet the United States and its allies have pointedly struggled to develop credible police forces in the past decade in Afghanistan and Iraq. We argue that there is a fundamental misunderstanding in the approach to police advising in high conflict areas, and that the critical factors in training police in a high conflict environment are not methodological in nature, but concern rather who is trained, as well as where, when, and how they are used in particular environments.

This conceptual confusion was highlighted by a recent and authoritative work by two icons of police studies, David Bayley and Robert Perito, in *The Police in War*. The authors criticized the US military for its use of police as 'little soldiers' in the combat zones of Iraq and Afghanistan, a valid critique when one considers the severe casualties that police suffered in these wars.[1] Yet their recommendation to only put new police into areas that have been cleared and secured is somewhat simplistic: what about policing requirements in unsafe areas? How do partner units keep police safe when insurgents invariably creep back into these cleared areas when a shift of government focus into another area allows insurgents back into safe areas? Now

1 Bayley, David and Robert Perito, *The Police in War: Fighting Insurgency, Terrorism, and Violent Crime* (Boulder: Lynne Rienner, 2010).

starved of resources and supporting security units, the new policing mechanisms are ripe for failure.

This is the paradox of policing in high conflict zones. On the one hand, police are strongly preferred over the military in the maintenance of order among the civilian population. On the other, they are incapable of defeating trained insurgents who not only bring to bear heavy weapon systems such as mortars and rockets, but can strike at will in contested areas against thinly manned and spread-out pockets of lightly armed police. The difficulty of solving this wicked problem inspires us to examine the issue of policing in heavy conflict zones in five key areas: the level of disorder, the type of law regime, the type of policing unit, the makeup of the units, and the role or roles of the advisor. Gaining an understanding of how all five variables interact to affect policing in conflict zones is critical to the development of improved police advising doctrine and a greatly needed improvement in the corresponding effectiveness of police forces.

Of the five factors, the level of disorder should play the determinant role in shaping the various ways that police units are built, manned, trained, operate, and advised. This chapter begins with a discussion of the five factors for the purpose of defining possibilities and combinations that produce an effective police force that provides security for the population and enhances the government's efforts in support of the populace. Two case studies of police formation and advising in Iraq and Afghanistan are then presented to highlight the presence of these variables in a dynamic environment. This analysis will highlight the ways in which an analysis of both case studies support the model outlined below, allowing for future testing of the model on an expanded set of case studies or on current problem sets.

An Ideal Typology in the Conflict-Policing Spectrum

Level of Disorder	Law Regime	Policing Unit	Unit Makeup	Advisor Role
Low	Rule of law	Law and Order	Representative or Unrepresentative	Professionalization
Medium	Mixed	Mixed; Police and Paramilitary	Directed	Protection
High	Extra-Legal	Military	Healthy Mix	Preservation

The Levels of Disorder: Low, Medium, High

Low levels of disorder allow the police to focus on their primary job of maintaining order in the face of few threats and with a high level of support for civilian property rights. In medium level disorder, there are occasional serious threats to police units; the civilian population is subject to alternative and competing governmental influence by insurgent or criminal elements able to deliver extra-legal sanctions to enforce their new norms and values. In high levels of disorder, there is a frequent occurrence of serious violence directed at government officials, police, and civilians that support the government. At this point, certain areas have been ceded to rival governance factions and the police are unable and/or unwilling to enter these areas out of fear.

The Type of Law Regime: Rule of Law, Mixed, Extra-Legal

Strong support for the rule of law by both the population and the government and its proxies reflect the optimal environment for the utilization of law and order police to protect life and property. A mixed law regime depends on the ability of well-trained police forces to differentiate normal crime versus anti-government inspired violence, which in turn has to be treated differently with some rights of the latter infringed in order to protect key personnel, infrastructure, and the population. Importantly, the rule of law is maintained whenever possible and the transparency of the police is high. In the extra-legal regime, military law and the law of armed conflict take priority over the rule of law, and this includes lower standards of evidence for detention and modified habeas corpus rules. The decision to operate in this regime must be made by the proper political authority.

Increased levels of disorder correspond with an inversely declining adherence to strict rule of law by government forces as well as the increased participation of military-style units. Ideally, law and order police should be limited to rule of law activities while paramilitary and military forces operate in other regimes. This division of labor would preserve the police unit's legitimacy in future law and order policing activities once the emergency has been resolved and symptoms of disorder drop to more normal levels.

The Type of Police Unit: Law and Order, Paramilitary, Military

Law and order police are necessary to recreate the existing order through routine law enforcement.[2] This type of policing is defined best by David Bayley and Clifford Shearing as the 'self-conscious process whereby societies designate and authorize people to create public safety'.[3] In contrast, paramilitary forces are trained combatants used to augment law and order police in order to field capabilities needed to defeat robust threats.[4] These units can be either militarized special police units (Emergency Response Units) or hastily trained government-sanctioned militias designed to act in times of emergency. The utilization of regular military forces for security in an

2 Marenin, Otwin, 'Changing Police, Policing Change: Towards More Questions', in Marenin, Otwin (ed.), *Policing Change, Changing Police: International Perspectives* (New York, NY: Garland Press, 1996), pp. 313-325.

3 Bayley, David and Clifford Shearing, 'The Future of Policing', *Law and Society Review* (1996), p. 586.

4 Dubik, James, *Creating Police and Law Enforcement Systems: Best Practices in Counterinsurgency*, Report 4 (Washington DC: Institute for the Study of War, 2010).

area is focused on controlling key territory and defeating security threats to the government—particularly those that are controlling and administering territory in competition with the existing regime.

Law and order police thrive in low threat environments where they can focus on administering order in the community and not combatting violent cell members planning acts of violence against the government. Higher levels of disorder require the introduction of paramilitary units to protect the police, government infrastructure, and certain elements of the population from capable and organized threats to order. Finally, the military is introduced in situations where the anti-government threat more resembles capable military units that are no match for regular police.

Unit Makeup: Representative, Directed, Unrepresentative

A police unit with a representative makeup reflects the ethnicities or racial background of the local community and region to avoid perceptions of foreign interference in local affairs. Directed representation is used to target particular groups for inclusion into local policing units for policy purposes, usually by coopting already built local militias or the use of quotas. An unrepresentative makeup includes the deliberate use of out of area recruits or units for loyalty or political reasons.

Employment in low levels of disorder could either be representative or unrepresentative, depending on local ethnic or racial divides. For example, most metropolitan police departments strive to reflect their community, while rural policing is sometimes done by external state agencies in order to avoid a conflict of interest.[5] With an elevated threat, directed makeup reflects proactive measures taken to augment local security forces with existing paramilitary and militia units. These actions might display a preference toward a particular ethnic group to co-opt tribes in order to incentivize loyalty to the government. Emergency situations with high levels of violence require a healthy mix of forces, which might include outside forces from more stable areas that don't reflect local demographics.

Advisor Roles: Professionalization, Protection, Preservation

Civilian police advisors working on the professionalization of local police units teach culture-appropriate policing and administrative tasks, especially criminal investigation techniques. When protection of the police becomes a necessary focus, survival skills, advanced weapons training, and small unit tactics take precedence in instruction over normal policing tasks. Finally, advisors preserve future police capabilities when they decide to withdraw police from dangerous areas until the area is sufficiently pacified in order to preserve human capital with specialized policing skills and training.

5 Marenin, Otwin, 'Policing the Native Villages of Alaska', *Rural Society*, 1:1 (1991).

The lower the threat environment, the easier it is for advisors to focus on teaching necessary law and order skills. As the threat increases, police, as key representatives of state security, must be protected, provided additional resources, and taught advanced survival skills in order to sustain operations in an increasingly lethal environment. The most difficult decision for an advising unit would be to pull out police units from an untenable security situation. Since police often have two to three times the amount of training that regular military members have, it is advisable to consider protecting that investment over leaving police to be killed in isolated police stations and checkpoints vulnerable to insurgent mass assaults. This dynamic is illustrated in both of the descriptive case studies of police units in war, with further discussion in the conclusion of what kind of criteria should be used to make these politically difficult decisions.

Now that a relatively holistic framework for police advising has been presented, we present two recent case studies to trace the factors described above in coalition efforts to stabilize the new governments of Iraq and Afghanistan after the transition from authoritarian-style governments to developing democracies with community-style policing and respect for individual rights. Both of these efforts observed a gradual increase in violent activity designed to disrupt efforts to develop functional government services, which included the delivery of professional police services for communities. After the creation of auxiliary police units and the introduction of military units into the areas, the areas stabilized for a temporary period before relapsing. Police advising played a key role in these events.

Case Study: Iraq (2003-2014)

The town of Jurf ah Sakhr, which means rocky bank in Arabic, sits on the western side of the Euphrates River about 50 miles south of Baghdad. The district of Jurf is largely agricultural with a network of canals from the river supporting a robust date crop. The area had been the home of the Baathist era Medina Republican Guard Division and its overwhelmingly Sunni population was strongly sympathetic to the previous regime and suspect of the new national and provincial governments—which under democratic conditions would be dominated at the national level by the majority Shia population.[6] After the invasion of 2003, the original police force operated in the town much as it did during Saddam's reign, although plans to provide a coalition civilian police advisor were neither timely nor feasible due to the rapidly deteriorating

6 The Sunni population of Jurf district did not necessarily support the Ba'ath Party but did identify strongly with an Iraqi state led predominantly by Sunnis and with the greater Sunni Arab region. The rise of a Shia led political coalition to control of the government led to a sense of dispossession in this and other Sunni communities, which fueled the insurgency against the Iraqi government and its coalition partners. 'Triangle of Death South of Baghdad: Bounties Offered for Killing of Shiites, Westerners', *Associated Press* (19 Nov. 2004).

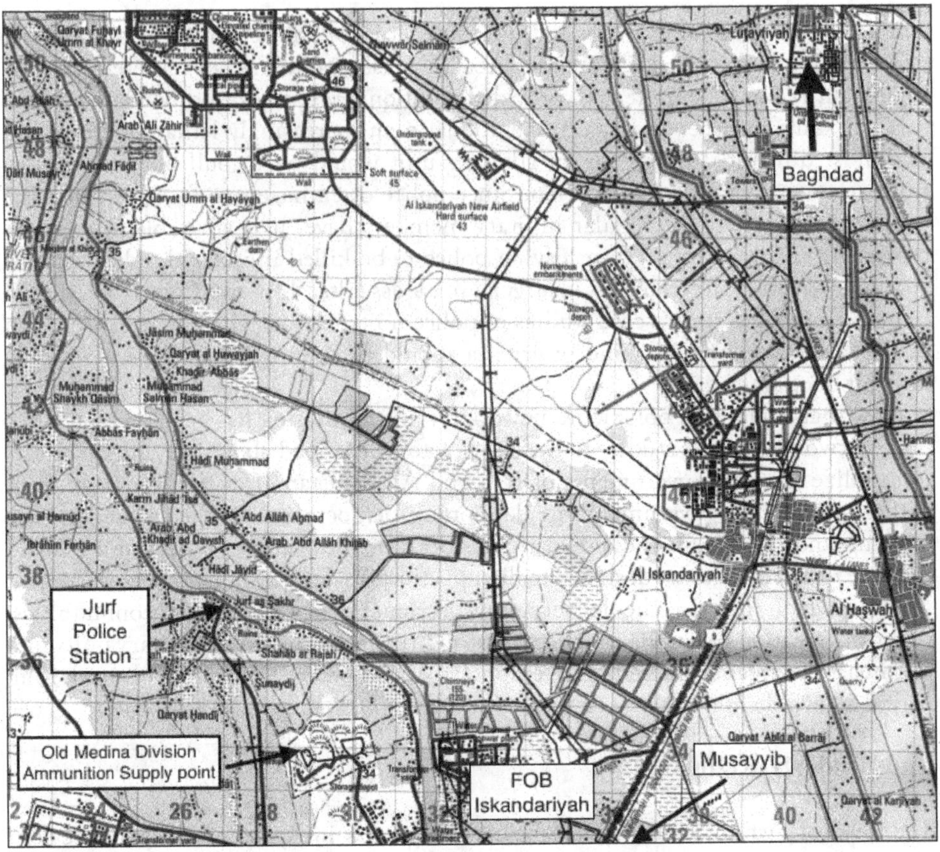

Map of North Babil Province, Iraq (author's collection)

conditions. Before 2003, the Jurf police force had functioned more as facilitators for the local tribal sheikhs in the administering of local disputes and justice.[7] After the invasion, Coalition forces stationed on the eastern side of the river across from 'Jurf' focused most of their effort in 2003-2004 on securing important facilities and lines of communication that led from Kuwait to Baghdad and beyond. Pacification of areas west of the Euphrates was not a priority for the thinly spread units that were constantly adjusting to more important missions as certain areas of Iraq such as Fallujah to the northwest and Najaf to the south fell into disorder.[8] As a result, the

7 This mediation role of the police was more common in rural areas dominated by tribes than urban areas that relied more on the police for law enforcement. Interview with a Jurf tribal sheikh who requested anonymity (18 March 2016).

8 Estes, Kenneth, *US Marines in Iraq: 2004-2005: Marines into the Fray* (Washington DC: United States Marine Corps, 2011), pp. 39-47.

Army unit originally stationed at the nearby Musayyib power plant in 2003 paid Jurf little attention and eventually defunded its only reconstruction project due to the high levels of hostility directed toward the Coalition in the local area.[9] The Marine unit that arrived in the summer of 2004 reported that 80 percent of its patrols to the town to check on the police and city council resulted in contact with the insurgents of the Islamic Army of Iraq, the dominant resistance faction in the district.[10] A Marine Civil Affairs officer who remarked to the press at the time summed up the coalition attitude toward Jurf: 'we basically told him (a local Jurf medical official) if they support the enemy they will get nothing but death and destruction. If they support us, we will work hard to improve their standard of living'.[11]

Jurf Police Station after its first destruction, taken in Aug 2004 by photojournalist Brian Palmer

9 Bathon, Zachary, '24th MEU, 3rd CAG Marines Visit Jurf as Sakhr' (19 August 2004).
10 The Iraqi insurgency was a fragmented and localized one, with different groups vying for power in particular areas based on family or tribal connections and relative power. The goal often was to dominate commercial activities in their area for economic gain. See 'Gunmen raid police station near Baghdad', *USAToday* (11 June 2004).
11 Bathon, '24th MEU, 3rd CAG Marines visit Jurf'.

In the summer of 2004 the police station in Jurf ah Sakhr was overrun by Islamic Army insurgents and deliberately destroyed.[12] The police chief, a local Sunni from the Janabi tribe who had recently been selected by the Iraqi Police to take over the prestigious Hillah SWAT, was publically executed in front of the townspeople as a warning to the citizens not to work with the new government of Iraq or the Coalition.[13] This was part of a synchronized campaign as police stations in the nearby towns of Yusifiyah, Latifiyah, Haswah, and Musayyib had all been destroyed.[14] The second battle of Fallujah (December 2004) forced counterinsurgent forces to pay increased attention to Jurf ah Sakhr as it provided a safe area for insurgents to stage attacks against Fallujah and Baghdad to the north and Shia cities to the south.[15] The replacement for the Marines, an Army National Guard unit from Mississippi, made plans for a new police station in Jurf; in the meantime, there was a limited police presence and no Iraqi Army or Coalition forces stationed in the town during 2005.[16] That summer, a temporary police station across the street from the previous one was attacked with a car bomb and destroyed by several improvised explosives placed inside the station by unknown perpetrators. This was the second police station destroyed in as many years in Jurf ah Sakhr.

The large ammunition depots that had once supported the Medina Division, abandoned and unguarded during the first months of the occupation, provided the insurgents an almost endless supply of weapons, munitions, and explosives, fueling an ever deteriorating security situation.[17] For example, one Iraqi Army raid on a cache near Jurf that year unearthed three tons of explosives, 155 mortar rounds, and over 250,000 rounds of small arms ammunition.[18] Despite this continued instability, the Iraqi Police were able to protect the poll workers in support of the December 2005 national election that witnessed a relatively high turnout in Jurf despite the nationwide

12 Palmer, Brian, photo of destroyed Jurf police station from his photo blog with mention of the executed police chief Abd Yaseen Gudeb al Janabi.

13 Interview with anonymous Jurf tribal sheikh (18 March 2016). This execution infuriated the local Janabi tribe and caused problems between the tribe and the Islamic Army of Iraq (IAI).

14 24th Marine Expeditionary Unit, 'ING Repel Attack on Police Station South of Baghdad: Iraqi Security Forces and US Marines Capture 72 Suspected Militants in Past 24 hours', Defense Video & Imagery Distribution System (2 February 2005).

15 Estes, 'Marines into the Fray', pp. 39-47.

16 The Jurf police took to operating out of nearby Tahrir Police Station in Musayyib, a mostly Shia town just south of Jurf that hosted district administration after 2003. Interview with Colonel Patrick Donahoe, 1-67 Combined Arms Battalion Commander in Jurf ah Sakhr from December 2005-November 2006 (12 February 2016).

17 Salo, Edward, and F. Patricia Stallings, *Captured Enemy Ammunition and Coalition Munitions Clearance Mission, 2003-2008* (Huntsville: The US Army Engineering and Support Center, 2013), pp. 1-7.

18 Entry for 25 March 2005, *Terrorism Incident Reference, Iraq: 2000-2005* (Arlington: IntelCenter, 2008), p. 309.

Sunni boycott.[19] The high level of violence in the Jurf area, which mirrored conditions across the river in Iskandariyah, Yusifiyah, Latifiyah, and Mahmudiyah, caused the Coalition to prioritize garrisoning this particular area with an armored brigade from the 4th Infantry Division in late 2005.[20] The commander of the battalion assigned to the area inherited the plans for a new forward patrol base for American and Iraqi forces next to the site of the future police station—a third one—which would be built on the location of the original.[21]

Iraqi policeman at a newly constructed checkpoint on the road to Jurf ah Sakhr in 2005 – (US DOD)

The 1-67 Armor's plan to secure Jurf consisted of a string of Iraqi Police checkpoints on the routes into Jurf from Musayyib, which were manned by 'mostly petrified Shia police'.[22] The US commander met with local Sunni dignitaries from Jurf to recruit their sons into the police and conducted joint patrols with the police stationed at the various checkpoints in Jurf district. His plan was to eventually create a mixed police

19 Omar, 'We Got our Purple Fingers', *Iraq the Model,* web blog (12 December 2005).
20 Gettleman, Matthew, 'In Iraqi Divide, Echoes of Bosnia for US Troops', *New York Times* (16 Apr 2006).
21 Army News Service, 'Coalition Builds Base at Jurf as Sukhr' (21 March 2006).
22 Donahoe interview.

force with a balanced sectarian makeup.[23] Two armored companies with infantry support operated from the patrol base in Jurf ah Sakhr and another one north of the town center to interdict insurgent movement along the Euphrates River and the western bank. The fighting was heavy during 2006, with the battalion suffering 17 soldiers killed in and around Jurf.[24] As the battalion's tour came to a close, it seemed like progress was around the corner. On 18 September, General Qais Hamza, the Babil provincial police commander, cut the ribbon on the new police station in Jurf.[25] A week after its grand opening, a foreign fighter drove a car bomb through the open gate and leveled the police station, killing two and wounding four policemen as well as several American soldiers in their adjacent base.[26] As 2006 ended, the citizens of Jurf once again had no police to secure government services in their town, and trips to nearby Musayyib were more dangerous than ever as sectarian violence peaked.

Babil Police General Qais cuts the ribbon with Lieutenant Colonel Donohoe, USA at the new Jurf Police Station in September 2006 (US DOD)

23 Morin, Monte, 'Third Time's No Charm for Iraqi Police Station', *Stars and Stripes* (28 September 2006).
24 Donahoe interview.
25 Reyes, Edgar, 'Jurf ah Sakhr Residents Celebrate Opening of IP Station', Defense Imagery Distribution System (18 September 2006).
26 Armed Forces Press Service, 'US Soldiers Stop Baghdad Bomber; Iraqi Police Catch Two Killers', US Department of Defense (26 September 2006).

By 2007, the American presence in Jurf was so precarious that the isolated patrol base north of the town designed to interdict insurgent movement toward Jurf was evacuated due to its untenable position in a hostile area. One company of American paratroopers operated in Jurf and eventually partnered with an Iraqi Army platoon garrisoning Jurf from the ruins of the third police station.[27] The introduction of Iraqi Army units in the absence of police was a new twist on the plan to secure Jurf ah Sakhr. Midway through the year a local delegation approached the Americans with a proposition of forming a Sunni militia to combat the growing influence of the Islamic State of Iraq in the town, a politico-military front formed in October 2006 that incorporated the entity formerly known as Al Qaeda in Iraq along with several other Sunni insurgent groups. This front had been responsible for the Sudanese suicide bomber who had leveled the police station that same month.[28] Most of the militia, or Sons of Iraq as they were called, came from the local Sunni Janabi tribe and from the local wing of the Islamic Army of Iraq—which reluctantly put down its arms and reconciled with the Iraqi government as part of the associated Awakening (*Sahwa*) movement that had spread from Anbar province from the north.[29]

Sunni member of the Sahwa in Jurf ah Sakhr (Thomas Westphal)

27 1-501 Parachute Infantry Regiment replaced 1-67 Armor in November 2006.

28 Seifert, Katherine and Clark McCauley, 'Suicide Bombers in Iraq, 2003-2010: Disaggregating Targets Can Reveal Insurgent Motives and Priorities', *Terrorism and Political Violence*, 26:5 (2014), pp. 803-820.

29 Cottam, Martha and Joe Huseby, *Confronting al Qaeda: The Sunni Awakening and American Strategy in al Anbar* (Lanham, MD: Rowman & Littlefield, 2016).

Sahwa checkpoint in Jurf ah Sakhr in 2010 (Thomas Westphal)

The *Sahwa* cadre, essentially a paramilitary group of tribal men and former insurgents, used their intimate knowledge of insurgent dynamics to root out the local cells of the Islamic State of Iraq throughout Jurf ah Sakhr district.[30] After several pitched battles, the violence in the area declined significantly and government services began to return to Jurf—which had operated without a local government for several years at that point. For example, the local government agency responsible for maintaining water treatment facilities refused to visit Jurf's plant and change out its filtration system, and as a result the citizens of the town had been reduced to drinking untreated river water for three years. By the summer of 2007, these dysfunctions were remedied as government services returned to the area due to lower levels of violence.[31]

With the return of government functions came the police. The police chief from the district seat of Musayyib, an Iraqi Shia and former Army officer turned policeman, reestablished a Jurf police force and skillfully integrated it with the paramilitary and Iraqi Army forces operating in Jurf.[32] The new security environment allowed the

30 Cigar, Norman, *Tribal Militias: An Effective Tool to Counter Al Qaida and its Affiliates?* (Carlisle, PA: Strategic Studies Institute, US Army War College Press, November 2014), p. 14.
31 Author's observation, Jurf ah Sakhr, Fall 2007.
32 Shishkin, Philip, 'Brothers in Arms: Sheik Backs US, Sibling is Suspect', *Wall Street Journal* (14 September 2007), p. A1.

police to conduct community patrols and adjudicate normal disputes among citizens. Jurf was peaceful again, and economic activity picked up with trade between Sunni Jurf and mostly Shia Musayyib.[33] Key to this change was the mobilization of a popular paramilitary force from the community that was willing to work with the government in return for services.

Iraqi police and military near Jurf ah Sakhr receive training on new weapons, 2011 (Thomas Westphal)

Unfortunately, the idyllic environment was only temporary, and in late 2008 an Islamic State assassination squad killed one of the founders of the paramilitary *Sahwa* (and a former leader in the Islamic Army resistance movement).[34] That was the start of a multi-year campaign that saw the paramilitary force decimated by 2011 and the police and Army units stationed in Musayyib under constant attack as they patrolled Jurf ah Sakhr.[35] The loss of effectiveness by the *Sahwa* led to mistrust between the Sunni paramilitaries and the mostly Shia Iraqi security forces, especially once the Americans withdrew from the Jurf district in late 2011—one of the last areas to be

33 Perdue, William, 'Road Opening Symbolizes Security', Defense Video & Imagery Distribution System (6 April 2008).
34 Sauret, Michel, 'From Insurgent to Community Leader; Iraq Loses a Hero', Fourth Infantry Brigade Combat Team, Third Infantry Division Public Affairs (24 Oct 2008).
35 Whiteside, Craig, 'Small Ball Warfare: An Effective Way to get Back into a Ballgame', *War on the Rocks* (April 2015).

vacated.[36] By 2013, the area was under Islamic State control and garrisoned by large, company-sized insurgent forces that defeated many of the government's attempts to regain a foothold in Jurf. For the third time since 2003, the police had been forcibly ejected from the area. Many of the new policemen were killed or wounded, and others fled during the fierce campaign. In 2014 after numerous failed military clearing operations in Jurf district, the government allowed distinctly Shia elements of the *Hash'd al Shaabi*, a volunteer militia force created after the fall of Mosul, to relocate the local civilian population and to garrison the area under martial law. The impetus for this emergency action centered on the political demands of safeguarding the Shia pilgrimage route from Baghdad to the holy city of Karbala, which passed through Musayyib. Because of this sectarian sensitivity and the animus toward Jurf's continual flirtation with Sunni extremists that frequently attacked the pilgrims, the area remains depopulated as of 2016.[37]

Iraq Case Study Summary and Discussion

The following chart captures the evolution of the police force in Jurf ah Sakhr over time, according to the categories of the conflict-policing typology advanced earlier:

Description	Time Period	Level of Disorder	Law Regime	Policing Unit	Unit Makeup	Advisor Role
Existing Police Force	2003-Summer 2004	Low but deteriorating	Martial	Law and order	Representative (Sunni)	None
New Police Force	Fall 2004-Oct 2006	High	Mixed	Law and Order & Military	Unrepresentative (Shia)	Survival
No Police Force	Oct 2006-Summer 2007	High	Mixed	Military only	N/A	Preservation
Integrated Police Force	Summer 2007-2011	Low but deteriorating	Rule of Law	Law and Order, Paramilitary, Military	Healthy Mix	Professionalization

36 Interview with Captain Thomas Westphal, platoon leader in Hamiya, Iraq south of Jurf ah Sakhr, from Aug 2010-Aug 2011 (February 2016).

37 Wing, Joel, 'The Clearing of Iraq's Jurf Al-Sakhr, Babil and Its Impact', *Musings on Iraq*, web blog (15 January 2015). For the Islamic State's targeting of pilgrims along the road, see Whiteside, Craig, 'A Case for Terrorism as Genocide in an Era of Weakened States', *Dynamics of Asymmetric Conflict: Pathways toward Terrorism and Genocide*, 8:3 (2015).

Militarized Police Force	2011-2013	High	Mixed	Specialized Police, Military	Unrepresentative (Shia)	Preservation
Hash'd al Shaabi	2014 to date	High	Extra-legal	Paramilitary	Unrepresentative (Shia)	None allowed

The original Iraqi police unit in Jurf ah Sakhr was left in an untenable situation as the level of disorder rose after 2003, a fact acknowledged by the coalition partner unit in their reluctance to visit the location and establish a viable partnership. Unconscionably, the police were left in a position that these combat units deliberately avoided, with predictable consequences. The disorder increased to the point that two consecutive police stations were destroyed and a very valuable police chief executed by insurgents in a public ceremony that underscored the lack of government control of the area. The fact that this extreme violence targeting police happened all over the this particular region south of Baghdad—nicknamed the 'triangle of death' for its instability and sectarian warfare—indicated that this failure was widespread among all advisor units and coalition partners and not unique to those who had responsibility for Jurf ah Sakhr.[38] In fact, it was indicative of a theater-wide botched approach to supporting police units in unstable regions.

The permanent stationing of coalition professional combat forces into Jurf district in late 2005—when episodes of violence were reaching emergency levels—was a necessary step in providing protection to a newly developed police force, but by then it was too late. This belated effort was foiled by the destruction of the third police station—which was literally next to a robust coalition patrol base equipped with tanks. At this point the police were permanently removed from the town with the exception of some vulnerable police checkpoints that served as a buffer between the area and its Shia neighbors to the south.

Once violence ebbed after the *Sahwa* movement defeated the Islamic State movement cells in Jurf ah Sakhr, law and order police were reintroduced to Jurf ah Sakhr as life returned to normal in 2008. The subsequent setbacks and the methodical return of the Islamic State after 2008 was facilitated by the failure of the paramilitary Sahwa to control their area and protect the police, and securing Jurf became a mostly military task once again.

The rule of law issues in Jurf ah Sakhr revolved around the lack of government services, which forced the police to represent a state that did not provide for its citizens. The perception of the police as representatives of the state in an area in which control had been forfeited to the regime's challengers, coincided with the selection of police as easy targets and symbols of the fading control of the government in Jurf. As violence

38 This appellation described the Sunni areas south of Baghdad; the key cities were mentioned in the Jurf case study.

levels rose again after 2009, police behavior in turn became more heavy handed and extralegal—which aligned with the Islamic State's influence campaign depicting the security forces as Shia occupiers that persecuted the local Sunni population of Jurf.

Law and order police only thrived in Jurf during periods of relative stability, but were decimated on several different occasions—which made the future employment of these types of units more difficult on each occasion due to long memories. In fact, the loss of the original police force with its Sunni representation and trained leadership was never overcome. Paramilitary forces and military forces were necessary to reduce violence in Jurf eventually, and even this had little impact until a popular shift in support of the population occurred in the form of the tribal uprising against the Islamic State. Unfortunately, even a Sunni police force made up of the *Sahwa* was no guarantee of security as after 2008 the locals were coopted from within by a fierce counterattack campaign by the Islamic State, which by 2011 had infiltrated the *Sahwa's* ranks and eliminated key leaders. The idea that the simple remedy of providing a police force of representative makeup would solve the security issues of Jurf and secure the loyalty of a similar population was incorrect and in fact hid a serious liability: susceptibility to penetration and divided loyalty.

The role of advising and partnering units in Jurf was almost solely limited to teaching survival skills to police in one of the most dangerous areas in Iraq. The resultant failure to teach professionalization skills was exacerbated by the loss of experienced police over time and the utilization of auxiliary police forces with no training after 2008. The presence of an indigenous police force failed to prevent the Islamic State's clandestine campaign from dominating the town after 2011, suggesting that simple police presence does not translate into government control.

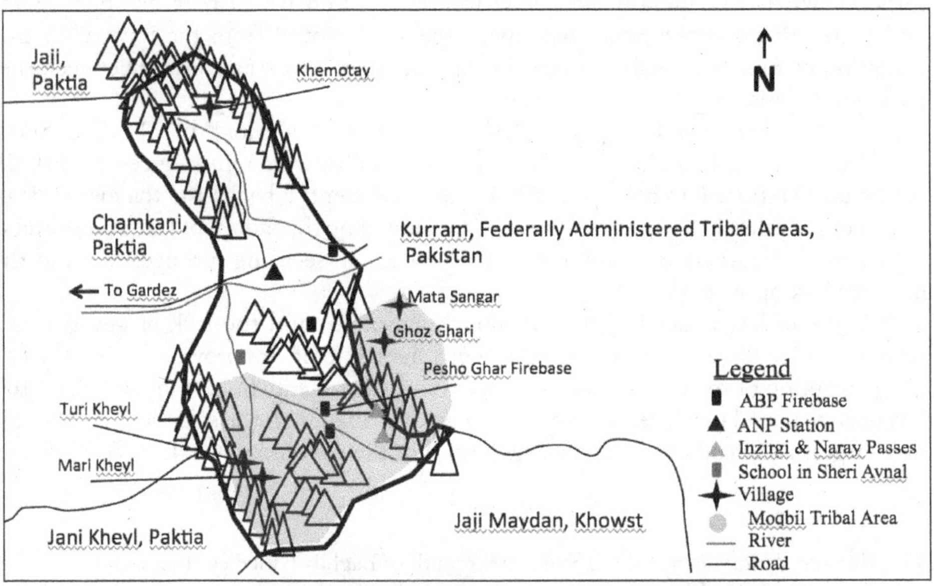

Dand Wa Patan District, Paktia Province

Case Study: Afghanistan (2009-2015)

In late August 2010, Afghanistan's president, Hamid Karzai, signed a decree permitting the implementation of the Afghan Local Police (ALP) program, a concept whereby locals would be trained and armed to provide security for their villages under the oversight of the Afghan National Police (ANP).[39] Since 2006, Afghanistan had witnessed a resurgence of the Taliban and its allies—namely the Haqqani Network and Hezbi Islami Gulbuddin—in the form of an insurgency that was particularly pervasive in the provinces of southern and eastern Afghanistan. After several other failed local security force initiatives to combat the insurgency in rural Afghanistan, the ALP program found support among the top military leadership of the North Atlantic Treaty Organization's (NATO) International Security Assistance Force (ISAF), particularly among the commanding general at the time—General David Petraeus—as well as top Afghan political leadership.[40] While the program would gradually be transferred to the Ministry of the Interior based on the maturity of the individual district's program and the ministry's ability to manage it, for the time being, the program's implementation was conducted under the purview of the Combined Forces Special Operations Component Command—Afghanistan. Dand Wa Patan, a militarily significant border district in Paktia Province, was one of the first six districts approved for a *tashkil* of approximately 225 ALP.[41]

Media reporting on developments in Dand Wa Patan is scarce prior to 2010 and most reporting on insurgent activity prior to that time was in US military channels. US Special Forces were the sole coalition force operating in the five districts that make up northeastern Paktia until the summer of 2009 when they were joined at Firebase Chamkani by a US Army military police platoon to conduct additional professionalization training for Paktia's police. The district's first dedicated coalition combat force arrived at the end of 2009 when a US Army National Guard infantry company was positioned at the main border patrol station in an advisory role. Despite an absence of reporting, it was apparent to the coalition that insurgent activity in northern Paktia province was on the rise as the year 2010 saw a sharp upturn in violence in the district.

Due to the district's location on the border with Pakistan, Dand Wa Patan served as an important transit zone for Haqqani fighters departing from safe havens in Kurram and North Waziristan for insurgent operations around Gardez and Kabul.[42] Dand

39 Saum-Manning, Lisa, *VSO/ALP: Comparing Past and Current Challenges to Afghan Local Defense* (Santa Monica, CA: RAND Working Paper, December 2012), p. 1.

40 Ibid.

41 A *tashkil* prescribes the unit organization, number of personnel, and equipment necessary to perform an assigned mission in a specific operational or geographical area.

42 Dressler, Jeffrey, 'The Haqqani Network: A Strategic Threat' (Washington, DC: Institute for the Study of War, March 2012), pp. 20-22. This is not to suggest that the insurgency is largely made up of non-Afghans. To the contrary, the bulk of the insurgency is Afghan

Wa Patan has four crossing points that are negotiable by vehicle; the most notable for insurgent activity was and remains the unguarded mountain Inzirgi pass from Mata Sangar and Ghoz Ghari, Pakistan, to villages in the south. In addition to this unsecured vehicle crossing point, the insurgency benefited from the strong tribal support of the Moqbil tribe in lower Dand Wa Patan and the Pakistani villages of Matar Sangar and Ghoz Ghari. Insurgents reacted energetically to any infringement on the district's southern transit zone while the 'ratlines' (infiltration routes) were active typically in order to maintain freedom of movement. To that end, insurgents targeted security personnel in Dand Wa Patan with improvised explosive devices (IEDs), direct fire, mortars, rockets, and suicide bombers.[43]

The start of a noticeable surge in violence began on 11 February 2010 when a suicide bomber was escorted by infiltrators onto the main border police firebase. Fortunately, stray dogs—cared for by the American advisors—attacked the suicide bomber as he made his way toward the American housing area, causing him to panic and detonate prematurely, wounding five soldiers.[44] This same firebase witnessed numerous rocket and mortar attacks throughout the spring and summer of 2010. Additionally, the border police firebases in Shepula and Pesho Ghar were routinely attacked by indirect and direct fire. On 28 May 2010, the district ANP chief was almost assassinated when a mine detonated under his vehicle just south of the school in Sheri-Avnal.[45] He was severely wounded, but survived, while five others were killed.[46] On 27 August 2010, two border police were killed and another three injured in an IED attack.[47]

At the end of the summer of 2010, the ALP program was initiated to assist local police and border patrol units in protecting themselves from the rising levels of violence. To begin the program, the local government and *shura*, or council of elders, first planned to disperse the ALP throughout the district and help Afghan and Coalition security forces with the vetting of proper candidates.[48] The *shura*'s allocation of ALP was done uniformly across the five tribes of the district and would eventually correspond roughly to the population size of each village.[49] Unfortunately, this left some of the smallest, most vulnerable villages woefully undermanned in proportion

and relies on Afghans; however, insurgents enjoy safe haven from pursuing security forces in Pakistan.

43 Former border patrol advisor US Army Major Paul Bosse, telephone interview by author (29 February 2016).

44 'Taleban Say 20 Foreign Troops Killed, Injured in Suicide Attack in Afghan East', *BBC Monitoring South Asia* (11 February 2010).

45 'Five Policemen Killed in Clash with Taleban in Afghan East', *BBC Monitoring South Asia* (29 May 2010).

46 Ibid.

47 'Blast Kills Two Policemen, Wounds Three Others in Afghan Southeast', *BBC Monitoring South Asia* (27 August 2010).

48 Bosse, telephone interview.

49 Former Dand Wa Patan ALP advisor, US Army Major, telephone interview by author (26 February 2016).

to the insurgent threat they faced. As for vetting, there was no prescribed procedure: candidates were vetted initially with biometrics and through local information to prevent infiltration.[50] Later in the program's development, tribal elders were relied upon to nominate members of their tribes for ALP training with the ANP, the Afghan National Directorate of Security, and ISAF security forces adding additional layers of vetting. Next, trainees were instructed on small arms marksmanship, radio communications, checkpoint security, basic light infantry tactics, first aid, searches, detentions, and IED detection.[51] The Dand Wa Patan ANP meanwhile instructed the ALP on the laws of Afghanistan and their role and responsibilities as an ALP member.[52] After completing three weeks of training, each trainee had to pass a skills test in order to graduate.[53] Training proceeded apace and the *tashkil* for Dand Wa Patan was filled by March of 2011 when a request was submitted to increase the *tashkil* to 350 ALP for the district; this staffing increase was completed by October of 2011, and refresher and on-the-job training continued through 2012.

By the spring of 2011, it was apparent the Moqbil ALP faced a concerted and twofold intimidation campaign from within the tribe as well as from the insurgency. Roughly four Moqbil ALP members from the vulnerable villages of Tsirgay and Tayara Lagada gave their AK-47s to insurgents after being threatened.[54] In a raid in October 2011 conducted by the Afghan Commandos in the Moqbil area, several ALP weapons were destroyed and others confiscated because the local ALP were mistaken for insurgents, which led to questions about their loyalty to the government.[55] Eventually, Moqbil tribal elders secretly negotiated with the local Haqqani Network commander to nominally retain their ALP affiliation, but under the condition that the ALP would not patrol, report enemy activities, or resist insurgents transiting the area. In return, these ALP units would not be targeted or coerced.

By the end of 2012, the advisors to the ALP in Dand Wa Patan had relocated to begin an ALP program in a different district and the paramilitary force was transferred to the ANP for oversight.[56] In January of 2013, according to Paktia Security Commander Major General Zalmay Oryakhel, the people of Paktia had voiced their satisfaction with the ALP in Jaji, Chamkani, and Dand Wa Patan and

50 Bosse, telephone interview.
51 Gaitley, Scott J., 'Securing Dan Patan: A US Infantry Squad's Counterinsurgency Program in an Afghan Village', in Wright, Donald P. (ed.), *Vanguard of Valor*, Vol. II (Fort Leavenworth, KS: Combat Studies Institute Press, US Army Combined Arms Center, 2011), pp. 136-137.
52 Ibid.
53 Ibid.
54 Bosse, telephone interview.
55 Former Dand Wa Patan ALP advisor, US Army Master Sergeant, telephone interview by author (24 February 2016).
56 Afghan citizen, correspondence to author (16 March 2016).

Afghan Local Police graduation with US Special Forces advisors in 2012 (Nick Kramer)

Afghan Local Policeman graduates from training (Nick Kramer)

had requested the program be expanded to other districts in the province.[57] Certainly, security in upper and central Dand Wa Patan had improved greatly from spring 2011 through 2014, resulting in a decline in overall insurgent activity and a reduced threat to security forces, but heavy insurgent activity still persisted in the south. In an effort to interdict insurgents crossing into Afghanistan from safe havens in Kurram through the Inzirgi pass, coalition forces built a firebase two kilometers south of the border patrol firebase at Pesho Ghar, an effort that cost $3 million.[58] During the summer of 2014, after the coalition infantry company that had advised and secured the border patrol throughout Dand Wa Patan withdrew from the district, insurgents attacked the newly built firebase killing and wounding several policemen and causing them to abandon the location.[59] The insurgents subsequently burned down the base in November 2015 and reestablished complete control of lower Dand Wa Patan.[60]

By 2013, a significant shortcoming that the ALP program in Dand Wa Patan faced after the withdrawal of all coalition military forces was the lack of a capable Afghan force to effectively partner with in order to counter the insurgency while maintaining order. The National Police were chronically undermanned, poorly trained, ill-equipped to provide security for the district,[61] and most were from Logar province, a point of friction with the local community due to the fact that they lacked any political, familial, or tribal leverage over the police.[62] The police lacked the necessary training and weaponry—mainly indirect fire capabilities—that would give them a comparative advantage against the insurgency.[63] What medium weapons the ANP did have were typically safely locked away at the ANP station and only utilized in special circumstances.[64] The ANP also rarely patrolled south of the Chamkani River or north of Stiya as a result of insurgent operations.[65]

The police partners in the specialized border police, in addition to being infiltrated, were also corrupt and ineffective in securing the infiltration routes into the district. Beyond demanding bribes at border crossings from commercial traffic, the border police ran a vehicle theft racket that led to cars being stolen in Chamkani and Dand Wa Patan districts and sold in Pakistan and vice versa.[66] Furthermore, this same

57 'Afghan East Residents Call for More Local Police', *BBC Monitoring South Asia* (21 January 2013).
58 Afghan citizen, correspondence (April 2016).
59 Ibid.
60 'Five police wounded as Taliban torch security post in Paktia', *Pajhwok Afghan News* (1 November 2015).
61 Bosse, telephone interview.
62 Former Dand Wa Patan ALP advisor, US Army Sergeant First Class, telephone interview by author (20 February 2016).
63 Bosse, telephone interview.
64 Former ALP advisor in Dand Wa Patan, US Army Warrant Officer, telephone interview by author (26 February 2016).
65 Bosse, telephone interview.
66 US Army Warrant Officer, telephone interview.

outfit was suspected of being involved in and profiting from the arms smuggling trade from Pakistani villages like Sadda and Turi Mangal.[67] As a result, the border police were widely seen as a predatory organization by the local community. And like the local national police force, the border police was chronically undermanned and poorly equipped to counter the local insurgency. The *kandak* (battalion) concentrated its efforts on the major border crossing and on observation posts along the border stretching north to Khemotay and south to Pesho Ghar.[68] The furthest the border police routinely ventured without US support was the Pesho Ghar firebase, and then only to rotate out the *koi*, or company, that was stationed there.[69] This meant that the Inzirgi pass was left unguarded. The lack of patrolling by both the police forces ceded large areas to the insurgency and its networks, particularly in the south where the Haqqani Network's influence was strongest.

The insurgents' freedom of maneuver in Dand Wa Patan district led to a surge in levels of violence highlighted by several days of fighting between insurgents and Afghan security forces in early 2015. On 14 January 2015, four intelligence personnel and an ABP commander were killed in the Inzirgi area.[70] By 11 September 2015, Afghan security officials reported that insurgents seized two ABP checkpoints in Dand Wa Patan, killing six ABP and kidnapping three others over several days.[71] Two days later, security officials announced a major operation to push back the insurgents and retake the checkpoints.[72] Among the security forces mentioned participating in the operation were the ALP. But by mid-November, additional sustained fighting was reported as insurgents attempted to capture the district center and seized several ABP checkpoints in the process.[73] Eventually, Afghan security forces retook the ABP

67 Ibid.

68 Bosse, telephone interview. A *kandak* refers to a battalion-sized element, which is roughly 400-700 personnel based on the unit's mission. In Dand Wa Patan, the actual number of personnel in the *kandak* was always elusive because several ABP allocated to Dand Wa Patan were held in Gardez as a quick reaction force and to increase security in the provincial capital. The exact number of personnel in the *kandak* was also difficult to ascertain because of 'ghost soldiers', or personnel who were named on the *kandak*'s rolls, but in reality did not exist, so the kandak's leadership could collect the salaries of these imaginary policemen.

69 Bosse, telephone interview. A *koi* refers to a company-sized element, which is roughly 80-120 personnel based on the unit's mission. An ABP *koi* was typically much less as a result of the aforementioned reasons and in actuality numbered around 40 personnel.

70 'Taleban Say Four Intelligence Personnel, Police Commander Killed in Afghan East', *BBC Monitoring South Asia* (14 January 2015).

71 'Pakistan-Based Militants Capture Two Afghan Border Posts in Southeast', *BBC Monitoring South Asia* (11 September 2015).

72 'Afghan Commander Vows to Inflict Serious Casualties on Insurgents in East', *BBC Monitoring South Asia* (13 September 2015).

73 'Programme Summary of Afghan Bost Radio News in Pashto 1630 Gmt 1 Nov 15', *BBC Monitoring South Asia* (18 November 2015).

checkpoints and repulsed the assault on the district center, but these events marked a significant downturn in the district's security.[74]

The loosening of government control in the district coincided with the introduction of a new, more radical element to the Afghan insurgency. In late December, the 'Khorasan Province of the Islamic State' announced their presence in Paktia via a video showing militants attacking government facilities in Jaji District, which is immediately north of Dand Wa Patan.[75] In early 2016, unknown militants hoisted black flags above their positions in Dand Wa Patan and announced their allegiance to the Islamic State, ushering in what could be a deadlier new phase of fighting for the district.[76]

Case Study Summaries and Discussion

The chart below traces the evolution of the Afghan Local Police in Dand Wa Patan and evaluates each period according to the variables in the conflict-policing typology:

Description	Time period	Level of Disorder	Law Regime	Policing Unit	Unit Makeup	Advisor Role
Existing police force (ANP/ ABP)	Prior to 2010	Low but deteriorating	Rule of Law	Law and Order & Specialized Police Unit (Border)	Unrepresentative	Professionalization
Creation of ALP	Fall 2010-Dec 2012	Medium	Mixed	Law & Order, Specialized, Paramilitary Military	Healthy Mix	Survival
Afghan Lead	2013-2014	Low	Mixed	Lay & Order, Specialized, Paramilitary Military	Healthy Mix	Professionalization
Regression	2015-to date	Medium	Mixed	Law & Order, Specialized, Paramilitary Military	Healthy Mix	Survival

In Afghanistan, the resurgence of the Taliban after 2006 made the Afghanistan National Police and Border Police in the region—widely dispersed across a rural area—very vulnerable to attack. The insurgents' view of the importance of these lines

74 'Programme Summary of Afghan Bayan Radio News in Dari 1330 GMT 2 Nov 15', *BBC Monitoring South Asia* (12 November 2015).

75 'Sources report presence of hundreds of IS militants in Afghan province', *BBC Monitoring South Asia* (27 January 2016).

76 Ibid.

of communication from Pakistan to the populated areas was reflected in an increase in violence after 2010 that spurred the creation of the Afghan Local Police as a solution. Over time, this paramilitary force was able to decrease the level of violence in the Dand Wa Patan district.

Taliban and Haqqani network cooption and infiltration of the ALP auxiliary, the structural deficiencies within the police and border units, and the withdrawal of coalition partner units in 2013 saw the dramatic rise of security issues. By 2015, the loss of checkpoints and the destruction of a brand new firebase were clear indications that security problems had erased any gains in the district seen by the employment of the paramilitary ALP.

The ALP's subsequent infiltration by the Haqqani network in certain tribal locations cast doubt on its legitimacy as a security force capable of enforcing order on behalf of the Afghan government. In this case, both representative and unrepresentative units had difficulties establishing legitimacy for different reasons, one because they were too familiar with local power groups and the other due to its foreign nature in the district. In addition, the blatant corruption of the border police and their involvement in criminal activity negated any progress in establishing the rule of law as a societal norm. Efforts to professionalize the force, however well intentioned, were unable to overcome structural factors in the makeup, education, and socioeconomic background of the advised police units.

Comparative Analysis

High levels of social disintegration created violent environments in Iraq and Afghanistan that made policing difficult and at times impossible. The government's inability to control rural locations and even the occasional urban center often prompted the use of police to project the appearance of government presence even when it was unsupportable. Why do counterinsurgents emphasize the use of police over other instruments in locations that are clearly unsupportable and dangerous? Some of this is due to a poor understanding of the theory behind order maintenance and the role of police. The insurgency scholar Richard Clutterbuck writing on the Malaysian crisis said:

> the government won the war in Malaya in the 1950s firstly because they provided adequate protection for the people in the form of a police post in every village; secondly because this gave that element of the population which did not want a communist victory, or which was apathetic and wished to be rid of war, sufficient confidence to be prepared to give information.[77]

77 Clutterbuck, Richard, *Guerillas and Terrorists* (London: Faber and Faber Limited, 1977), p. 42.

It is clear that the emphasis on local policing as a counter to insurgency as a legacy of the successful Malaysian counterinsurgency influenced the coalition strategies in Iraq and Afghanistan. However, there are substantial differences between the low capability of the communist forces in Malaysia and the ability of insurgents in Iraq and Afghanistan to utilize heavy machine guns, mortars, rockets, artillery rounds, and large truck bombs to level police stations. Writing on Northern Ireland, Clutterbuck described how an effective police training program could relieve the strain on a constantly deployed Army as they relieved them 'in all but the most violent areas, and eventually in those as well'. The police are the solution to returning areas to effective government control after periods of increased violence, but the reintroduction should be slow and methodical, and based on a 'conditions based approach'.[78] This conditions based approach was not witnessed in either case study, where law and order police units were continually victimized by more powerful insurgent groups. The small unit nature of policing made senior ranking police officers particularly vulnerable. Both Jurf ah Sakhr and Dand Wa Patan lost important chiefs and had prestigious facilities destroyed by insurgents seeking to humiliate the government. The introduction of paramilitary forces in both case studies made an impact on the security situation, at least for a temporary period. In Jurf ah Sakhr, the loss of key law and order policing with close ties to the community early in the campaign might have had an impact later when outsiders were forced to police the community. When violence was low, local police units flourished along with revived economies and improved community relations. The return of high levels of violence, in turn, made these gains illusory.

When military units were required to protect police units during these periods of increased threat, the police thrived. Alternately, their precipitous withdrawal in several cases doomed local police units who proved unable to provide for their own security in the face of more heavily armed insurgents. The case studies indicate that police were never pulled out of dangerous locations to preserve them for future employment. Instead, the Jurf case shows that the government forces left lightly armed police forces in place long after they were no longer viable, and abrogated the decision to the insurgents on the ultimate disposition of local police, which often led to the decimation of the units, their facilities, and their leaders.

The sectarian, ethnic, and local participation in the police or paramilitary force was not as crucial a variable as one might have predicted. Representative units were often co-opted by local insurgents due to familial or tribal ties. Instead, when counterinsurgents used a healthy mix of locals and foreigners (the directed makeup), auxiliary policing forces in the Sahwa and ALP were able to defeat their fellow tribesmen in both cases, although gains were temporary in nature and subject to a slow degradation over time. This calculated method of recruiting auxiliary forces, depending on the local security situation, seemed to be an ideal solution but was rarely achieved for a variety of reasons—usually a lack of trust between friendly

78 Ibid., p. 74.

forces or unhelpful sectarian engineering by politically influenced and partisan higher level commanders far from the fight. Unrepresentative units did not fare well within assigned districts due to a lack of knowledge of the area and the perception of police brutality against local members of the communities.

Coalition units rarely conducted high-level police professionalization training of its partners in blue, mostly due to the immediate demands of teaching survival skills in a dangerous environment for police. In addition, there was neither the expertise to conduct it due to a lack of civilian police advisors, or the will to embed fulltime advisors in shady, sectarian influenced police units. Furthermore, the casual and frequent abandonment of experienced police professionals to insurgent violence created a measurable skills gap that eventually became impossible to overcome in what looks to be a generational struggle.

While teaching skills related to individual force protection is a strength of military units that are conducting the preponderance of police advising in high combat zones, this is not as important as providing protection to vulnerable police units and their auxiliaries. When commanders located coalition units near police stations and checkpoints, the police were able to function more effectively. Likewise, preservation of the police as an advising principle was severely lacking. The case studies clearly show that the loss of policing experience cannot be overcome in the short term and regeneration of police forces requires a significant amount of time. In fact, even if paramilitary forces are used to buy time for the development of police forces, the lack of experienced police leadership and management is probably the key factor that caused both the police in Iraq and Afghanistan to suffer a relapse in security as the enemy recovered and adjusted to the presence of additional security forces in their core areas and movement zones. The loss of police early in the campaigns due to systemic poor environmental risk assessments and a lack of appreciation for the value of police operations and human capital was a deficit that could not be overcome in less than a dozen years. The long-term impact of the loss of experienced and capable police leaders to attrition has a follow on effect on the failure to promote leaders that establish positive organizational norms to combat corruption, infiltration, and sectarian behavior in the ranks.

Conclusion

Too often the discussion of police advising is one about teaching the right skills and attitudes to the right candidates. This chapter instead examines the often faulty assumptions regarding the employment and protection of police in dynamic environments, which has resulted in the unacceptable losses of untold thousands of police in Iraq and Afghanistan. It is time that security sector analysts came to terms with the fact that much of this is due to poor advising decisions based on these faulty assumptions. While police are very important elements for maintaining order, they are demonstrably incapable of doing what most counterinsurgents unfairly expect them to do once violence levels escalate beyond the norm in a particular environment—particularly when that violence is not criminally inspired but deliberately focused against the state's legitimacy and sovereignty. This confuses law and order policing with counterinsurgency, where the focus of the incumbent's efforts is to protect pro-government populations and reinforce loyalty to the government.

Effective police advising starts with an understanding of the conditions in which police unit development is occurring, as well as the efficacy of the rule of law in the context of the situation. Do judges exist to prosecute criminals and insurgents? Are detention facilities functioning properly? Are witnesses intimidated into not testifying? Police (and their families) who arrest dangerous insurgents only to see them released immediately face a personal security dilemma. Expectations that they will continue to function as police in these situations are unrealistic and dangerous, if not immoral.

Governments often rely on paramilitary units in civil war environments due to the need for additional manpower that is cheap and available. The benefit they provide is equal to their cost; expecting long lasting results from the temporary benefit paramilitary police auxiliaries produce is as dangerous as not fielding them for state sovereignty reasons—depending on the severity of the emergency. Police advisors in dynamic environments must have a detailed plan on the eventual transfer of responsibility to the state once the crisis has subsided. The fact that both Iraq and Afghanistan are still dominated by militias of all types more than a decade later illuminates both the natural need for paramilitaries and their enduring presence—even after they are no longer wanted.

Another paradox of police advising is that police units don't always benefit from being locally recruited. In fact, local dynamics can undermine a police unit more effectively than any other factor. Local leaders and tribal sheiks push their loyal followers into developing police units often for control purposes, which might be counter to the state's needs or the effective support for rule of law in the area. Police advisors must evaluate these local conditions and factors and make calculated decisions on the makeup of new police and paramilitary units.

Finally, the advisor's role is hugely complex and extends far beyond skills and attitudinal training. The advisor must ensure that the focus (professionalization, protection, or preservation) of the training and effort is appropriate to the environment the trained unit faces. Advisors must make the tough call when police units should be pulled from dangerous areas; if one cannot safely embed with the police or finds it difficult to access the police station—then the police unit probably shouldn't be there. A long term focus on preserving the critical experience of senior police leaders and saving them from their own best intentions is the true benefit a thoughtful advising team brings to their police partners.

12

Contracted Foreign Advisors in the Abu Dhabi Police Force: Explaining Their Enduring Presence, 2002-2015

Athol Yates

Introduction

The UAE is a truly unique example of what are sometimes called Middle East and North Africa (MENA) countries. While it shares its Arabic and Islamic roots with other Arabic nations, and oil resources with other Arabian Gulf countries, the UAE's history, culture, and leadership has resulted in it developing in a remarkably different way than other MENA countries. Today it is characterized by a dynamic and diversifying economy, optimistic national culture, and high incomes for both nationals (Emiratis) and non-nationals when they are compared to their home countries. These factors, plus its good business environment, advanced air transport infrastructure, tolerance for other nationalities, and moderate Islamic values have resulted in it topping many regional rankings. For example, it was first in the MENA region in both the 2015 Global Competitiveness Report index and the 2015 Travel and Tourism Competitiveness Index.

While its economic and tourism miracles are impressive, no less remarkable is its security achievements. Unlike surrounding Gulf countries that have experienced three major wars, several revolutions and civil wars, and numerous terrorist attacks, the UAE has largely been immune. Despites its very high levels of foreign workers and numbers of illegal immigrants, it has maintained a consistently low crime rate, strong feelings of security and safety among both nationals and foreigners, and a very high level of political stability. Its considerable security, safety, and stability achievements are reflected in it topping the MENA's raking for the 2015 World Justice Project's Rule of Law Index. A more specific measurement of policing outcomes is the Index's ranking for 'Order and Security', which 'measures various threats to order and security including conventional crime, political violence, and violence as a means to redress personal grievances'. The UAE was ranked sixth in this measure after Japan, Denmark, Finland, Singapore and Uzbekistan.[1]

One contribution to this success has been the small number of Western retired police officers who have been contracted individually by UAE police and security organizations since 2002. This chapter examines the largest group of these expatriates—those who have been embedded in the UAE's largest police service, the Abu Dhabi Police (ADP). In doing so, it tells the story of how these officers have contributed to modernizing the ADP which has, in turn, contributed significantly to the outstanding security achievements of the nation. The focus on Western expatriates does not mean other groups of foreigners employed by the ADP, such as other Gulf Arabs and South Asians, have not also made similarly important contributions, but these contributions require a separate study.

For the purpose of this chapter, expatriates are defined as those who permanently reside in the UAE for a minimum of two years, and who originate from European countries. Another defining criterion of the study's population is that the expatriates must be embedded in the ADP, and work within the Emirati chain of command. The term 'expatriate' is henceforth used to mean this group.

It is also important to note that expatriates are only part of the foreign expertise that the UAE police services has taken advantage of to achieve an accelerated evolution. They get international know-how from a variety of sources, including by sending Emirati officers to foreign countries in order to study policing, hosting visits by foreign police experts, hiring Western consulting and contracting companies, and accepting seconded foreign police and security bureaucrats. All of these methods are common to police services around the world. What is unique about the ADP is that for a modern police force, it has engaged a significant number of expatriates for over a decade. Consequently, this chapter focuses on explaining this phenomenon. In doing so, it tells the story of how the ADP's leadership has used strategic management as a driver for organization modernization.

In discussing expatriates, it is essential to recognize that they are ultimately just a small part of the ADP, making up less than 0.5 percent of the workforce. The ADP is entirely run and officered by Emiratis, who determine the ADP's policy, strategy, and initiatives. Emirati police personnel direct the expatriates, and Emiratis choose to accept an expatriate's advice or not.[2] Expatriates have no formal executive authority

1 World Justice Project, *Rule of Law Index 2015* (Washington, DC: World Justice Project, 2015), p. 28.

2 Rejecting advice was not uncommon and should not be seen as a failure of the advisor. Often it was because the advisor was not aware (nor could be) of Emirati cultural or organizational factors which made the suggested course of action inadvisable. Major General Al Nuaimi writes about one example of this. During discussions about why staff resisted organizational change, the expatriates, based on their experience, believed a primary reason was a fear of losing their jobs. However, Major General Al Nuaimi stated, this 'judgement [by expatriates] is based on the economic and social environment

to make decisions, allocate resources, or order others to take action, except in unique circumstances.

The Challenges Facing the ADP Before 2001

In 2001, the Director-General of the ADP, Sheikh Saif bin Zayed Al Nahyan, issued instructions that the organization would abandon its existing management approach with its problems as discussed below, and replace it with one based around achieving a strategic vision.[3] The decision to adopt strategic management was one of the most significant in the organization's history as it has become central to the ADP's rapid modernization post-2001. Strategic management is defined as 'a deliberative, disciplined approach to producing fundamental decisions and actions that shape and guide what an organization (or other entity) is, what it does, and why'.[4] This decision would also become the catalyst for the engagement of expatriates. So what drove this reform?

The fundamental motivation for modernizing was that in the 1990s the police service was failing to meet the expectations of the government and the population. Specifically, the ADP was not keeping pace with new safety and security challenges that had arisen from the Emirate's extremely fast rate of developmental and demographic change.

The rate of development of Abu Dhabi has been phenomenal over the last 40 years. While today Abu Dhabi is a modern city with dozens of skyscrapers, multi-lane freeways, and huge shopping malls, just 50 years ago, in 1965, it was referred to as 'simply a coastal village of 4,000 inhabitants, with hardly any vegetation and no potable water other than that produced by two unreliable distillation plants of limited capacity'.[5] And this was an improvement over what it had been five years before when the only major permanent building was the fort and residence of the Ruling Sheik, with the vast majority of other structures being palm frond huts. Fresh water was carried in by barge or mule, and the diet was centered on local fish, dates, and camel. The city's population in the early 1960s was predominately Arabs from the region.

Everything changed with the discovery of oil. Oil exploration and drilling teams started to arrive in small numbers in the late 1950s, and by 1962 the Emirate had exported its first crude oil. By the mid-1960s, large numbers of foreign workers

prevailing in their countries, which differs completely from the nature of the UAE society.' In the UAE, given the shortage of Emiratis, there is no intention of reducing employee numbers or conditions. Al Nuaimi, Nasser, *Change Management from a Practical Perspective*, Part I (Abu Dhabi: Centre of Research and Security Studies, 2010), p. 70.

3 Al Nuaimi, *Change Management*, Part I, p. 64.

4 Bryson, John M., *Strategic Planning for Public and Nonprofit Organizations* (4th ed.) (San Francisco: Jossey-Bass, 2011), pp. 7-8.

5 Maitra, Jayanti and Afra Al-Hajji, *Qasr Al-Hosn: the History and Rulers of Abu Dhabi, 1793-1966* (Abu Dhabi: Centre for Documentation and Research, 2001), pp. 249-248.

started to arrive to assist in constructing the oil extraction and associated export infrastructure such as storage facilities and ports. The influx of oil revenues, coupled with the demand for roads, housing, water, electricity, medical facilities, and schools by both nationals and foreign workers, led to a construction and trading boom. This started a massive wave of immigration, and by 1971 the population of Abu Dhabi city had exploded tenfold to 55,000. Of these, 41,000, or 74 percent, were expatriates, mainly from Pakistan (12,700), Oman (9,300), India (8,300), Jordan (3,400), Palestine (1,500), Iraq (1,300), and the UK (1,200).[6] Most were low skilled laborers. The vast majority were male, single, aged between 20 and 40, who sent their income back to their home country to support their families there. The local Emiratis made up just 26 percent of the population and thus were in the minority. This new demographic—one characterized by the majority of the population being expatriate, male, single, young, and from developing countries—set the population pattern for the Emirate to the present day.[7] The influx of foreigners accelerated in the late 1970s and early 1980s as massive oil-generated funds were injected into civil infrastructure across the Emirate and especially into Abu Dhabi's high-rise development. Growth slowed in the late 1980s but resumed in the mid-1990s when the older buildings in the city were replaced with modern high rises and villas. A further population boom started in the early 2000s when large scale development projects like Yas Island were begun.[8]

The massive economic growth and demographic changes created considerable anxiety within the minority Emirati population. An ongoing concern has been that these expatriates could overwhelm the nation, both physically and culturally. The physical form could include strikes at oil fields that would hold the nation's economy ransom, destructive protests due to foreign groups transplanting their domestic tensions to the UAE, and foreign governments using their nationals as a tool for subversion. At a cultural level, the large numbers of foreigners could spread new cultural norms to nationals, which would lead to the breakdown of traditional family, tribal, and Islamic values. Anxiety also increased due to the appearance of new crimes, such as drug importation and human smuggling, as well as problematic legal issues such as contractors taking advantage of the Emiratis' lack of commercial experience to massively overcharge for goods and services.

The rapid growth and the demographic changes meant huge new challenges for the ADP. The most obvious was the need for a massive expansion in policing services. Not only did the volume of services need to increase in line with the population

6 Abu Dhabi Defence Force, *Abu Dhabi Town. Present and Expected Population to the Year 2,000* (Abu Dhabi, 1971), p. 8.

7 In 1960 the population was 19,908 (44 percent noncitizens), in 1970 it was 66,713 (61 percent), in 1980 it was 420,455 (79 percent), in 1990 it was 713,702 (76 percent), in 2000 it was 1,112,716 (75 percent), in 2010 it was 1,967,659 (78 percent) and in 2013 it was 2,453,096 (80 percent). Statistic Centre Abu Dhabi, *Abu Dhabi Over Half A Century* (Abu Dhabi, 2012), p. 2.

8 'Abu Dhabi population grows tenfold in 36 years', *Khaleej Times* (6 November 2012).

growth, but they also needed to be provided in a culturally appropriate manner. Given the large number of languages spoken by the foreign groups, finding Emirati police officers who could speak multiple languages was a challenge. In addition, many foreign nationals would not voluntarily contact police due to prior negative experiences dealing with the police in their home country, or because they were undocumented. This required a different range of police services to be provided. Another challenge was developing capabilities to understand, investigate, and prosecute categories of crimes previously unknown in the Emirate. A final challenge was updating the legal system, including the criminal code, to reflect not only the new demographics but also the types of crimes and incidents arising from the integration of the UAE into the modern global economy.

When the ADP was established in 1957, the main roles of the police were to protect and enforce decisions by the ruling Sheikh, and provide security on the outskirts of Abu Dhabi town. The police were generally not responsible for the prevention of crime and dispute settlement. Instead, social order was maintained and punishment meted out under long-established tribal practices and Islamic law.

Tribal law is based on inherited customs and traditions. It was limited in scope in so far as it only addressed those issues that related to the people's personal and historical experience. While the basic elements of tribal law remained constant, its application varied with time and location. It was unwritten. Following the conversion of the people of Arabian Peninsula to Islam, Islamic legislation (Sharia) became the preeminent law. Unlike tribal law, Sharia is a body of moral and religious doctrines which can be applied to previously unexperienced situations. It overrules tribal law if they are in conflict. The effectiveness of the tribal and Islamic traditions relies on the population having a shared understanding of and respect for the traditions and the adjudicating power of certain individuals to make and enforce decisions. If this understanding and respect is absent, or if new types of disputes and crimes arise that are difficult to resolve under tribal or Sharia law, then the traditional approach to dispute resolution and crime prevention becomes less effective. To address some new safety and security challenges, such as road rules and strikes, legislation, regulations, and decrees were issued. Those relating to crimes were consolidated into the UAE Penal Code of 1987. This code balanced the desire for laws to reflect Sharia principles with modernization based on adopting Western approaches, laws, and institutions.[9]

Despite the existence of the Penal Code, traditional values arising out of tribal and Islamic traditions were still being reflected in the application of policing well into the 1990s. This is seen in the following statement by Colonel (Dr.) Khalifa Rashid Al Shaali, Director-General of the Ajman Police:

9 Al-Muhair, Butti, 'The Islamization of Laws in the UAE: The Case of the Penal Code', *Arab Law Quarterly*, 11:4 (1996), p. 350.

> Emirates society inherited tribal law, and with this heritage it inherited the concept of revenge as a legitimate right owed to the victim or his family forever. Revenge did not vanish completely after unification in 1971. It continued to exist in some areas despite the authorities' efforts. The negative effects of this antisocial phenomenon...can still be seen today, especially as the authorities prefer to step away from most cases that involve revenge and therefore, allow the disputing parties to solve their cases in accordance with tribal tradition.[10]

Colonel Al Shaali noted in 1999 that the response to the challenges arising from the economic growth and demographic changes by the police had 'led to the creation of more and more rules, regulations, and laws to reorganize and strengthen the internal security system'. However, he stated that these measures failed as they responded to criminal actions while 'attention should have been focused on the root of the problems. That is, the main criminal, social, and political phenomena that produced the criminal activities in the first place'.[11]

At an operational level, there was also a realization that policing tactics and doctrine were inadequate for addressing the changed conditions. For example, the official publication celebrating the 50 year anniversary of the ADP stated that in the 1990s, 'short-term preventative aspects such as patrols and fast paced reaction following a crime are necessary but no longer sufficient to meet the needs of society'.[12] Another problem identified in 1996 by General Sagr Ghubash, then the Undersecretary of the Ministry of the Interior, was that 'Crime prevention is not receiving the attention it needs'.[13] There was also great concern about the high number of road fatalities and injuries.

Within the ADP itself, there were a number of significant problems that impeded the organization's effectiveness. A comprehensive list identifying the problems of the late 1990s was produced by Major General Nasser Salem Saif Lakhraibani Al Nuaimi. His list can be grouped into three main areas. Firstly, the existing organization structure was outdated and not 'compatible with contemporary administrative systems'.[14] At the turn of the century, the ADP had about 17 variously sized organizational elements (e.g., directorates and departments) which were directly accountable to the Director-General. This large number of elements reporting to a single person caused management overload. In addition, as they were geographically dispersed, communication, coordination, and supervision between these organizational structures and the Director-General was difficult. Another organizational structural

10 Al Shaali, Khalifa Rashid, 'Crime Control, Policing and Security in the United Arab Emirates' (PhD dissertation, University of Wales at Aberystwyth, 1999), p. 50.
11 Al Shaali, *Crime Control*, p. 2.
12 Abu Dhabi Police, *Fifty Years of Progress, 1957-2007* (Abu Dhabi, 2007).
13 Al Shaali, Khalifa Rashid and Neil Kibble, 'Policing and Police Accountability in the UAE: The Case for Reform', *Arab Law Quarterly*, 15:3 (2000), p. 296.
14 Al Nuaimi, *Change Management*, Part I, p. 65.

defect was the lack of a defined and rationalized high command structure which allowed proper supervision and coordination.

Secondly, the organization did not reflect modern management practices. Problems included the lack of a clear vision and goals for the organization, an inability to measure organizational performance, insufficient interagency cooperation, poor human resource management, and an absence of job descriptions detailing specific individual responsibilities.

Thirdly, the ADP did not reflect modern policing practices. Specifically, the culture of the organization was focused on remedial action rather than a proactive approach. In addition, its services at the local level were fragmented rather than delivered via a comprehensive police station arrangement. There was also a lack of security data, making evidence-based policing decisions difficult, in addition to no effective community policing focus.

There were also a number of structural issues facing the ADP. These included the low educational standard of police personnel and the ADP's militarized culture. Historically, the UAE police services, like the military, have been attractive for Emiratis due to its providing secure employment, prestige, and minimal educational requirements. Due to widespread illiteracy in the 1960s (it was 90 percent in 1968 and nearly 15 percent in 1995),[15] police recruitment did not mandate specific education levels.[16] While education levels improved in the 2000s, the legacy of personnel with minimal educational backgrounds is reflected in the findings from a 2007 Abu Dhabi Executive Council report which noted that 'surveys of staff of the General Directorate [of the ADP] have revealed significant numbers with inadequate literacy and communication skills'.[17] This observation is reinforced by researchers from the UAE's Sheikh Saud Bin Saqr Al Qasimi Foundation for Policy Research. In their 2014 study of Emirati male education, they noted that both the police and military have 'at least until recently, accepted boys without a secondary school diploma'.[18]

Another structural issue of the 1990s was the ADP's militarized culture. The ADP, like other UAE police services, reflected its military heritage. This was due to the fact that they were established primarily by British military officers. This military heritage had long resulted in the police giving far more emphasis to internal security and stability rather than law enforcement, community policing, and crime prevention.

The military roots of the ADP can be readily seen today. For example the ADP has a military rank structure. The military heritage can also be seen in the ADP's organizational culture. ADP Major Saif Salem Al-Nuaimi, when conducting interviews with ADP personnel on change management in 2011, described the ADP

15 Statistic Centre Abu Dhabi, *Abu Dhabi Over Half A Century*, p. 25.
16 Abu Dhabi Police, *Fifty Years of Progress, 1957-2007*, p. 23.
17 The Executive Council, *Policy Agenda 2007-2008: The Emirate of Abu Dhabi*, pp. 61-62.
18 Ridge, Natasha and Samar Farah, *The 30%: Who Are the Males in Higher Education in the UAE?*, Policy Paper No. 3 (Ras Al Khaimah, Sheikh Saud Bin Saqr Al Qasimi Foundation for Policy Research, 2012), p. 2.

as having a paramilitary organizational culture.[19] This can be seen in the quotes provided by interview subjects: 'Leaders motivate employees to bring about change because they are asked to do so; on the other hand, as it's a *paramilitary* organization, everyone takes orders to do their job properly', 'Changes are implemented with ease due to the *military ethos*', and 'Sometimes *rank* plays a big role in motivating change' (author's italics).[20]

One reason why a militarized police can be problematic is that its culture can result in police being trained to obey orders automatically rather than acting with discretion and common sense. It could also be argued that militarized police are more likely to use excessive force. Another issue with a militarized culture is that it encourages an attitude of exceptionalism with its accompanying belief that they must take the lead and only rely on themselves, thus undermining responsibility sharing and building cross-agency coordination, both of which are essential to controlling and preventing crime.[21]

The situation of a police service not staying in step with its changing environment is not unique to the UAE. For example, this situation occurred in the British Police Services of the early 1990s. At that time the public was losing confidence in the United Kingdom's (UK) police due to rising crime crates, poor arrest rates, perceived diminishing police capability, and irregularities in police behavior characterized by the convictions of the Birmingham Six.[22] While there is no evidence that there was such a similar crisis of confidence in the ADP at that time, the above list of challenges required major changes within the ADP to ensure that it maintained the confidence of the rulers, nationals, and foreigners living, visiting, and investing in the country.

The Initiation of Strategic Planning

Given the range of challenges detailed above, Sheikh Saif Al Nahyan recognized these problems could not be effectively addressed through the historical approach of incremental change. Consequently, he decided to pursue radical transformation based around strategic management (also referred to as strategic planning). This methodology provided the guiding mechanism by which the ADP would be modernized. It would provide the basis for developing goals, targets, initiatives, organizational restructuring, employee development, and technological deployment. Importantly, it would unify

19 Al Nuaimi, Nasser, *Change Management from a Practical Perspective*, Part II (Abu Dhabi: Centre of Research and Security Studies, 2013), p. 96.
20 Al-Nuaimi, *Change Management*, Part II, p. 272.
21 Al Shaali and Kibble 'Policing and Police Accountability', p. 296.
22 This case involved six Irishmen being sentenced to life imprisonment in 1975 in England for the 1974 Birmingham pub bombings which killed 32 and left hundreds injured. However, in 1991, their convictions were declared unsafe and quashed due to fabrication and suppression of evidence by police.

and refocus existing improvement efforts such as employee development and building a professional police culture.

Major General Nasser Al Nuaimi stated that 'Strategic planning as a continuous process is instrumental in enhancing efforts to identify the positive targets we all aspire to attain, according to a methodic [methodological] and scientific vision to achieve excellent results'. Al Nuaimi was tasked by Sheikh Saif Al Nahyan personally to implement the strategic management approach in the ADP.

When the ADP started introducing strategic management in a systematic manner around the turn of the millennium, strategic planning was very uncommon in the UAE. In a 2001 assessment of strategic planning in the UAE's private sector, Al-Shaikh concluded that the 'prevalence of strategic planning in the UAE is rare'.[23] The only Abu Dhabi agency identified as having applied a strategic planning methodology at a more strategic level prior to the early 2000s was the Environment Agency Abu Dhabi.[24] The consequence for the ADP of the UAE's lack of experience with strategic planning was that there was no pool of Emiratis to draw upon who had practical knowledge and experience of this methodology.

There were three approaches used by the ADP to address this issue: improved training for ADP personnel, utilizing consultants, and engaging expatriates as employees. As an example of the first approach, Cambridge University was contracted to run a year-long program that led to the award of a strategy diploma for the ADP's senior leadership.[25] Consultants were also used in developing strategic reform initiatives. In 2002 the first expatriate was hired. Hiring expatriates with experience in strategic management was logical as they could not only offer their experience to support the ADP personnel's academic training in strategic management, but they could also assist the ADP in becoming a more 'informed buyer' of strategic management consulting services.

The engagement of the first expatriate in 2002 signaled the beginning of the contracted foreign expatriate phenomenon in the ADP. Their presence can be divided into two phases. The first from 2002 to 2005 involved a handful of expatriates primarily working on building knowledge among the ADP leaders of strategic planning and facilitating the development of the ADP's first strategic plan. The second phase from 2005 to the present involved engaging a large number of expatriates and deploying them to provide advice, operational support, and mentoring and training across the strategic and tactical policing domains.

23 Al-Shaikh, Fuad N., 'Strategic Planning Process in Developing Countries: The Case of United Arab Emirates Business Firms', *Management Research News*, 24:12 (2001), p. 11.

24 An agency which had previously developed a strategic plan was Environment Abu Dhabi. It had produced a five-year strategic environment action plan covering 2000-4. See Environment Agency Abu Dhabi, *Policies and Regulations of Abu Dhabi Emirate* (Abu Dhabi, 2009), p. 25.

25 Al Nuaimi, *Change Management*, Part I, p. 72.

The First Group of Expatriates (2002-5)

The first expatriate recruited specifically for his strategic management expertise was Gerry O'Connell.[26] O'Connell served with the United Kingdom's police for 35 years, retiring as Deputy Chief of the Lancashire Constabulary, the UK's sixth largest police service. While widely experienced in the field of policing, it was his knowledge and experience in strategic and program management that proved most important to the ADP. Previously, he had led a two-year program of reform starting in 1996 at the Lancashire Constabulary. It had involved implementing the San Diego model of preventive policing and led to a complete transformation of the Lancashire Constabulary.[27] The effectiveness of the reform was reflected in it being named the best performing UK Police Force in 2002-3.[28]

O'Connell also led a review of Metropolitan Police Service (MET) corporate strategy. His work at the MET involved a major study of organizational development, identifying strengths and weaknesses, and giving advice to high level managers about organizational improvements. His experience was backed up by his academic background, including postgraduate degrees in business from the Manchester Business School and criminology from Cambridge University. His academic thesis focused on organizational change at the MET. Upon retiring, he worked as a Senior Lecturer in Strategic Management at the Institute of Criminal Justice Studies, University of Portsmouth, UK. In that position he advised several foreign police forces, and met senior ADP officers in Abu Dhabi on one visit by the university delegation. This introduction led to him being offered a position at the ADP.

O'Connell's principal role was to assist with strategic reform, working directly under Major General Nasser Al Nuaimi's performance and management team. Initially, O'Connell focused on laying the foundations of strategic planning within an overall framework of program and project management. This involved augmenting the capabilities of Major General Nasser Al Nuaimi's team so that its members would

26 Technically the first expatriate engaged was Chris Cole. He was a former UK Cheshire Police officer working at that time for Police Staff College, Bramshill, which became part of the National Police Improvement Agency (NPIA) and is now the College of Policing. When he was recruited, he was working out of ADP premises coordinating Police Staff College training for the ADP. He was hired by the ADP in 2002, but within a few months he moved from ADP to MoI where he worked on other projects. He left the MoI in 2012.

27 The San Diego model was developed in the 1970s and 1980s and emphasized community policing and problem-oriented policing. It stands in contrast with the more forceful and confrontational US policing models of that time: the Los Angeles Police Department model which focused on enforcement, specialization, and robustness, and the York City Police Department model which emphasized zero tolerance as seen in the broken-windows theory and quality of life enforcement.

28 BBC, 'First police performance grades' (14 June 2004), <http://news.bbc.co.uk/2/hi/uk_news/england/3803047.stm> (accessed 6 January 2016).

lead the development of the ADP's strategic planning. Crucial to their early success was explaining strategic planning concepts and practices in Arabic. This was done by a team of bilingual Arab consultants (notably Dr. Sabbah and an Iraqi quality expert, Talal Galliani) who O'Connell credits as responsible for much of the initial achievements of strategic planning in the ADP.[29]

During 2002 and much of 2003, O'Connell worked mostly with a team of Emirati officers who had been selected for fast track promotion. The hard work of these gifted officers, plus support from others, O'Connell insists, resulted in the strategic reform efforts that attracted the attention of the national leadership. Consequently, the ADP's strategic reform program was accelerated. This led to the number of expatriates being increased and some 35 international consultants also being engaged.[30]

In 2003 the next expatriate, Rod Degnan, was hired. Degnan was a 30-year veteran of the UK's Merseyside Police, retiring as a Police Superintendent in 2003. During his British policing career, he gained wide experience across operational areas including territorial policing (policing in a geographic area), running training courses, and human resource management, including selecting staff for the UK National Crime Agency's Serious Crime Analysis Section.[31] Prior to taking up the ADP advisor position, Degnan had worked previously in Abu Dhabi running police training courses on behalf of the UK Police Staff College, Bramshill. His work in the years immediately after his arrival was mainly concerned with assisting in strategic management, and because of his human resource experience, he became heavily involved in the recruiting of expatriates needed to resource the ADP's strategic management agenda. In 2004, another expatriate was hired, Mike Speakman, a former Deputy Chief Constable of the Humberside Police (UK).

Emirati police officers, supported by these expatriates and consultants, continued to build the strategic plan, which led to reengineering business processes, building a new organizational structure, and writing human resource plans, and an organization wide management change strategy. One reflection of the importance of O'Connell's expatriate team involved his decision to give monthly presentations to Sheik Saif Al Nahyan on the progress of reforms, who also sought his advice on strategic issues.

A key result of their work was the ADP's first strategic plan. It covered the five year period from 2003 to 2008. This plan had all the archetypical components of a strategic plan, notably a vision statement, a mission statement, organizational values, and strategic objectives. The vision and mission statements were at the apex of the plan as their intent cascaded down through the organization in the form of strategic

29 Email from O'Connell, Gerry, 'Re: Interview on your role in the Abu Dhabi Police', 19 January 2015.

30 Gerry O'Connell Associates Ltd., 'Achievements', <http://www.gocassociates.com/acheive.htm> (accessed 6 October 2015).

31 Rodneydegnanwrites.com, 'Author's Biography', <http://www.rodneydegnanwrites.com/authors-biography.html> (accessed 1 June 2015); LinkedIn Profile, <https://www.linkedin.com/pub/dr-rodney-h-degnan/33/ab7/383> (accessed 1 June 2015).

objectives, priorities, strategic goals, key performance indicators, and strategic initiatives. The strategic plan provided a road map to deliver the ADP's mandate through explicitly linking every level of strategy—from the vision to the activities of individuals.

Another major change was the restructuring of the organization starting in 2003. Reflecting police structural trends in the West, the ADP was structured into functional and support groups. Four main functional areas were created (the General Directorates of territorial policing, operational support, security and special response, and technical support) and two support areas (the General Directorates of finance and human resources).

These reforms had ramifications outside of the ADP. Given that the ADP was the first significant Abu Dhabi organization to implement holistic strategic management, its experience was a key driver in strategic management planning being introduced at the Emirate government level in the late 2000s, and this methodology eventually became mandatory for all Abu Dhabi government entities.

The Second Group of Expatriates (2005-2008)

Following the release of the first strategic plan, the next stage was for each of the ADP's General Directorates to develop their own cascading strategic plans. This required the leadership of these General Directorates and their responsible units to gain the strategic management skills to formulate plans and implement initiatives. To facilitate this process, and given the success of the small group of expatriates' involvement in the initial strategic reforms, Sheik Saif Al Nahyan agreed to expand the use of expatriates and to assign them to the General Directorates.

Starting in 2005, and over an 18 month period, the ADP recruited ten advisors. Their primary role was to provide mentorship and management assistance to a small group of senior police officers. The use of foreign expertise was part of Sheik Saif Al Nahyan's agenda, which 'stressed the proper utilization or expertise and practices of advanced countries in the police domain'.[32] The adoption of foreign practice can be seen in various areas of the ADP. For example, the regulation of the private security sector was derived from the Canadian approach, civil defense (fire and rescue) was based on the German model, and strategic management and organizational development reflected British practices.[33]

Based on the anticipated nature of their work, the advisors were generically known as 'mentors'. Initially, the expatriates were paired with English-speaking Emirati police lieutenants who assisted in introductions and worked closely with them, enabling the expatriates to make a contribution rapidly. The decision on where to locate the advisors was directed by Al Nuaimi, and initially this was the result of a top-down approach,

32 Al Nuaimi, *Change Management*, Part I, p. 36.
33 Ibid., p. 98.

that is, Al Nuaimi's Strategy Directorate assessed where advisors should be placed in the organization. Over time, as the value of the expatriates was demonstrated, ADP managers started requesting them. The contributions of expatriates were particularly valuable in meeting the requirements of the new strategic plan such as specifying key performance indicators and developing action plans to close identified gaps in performance. Their numbers subsequently grew, and to better reflect their role, they were renamed 'Strategic Advisors'. These advisors typically worked with the heads of Directorates, often at the Lieutenant Colonel level or above. Strategic Advisors were normally former middle to senior level police officers, commonly Chief Superintendents and Superintendents. They were required to have a minimum of a Bachelor's degree, but a relevant Master's degree was preferred. International experience was also desired but not essential.[34]

In 2007, Abu Dhabi started recruiting a new type of advisor. Initially known as 'Tutors', and later as 'Tactical Advisors', their work typically involved training, including mentoring trainers, identifying training needs, developing training material, delivering training, and accompanying ADP police personnel on operational tasks as operational advisors. Tactical Advisors normally worked with a Captain or Major who headed up a section or local police area. Tactical Advisors were commonly former Inspectors with considerable operational experience who were qualified in police specialties and disciplines such as the use of firearms and maintaining public order.

These two types of expatriates—Strategic Advisors and Tactical Advisors—remained active in the ADP at the time of this writing in 2016. Advisors do not wear ADP uniforms. Most wear formal business attire, unless involved in field activities, when they dress more casually. Advisors do not have any formal rank within the ADP.

The former leader of the ADP's expatriate team from 2008 to 2011, Steve Watts, described the difference between the two types of advisors:

> [Strategic Advisors are working on] particular projects and working in support of the force's performance indicators and targets, such as reducing overall crime and the number of deaths on the roads. The others [Tactical Advisors] have been deployed as trainers and mentors, teaching specialist subjects such as crime and crime-scene investigations, firearms, traffic response, patrol and public order. Their roles can involve shadowing and supporting officers in the field.[35]

Together, these two types of advisors provide a comprehensive approach to assisting with implementing the ADP's strategic goals. That is, Strategic Advisors contribute

34 International Corrections and Prisons Association 2014, Job Opportunity: Juvenile Custody Advisor, Abu Dhabi. Posted by Ross Toomer (29 January 2014), <http://www.icpa.ca/forums/topic.php?s=&t=439> (accessed 27 September 2014).

35 'Police Train with UK officers', *The National* (30 April 2009), <http://www.uaeinteract.com/docs/Police_train_with_UK_officers/35506.htm> (accessed 25 September 2015).

through a top-down approach by advising and mentoring senior officers in development of strategic plans and initiatives in their areas. Tactical Advisors aid them through a bottom-up approach via training and operational support and mentoring, which builds the systems and services to achieve the strategic objectives and priorities.

Another indication of the direct link between expatriates and the ADP's strategic plan is contained in Abu Dhabi's first whole-of-government policy agenda. The *Policy Agenda 2007-2008: The Emirate of Abu Dhabi* identified six initiatives to advance the modernization of the ADP. The first was the 'Establishment of a team of senior international advisory experts'.[36]

A final indicator of the link can be seen in a 2009 article in *The National* newspaper. It stated that 'More than 50 former senior British police officers are assisting Abu Dhabi Police in a modernization programmer designed to transform the force over the next five years into one of the most effective in the world. Each [advisor] is tackling particular projects and working in support of the force's performance indicators and targets, such as reducing overall crime and the number of deaths on the roads'.[37]

The need for strategic management skills in Strategic Advisors, and to a lesser degree in Tactical Advisors, is reflected in job advertisements for advisors. Based on an analysis of web-based job ads from 2009 to 2014, Table 1 details the skills mentioned in ads, divided into strategic skills and policing specializations.

Expatriates are directly accountable to the Emirati police officers they are assigned to. The expatriates also report through the ADP advisor team leader. The team leaders were Gerry O'Connell (2002-7), Paul Blewitt (January 2007 to late 2008),[38] Steve Watts (September 2008 to November 2011), Rod Degan (2011 to 2015) and Alan Betts (2015-).

The responsibilities of team leaders have varied with time, need, and personality. They have always involved some form of centralized coordination, leadership and management of the advisors, and at a minimum included logistics management of the expatriates such as organizing air tickets, contracts, and accommodation for newly arrived personnel. It could also include organizing induction sessions, assisting with settling in, and troubleshooting expatriate-principal problems.

From 2009, the formal Team Leader of the expatriates for both the Ministry of the Interior (MoI) and the ADP was the British former police officer, Sir Ronnie Flanagan. He was engaged as the personal advisor to Sheik Saif Al Nahyan. Like the other expatriates, he had considerable strategic management and reform expertise. Before accepting this post, Flanagan was the most senior police officer in the UK, being Her Majesty's Chief Inspector of Constabulary (HMIC) for England, Wales,

36 The Executive Council, *Policy Agenda*, pp. 62-63.

37 'Police Train', *The National*.

38 Paul Blewitt was an Assistant Chief Constable of West Midlands Police before accepting the position as team leader in the UAE. In late 2008, he transferred to MoI, where he led the recruitment and establishment of a team of seven expatriate police advisors in the northern Emirates. He left the MoI in January 2010.

Table 1: Strategic skills and policing specializations identified in job advertisements for ADP advisor positions

Strategic Skills	Policing Specializations
• Balanced score card	• Operational & community policing
• Strategic planning & performance	• Counter terrorism
• Finance & budgeting	• Crime scene
• Human resources & training	• Crime investigation & intelligence
• Education and training technology	• Criminal biology
• Project & programm management	• Data security, vetting & protective marking
• Strategic planning & performance management	• Diplomatic & VIP protection
• Professional standards	• Documents
• Management training	• Electronic crimes
• Strategy	• Explosive
• Education and training	• Financial control
• Quality	• Fire analysis
• Human resources	• Firearms & public order
	• Fingerprints
	• Forensic evidence & crime scene
	• Handwriting
	• Police training
	• K9
	• Legal
	• Music
	• Public order & major events
	• Rescue
	• Roads and traffic engineering
	• Roads policing
	• Toxins and drugs
	• Traffic enforcement
	• Weapons

and Northern Ireland from 2002. The HMIC independently assesses police services and policing across the UK, and reports publicly on the performance of each police service. This scrutiny aims to drive improvements in the services.[39]

Prior to serving as the HMIC, Flanagan was Chief Constable of the Police Service for Northern Ireland and its predecessor, the Royal Ulster Constabulary. His 31 year career in Northern Ireland police services spanned the Northern Ireland peace process, which culminated in the 1998 peace accord between nationalist and loyalist factions. Consequently, he led the change management processes that transformed the militarized Royal Ulster Constabulary into the civilianized Police Service for Northern Ireland. He also had Middle East experience as the British government asked him in 2005 to produce recommendations on reforming police operations in southern Iraq. As the ADP and MoI were undergoing extensive change in the late 2000s, Sir Ronnie Flanagan's change management experience may have been particularly attractive when coupled with his breadth of experience across policing areas. One of his most significant contributions was his 2008 *Review of Policing* commissioned by the UK's Home Secretary. Its recommendations centered on making the police more productive and accountable, which could only be done through major restructuring, greater strategic vision from the Home Office, more effective support from policing improvement entities, improved flexibility in resource allocation, and better performance management systems. The UK government accepted all of his recommendations.[40]

Over time, the employment of advisors became more strategic and top-down to align this with the gaps identified in the strategic plan, and the performance management tool known as balanced scorecard that was introduced in the late 2000s. This more structured planning involved identifying the areas where expatriates were required, and the specific skillset they would need. This led to more targeted recruiting. Another sign of a more strategic approach to the use of expatriates was seen in the introduction in 2009 of a formal process to justify the need for a new position. This involved the police section, which wanted an expatriate advisor to build a business case and submit it to the police strategy department for review. There were about 45 expatriates in 2008, 75 in 2011, and 80 by the middle of 2015.

Conclusion

As a mechanism to accelerate strategic reform and modernization of a police service, the ADP's direct hiring of large numbers of expatriates has been a truly innovative idea. The presence of expatriates in a foreign police force is normally associated with the rebuilding of a failed state. However, as a relatively modern police force, the ADP

39 'New ideas from an old hand', *The National* (14 February 2009), <http://www.thenational.ae/news/uae-news/new-ideas-from-an-old-hand#full> (accessed 10 August 2015).
40 Ibid.

has used the technique to assist its accelerated evolution targeted at the goal put forth in the ADP's 2008-12 Strategic Plan of becoming 'the most operationally effective police force possible in one of the safest countries of the world'.

The idea and ongoing engagement of expatriate advisors is a testament to the vision of Sheikh Saif Al Nahyan and Major General Nasser Al Nuaimi. They saw the benefits that the expatriates could deliver, socialized the concept within the ADP, and have continued to support their presence. Equally, the success of the project reflects extremely well on the pragmatic attitude of the Emirati police, and at a broader societal level, the tolerance and even welcoming of people of other nationalities, ethnicities, and religions. This ADP experience may provide a model for other developed police services wanting to leap-frog stages of organizational evolution.

13

Expeditionary Police Advising: Some Conclusions, Problems, and Lessons Learned

Donald Stoker and Edward B. Westermann

Introduction

As we've seen in the preceding chapters, the experience of police expeditionary advising is far deeper and more varied than previous works on advising have revealed (including our own). A comprehensive, analytical history is clearly needed. But from what we do know we can draw at least a few tentative conclusions. Two obviously important questions to ask are: Why do police advisory missions succeed? And why do police advisory missions fail?

Police Advising: Creating Success

One of the building blocks for succeeding with a police advisory mission is to first assess the situation to gain an understanding of the environment in which the mission will take place. Examine as much as practicable the history and culture of the recipient, with a special focus on the history of policing in the nation. Arguably, the fundamental issue is determining whether the environment is permissive or non-permissive, meaning whether or not the environment is a warzone, which will usually mean a counterinsurgency environment. The sponsoring state must understand whether or not the building of the police force is supposed to take place under relatively stable conditions such as some post-hostility operations where there is no significant active enemy force, or the occupation of a state in which the population has generally accepted defeat, or whether the security situation is still very unstable and is afflicted by the presence of a significant insurgency.

A critical factor contributing to success in creating police is a stable security environment. The 1911-1914 Swedish police mission to Persia succeeded partially because the nation was largely peaceful. It also already possessed a generally legitimate government. The Swedes developed a professional gendarmerie—not a militia (which would have been unprofessional, poorly disciplined, and difficult to control)—and not a weak police force unable to defend itself against the rebel nomads and large bandit gangs which were its sometime opponents.[1]

Other successful police training missions have occurred in post-hostility situations where security was assured and the populace receptive. After the Second World War, the US and its allies were able to create professional, democratic police forces in Japan, Austria, Italy, and Germany. In some ways though, these were ideal conditions because of the scale of resources possessed by the conquering powers, and the absence of any resistance group the population considered legitimate. All of these states also possessed well developed civil societies and had accepted norms of behavior and expectations in regard to law enforcement.

But suppose this is not the case? In their chapter on Iraq and Afghanistan, Kramer and Whiteside point out that 'The police are the solution to returning areas to effective government control after periods of increased violence, but the reintroduction should be slow and methodical, and follow a "conditions based approach".' So if there is violence, how do you decide whether or not to use police? Kramer and Whiteside give us a simple key to determining when to use soldiers rather than police: 'if one cannot safely embed with the police or finds it difficult to access the police station—then the police unit probably shouldn't be there'.

In Afghanistan in 2011-2013, Dutch advisors in Kunduz focused on community policing and the initial results were generally well regarded. The new force even included female members. But the problem is that one can't successfully do this—especially over the long term—in an environment with active and effective enemy militia, guerrillas, or regular enemy combat forces because these units will simply overpower and kill the local police. This, unfortunately, proved the case in Kunduz. The police needed stronger support units that could protect them from insurgents and hostile militia.

Another critical factor for the success of police advising is to construct the right type of policing tool for the situation at hand. What—exactly—this means can be difficult to decipher as there is no one solution to any particular problem. In 1990s Haiti for example, Haiti needed a decentralized police force built more on the US model because the people distrusted the state security organs and feared the police would become an instrument of repression just like the hated army. Independent local forces, then regional forces, then a state force to handle customs, border security, etc., might have been a better model than a paramilitary constabulary-style force because this would disperse state power. Despite being more expensive and duplicating effort,

1 Fazlhashemi, Mohammad, 'Sweden ii. Swedish Officers in Persia, 1911-1915', *Encyclopedia Iranica*, <http://www.iranicaonline.org/articles/sweden-ii> (15 Aug. 2006).

it stood a better chance of actually working by providing security and protection for citizens. Insuring stability and security critical.

Another important factor is to ensure that the correct branch of government is controlling the police force. This can be very difficult to decide. Generally, police forces should be under either the Ministry of the Interior or under the Ministry of Defense. Which is better depends upon the situation the nation faces. Having the police advised, created, and controlled by the defense ministry can act as a break on politicization and corruption, especially at the local level. But they must still be oriented towards traditional police duties rather than standard military functions. The successful effort in the Philippines against the Huks (1946-1954) probably required the placing of the police under the Ministry of the Defense to ensure the new force was apolitical and not a tool for repressing the opponents of whatever political party held power. There can also be legal reasons for doing so in the eyes of the sending or receiving state. Here, placing the police in the Defense Ministry chain allowed the US to use military aid resources to train the constabulary. In the 1990s, though, doing this would have created suspicion. In Iraq after 2003, placing the police under what became a politicized and habitually Shia-controlled interior ministry made it easier to turn the police into a weapon for political retaliation and sectarian murder.[2] But, based on the post invasion conditions and existing ethnic and religious rivalries, this could very well have happened in Irag regardless of who ran the police.

One of the downsides to having police forces advised by the military is that this often leads to the militarization of policing (by which we mean turning the policing force into a military or quasi-military entity). This tends to occur in the face of an internal or external threat, particularly in a counterinsurgency environment. But the problem with militarization is that it too often results in the failure to develop a police force suitable for performing the critical day-to-day policing duties necessary for the smooth functioning of civil society.

Police and Counterinsurgency

Some believe that counterinsurgency is only or primarily a policing problem. Using this as a blanket response to insurgency is just as misguided as saying that police have no role in counterinsurgency. Generally, treating fighting in an insurgency as a criminal offense is a recipe for failure and for getting police killed for no gain. Police are certainly invaluable in a counterinsurgency environment. They provide intelligence support, situational awareness, security, reinforce the rule of law, aid state building, and the list goes on. Police can even effectively combat insurgents. But this is primarily the job of regular military units who are better trained, equipped, and supported for this task. Police can do it—and certainly should if the opportunity

2 Hammes, T.X., 'Raising and Mentoring Security Forces in Afghanistan and Iraq', *Orbis*, 60:1 (Winter 2016), pp. 316-317.

arises—but to make this the primary job of the police is to put the force's members into a situation they usually are not properly prepared to handle.

Sometimes police are used as auxiliaries to the army in counterinsurgency situations. This, historian William Rosenau points out, is 'ultimately self-defeating' because it 'leads inexorably to the neglect of what should be the primary police mission: the protection of the public from serious crime'. Rosenau gives us an example of misuse by citing a former Afghan police chief. This Afghan police official lamented that he and his men had been used as 'little soldiers', noting that they did 'extra work that is not police work. Firing rockets is not the job of police'.[3] In a counterinsurgency environment, 'Good police are most often the ones killed first'. If one is unfortunate enough to have the added obstacles of low pay, corruption, poor leadership, and little support from above, building a police force becomes 'the very definition of a Sisyphean task'. Moreover, 'Local police are not trained, armed, equipped, or organized to defeat insurgent attacks. Secure conditions must exist before local police can do their job'.[4]

During the Malaya (1948-1960) and Cyprus (1955-1959) insurgencies the police had daily contact with the civilian population, in both cases the well from which the guerrillas drew their support. Also, in both situations the military generally conducted offensive military operations, but since the insurgent groups were generally small, the armies rarely deployed units of brigade or battalion size. The army also acted in support of police operations. In general, the action was small scale and resembled policing tasks.[5]

What was more important to the success or failure of the counterinsurgency efforts here was not the force size, but the quality and quantity of the intelligence gathered.[6] Because of their constant contact with the population, the police are often a prime source of intelligence in a counterinsurgency environment. Unlike their ultimately successful compratriots in Malaya, the British police in Cyprus lacked a 'Special Branch'—and paid for this failure.[7] Not surprisingly, the role of the police in gathering intelligence is a critical element of the British Army officer Frank Kitson's theory of counterinsurgency.[8]

Sometimes governments misunderstand the role of police and use them as counterinsurgency forces when the insurgents are much stronger than the police sent

3 Rosenau, William, *'Low-Cost Trigger-Pullers': The Politics of Policing in the Context of Contemporary 'State Building' and Counterinsurgency* (Santa Monica: RAND, 2008), pp. 1-2, 27.

4 Dubik, James M., 'Creating Police and Law Enforcement Systems', *Best Practices in Counterinsurgency*, Report No. 4 (Washington, DC: Institute for the Study of War, Oct. 2010), pp. 2, 6.

5 Corum, James S., *Training Indigenous Forces in Counterinsurgency: A Tale of Two Insurgencies* (US Army War College, Carlisle, PA: Strategic Studies Institute, March 2006), p. 3.

6 Ibid., p. 36.

7 Ibid., pp. 31-33.

8 Kitson, Frank, *Low Intensity Operations: Subversion, Insurgency, and Peace-keeping* (Harrisburg, PA: Stackpole Books, 1971).

against them. Putting the police in the lead can be an effective approach. It puts a more civilian face on things because the police are actually in control. But this will only work if the insurgency is so small in scale that the police can handle problems most of the time.

Police are often used as the holding force in counterinsurgency operations after the regular army has cleared an area of insurgents. But what is often forgotten here is that the insurgents sometimes come back. When they do, the army must return to deal with them. If they do not, the existing police will be at great risk. If you lose your valuable human capital replacing it is very difficult. In Iraq and Afghanistan, Kramer and Whiteside show us that the military forces withdrew too soon.

Generally, creating a police force under combat conditions is a bad option and is very likely to lead to failure of the force, failure for its creator, the discrediting of the government for which it is intended to build support, and disaster for the population. Win the war first, or at least secure the area. Then build the police. Don't send a cop to do the soldier's job, and try to avoid employing soldiers as police. Send in the army if the insurgents reappear. We also understand that this is the ideal.

The Militia or Home Guard Problem

Militia, Home Guard, or similar paramilitary forces are often used as stop-gap security services to work as police or to make up for shortfalls in troop strength. Building regular forces is better than building militia as regular forces are more reliable and accountable. But as Brookings scholar Vanda Feldab-Brown observes, sometimes using or supporting a militia constitutes 'the least bad option...because formal military and police forces are totally corrupt, collapsed, or antagonistic'. Militia also have an unfortunate tendency to 'go rogue' and can become part of the problem instead of the solution. Felbab-Brown wisely points out that one 'needs from the very beginning to build into the effort a consideration of how to end and roll them back'.[9]

During the Malayan Emergency (1948-1960) one of the tools the British used was the creation of village Home Guards to provide local security at night by doing things such as taking shifts in the watchtowers. There were perhaps 100,000 men serving in such a capacity by 1951. It was greatly expanded as the war went on, and even included 50,000 members of the Chinese community, the primary source of insurgent support. The village Home Guards emerged as a force that could take over static security duties and thus free-up army and police units for more active work, while also assisting in 'Malayanization' of the struggle. Each state in Malaya eventually had

9 Felbab-Brown, Vanda, 'The Dubious Joys of Standing Up Militias and Building Partner Capacity: Lessons from Afghanistan and Mexico for Prosecuting Security Policy Through Proxies', *Brookings* (21 July 2015), pp. 1-2, 21.

training camps to provide basic military instruction to Home Guard members. It is generally considered to have been a success.[10]

The best way to use militia might be to revive the eighteenth and nineteenth century practice of *Petite Guerre*, or Little War or Partisan War, as it was sometimes called. These doctrinal approaches treated militia as quasi-soldiers—which is what militia are—rather than super-police. This, though, is certainly not the answer in every situation where militia use might arise as each is different. One should be careful of the short-term fix of relying on paramilitary units, they may cause long-term problems.

Failure

We also know that often police advising missions fail, and there is usually plenty of blame to go around when they do. Indeed, policing expert David Bayley notes that at least in regard to US efforts, 'As a general proposition, American foreign assistance has not been shown to contribute significantly or consistently to reforming police institutions abroad'.[11] Similarly, policing scholar Robert Perito writes that 'Between *Operation Just Cause* in Panama and *Operation Iraqi Freedom* more than a decade later, the United States established a pattern of failing to deal with large-scale breakdowns in public order that occurred after international interventions'.[12] When this occurs the sending nation will incur the political and prestige costs of this failure.

One of the reasons for the failure of police expeditionary advising is that the police forces are used incorrectly. For example, the post-First World War Haitian Gendarmerie was used for tasks other than its primary one—policing—such as running hospitals, managing how civil servants were paid, and counterinsurgency operations from 1919-1921.[13]

Limiting the power of the advisors can also contribute to failure. The US Marines who ran the gendarmerie mission to Haiti in the 1920s and 1930s could give orders and ensure compliance. The Marines in the 1959-1963 Haiti mission could only provide advice, nothing more. This made a big difference. Moreover, the interference of Haitian leader François Duvalier and weak US policy direction,

10 Corum, James S., 'Building the Malayan Army and Police—Britain's Experience During the Malayan Emergency, 1948-1960', in Gott, Kendall D. (ed.), *Security Assistance: US and International Historical Perspectives* (Leavenworth, KS: Combat Studies Institute Press, 2006), pp. 305-307.

11 Bayley, David H., *Changing the Guard: Developing Democratic Police Abroad* (Oxford: Oxford University Press, 2006), p. 109.

12 Perito, Robert M., *US Police in Peace and Stability Operations* (Washington, DC: United States Institute of Peace, 2007), p. 11.

13 Mihara, Robert 'Employment of the Philippine Constabulary (1901-1917) and Hatian Gendarmerie (1916-1934) in Civic Tasks, Such as Anti-Corruption, Against the Background of Counterinsurgency Campaigns', in Gott (ed.), *Security Assistance*, pp. 404-410.

meant that sometimes the US did not push back against Duvalier's actions, which also played a part.[14]

The failure to develop proper police forces in Iraq after 2003 was particularly pronounced. The US built a police force not aligned with the culture and that became a political tool used for ethnic cleansing. Arguably, in Iraq the police forces should have been under the Ministry of Defense instead of the Interior. Having them responsible to the Ministry of the Interior ensured their politicization.

In Afghanistan since 2001 we've seen an ever multiplying alphabet soup of police organizations created and trained by dozens of military and civilian organizations from dozens of nations. One could argue that there are simply too many forces, and that too often the West has tried to impose its own idea of policing on Afghanistan without seriously considering whether the ideas are applicable. Today, in 2018, Afghanistan still suffers from an active insurgency and a dysfunctional police organization.

As we touched on before, another reason for failure is that sometimes the regular army units are withdrawn too early. Kramer and Whiteside give us an example of the effects of this in Dand Wa Patan in Afghanistan. They note that 'withdrawal of coalition partner units in 2013 saw the dramatic rise of security issues. By 2015, the loss of checkpoints and the destruction of a brand new firebase were clear indications that security problems had erased any gains in the district seen by the employment of the paramilitary ALP'.

Another critical element in the success of expeditionary police advising is the simultaneous creation of supporting judicial and corrections systems. These are critical for building a successful police force as the police must know that their work and the risks that they take will have positive results. This also produces credibility and confidence among the population at large.[15] The British forces who established the local police force in Shkodra, Albania, in 1913 were prescient enough to set up courts at the same time as they established the police.[16]

On a related note: one also must have a judicial and legal solution to the problem of captured insurgents and terrorists. During the Hukbalahap (Huk) Rebellion in the Philippines (1946-1954), the Philippine government resisted necessary judicial reforms. Before the closing of a legal loophole, the government had to have a captured insurgent before a judge in six hours, and charge him within 24. This was virtually impossible and it was not unusual for captured Huks to be back with their units within 72 hours. This undermines the morale and effectiveness of the forces who are risking their lives to put the guerrillas away. With the memory of the brutal Japanese

14 Williamson, Charles T., *The US Naval Mission to Haiti, 1959-1963* (Annapolis, MD: Naval Institute Press), pp. 345-350.

15 Phelps, James R., 'Lessons in Developing Democratic Police from Post-Second World War Successes', *International Journal of Comparative and Applied Criminal Justice*, 34:1 (Spring 2010), p. 130.

16 Schmidl, Erwin, 'The International Operation in Albania, 1913-14', *International Security*, 6:3 (Autumn 1999), pp. 5-6.

occupation still fresh in the minds of the people, the government was reluctant to suspend habeas corpus because it feared a public outcry. This changed after a raid on the guerrilla politburo office in Manila furnished information that the insurgency was larger and more dangerous than the government realized.[17]

During the US mission to Haiti in the mid-1990s, the US made the mistake of providing too little funding to the judiciary and penal system by providing 80 percent of funds to the police. One author notes that 'There is little point in creating a functional police force if there is no functional judiciary and penal system'. Failing to do this destroys the faith of both the police and the population because judicial failures destroy or negate the results of good police work. This occurred in Haiti as people saw that arrests didn't result in curbing instability or violence in the country. This also contributed to the police taking matters into their own hands (which produced abuses) because the police knew they would soon see the perpetrator back on the street if they did not.[18]

George Frerks and Niels Terpstra also show us—as does Mark Moyar—the importance of establishing a justice system to accompany the construction or reform of police forces. Not doing this weakens the chances of police advising being effective. The weakness and corruption of the Afghan justice system fueled increasing use of Taliban courts in the province.[19] In the words of counterinsurgency expert Bernard Fall when writing about the penetration of the Communist Vietcong in the South Vietnamese countryside: 'When a country is being subverted it is not being outfought; it is being out-administered'.[20] In a similar respect, the US has never figured out a controversy-free means of dealing with prisoners captured during the so-called 'Global War on Terror'. The prison at Guantanamo Bay has not proven the most politically beneficial solution.[21]

Sometimes expeditionary police advising missions fail because of poor decisions made by the sending nations. Policing scholars Nathan Pino and Michael Wiatrowski argue that the two developed world policing models that are exported abroad—community policing and professional policing—are inappropriate for developing nations because the practices of these two approaches have 'not adequately addressed the following issues: human rights, equity, co-production with the citizenry and other public and private sector organizations, accountability, openness, and organizational change, to name a few. Instead of trying to import these models of policing, nation

17 Ladwig, Walter, 'When the Police are the Problem: The Philippine Constabulary and the Hukbalahap Rebellion', in Fair, C. Christine and Sumit Ganguly (eds), *Policing Insurgencies: Cops as Counterinsurgents* (Oxford: Oxford University Press, 2014), p. 39.
18 Mobekk, Eirin, 'International Involvement in Restructuring and Creating Security Forces: The Case of Haiti', *Small Wars & Insurgencies*, 12:3 (Autumn 2001), pp. 107-108.
19 See the contribution in this volume by Georg E. Frerks and Niels Terpsta.
20 Fall, Bernard B., 'The Theory and Practice of Insurgency and Counter-Insurgency', *Military Review* (Sept.-Oct. 2015), pp. 47-48.
21 I am indebted to my colleague Michael W. Jones for the Guantanamo point.

states ought to create their own versions of democratic policing based on international standards tailored to their own goals and needs'.[22] Pino and Wiatrowski make this particularly clear by noting that 'Many countries export their models of policing unilaterally or through UN missions, and in some cases have imposed their models on these countries. Many have been complicit in the para-militarization of police forces and the equation of security forces with police forces. This has limited, in part, the chances that police forces can be democratized. All of the above issues have retarded the building of social and human capital and citizen-police interaction and cooperation within a developing democratic model'.[23]

Another problem is that nations 'which bring developmental assistance frequently do so through the lens of their own national experience, which may be inapplicable or irrelevant'. The policymakers of the John F. Kennedy administration, 'in attempting to export the American police model, ... failed to consider whether US notions about internal security were appropriate for fractious and unstable regions of the world'. Kennedy, his advisor Robert Komer, and other key members of the administration looked at past counterinsurgency successes in Greece, the Philippines, and Malaya, and drew the lesson that by helping the local governments militarily and economically, success against Communist insurgents could be assured. Since providing policing and paramilitary assistance had worked so well in these earlier cases, it was deemed that it must certainly work well elsewhere. The Malayan victory had a particularly attractive draw. But they dismissed the failure of the French created village militias in Vietnam, or simply deemed it irrelevant. Only British successes mattered as they were America's Anglo-Saxon cultural brethren and counterinsurgency campaigns by other European states were considered tainted by imperialistic self-interest. They ignored the fact that British forces in Malaya ran the show and behaved as a colonial power. The Kennedy administration though, wanted to work through local leaders such as Ramon Magsaysay in the Philippines and Ngo Dinh Diem in Vietnam.[24]

In some cases, the advising or creating force misunderstands or simply ignores the wishes of the local inhabitants. For example, locals in Iraq in 2003 sometimes set up their own government and security forces, only to be forced by the US to disarm and disband them or see some of the leaders arrested. This practice was all the more counterproductive when these local forces observed former Baath Party members

22 Pino, Nathan and Michael D. Wiatrowski, 'Policing and Police Reform in the US: Adequate for Export?', in Pino, Nathan and Michael D. Wiatrowski (eds), *Democratic Policing in Transitional and Developing Countries* (Aldershot, Hampshire: Ashgate, 2006), p. 43.

23 Pino, Nathan and Michael D. Wiatrowski, 'Conclusion', in Pino, Nathan and Michael D. Wiatrowski (eds), *Democratic Policing in Transitional and Developing Countries* (Aldershot, Hampshire: Ashgate, 2006), p. 212.

24 Rosenau, William, 'The Kennedy Administration, US Foreign Internal Security Assistance and the Challenge of "Subterranean War", 1961-63', *Small Wars & Insurgencies*, 14:3 (2003), pp. 65, 87.

being installed because US government officials believed that these supposedly better skilled people were needed to ensure a quick return to order.[25]

Reformers can also sometimes put the cart before the horse. Pino and Wiatrowski note that 'Reforming policing into a democratic form is not likely to succeed unless we also work on democratizing the state and its institutions in general'.[26] One must first have a democratizing state and society before one can rationally expect the creation and development of a democratic police force.

We also have the problem of believing that simply throwing a large number of people at the problem—meaning police—provides an easy solution. In a counterinsurgency situation this is always part of the answer, but the problem can be the quality of the people, meaning: how well trained and prepared are these police? In response to the Malayan Emergency (1948-1960) the British rapidly expanded their police forces, but provided little or no training because of their dire need. For the next three years the British essentially made little progress against the communist insurgency. The British then brought in the best people they could find to train the Malayan police, which helped turn the tide in their favor. This was one of the reasons for their success.[27]

In Iraq, the initial police advisory efforts also threw great numbers of people at the problem of instability and insurgency. But the people thrown at the problem were poorly trained and not equipped to do the job. The result was a number of very short training programs that produced poorly trained police who were then often thrust into a non-permissive environment where too often they had to fight better armed and prepared insurgents.[28]

Another potential source of failure is the ability of the host nation to institute needed reforms or modernization, or even build a workable police force. Political scientist Sidharth Kaushal examines this issue in relation to naval advising, but the idea is no less applicable in the police advising realm.[29] Sometimes, the ground on which the advisors have to build is so barren or corrupt that it may be all but impossible for their efforts to bear productive fruit. At other times the host state may lack the organizational and structural ability to benefit from the mission. Some use

25 Pino, Nathan and Michael D. Wiatrowski, 'Introduction', in Pino and Wiatrowski (eds), *Democratic Policing in Transitional and Developing Countries*, p. 4.

26 Pino, Nathan and Michael D. Wiatrowski, 'Implementing Democratic Policing and Related Initiatives', in Pino and Wiatrowski (eds), *Democratic Policing in Transitional and Developing Countries*, p. 113.

27 Corum, 'Building the Malayan Army and Police', pp. 293-294, 299-302.

28 Bayley, David H. and Robert M. Perito, *The Police in War: Fighting Insurgency, Terrorism, and Violent Crime* (Boulder, CO: Lynne Riener Publishers, 2010), pp. 10-11; Hammes, 'Raising and Mentoring Security Forces in Afghanistan and Iraq', pp. 312-313.

29 Kaushal, Sidharth, 'Adoption Capacity Theory and Naval Doctrine: A Theory of Success and Failure in Naval Advise and Assist Missions to Modernizing States', in Stoker, Donald and Michael T. McMaster (eds), *Naval Advising and Assistance* (Solihull: Helion, 2017), pp. 41-67.

the numerous failed missions to Haiti as an example of this problem; others could point to Afghanistan after 2001, or Iraq after 2003.

Doing what is necessary to make the police effective in their jobs, as well as in counterinsurgency operations, might adversely affect the personal interests of the government or people in power. De-politicizing the Filipino police meant that the ruling Liberal Party could not use it to make sure elections went their way. This was one of the primary reasons for government resistance to police reform. The party providing outside aid may have to lean on or coerce their client to implement the necessary reforms.[30]

Police corruption always makes the job of the advisor more difficult. Mark Moyar makes this clear in his contribution. The police are often the first and sometimes the only arm of the state with which the people interact. During the Malayan Emergency (1948-1960), the Malayan police, especially the local, rural police, were notoriously corrupt.[31] It is believed that police are better for interacting with the civilians during counterinsurgency because they are more accustomed to doing so and are used to accomplishing the mission with the minimum necessary force. Thus, it is thought, they are less likely to alienate the population. But if the police are corrupt and abusive this does not hold true. Adequate pay and training cut-down on corruption and help to prevent abuses of the population. The police recruits should be properly vetted, properly trained, given good equipment and quarters, and paid a living, competitive wage. All of these steps will reduce corruption and abuses. It is cheaper in the long run—both in blood and money—to do things right.[32]

Another obstacle can be sectarian or ethnic tensions. Not addressing these—or failing to understand their relevance—can contribute to failure. During the Malayan Emergency (1948-1960), beginning in 1952 British leaders launched a concerted effort to recruit Chinese citizens as part of their effort to create a multi-ethnic police force. The Chinese had traditionally faced official discrimination at the hands of the Malay majority, something that partially fed Malaya's Chinese-based insurgency. Although this was not as successful as British leaders hoped, it was a step toward integrating the police within the broader demographics of Malayan society.[33] In contrast, in Cyprus Britain failed to create a multi-ethnic police force. The insurgents came to be seen by the Greek population of Cyprus as the only line of defense against a corrupt, brutal Turkish police. This is the opposite effect that should be produced.[34]

The lesson here can be carried over to sectarian differences. In Iraq (2003-2011), the police became a Shia-controlled tool, one often used for ethnic cleansing and mass murder. This undermines nation building efforts and destroys support for

30 Ladwig, 'When the Police are the Problem', p. 40.
31 Corum, 'Building the Malayan Army and Police', pp. 293-294.
32 Corum, *Training Indigenous Forces in Counterinsurgency*, p. 39; Ladwig, 'When the Police are the Problem', pp. 39-40.
33 Corum, 'Building the Malayan Army and Police', pp. 303-304.
34 Corum, *Training Indigenous Forces in Counterinsurgency*, pp. 45-46.

the government by crushing its credibility as an honest broker. This type of police organization feeds insurgencies instead of weakening them.

Kramer and Whiteside offer the following relevant lesson in building police forces from their examination of events in Iraq and Afghanistan: 'A healthy mix of locals and foreigners seemed to be an ideal solution but was rarely achieved for a variety of reasons—usually a lack of trust or deliberate sectarian engineering by partisan commanders'. Local recruitment is not always the best answer. Sometimes mixing locals with those from other areas is better.

Militarization

Internal and external security fears often drive the militarization of police forces. The Philippine Constabulary established by the US in the wake of its 1898 seizure of the Philippines, and the Haitian Gendarmerie the US established during the First World War, both became militarized because of security fears. The Filipinos feared an increasingly aggressive Japan and internal unrest, while Haitian leaders worried about threats from the Dominican Republic and an internal insurgency.[35]

Sometimes the militarization of police forces can cause as many problems as it solves. Unfortunately, as policing expert Robert Perito writes, 'Militarization of the police will produce a force that is inconsistent with the country's long-term needs'. Some experts believe that putting the US military in charge of training Iraqi police forces produced militarized police structures unable to perform law enforcement tasks and which could not meet Iraq's post-conflict policing needs.[36] The US police advising mission to Brazil was used to promote US interests during the Cold War, which specifically meant the prevention of Communist insurgent activity. But the US helped militarize a police force that before Brazil's transition to democracy in the 1980s had become an instrument of repression. The people grew to distrust the police and withdrew their support.[37]

The Filipino experience dealing with the Huk Rebellion (1946-1954) reveals the counterintuitive reality that paramilitary police formations in counterinsurgency are not necessarily the best answer. 'In this instance', as historian Walter Ladwig shows, 'the confused paramilitary nature of the PC [Philippine Constabulary], combined with the limited ability of the Philippine government to professionalize the force, rendered it poorly prepared to carry out either police or military missions. The effectiveness of the PC in COIN was only realized once it was bifurcated into a dedicated policing agency and a regular military force'.[38]

35 Mihara, Robert, 'Lesser Victories: A Study of the Philippine Constabulary and Haitian Gendarmerie' (MA thesis, Texas A&M University, 2007), pp. 101-102.
36 Perito, *The Iraq Federal Police*, p. 13.
37 Pino, Nathan and Michael D. Wiatrowski, 'Assessing the Obstacles', in Pino and Wiatrowski (eds), *Democratic Policing in Transitional and Developing Countries*, p. 37.
38 Ladwig, 'When the Police are the Problem', pp. 20, 39.

We also know that there is very often a direct link between using police for counterinsurgency and police militarization. In some ways this is perfectly understandable because of the desire to give the police the means to defend themselves from sometimes more heavily-armed insurgents, coupled with governmental insistence (and sometimes dire need) to use the police as a counterinsurgency force rather than a policing force. During the Malayan Emergency (1948-1960), British officials up-gunned the police, even supplying them with armored cars.[39] But the police at this point often cease to be police, an alternative approach that includes significant risk.

In counterinsurgency situations in particular, sometimes police forces evolve into paramilitary formations unintentionally because they are pushed to do far more than what they were intended to do.[40] One counter to militarization might be having the police trained by police and not by soldiers, as was done during the Malayan Emergency.[41]

Building Effective Police Forces Takes Time—Sometimes A Lot of Time

It is important to keep in mind that to build and put in the field a civilian police force can easily take a year or more *after* the end of combat operations.[42] One year would be considered short. It took much longer to build police forces in Iraq, West Germany, Japan, Kosovo, and Timor-Leste. In 2008, ten years after it began, 2,000 foreign police were still in Kosovo. The UN police forces were pulled out too early from Timor-Leste and the state's leaders begged for their return.[43]

Moreover, training an effective police force, particularly an effective cadre of leaders, will take time *and* be expensive. Policing expert Otto Marenin noted that: 'What the police are, what they do, and what their work means to society have to be built from the bottom up'.[44] In Malaya, senior leaders were sometimes sent abroad for courses lasting from six months to one year. Though expensive, this approach proved successful in professionalizing these forces and building expertise. What is also critical to remember here is that during the time it takes to train and develop a professional police force, the army will have to carry the security load.[45]

Retired US Army Lieutenant General James M. Dubik (who had experience in police advising in Haiti, Iraq, and Afghanistan), urges the creation of a national army as well as a national level paramilitary force that can deal with insurgents. These

39 Corum, 'Building the Malayan Army and Police', p. 301.
40 Ladwig, 'When the Police are the Problem', p. 20.
41 Corum, *Training Indigenous Forces in Counterinsurgency*, p. 40.
42 Pino and Wiatrowski, 'Implementing Democratic Policing and Related Initiatives', p. 112.
43 Phelps, James, 'Lessons in Developing Democratic Police from Post-Second World War Successes', p. 131.
44 Marenin, Otwin, review article, 'Police Performance and State Rule: Control and Autonomy in the Exercise of Coercion', *Comparative Politics*, 18:1 (Oct. 1985), pp. 101-122.
45 Corum, *Training Indigenous Forces in Counterinsurgency*, pp. 42-43.

should be supported by local police forces. His key point: 'Local police are not trained, armed, equipped, or organized to defeat insurgent attacks. Secure conditions must exist before local police can do their job'. The creation of both the national and local police forces requires the creation of the necessary training and administrative systems and physical infrastructure, as well as the important judicial and penal institutions to support the work of the police. The entire law enforcement system must be built. Critically, it takes a long time to build a trusted judicial system. This must usually be done in a phased manner, and all of it should be done under one governmental wing—if possible. An interim solution that meets the situation on the ground must be established. All of this must complement the host nation's culture and the environment, but ultimately security is the prime requisite for building a successful police force.[46] It is difficult to disagree with General Dubik's recommendations, and his article on this should be read by everyone with a serious interest in police advising.

If Nothing Ever Works, Then What Do We Do?

One of the reasons advising—including police advising—is important is because of the qualms of US policymakers regarding overseas involvements and interventions. But advising in the George W. Bush and Barack Obama years—particularly the building partner capacity plank—has too often proven an abysmal, abject, and humiliating failure, something supported by numerous examples: the violent sectarianism of Iraqi police; the collapse of Iraq's forces in 2014 in the face of the Islamic State's advance; Yemen's collapse in 2015 (shortly after President Obama made a speech touting Yemen as an administration success); the Afghani loss of Kunduz to the Taliban in October 2015; and the debacle of training a Free Syrian Army that failed to produce an army. If the US is going to fight its wars by having forces it is advising carry the weight, then US political and military leaders have much to learn about how to fight this way.

This advice from General Dubik offers the perfect ending: 'Creating police is actually about fielding police under the right conditions while creating a local-to-national security and law enforcement scheme that reflects the history and culture of a nation and adheres to that nation's idea of what is just'.[47]

46 Dubik, 'Creating Police and Law Enforcement Systems', pp. 2-3.
47 Ibid., p. 8

Select Bibliography

Abbas, Hassan, *Reforming Pakistan's Police and Law Enforcement Infrastructure* (Washington, DC: United States Institute of Peace Press, 2011).

Abu Dhabi Police, *Fifty Years of Progress, 1957-2007* (Abu Dhabi, 2007).

Agyeman-Duah, Baffour, *The United States and Ethiopia: Military Assistance and the Quest for Security, 1953-1993* (Lanham, MD: University Press of America, 1994).

Aguilar, Sérgio Luiz Cruz, 'South Atlantic: Brazil-Africa Relations in the Field of Security and Defense', *Austral: Brazilian Journal of Strategy and International Relations*, 2:4 (July-Dec. 2013), pp. 47-68.

Ahern, Thomas, *Vietnam Declassified: The CIA and Counterinsurgency* (Lexington: University of Kentucky Press, 2010).

Akhund, Nadine, 'Stabilizing a Crisis and the Mürzsteg Agreement of 1903: International Efforts to Bring Peace to Macedonia', *Hungarian Historical Review*, 3:3 (2014), pp. 587-608.

Aldous, Christopher, *The Police in Occupation Japan: Control, Corruption, and Resistance to Reform* (London: Routledge, 1997).

Alexander, R.C., III, 'Reform of the Police System During the Occupation of Japan, 1945-1952' (MA thesis, Washington University 1966).

Al-Khalidi, Suleiman, 'Jordanian Officer Shoots Dead Two Americans, One South African at Security Training Site', *Reuters*, 9 Nov. 2015.

Al Shaali, Khalifa Rashid, 'Crime Control, Policing and Security in the United Arab Emirates' (PhD dissertation, University of Wales at Aberystwyth, 1999).

Al Shaali, Khalifa Rashid and Kibble, Neil, 'Policing and Police Accountability in the UAE: The Case for Reform', *Arab Law Quarterly*, 15:3 (2000), pp. 272-303.

Anderson, David M., 'Policing the Settler State', in Engels, Dagmar and Shula Mars (eds), *Contesting Colonial Hegemony: State and Society in Africa and India* (London: British Academic Press, 1994).

_____, and David Killingray (eds), *Policing and Decolonisation: Politics, Nationalism, and the Police, 1917-65* (Manchester: Manchester University Press, 1992).

Andrade, Dale, *Ashes to Ashes: The Phoenix Program and the Vietnam War* (Lexington: Lexington Books, 1990).

_____ and James H. Willbanks, 'CORDS/Phoenix: Counterinsurgency Lessons from Vietnam for the Future', *Military Review* 86:2 (March-April 2006), pp. 9-23.

Arfsten, D.P., J.F. Moralez, L.L. Chester Jr., P. Mohamad, and T.H. Weber, 'Drug Use among the Afghanistan National Police: A National Assessment', *Military Medicine*, 177:1 (2012), pp. 85-90.

Arne, T.J. *Svenskarna och Österlandet* (Stockholm: Natur och Kultur, 1952).

Attewell, Wesley, 'Ghosts in the Delta: USAID and the Historical Geographies of the Vietnam's 'Other War'', *Environment and Planning A*, 47 (2015), pp. 2257-2275.

Aussaresses, Paul, *The Battle of the Casbah: Terrorism and Counter-Terrorism in Algeria, 1955-1957* (New York: Enigma Books, 2002).

Bailey, John and Lucía Dammert (eds), *Public Security and Police Reforms in the Americas* (Pittsburgh: University of Pittsburgh Press, 2006).

Balko, Radley, *Rise of the Warrior Cop: The Militarization of America's Police Forces* (New York: Public Affairs, 2013).

Bayley, David H., *Changing the Guard: Developing Democratic Police Abroad* (Oxford: Oxford University Press, 2006).

_____, *Democratizing the Police Abroad: What to Do and How to Do It* (Washington, DC: US Department of Justice, 2001).

_____, *Patterns of Policing: A Comparative International Analysis* (New Brunswick, NJ: Rutgers University Press, 1985).

_____, *Policing for the Future* (Oxford: Oxford University Press, 1994).

_____, and C. Shearing, 'The Future of Policing', *Law and Society Review*, 30 (1996), pp. 585-606.

Bayley, David H., and Robert M. Perito, *The Police in War: Fighting Insurgency, Terrorism, and Violent Crime* (Boulder, CO: Lynne Riener, 2010).

Beaumont, R.A., 'Almanac: The Constabulary Function Dilemma', *Military Review*, 79:1 (1999), pp. 57-60.

Beckett, Ian F.W., 'Robert Thompson and the British Advisory Mission to South Vietnam, 1961–1965', *Small Wars & Insurgencies*, 8:3 (1997), pp. 41-63.

Bergin, Anthony and Karl Claxton, 'Shock Without Awe: Military Lessons of the Regional Assistance Mission to the Solomon Islands', *PRISM*, 5:3 (2014), pp. 161-173.

Berman, Larry, *Planning a Tragedy: The Americanization of the War in Vietnam* (New York: W.W. Norton and Co., 1982).

Bessel, Richard, 'Militarisierung und Modernisierung: Polizeiliches Handeln in der Weimarer Republik', in Lüdtke, Alf (ed.), *'Sicherheit' und 'Wohlfahrt': Polizei, Gesellschaft und Herrschaft im 19. und 20. Jahrhundert* (Frankfurt am Main: Suhrkamp, 1992), pp. 323-343.

______, 'Policing in East Germany in the Wake of the Second World War', *Crime, History and Societies*, 7:2 (2003), pp. 5-21.

Black, Jeremy, *Insurgency and Counterinsurgency: A Global History* (London: Bloomsbury, 2016).

Blake, Philip, 'Cordon and Search', in *Infantry Magazine* (ed.), *A Distant Challenge: The US Infantryman in Vietnam, 1967-1972* (Nashville: The Battery Press, 1983), pp. 39-43.

Blood, Philip, *Hitler's Bandit Hunters: The SS and the Nazi Occupation of Europe* (Washington, DC: Potomac Books, 2006).

Bowling, Ben, and James Sheptycki, *Global Policing* (London: Sage, 2012).

Brewer, John D., *The Royal Irish Constabulary: An Oral History* (Belfast: Institute of Irish Studies, 1990).

Cable, Larry E., *Conflict of Myths: The Development of American Counterinsurgency Doctrine during the Vietnam War* (New York; New York University Press, 1986).

Calixte, D.P., 'Garde d'Haiti: Its Progress and Future Plans', *Marine Corps Gazette*, 20:1 (Feb. 1936), p. 16-17, 63.

Caldwell, William B., and Nathan K. Finney, 'Building Police Capacity in Afghanistan: The Challenges of a Multilateral Approach', *PRISM*, 2:1 (Dec. 2010), pp. 121-130.

Call, Charles T. (ed.), *Constructing Justice and Security After War* (Washington, DC: United States Institute of Peace Press, 2007).

_____, 'War Transitions and the New Civilian Security in Latin America', *Comparative Politics*, 35:1 (October 2002), pp. 1-20.

Carafano, James Jay and Richard Weitz, *Mismanaging Mayhem: How Washington Responds to Crisis* (Westport: Praeger, 2007).

Carland, John M., 'Document of Note: Winning the Vietnam War: Westmoreland's Approach in Two Documents', *The Journal of Military History*, 68:2 (April 2004), pp. 553-574.

Carlberg, Eric, *På uppdrag i Persien. Glimtar från en trettioårig vistelse under solens och lejonets tecken* (Stockholm: Natur och Kultur, 1962).

Carter, L. and K. Connor, *A Preliminary Investigation of Contemporary Afghan Councils* (Peshawar: ACBAR, 1989).

'Cent cinquante gendarmes français en mission en Afghanistan', *Le Monde*, 16 November 2009.

Chapman, Brian, *Police State* (New York: Praeger, 1970).

Chapman, Jessica, *Cauldron of Resistance: Ngo Dinh Diem, the United States, and 1950s Southern Vietnam (Ithaca*: Cornell University Press, 2013).

Chappell, Duncan and John Evans, 'The Role and Functions of Civilian Police in United Nations Peace-Keeping Operations', *Commonwealth Law Bulletin*, 24:3-4 (August 2010), pp. 1248-1316.

Cigar, Norman, *Tribal Militias: An Effective Tool to Counter Al Qaida and its Affiliates?* (Carlisle: Strategic Studies Institute, US Army War College Press, November 2014).

Clarke, Jeffrey, *Advice and Support: The Final Years, 1965-1973* (Washington, DC: Center for Military History, 1988).

Clayton, Anthony and David Killingray, *Khaki and Blue: Military and Police in British Colonial Africa* (Athens, OH: Ohio University Center for International Studies, 1989).

Clemens, Peter, 'Captain James Hausman, US Military Advisor to Korea, 1946-48: The Intelligent Man on the Spot', *The Journal of Strategic Studies*, 25:1 (Mar. 2002), pp. 163-198.

Cline, Lawrence E., 'The New Constabularies: Planning US Military Stabilization Missions', *Small Wars and Insurgencies*, 14:3 (2003), pp. 158-184.

Clutterbuck, Richard, *Guerillas and Terrorists* (London: Faber and Faber Limited, 1977).

Coburn, N., *Informal Justice and the International Community in Afghanistan* (Washington, DC: United States Institute of Peace, 2013), <http://www.usip.org/publications/informal-justice-and-the-international-community-in-afghanistan>.

Comber, Leon, *Malaya's Secret Police: The Role of Special Branch in the Malayan Emergency* (Singapore: Institute of Southeast Asian Studies, 2008).

Cooperation for Peace and Unity, *2014 Final Assessment Report of the Dutch Integrated Police Training Mission in Kunduz* (Kabul: Cooperation for Peace and Unity (CPAU), 2015).

Corum, James S., 'Building the Malayan Army and Police—Britain's Experience During the Malayan Emergency, 1948-1960', in Gott, Kendall D. (ed.), *Security Assistance: US and International Historical Perspectives* (Leavenworth, KS: Combat Studies Institute Press, 2006), pp. 291-313.

_____, *Training Indigenous Forces in Counterinsurgency: A Tale of Two Insurgencies* (Carlisle, PA: Strategic Studies Institute and US Army War College Press, 2006).

Cottam, Martha and Joe Huseby, *Confronting al Qaeda: The Sunni Awakening and American Strategy in al Anbar* (Lanham, MD: Rowman and Littlefield, 2016).

Cronin, Stephanie, *The Army and the Creation of the Pahlavi State in Iran, 1910-1926* (New York: I.B. Tauris and Company, 1997).

Daddis, Gregory A., 'CORDS in Charge: Organizing for Pacification Support in the Vietnam War', in Seidule, Ty and Jacqueline Whitt (eds), *Stand Up and Fight! The Creation of US Security Organizations, 1942-2005* (Carlisle, PA: Strategic Studies Institute and US Army War College Press, 2015), pp. 139-158.

DeRouen, Karl and Uk Heo, *Defense and Security: A Compendium of Armed Forces and Security Policies* (Santa Barbara, CA: ABC-CLIO, 2005).

Diedrich, Torsten and Rüdiger Wenzke, *Die getarnte Armee: Geschichte der Kasernierten Volkspolizei der DDR, 1952-1956* (Berlin: Christoph Links Verlag, 2001).

Dimitrijevic, Bojan, 'The Mutual Defense Aid Program in Tito's Yugoslavia, 1951-1958, and its Technical Impact', *The Journal of Slavic Military Studies*, 10:2 (June 1997), pp. 19-33.

Dirkx, T., *At the Margins of the State: Intervention-induced Opportunities for Arbakai Militias in the Context of the Dutch Integrated Police-Training Mission, in Kunduz Province, Afghanistan* (Kabul: CPAU, 2013).

Dobbins, James, Seth G. Jones, Keith Crane, Andrew Rathmell, Brett Steele, Richard Testschik, and Anga Timilsina, *The UN's Role in Nation-Building: From the Congo to Iraq* (Santa Monica, CA: RAND, 2005).

Dobbins, James, John G. McGinn, Keith Crane, Seth Jones, Rollie Lal, Andrew Rathnell, Rachel Swanger, and, Anga Timilsina, *America's Role in Nation Building: From Germany to Iraq* (Santa Monica, CA: RAND, 2003).

Dubik, James M., 'Creating Police and Law Enforcement Systems', *Best Practices in Counterinsurgency*, Report No. 4 (Washington, DC: Institute for the Study of War, Oct. 2010).

Dwan, Renate, *Executive Policing: Enforcing the Law in Peace Operations* (Oxford: Oxford University Press, 2002).

Eide, Espen Barth Holm and Tor Tanke Holm (eds), *Peacebuilding and Police Reform* (London: Frank Cass, 2000).

Elliot, David W.P., 'Hanoi's Strategy in the Second Indochina War', in Werner, Jayne S. and Luu Doan Huynh (eds), *The Vietnam War: Vietnamese and American Perspectives* (Armonk, NY: M.E. Sharpe, 1993), pp. 79-83.

Ellison, Graham and Conor O'Reilly, 'From Empire to Iraq and the "War on Terror": The Transplantation and Commodification of the (Northern) Irish Policing Experience', *Police Quarterly*, 11:4 (May 2008), pp. 395-426.

Ellison, Graham and Jim Smyth, *The Crowned Harp: Policing in Northern Ireland* (London: Pluto Press, 2000).

Emsley, Clive and Barbara Weinberger (eds), *Policing Western Europe: Politics, Professionalization, and Public Order, 1850-1940* (Westport: Greenwood Press, 1991).

Etzioni, Amitai, 'A Self-Restrained Approach to Nation-Building by Foreign Powers', *International Affairs*, 80:1 (Jan. 2004), pp. 1-17.

Evans, E.C., *The Development of Japan's Police System from Prewar to Present Time* (BA thesis, Harvard University, 1977).

Fair, C. Christine and Sumit Ganguly (eds), *Policing Insurgencies: Cops as Counterinsurgents* (Oxford: Oxford University Press, 2014).

Fazlhashemi, Mohammad, 'Kolonialt medvetande utan kolonier. Svenska officerare på uppdrag i 1910 talets Persien', in Berg, Magnus and Veronica Trépagny (eds), *I andra länder: historiska perspektiv på svensk förmedling av det främmande: en antologi* (Lund: Historika Media, 1999), pp. 111-134.

_____, 'Officerare och ingenjörer i civilisationens tjänst', *Lychnos, Årsbok för idé- och lärdomshistoria* (Uppsala: Lärdomshistoriska, 2001).

_____, 'Sweden ii. Swedish Officers in Persia, 1911-1915', *Encyclopedia Iranica* (15 Aug. 2006), <http://www.iranicaonline.org/articles/sweden-ii>.

Felbab-Brown, Vanda, 'The Dubious Joys of Standing Up Militias and Building Partner Capacity: Lessons from Afghanistan and Mexico for Prosecuting Security Policy Through Proxies', *Brookings* (21 July 2015), pp. 1-12, <https://www.brookings.edu/research/the-dubious-joys-of-standing-up-militias-and-building-partner-capacity-lessons-from-afghanistan-and-mexico-for-prosecuting-security-policy-through-proxies/>.

Fijnaut, Cyrille (ed.), *The Impact of World War II on Policing in North-West Europe* (Leuven Belgium: Leuven University Press, 2004).

Fisher, Christopher, 'The Illusion of Progress', *Pacific Historical Review*, 75:1 (2006), pp. 25-51.

Fleming, Robert and Hugh Miller, *Scotland Yard* (London: Michael Joseph, 1994).

Foran, W. Robert, *The Kenya Police, 1887-1960* (London: Hale Publishing, 1962).

Fosdick, Raymond, *European Police Systems* (Montclair, NJ: Patterson Smith, 1969).

Gaitley, Scott J., 'Securing Dan Patan: A US Infantry Squad's Counterinsurgency Program in an Afghan Village', in Wright, Donald P. (ed.), *Vanguard of Valor*, Vol. II (Fort Leavenworth, KS: Combat Studies Institute Press, US Army Combined Arms Center, 2011), pp. 125-146.

Galula, David, *Counterinsurgency Warfare: Theory and Practice* (Westport, CT: Praeger, 2006).

Giustozzi, Antonio, and Mohammad Isaqzadeh, 'Afghanistan's Paramilitary Policing in Context: The Risks of Expediency', *Afghan Analysts Network Thematic Report*, 7 (November 2011), pp. 1-36.

_____ and _____, *Policing Afghanistan: The Politics of the Lame Leviathan* (New York: Columbia University Press, 2012).

Giustozzi, Antonio and Artemy Kalinovsky, with Paul Robinson, Bob Spencer, and Alfia Sorokina, *Missionaries of Modernity: Advisory Missions and the Struggle for Hegemony in Afghanistan and Beyond* (London: Hurst, 2016).

Goldsmith, Andrew and James Sheptycki (eds), *Crafting Transnational Policing: Police Capacity-Building and Global Policing Reform* (Oxford: Hart Publishing, 2007).

Goldwert, Marvin, *The Constabulary in the Dominican Republic and Nicaragua: Progeny and Legacy of United States Intervention* (Gainesville, FL: University of Florida Press, 1962).

Gómez Rojas, Claudia Patricia, and Estela Baracaldo Méndez, 'La Corresponsabilidad: Una Estrategia para la Convivencia y la Seguridad Ciudadana en la Policia Nacional de Colombia', *Urvio: Revista Latinoamericana de Seguridad Ciudadana*, 2 (September 2007), pp. 99-111.

Goodhand, J., 'Corrupting or Consolidating the Peace? The Drugs Economy and Post-conflict Peacebuilding in Afghanistan', *International Peacekeeping*, 15:3 (2008), pp. 405-423.

Gordon, Sandy, 'Policing Terrorism in India', *Crime, Law, and Social Change*, 50:1 (June 2008), pp. 111-124.

Goslinga, Gorrit T.A., 'The Dutch in Albania (A History of the First Albanian Gendarmerie Organized and Directed by Dutch Officers, 1913-1914)' [Part 1], *Shêjzat*, 15:4-6 (1971), pp. 117-130.

_____, 'The Dutch in Albania (A History of the First Albanian Gendarmerie Organized and Directed by Dutch Officers, 1913-1914)' [Part 2], *Shêjzat*, 15:7-9 (1971), pp. 224-238.

_____, 'The Dutch in Albania (A History of the First Albanian Gendarmerie Organized and Directed by Dutch Officers, 1913-1914)' [Part 3], *Shêjzat*, 16 (1972), pp. 14-51.

Gott, Kendall D (ed.), *Security Assistance: US and International Historical Perspectives* (Leavenworth, KS: Combat Studies Institute Press, 2006).

Government Accountability Office, *Afghanistan Security: Efforts to Establish Army and Police Have Made Progress, but Future Plans Need to be Better Defined* (Washington, DC: GAO, 2005).

Government of Pakistan, *Police Organization in Pakistan* (Lahore: Commonwealth Human Rights Commission of Pakistan, 2010).

Gwynn, Charles, *Imperial Policing* (London: Macmillan, 1939).

Gyllenhaal, Lars and Lennart Westberg, *Svenskar i krig, 1914-1945* (Lund: Historiska Media, 2004).

Haberfeld, M.R. and Ibrahim Cerrah (eds), *Comparative Policing: The Struggle for Democratization* (Los Angeles, CA: Sage, 2008).

Hammes, T.X., 'Raising and Mentoring Security Forces in Afghanistan and Iraq', *Orbis*, 60:1 (Winter 2016), pp. 277-344.

Hancock, L., *Women and the Afghan Police,* Oxfam Novib Policy Paper (The Hague: Oxfam Novib, 2013).

Hansen, Annika, 'Civil-Military Cooperation: The Military, Paramilitaries, and Civilian Police in Executive Policing', in Dwan, Renata (ed.), *Executive Policing: Enforcing the Law in Peace Operations* (Oxford: Oxford University Press, 2002), pp. 67-84.

Harvey, A.D., 'Who Were the Auxiliaries?' *Historical Journal*, 35:3 (September 1992), pp. 665-669.

Hashimoto, Chikara, 'British Security Liaison in the Middle East: The Introduction of Police/Security Advisers and the Lebanon-Iraq-Jordan 'Anti-Communist Triangle' from 1949-1958', *Intelligence and National Security*, 27:6 (Dec. 2012), pp. 848-874.

Havron, M. Dean, William Chenault, James Dodson, and A. Terry Rambo, *Constabulary Capabilities for Low-Level Conflict* (Washington, DC: Office of Naval Research, 1969).

Herrington, Stuart, *Silence was a Weapon: The Vietnam War in the Villages* (New York: Presidio Press, 1982).

Hewad, G., *Legal, Illegal: Militia Recruitment and (Failed) Disarmament in Kunduz* (Kabul: Afghan Analyst Network (AAN), 2013).

Hills, Alice, *Policing Africa: Internal Security and the Limits of Liberalization* (Boulder, CO: Lynne Rienner Publishers, 2000)

_____, *Policing Post-Conflict Cities* (London: Zed Books, 2009).

Hoelscher, Kristian and Per M. Norheim-Martinsen, 'Urban Violence and the Militarisation of Security: Brazilian 'Peacekeeping' in Rio de Janeiro and Port-au-Prince', *Small Wars and Insurgencies*, 25:5-6 (October 2014), pp. 957-975.

Holland, Jack and Susan Phoenix, *Phoenix—Policing the Shadows: The Secret War against Terrorism in Northern Ireland* (London: Hodder and Stoughton, 1996).

Huggins, Martha K., *Political Policing: The United States and Latin America* (Durham, NC: Duke University Press, 1998).

Hulsander, Robert and Jake Spivey, 'Village Stability Operations and Afghan Local Police', *PRISM*, 3:3 (June 2012), pp. 125-138.

Human Rights Watch, *'Just Don't Call it a Militia': Impunity, Militias, and the 'Afghan Local Police'* (New York: Human Rights Watch, 2011).

Hunt, Richard, *Pacification: The American Struggle for Vietnam's Hearts and Minds* (Boulder: Westview Press, 1995).

Hutchison, W.E. (ed.), *History of the Nonmilitary Activities of the Occupation of Japan: Legal and Judicial Reform (1945-1951)* (Japan, Supreme Commander of the Allied Powers, General Headquarters, Undated).

Ince, Matthew, 'The EU's Afghan Police Mission: Failing to Meet Commitments', *Small Wars Journal* (12 Mar. 2011).

Ineichen, Markus, *Die schwedischen Offiziere in Persien (1911-1916)* (Bern: Peter Lang, 2002).

International Crisis Group, 'Policing in Afghanistan: Still Searching for a Strategy', *Crisis Group Asia*, Briefing No. 85 (18 Dec. 2008).

_____, 'Reforming Afghanistan's Police', *Crisis Group Asia*, Report No. 138 (30 Aug. 2007).

_____, 'The Future of the Afghan Local Police', *Crisis Group Asia*, Report No. 268 (4 June 2015).

_____, 'Women and Conflict in Afghanistan', *Crisis Group Asia*, Report No. 252 (14 October 2013).

Jafa, Yateendra Singh, 'Defeating Terrorism: A Study of Operational Strategy and Tactics of Police Forces in Jammu and Kashmir (India)', in Lowe, David, Austin Turk and Dilip K. Das (eds), *Examining Political Violence: Studies of Terrorism, Counterterrorism, and Internal War* (Boca Raton, FL: CRC Press, 2014), pp. 261-288.

Jayamaha, Dilshika, Scott Brady, Ben Fitzgerald, and Jason Fritz, *Lessons Learned from US Government Law Enforcement in International Operations* (Carlisle, PA: United States Army War College, 2010).

Johnson, Herbert A., Nancy Travis Wolfe, and Mark Jones, *History of Criminal Justice*, 4th ed. (Newark, NJ: Matthew Bender and Company, 2008).

Johnson, Robert and Timothy Clack (eds), *At the End of Military Intervention: Historical, Theoretical, and Applied Approaches to Transition, Handover, and Withdrawal* (Oxford: Oxford University Press, 2015).

Jones, Frank, *Blowtorch: Robert Komer, Vietnam, and American Cold War Strategy* (Annapolis: Naval Institute Press, 2013).

Jones, Seth G., Jeremy M. Wilson, Andrew Rathmell, and K. Jack Riley, *Establishing Law and Order after Conflict* (Santa Monica, CA: RAND, 2005).

Keller, Dennis E., *US Military Forces and Police Assistance in Stability Operations: The Least-Worst Option to Fill the US Capacity Gap* (Carlisle, PA: Strategic Studies Institute, Aug. 2010).

Kelly, Terrence, *Options for Transitional Security Capabilities for America* (Santa Monica, CA: RAND, 2006).

Kelly, Terrence, Seth Jones, James Barnett, Keith Crane, Robert Davis and Carl Jenson, *A Stability Police Force for the United States: Justification and Options for Creating US Capabilities* (Santa Monica, CA: RAND, 2009).

Kelly, Terrence, Nora Bensahel, and Olga Oliker, *Security Force Assistance in Afghanistan: Identifying Lessons for Future Efforts* (Santa Monica, CA: RAND, 2011).

Kenninson, Peter, and Amanda Loumansky, 'Shooting to Kill: Understanding the Police Use of Force in Combatting Suicide Terrorism', *Crime, Law and Social Change*, 47:3 (March 2007), pp. 151-168.

Kilcullen, David, *Counterinsurgency* (London: Hurst and Company, 2010).

_____, *The Accidental Guerrilla: Fighting Small Wars in the Midst of a Big One* (Oxford: Oxford University Press, 2009).

Kitson, Frank, *Low Intensity Operations: Subversion, Insurgency and Peacekeeping* (London: Faber and Faber, 1971).

Klare, M.T., *War Without End: American Planning for the Next Vietnams* (New York: Vintage Books, 1972).

Komer, Robert, *Organization and Management of the 'New Model' Pacification Program, 1966-1969* (Santa Monica: RAND, 1970).

_____, 'Was There Another Way?', in Thompson, Scott and Donaldson Frizzell (eds), *The Lessons of Vietnam* (New York: Crane, Russak & Comapany, Inc., 1977), pp. 211-230.

Kraska, Peter B. (ed.), *Militarizing the American Criminal Justice System: The Changing Roles of the Armed Forces and the Police* (Boston, MA: Northeastern University Press, 2001).

_____, and Louis J. Cubellis, 'Militarizing Mayberry and Beyond: Making Sense of American Paramilitary Policing', *Justice Quarterly*, 14:4 (December 1997), pp. 607-29.

_____, and Victor E. Kappeler, 'Militarizing American Police: The Rise and Normalization of Paramilitary Units', *Social Problems*, 44:1 (February 1997), pp. 1-18.

Krekvik, Ola, 'Transferring Responsibility for Security in Afghanistan: Norwegian Officers' Challenges When Cooperating With the Afghan National Security Forces' (MA thesis, University of Oslo, 2011).

Krongard, Howard J. and Joseph E. Schmitz, *Interagency Assessment of Iraq Police Training* (Washington, DC: Department of State and Department of Defense, 2005).

Kuzmarov, Jeremy, *Modernizing Repression: Police Training and Nation-Building in the American Century* (Amherst, MA: University of Massachusetts Press, 2012).

Ladwig, Walter C., 'Training Foreign Police: A Missing Aspect of US Security Assistance to Counterinsurgency', *Comparative Strategy*, 26:4 (October 2007), pp. 285-293.

_____, 'When the Police are the Problem: The Philippine Constabulary and the Hukbalahap Rebellion', in Fair, C. Christine and Sumit Ganguly (eds), *Policing Insurgencies: Cops as Counterinsurgents* (Oxford: Oxford University Press, 2014), pp. 19-45.

Lansdale, Edward G., *In the Midst of Wars: An American Mission to Southeast Asia* (New York: Harper and Row, 1972).

Lawrence, Mark, *Assuming the Burden: Europe and the American Commitment to War in Vietnam* (Berkeley: University of California Press, 2005).

Leeson, D.M., *The Black and Tans: British Police and Auxiliaries in the Irish War of Independence, 1920-1921* (Oxford: Oxford University Press, 2011).

Lefèvre, Mathieu, *Local Defence in Afghanistan* (Kabul: Afghan Analysts Network, 2010).

Liang, His-huey, *The Berlin Police Force in the Weimar Republic* (Berkeley: University of California Press, 1970).

Lindenberger, Thomas, *Volkpolizei: Herrschaftspraxis und* öffentliche *Ordnung im SED-Staat, 1952-1968* (Köln: Böhlau Verlag, 2003).

Long, Austin and Andrew Radin, 'Enlisting Islam for an Effective Afghan Police', *Survival*, 54:2 (April 2012), pp. 113-128.

Lowe, W.J., 'The War Against the RIC, 1919-21', *Éire-Ireland*, 37:3-4 (Fall/Winter 2002), pp. 79-117.

Lüdtke, Alf, *Police and State in Prussia, 1815-1850* (New York: Cambridge University Press, 1989).

Malcolm, Elizabeth, *The Irish Policeman, 1822-1922: A Life* (Dublin: Four Courts Press, 2006).

Malinowski, Tom and Charles O. Blaha, 'De-Militarizing Civilian Security in Mexico and the Northern Triangle', *PRISM*, 5:4 (2014), pp. 27-33.

Marcella, Gabriel, *Democratic Governance and the Rule of Law: Lessons from Colombia* (Carlisle, PA: United States Army War College, 2009).

Marenin, Otwin, 'Changing Police, Policing Change: Towards More Questions', in Marenin, Otwin (ed.), *Policing Change, Changing Police: International Perspectives* (New York: Garland Press, 1996), pp. 309-330,

_____, 'Police Performance and State Rule: Control and Autonomy in the Exercise of Coercion', *Comparative Politics*, 18:1 (October 1985), pp. 101-122.

_____, *Restoring Police Systems in Conflict Torn Nations: Process, Problems, Prospects* (Geneva: Geneva Centre for the Democratic Control of Armed Forces, 2005).

_____, 'United States Police Assistance to Emerging Democracies', *Policing and Society*, 8:2 (1998), pp. 153-167.

Martin, Simon, 'The Gendarme Mission in Albania, 1925-38: A Move on the English Chess Board?', *Contemporary European History*, 7:2 (July 1998), pp. 143-159.

Max Planck Institute for Comparative Public Law and International Law (MPIL), *Provincial Needs Assessment: Criminal Justice in Kunduz Province* (Heidelberg: Max Planck Institute, 2011).

McCoy, Alfred, *Policing America's Empire: The United States, the Philippines, and the Rise of the Surveillance State* (Madison, WI: University of Wisconsin Press, 2009).

McCrocklin, James H., *Garde d'Haiti: Twenty Years of Organization and Training by the United States Marine Corps, 1915-1934* (Annapolis, MD: Naval Institute Press, 1956).

McLeod, Abby and Sinclair Dinnen, 'Police Building in the Southwest Pacific—New Directions in Australian Regional Policing', in Goldsmith, Andrew and James Sheptycki (eds), *Crafting Transnational Policing: Police Capacity-Building and Global Policing Reform* (Oxford: Hart Publishing, 2007), pp. 295-328.

Mihara, Robert, 'Employment of the Philippine Constabulary (1901-1917) and Haitian Gendarmerie (1916-1934) in Civic Tasks, Such as Anti-Corruption, Against the Background of Counterinsurgency Campaigns', in Gott, Kendall D. (ed.), *Security Assistance: US and International Historical Perspectives* (Leavenworth, KS: Combat Studies Institute Press, 2006), pp. 391-420.

_____. 'Lesser Victories: A Study of the Philippine Constabulary and Haitian Gendarmerie' (MA thesis, Texas A&M University, 2007).

Miller, Edward, *Misalliance: Ngo Dinh Diem, the United States, and the Fate of South Vietnam* (Boston: Harvard University Press, 2013).

Miller, Paul D., *Armed State Building: Confronting State Failure, 1898-2012* (Ithaca, NY: Cornell University Press, 2013).

Millett, Alan R., *The War for Korea, 1945-1950: A House Burning* (Lawrence, KS: University Press of Kansas, 2005).

Millett, Richard L., 'Limits of Influence: Creating Security Forces in Latin America', *Joint Forces Quarterly*, 42:3 (2006), pp. 14-16.

Mobekk, Eirin, 'International Involvement in Restructuring and Creating Security Forces: The Case of Haiti', *Small Wars & Insurgencies*, 12:3 (Autumn 2001), pp. 97-114.

Moelker, R., 'The "Dutch approach" and the Expeditionary Formula', in Hansen, F.S. (ed.), *The Comprehensive Approach: Challenges and Prospects* (Copenhagen: Royal Danish Defence College, 2009), pp. 85-106.

Motter, T.H. Vail, *United States Army in World War II. The Middle East Theater. The Persian Corridor and Aid to Russia* (Washington, DC: Center of Military History, 1952, Reprint, 2000).

Moyar, Mark, *Phoenix and the Birds of Prey* (Lincoln: University of Nebraska Press, 1997).

_____, *Triumph Forsaken: The Vietnam War, 1954–1965* (New York: Cambridge University Press, 2006).

Mulcahy, Aogan, *Policing Northern Ireland: Conflict, Legitimacy and Reform* (Cullompton, Devon: Willan Publishing, 2006).

_____, 'The "Other" Lessons from Ireland? Policing, Political Violence and Policy Transfer', *European Journal of Criminology*, 2:2 (March 2005), pp. 185-209.

Mullick, Rehan and Rabia Nusrat, 'Policing and Institution Building in Iraq', in Nathan Pino and Michael D. Wiatrowski (eds), *Democratic Policing in Transitional and Developing Countries* (Ashgate: Aldershot, Hampshire, 2006), pp. 131-147.

Münch, P., *Local Afghan Power Structures and the International Military Intervention: A Review of Developments in Badakhshan and Kunduz Provinces* (Kabul: Afghan Analyst Network (AAN), 2013).

Mungi, Timothy, *Indigenous Police Forces in Counterinsurgency* (Fort Leavenworth, KS: United States Army Command and General Staff College, 2010).

Murphy, Peter, 'Why Military Advising was so Successful in Vietnam…for the Chinese: And What the US Can Learn From It', *Small Wars Journal*, <http://smallwarsjournal.com/jrnl/recent?page=7> (June 28, 2015).

Murray, Tonita, 'Police-Building in Afghanistan: A Case Study of Civil Security Reform', *International Peacekeeping*, 14:1 (2007), pp. 108-126.

Musa, Samuel, John Morgan, and Matt Keegan (eds), *Policing and COIN Operations: Lessons Learned, Strategies, and Future Directions* (Washington, DC: Center for Technology and National Security Police and Combatting Terrorism Technical Support Office, 2011).

Nagl, John, *Learning to Eat Soup with a Knife: Counterinsurgency Lessons from Malaya and Vietnam* (Chicago: The University of Chicago Press, 2002).

Ní Aoláin, Fionnula, *The Politics of Force: Conflict Management and State Violence in Northern Ireland* (Belfast: The Blackstaff Press, 2003).

Nyström, Per, *Fem år i Persien som gendarmeriofficer* (Stockholm: A. Bonniers, 1925).

Oakley, Robert, Michael J. Dziedzic, and Elliot M. Goldberg (eds), *Policing the New World Disorder: Peace Operations and Public Safety* (Washington, DC: National Defense University, 1998).

Oakley-Hill, D. R., 'The Albanian Gendarmerie, 1925-1938, and its British Organizers', in *Albania* (Roma: Comité National-Démocratic 'Albanie Libre', 1962), pp. 403-406.

Obaid, A., *The 2016 Insurgency in the North: Beyond Kunduz City—Lessons (Not Taken) From the Taleban Takeover* (Kabul: Afghan Analyst Network (AAN), 2016).

O'Brien, Kevin A., 'Military Advisory Groups and African Security: Privatized Peacekeeping?', *International Peacekeeping*, 5:3 (Autumn 1998), pp. 78-105.

Osland, Kari M., 'The EU Police Mission in Bosnia and Herzegovina', *International Peacekeeping*, 11:3 (Autumn 2004), pp. 544-560.

Ott, Robert C. (ed.), *Winning the Peace: An American Strategy for Post-Conflict Reconstruction* (Washington, DC: Center for Strategic and International Studies, 2004).

Ottaway, Marina, 'Democratization in Collapsed States', in Zartman, I. William, *Collapsed States: The Disintegration and Restoration of Legitimate Authority* (Boulder, CO: Lynne Rienner, 1995), pp. 235-249.

Özbek, Nadir, 'Policing the Countryside: Gendarmes of the Late 19th Century Ottoman Empire (1876-1908)', *International Journal of Middle East Studies*, 40:1 (January 2008), pp. 47-67.

Pach, Chester J., *Arming the Free World: The Origins of the United States Military Assistance Program, 1945-1950* (Chapel Hill, NC: The University of North Carolina Press, 1991).

Paris, R. and T.D. Sisk, *The Dilemmas of Statebuilding: Confronting the Contradictions of Postwar Peace Operations* (London: Routledge, 2009).

Perdomo, Jose R., *Colombia's Democratic Security and Defense Policy in the Demobilization of the Paramilitaries* (Carlisle, PA: United States Army War College, 2007).

Perito, Robert, M., *Afghanistan's Civil Order Police: Victim of Its Own Success* (Washington, DC: United States Institute of Peace, 2012).

_____, *Afghanistan's Police: The Weak Link in Security Sector Reform* (Washington, DC: United States Institute of Peace, 2009).

_____, *Reforming the Iraqi Interior Ministry, Police and Facilities Protection Service* (Washington, DC: United States Institute of Peace Press, 2007).

_____, *The Iraq Federal Police: US Police Building under Fire* (Washington, DC: United States Institute of Peace Press, 2011).

_____, *US Police in Peace and Stability Operations* (Washington, DC: United States Institute of Peace, 2007).

_____, *Where Is the Lone Ranger When We Need Him? America's Search for a Postconflict Stability Force* (Washington, DC: United States Institute of Peace Press, 2004).

Persson, S.A., 'Det svenska gendarmeriet i Persien', in Ådahl, Andreas (ed.), *Iran genom seklerna, en svensk antologi* (Stockholm: Norstedt, 1971).

Pfaff, Tony, *Development and Reform of the Iraqi Police Forces* (Carlisle, PA: Strategic Studies Institute, US Army War College, 2008).

Phelps, James R., 'Lessons in Developing Democratic Police from Post-Second World War Successes', *International Journal of Comparative and Applied Criminal Justice*, 34:1 (Spring 2010), pp. 119-137.

_____, *What Happened to the Iraqi Police? Applying Lessons in Police Democratization Successes in West Germany and Japan* (Durham, NC: Carolina Academic Press, 2010).

Pickering, Sharon, Jude McCulloch, and David Wright-Neville, 'Counterterrorism Policing: Towards Social Cohesion', *Crime, Law and Social Change*, 50:1 (September 2008), pp. 91-109.

Pino, Nathan and Michael D. Wiatrowski (eds), *Democratic Policing in Transitional and Developing Countries* (Aldershot, Hampshire: Ashgate, 2006).

______ and _____, 'Implementing Democratic Policing and Related Initiatives', in Nathan Pino and Michael D. Wiatrowski (eds), *Democratic Policing in Transitional and Developing Countries* (Aldershot, Hampshire: Ashgate, 2006), pp. 99-130.

_____ and _____, 'Policing and Police Reform in the US: Adequate for Export?', in Nathan Pino and Michael D. Wiatrowski (eds), *Democratic Policing in Transitional and Developing Countries* (Aldershot, Hampshire: Ashgate, 2006), pp. 43-68.

_____ and _____, 'The Principles of Democratic Policing', in Nathan Pino and Michael D. Wiatrowski (eds), *Democratic Policing in Transitional and Developing Countries* (Aldershot, Hampshire: Ashgate, 2006), pp. 68-97.

Pion-Berlin, David, 'Neither Military nor Police: Facing Heterodox Security Challengers and Filling the Security Gap in Democratic Latin America', *Democracy and Security*, 6:2 (2010), pp. 109-127.

Planty, Donald J., Robert M. Perito, *Police Transition in Afghanistan* (Washington, DC: United States Institute of Peace, 2013).

Pollack, Kenneth, *A Switch in Time: A New Strategy for America in Iraq* (Washington, DC: Brookings Institution, 2006).

Reiner, Robert, *The Politics of the Police*, 3rd edition (Oxford: Oxford University Press, 2000).

Richter, J.S., 'Exporting the Bobby: German Police and British Reform, 1944-1955', (PhD dissertation, Harvard University), *Dissertation Abstracts International*, No. 59 (2005), p. 1729.

Richter, J.S. '"Entpolizeilichung" der öffentlichen Ordnung: die Reform der Verwaltungspolizei in der British Besatzungszone 1945-1955', in Fürmetz, Gerhard, Herbert Reinke, and Klaus Weinhauer (eds), *Nachkriegspolizei: Sicherheit und Ordnung in Ost- und West-Deutschland 1945-1969* (Hamburg: Ergebnisse Verlag, 2001), pp. 35-50.

Ricks, Thomas M., 'US Military Missions to Iran, 1943-1978: The Political Economy of Military Assistance', *Iranian Studies*, 12:3/4 (Summer—Autumn, 1979), pp. 163-193.

Rosenau, William, *Acknowledging Limits: Police Advisors and Counterinsurgency in Afghanistan* (Alexandria and Quantico, VA: CNA and Marine Corps University Press, 2011)

_____, *'Low-Cost Trigger-Pullers': The Politics of Policing in the Context of Contemporary 'State Building' and Counterinsurgency* (Santa Monica: RAND, Oct. 2008).

_____, 'The Kennedy Administration, US Foreign Internal Security Assistance and the Challenge of "Subterranean War", 1961-63', *Small Wars & Insurgencies*, 14:3 (2003), pp. 65-99.

_____, *US Internal Security Assistance to South Vietnam: Insurgency, Subversion, and Public Order* (London: Routledge, 2005).

_____, McAdam, Melissa, Megan Katt, Gary Lee, Jerry Meyerle, Jonathan Schroden, Annemarie Randazzo-Matsell, with Cathy Hiatt, and Margoux Hoar, *United States Marine Corps Advisors: Past, Present, and Future* (Washington, DC: CNA, 2013).

Ruis, Edwin, *Vechtmissie: Nederlande Militairen in Albanie, 1913-1914* (Uitgever: Just, 2013).

Ruttig, T. *ANSF Wrong-Footed: The Taleban offensive in Kunduz* (Kabul: Afghan Analyst Network (AAN), 2014).

Ryder, Chris, *The RUC: A Force Under Fire* (London: Meuthen Publishing, 2004).

Sanders, Andrew, 'Northern Ireland: The Intelligence War, 1969-1975', *British Journal of Politics and International Relations*, 13 (2010), pp. 230-248.

_____, 'Operation Motorman (1972) and the Search for a Coherent British Counterinsurgency Strategy in Northern Ireland', *Small Wars & Insurgencies*, 24:3 (2013), pp. 465-492.

_____, 'The Role of Northern Ireland in Modern Anglo-American Relations: The US Department of State and the Royal Ulster Constabulary, 1979', *Journal of Transatlantic Studies*, 12:2 (2014), pp. 163-181.

Saum-Manning, Lisa, *VSO/ALP: Comparing Past and Current Challenges to Afghan Local Defense* (Santa Monica, CA: RAND, Dec. 2012).

Savich, Carl, 'International Intervention in Kosovo and Macedonia, 1902-1908', *Serbiana.com* (3 Sept. 2007), <http://www.serbianna.com/columns/savich/092.shtml>.

Schmidl, Erwin A., 'Police Functions in Peace Operations: An Historical Overview', in Oakley, Robert B., Michael Dziedzic, and Eliot M. Goldberg (eds), *Policing the New World Disorder: Peace Operations and Public Safety* (Washington, DC: National Defense University, 1998).

_____. 'The International Operation in Albania, 1913-14', *International Security*, 6:3 (Autumn 1999), pp. 1-10.

Schulte, W., 'Politische Bildung in der Polizei: Funktionsbestimmug von 1945 bis zum Jahr 2000' (PhD dissertation, University of Essen, 2003).

Scoville, Thomas, *Reorganizing for Pacification Support* (Washington, DC: Center for Military History, 1991).

Sedra, M., 'The Hollowing-out of the Liberal Peace Project in Afghanistan: the Case of Security Sector Reform', *Central Asian Survey*, 32:3 (2013), pp. 371-387.

Shepherd, David E., 'The Republic of Vietnam's National Police', *Military Review*, 51:6 (June 1971), pp. 69-74.

Siggemann, Jürgen, *Die kasernierte Polizei und das Problem der inneren Sicherheit in der Weimarer Republik* (Frankfurt/Main: Rita G. Fischer, 1980).

Simons, Anna, 'The Military Advisor as Warrior-King and Other "Going Native" Temptations', in Frese, Pamela R., and Margaret C. Harrell (eds), *Anthropology and the United States Military: Coming of Age in the Twenty-first Century* (New York: Palgrave MacMillan, 2003), pp. 113-133.

Simonsen, Sven Gunnar, 'The Role of East Timor's Security Institutions in National Integration and Disintegration', *The Pacific Review*, 22:5 (November 2009), pp. 575-96.

Sinclair, Georgina, *At the End of the Line: Colonial Policing and the Imperial Endgame, 1945-80* (Manchester: Manchester University Press, 2006).

Skinner, M., 'Counterinsurgency and State Building: An Assessment of the Role of the Afghan National Police', *Democracy and Security*, 4:3 (2008), pp. 290-311.

Sklansky, David, 'Police and Democracy', *Michigan Law Review*, 103 (2005), pp. 1699-1830.

Smith, David, 'Trusted Servants of the Population: The Public Safety Branch and the German Police in the British Zone of Germany', in Knafla, Louis A. (ed.), *Policing and War in Europe* (Westport, CT: Greenwood Press, 2002), pp. 145-170.

Smith, Scott and Colin Cookman (eds), *State Strengthening in Afghanistan: Lessons Learned, 2001-14* (Washington, DC: United States Institute of Peace, 2016).

Snajdr, Edward, 'Creating Police Partnerships with Civil Society in Kazakhstan Through US-Funded Domestic Violence Training: A Step Toward Democratic Policing', in Nathan Pino and Michael D. Wiatrowski (eds) *Democratic Policing in Transitional and Developing Countries* (Aldershot, Hampshire: Ashgate, 2006), pp. 179-197.

Sorley, Lewis, *A Better War: The Unexamined Victories and Final Tragedy of America's Last Years in Vietnam* (Orlando: Harcourt, 1999).

Sorley, Lewis (ed.), *Vietnam Chronicles: The Abrams Tapes, 1968-1972* (Lubbock: Texas Tech University Press, 2004).

Special Inspector General Iraq Reconstruction, *Hard Lessons: The Iraq Reconstruction Experience* (Washington, DC: USGPO, 2009).

Strandquist, Jon, 'Local Defence Forces and Counterinsurgency in Afghanistan: Learning from the CIA's Village Defense Program in South Vietnam', *Small Wars and Insurgencies*, 26:1 (2015) pp. 90-113.

Stromseth, Jane, David Wippman, and Rosa Brooks, *Can Might Make Rights? Building the Rule of Law after Military Interventions* (Cambridge: Cambridge University Press, 2006).

Sullivan, John P., 'Role of the Police Service in Establishing the Rule of Law in Transitional States', in Priniotakis, Manolis (ed.), *Countering Insurgency and*

Promoting Democracy (New York: Council for Emerging National Security Affairs, 2007), pp. 108-121.

Terpstra, N., *The Dynamics of Justice Provision in the Context of Irregular Warfare and Legal Pluralism* (Kabul: CPAU, 2013).

The Constabulary Story (Quezon City; Philippines: Public Information Office, 1982).

Thiessen, C., *Assessment of the Dutch Integrated Police-Training Mission in Kunduz, Afghanistan: 2013 Progress Report* (Kabul: CPAU, 2014).

Thomas, Lowell, *Old Gimlet Eye: The Adventures of Smedley D. Butler, As Told to Lowell Thomas* (New York: Farrar and Rinehart, 1933).

Thruelsen, Peter Dahl, 'Security Sector Stabilisation in Counterinsurgency Operations: The Case of Afghanistan', *Small Wars & Insurgencies*, 22:4 (2011), pp. 619-643.

Tollefson, Harold, *Policing Islam: The British Occupation of Egypt and the Anglo-Egyptian Struggle Over Control of the Police, 1882-1914* (Westport, CT: Greenwood Press, 1999).

Tondini, Matteo, *Statebuilding and Justice Reform: Post Conflict Reconstruction in Afghanistan* (London: Taylor and Francis, 2010).

Trinquier, Roger, *Modern Warfare: A French View of Counterinsurgency* (New York: Praeger, 1964).

Uildriks, Niels, *Policing Insecurity* (Lanham, MD: Lexington Books, 2009).

UNDP Afghanistan, *Police Perception Survey—2010: The Afghan Perspective* (Kabul: Aina Media, 2010), <http://www.undp.org.af/publications/KeyDocuments/2011/Police%20Perception%20Survey%20Book%202010%20FINAL%20(6th%20Jan%202011).pdf>.

UNMIT, 'Timor Leste—UNMIT—Background', in *UN Peacekeeping Current Operations*, <http://www.un.org/en/peacekeeping/missions/past/unmit/background.shtml>.

US Government, White House, 'Fact Sheet: US Support to Peace Operations 2015 Leaders' Summit on UN Peacekeeping', 28 Sept. 2015, <https://www.whitehouse.gov/the-press-office/2015/09/28/fact-sheet-us-support-peace-operations-2015-leaders-summit-un>.

US Marine Corps, *Small Wars Manual* (Washington, DC: USGPO, 1940, Reprint, 1987).

Vagts, Alfred, *A History of Militarism: Civilian and Military* (New York: Free Press, 1959).

Walton, Frank E. (ed.), *Survey of Philippine Law Enforcement* (Washington, DC: Office of Public Safety, Agency for International Development, Department of State, 1966).

Weinhauer, Klaus, *Schutzpolizei in der Bundesrepublik: Zwischen Bürgerkrieg und Innere Sicherheit* (Paderborn: Ferdinand Schöningh, 2003).

Westermann, Edward B., *Hitler's Police Battalions: Enforcing Racial War in the East* (Lawrence, KS: University Press of Kansas, 2005).

_____, 'Shaping the Police Soldier as an Instrument for Annihilation', in Steinweis, Alan, and Daniel Rogers (eds), *The Impact of Nazism: New Perspectives on the Third Reich and Its Legacy* (Lincoln: University of Nebraska Press, 2003), pp. 129-150.

Weber, Nathaniel R., 'United States Military Advising and Assistance Groups During the Cold War, 1945-1965' (PhD dissertation, Texas A&M University, 2016).

Wiest, Andrew and Michael Doidge (eds), *Triumph Revisited: Historians Battle for the Vietnam War* (New York: Routledge, 2010).

Wilhelm, Friedrich, *Die Polizei im NS-Staat: Die Geschichte ihrer Organisation im Überblick* (Paderborn: Ferdinand Schöningh, 1997).

Wilder, Andrew, *Cops or Robbers? The Struggle to Reform the Afghan National Police* (Kabul, Afghanistan: Afghanistan Research and Evaluation Unit, 2007).

Williamson, Charles T., *The US Naval Mission to Haiti, 1959-1963* (Annapolis, MD: Naval Institute Press, 1998).

Wilson, Jeremy M., 'Law and Order in an Emerging Democracy: Lessons from the Reconstruction of Kosovo's Police and Justice Systems', *Annals of the American Academy of Political and Social Science,* 605 (May 2006), pp. 152-177.

Wood, Jennifer, and Clifford Shearing, *Imagining Security* (Cullompton, UK: Willan Publishing, 2007).

Yasin, Muhammed, *District and Police Systems in Pakistan* (Lahore: Vanguard Books, 1999).

Zanker, Franzisca, 'A Decade of Police Reform in Liberia: Perceptions, Challenges, and Ways Ahead', *Centre for Security Governance SSR 2.0 Brief,* 4 (Sept. 2015), pp. 1-12.

Index

Index of People

Index of Places

Index of Police, Military, Civilian Agencies, Formations, Organisations, Units, Programs, Schools etc.

Index of General & Miscellaneous Terms